More from the Shaggy Man

Also by Leslie Evans

BOOKS
Shaggy Man's Ramblings
Outsider's Reverie
China After Mao. Chinese edition: *Mao Zedong yihou de Zhongguo*

More from the Shaggy Man

Essays by

Leslie Evans

Boryanabooks
Los Angeles

Published by   Boryana Books
                3941 Veselich Avenue, Suite 262
                Los Angeles, CA 90039
                www.boryanabooks.com

ISBN: 978-1492251095

Cover: Portrait of the Shaggy Man, by John R. Neill, from L. Frank Baum's
Tik-Tok of Oz (1914).

Contents

Preface

Here in this second Shaggy Man collection are fifteen essays written between May 2012 and August 2013. They appeared first on The Shaggy Man's Place (www.shaggman.com) and on my publisher's website, www.boryanabooks.com, as well as one from the socialist journal *Against the Current*. They range from the rightward evolution of the Republican Party to recent discoveries about the ancient Jewish religion known as Gnosticism.

"On the Track of the Elusive Baron Long" offers the only extensive biographical sketch of one of Southern California's most fascinating characters. I became interested in Baron Long from having written previously on the history of the little industrial city of Vernon just southeast of downtown Los Angeles. Surprisingly for a tiny town with virtually no residential district, composed of slaughterhouses, factories, and warehouses, Vernon before Prohibition hit in 1920 was the nightlife capital of Los Angeles. Two institutions were the cornerstones of its appeal: Jack Doyle's Saloon and its adjacent boxing arena, and Baron Long's Vernon Country Club. The Country Club is reputed to have been the first real night club in America, combining a restaurant with an orchestra and floor show. The Baron, as he was always called, was for years the bête noir of the *Los Angeles Times*, before he struck it rich with a string of night clubs, became part owner of the U.S. Grant Hotel in San Diego, then of the world class Agua Caliente hotel and racetrack in Tijuana, finally ending as the owner of the Biltmore Hotel.

There are two pieces on Peak Oil and the threat it poses to modern industrial civilization. "The Twilight of Industrial Society" reports on the Age of Limits conference held in May 2012 at a farm in the Appalachian Mountains near Artemas, Pennsylvania. There several prominent writers on the dangers of oil depletion spoke: former CIA analyst Tom Whipple; John Michael Greer, author of *The Echotechnic Future*; Gail Tverberg, who maintains the website Our Finite World (www.ourfiniteworld.com); and Dmitry Orlov, a Russian-born author who witnessed the collapse of the Soviet Union.

i

I returned to the subject in "The Controversy over America's Oil Future," which examines the claims that unconventional oil from hydraulic fracking and Canadian tar sands are compensating for the global declines in convention crude oil.

In "Symptoms of U.S. Decline" I collect and discuss the comparative statistics for the United States and other advanced countries on a wide range of indices: education, infrastructure, poverty, homelessness, health, upward mobility, economic inequality, and prison populations. These all show a sharply declining America in comparison to countries with a more humane social safety net, and bode poorly for U.S. economic competitiveness in a world were other countries are training a healthier and more highly educated younger generation. It also shows that conservative claims that Europe is in economic collapse because of unaffordable health and welfare benefits is a misnomer. The most serious problems are found in southern Europe: Greece, Italy, and Spain. From Germany northward into the Scandinavian countries the economies are in substantially better shape than the United States despite some of the most generous social safety nets on the planet.

"The Strange Case of Ahmad Kamal and How He Helped the CIA Invite Radical Islam into Europe" bridges two stories: The unhappy unexpected consequences of the American CIA's attempt in the early 1950s to enlist émigré Soviet Muslims in Munich, West Germany, to weaken the Russian hold on its Central Asian colonies, and the remarkable personal history of the American adventurer Cimarron Hathaway, who, under the pseudonym of Ahmad Kamal, devoted his life to fighting for the independence of the Muslim peoples of Soviet and Chinese Turkestan.

A short piece on Edmond Kovacs offers an appreciation of an old friend from my Trotskyist days who died in January 2010.

Two lengthy essays take up the modern history of the Jews. "The Left and the Jews," based mainly on Robert S. Wistrich's *From Ambivalence to Betrayal: The Left, the Jews, and Israel,* traces the attitude of the Marxist and anarchist Left toward the Jews, from early in the nineteenth century. Because the far Left vigorously opposed German National Socialism and because left-wing Jews have been prominent in leftist organizations, from Lenin's Bolsheviks down to today's Occupy movement, there is a widespread view that the Left is immune to antisemitism. In fact, the Marxist Left has from its founding been hostile to Jewish national identity, calling for an extreme assimilation that would eradicate any specifically Jewish culture or character. The Marxist parties in Germany in the 1890s went so far as to publicly welcome the rise populist antisemitic movements on the theory that these were objectively anti-capitalist. The abysmal consequence of this ultra-assimilationist politics has been the widespread leftist embrace of antidemocratic and antisemitic Arab and Iranian movements and bitter hostility toward the Middle Eastern Jews.

"Why the Middle East Is Always in Crisis" recapitulates David Fromkin's essential *A Peace to End All Peace*. This traces the, mainly British, Western interventions in the last days of the Ottoman Empire and the doomed states that were carved in the Middle East at the end of World War I. These, in the absence of the Turkish lid that held mutually hostile currents at bay, drew borders that placed Sunni Muslims under Shi'ite rule in Syria, Shi'ite Muslims under Sunni rule in Iraq, and laid the groundwork for herding the million native Middle Eastern Jews into Palestine, the majority of whose territory was put under the rule of an Arab prince and renamed Jordan.

"Bygone Days in West Adams" is based on a talk I gave to a neighborhood association at the western end of my own West Adams community on some of the grand old houses and their history. At the turn of the twentieth century West Adams was the edge of town, just being developed for the new rich, many of them self-made, when a former gunslinger and singing waiter could become the richest man in America on newfound oil and an Italian immigrant farm worker could found the largest winery in the country. By the time of the Depression, West Adams went into decline. The old mansions were broken up into boarding houses. After 1948 it become one of the prime African American communities in Los Angeles, and today has a plurality of recent Latino immigrants.

"The Hunger Ahead" reviews two books on the rising threat of world famine. As population continues its geometric spiral upward the Green Revolution of the 1970s has finally proven unable to keep up. Arable land is rapidly eroding, aquifers are being drained at an irreplaceable rate, global warming is reducing snow packs that feed major river systems. Middle Eastern and Asian countries arc buying up huge tracts of farmland in Africa and Brazil to guarantee their own peoples a food supply now that they are no longer self-sufficient, guarding their foreign farms with militarily armed mercenaries. Internationally stored grain reserves, once abundant, fall lower each year, while climate change offers more and more frequent heat waves, droughts, and floods that endanger still more the narrow margins that fend off catastrophe.

"The Hip Dictator and His Opponents" takes a look at the more modern style of dictator, the ones who are satisfied to rig elections to get 70 percent of the votes instead of the old 98 percent, and who send building and health inspectors to close down the offices of critics instead of shooting them or carting them off to mental hospitals. This piece also looks at the tactics of the mostly young rebels who have challenged and sometimes brought down even the new style demagogues.

The Shaggy Man of my title is a character from L. Frank Baum's Oz books. He appeared first in the fifth book, *The Road to Oz* of 1909. I have had an affection for Oz since I first heard of it, around the age seven. By the time I created my website almost sixty years later, I could no longer imagine my Oz avatar to be one of the American youths who find their way there, characters like Button Bright or Peter from Philadelphia. Not feeling magical, I wouldn't choose one of the mysteriously living automatons — the Scarecrow, Tin Woodman, or Jack Pumpkinhead. Not being a native, I wouldn't pick a Quadling, a Gillikin, a Winkie, or a Munchkin, however old they might be. That left the old American wanderer who found his way there while trying to avoid someone to whom he owed a debt in Butterfield, Kansas: the otherwise nameless Shaggy Man. Writing as the Shaggy Man, because he carried with him the Love Magnet, it reminds me to care about the problems of our world, while because he has long since moved on to the more peaceful and less contentious Oz I am reminded to stay calm about it.

And so to connect my avatar with my text, the final essay contains some thoughts about L. Frank Baum's Land of Oz and why we should still care about it.

West Adams, Los Angeles
September 1, 2013

On the Track of the Elusive Baron Long

I first heard of Baron Long twenty years ago. My wife Jennifer and I had bought a 1910 Craftsman house near USC in the West Adams section of Los Angeles and we were researching its history. We had discovered that from 1921 to 1958 it had been owned by a branch of the Furlong family, founders and effective co-owners of the small industrial city of Vernon five miles southeast of downtown Los Angeles, incorporated in 1905. I had worked in Vernon for a year in an electric motor repair shop in the early 1980s and knew it to live up to its motto, "Exclusively Industrial." Our research at the Los Angeles main library turned up a small out-of-print book, *Leonis of Vernon* by James Kilty, that revealed an extraordinary story of the little town's early days, when it was the hard-drinking center of Los Angeles night life, boxing capital of the nation, and the bane of the *Los Angeles Times* and at least some of polite society.

Our Furlongs, Thomas, city treasurer, who lived in our house, and his brother James, the mayor, who did not, played only walk-on parts in Kilty's book. Even Leonis, despite Kilty's sycophantic and repetitive praise, was little more than a shadowy land owner and idea man. The stars were Jack Doyle and Baron Long. Doyle owned Doyle's Central Saloon at Santa Fe and Joy Streets, where the hundred-foot bar was claimed to be the longest in the world, and there were thirty-seven bartenders, each with his own cash register. Doyle also owned the Vernon Arena, where championship bouts were fought to huge crowds. Baron Long was the proprietor of the Vernon Country Club, later recognized nationally as the prototype of the modern night club, haunt of the Hollywood stars, such as Charlie Chaplin, Fatty Arbuckle, Norma Talmadge, and Eddie Cantor. Jimmy Durante played piano there. This improbable juxtaposition of factories, meat-packing plants, and warehouses with a center of regional night life mostly ended with Prohibition in 1920 and has been long forgotten.

Last year in writing a critique of the *LA Times* coverage of the recent corruption scandals in Vernon I read most of their early articles on the town. Despite the paper's current assertions that Vernon had from the beginning been a hotbed of civic malfeasance, for a decade there seemed to be only a single villain: Baron Long and his notorious Vernon Country Club. At the heart of the paper's disapproval was the fact that Los Angeles back then was a dry town, and liquor was available in night spots only in two cities in Los Angeles County: Vernon and Venice. Baron Long owned restaurant-night clubs in both.

As I scanned the years of listings I discovered that Long rose from a small-time bad boy to a major player in night clubs, hotels, and horse racing. He bought the U.S. Grant Hotel in San Diego in 1919, was a partner in the $10 million Agua Caliente hotel, casino, and racetrack resort in Tijuana from 1928, the Monte Carlo of the Western Hemisphere, and capped his career in 1933, taking over the Los Angeles Biltmore Hotel, the largest hotel west of Chicago.

Long was a major influence in hotel and night club design, an impresario who discovered and promoted a number of major show business figures, including Rita Hayworth, and a close friend of film studio heads.

I looked for a biography and there was none. The closest for the Vernon days was a chapter in James Kilty's forgotten and poorly written paean to John Leonis. For the Agua Caliente period there is a good treatment in Paul J. Vanderwood's *Satan's Playground: Mobsters and Movie Stars at America's Greatest Gaming Resort*. For the rest, Baron Long is mentioned, sometimes only in a paragraph or a sentence, in a score of books, often presenting contradictory claims about him. I will try to reconstruct the Baron's colorful life, so intimately linked to the nightlife, entertainment, and leisure pursuits of Southern California and Tijuana. He puts me in mind of Tom T. Hall's country and western song where the old cowboy tells the poet who asks him about the meaning of life: "It's faster horses, younger women, older whiskey, and more money." All this applies double to Baron Long except the search for younger women. He remained loyal to his one wife for fifty years.

Baron Long — "Baron" was his given name — was born on August 8, 1883, in Fort Wayne, Indiana. His father was Mason Long, a Civil War veteran on the Union side and in his time a noted card sharp, gambler, and "a patron of the turf," who got religion a few years before Baron's birth and published a repentant memoir in 1878 consecrating his life to Christ.

According to James Kilty, the Baron graduated from DePauw University in 1905, worked as a newspaperman in New York, then migrated to San Francisco, where "he met a rich Chinese herb merchant and went to work for him as a herb salesman. He was very successful." Typically, Paul J. Vanderwood in his *Satan's Playground* has a different version of all this: Long went to Franklin College, did not go to New York, and in San Francisco, "became the pitchman for a traveling patent medicine company. Ogling sightseers remember the hefty, 6'4" 'Chinese coolie' who sold 'tiger fat,' good for whatever ailed one." His obituary in the *Los Angeles Times* has this episode taking place in New York, where it was a mail order business. Still another variant, certainly apocryphal, has him hitting New York when he left Indiana, becoming a song writer, and making $200,000 at it before heading to San Francisco.

An unsigned column in the December 11, 1920, San Jose *Evening News*, interviewed Henry Hirsch, a former roommate of the Baron from his San Francisco days:

"I knew Baron Long when he had millions less than he has now," Hirsch told the reporter.

> About six years ago I was living at the Elks' club in San Francisco. . . . A young fellow blew in one night. He said he wanted a room. As I happened to be the house man he looked me up. I told him we were full up. He said he would give $150 for a room. I all but fainted. I knew there were fellows who would sell their rooms for $5 or maybe $10. I happened to have a very large room, and I suggested we might move in another bed. He was agreeable, and we did. An hour later I happened to go down stairs into the card room, and this young man had got into a dice game and the sky was the limit. This young man was Baron Long. He told me he won a couple thousand that night, and he also told me afterwards that he was broke when he arrived, but he was a sport. . . . Long is of the kind that can be broke one day and millionaire the next. He is a plunger for fair.

Long moved on to Los Angeles. There he became friends with racecar driver Barney Oldfield (and is said to have raced him in an old jalopy), baseball great Frank Chance, and James J. Jeffries, a former boilermaker who rose to become world heavyweight boxing champion, 1899-1905. Long visited Vernon, where he met Jack Doyle and was impressed with the possibilities in a mostly alcohol-free county. He partnered with Jeffries to open the James J. Jeffries Athletic Club in Vernon. Long managed one fighter himself, later lightweight champion Freddy Welsh. A famous bout was held at the club on Labor Day 1908, when Billy Papke, the Illinois Thunderbolt, took the middleweight title from Stanley Ketchel, the Michigan Assassin, in a brutal eleven-round match, Jeffries refereeing. Jeffries and Long then built the first Vernon Arena, an open-air bleachers at 27th Street and Santa Fe Avenue that could seat 15,000. Jack London and Damon Runyon were both said to be regulars at Jack Doyle's Saloon and the Long-Jeffries arena.

The Baron was becoming a real life Damon Runyon character. Inevitably the two became friends. Runyon, the chronicler of gamblers, betters on horses, and minor mobsters, best remembered for the musical *Guys and Dolls*, based on his short stories, devoted several of his columns to Baron Long. To mix up the story a bit more, Runyon has the Chinese medicine episode take place in Los Angeles, not San Francisco, and after the Jeffries Athletic Club, not before. He claims the boxing venue went broke, and Long, happening on a Chinese drug store in LA, going into the Chinese herb business, telling Runyon, "I knew that the tribe of hypochondriacs never decreases. The herbs wouldn't hurt anybody, and might do them some good." Runyon added:

> He accumulated another couple of hundred thousand dollars, and one day started what later, became famous as the Vernon Country Club. . . . Baron Long was moving up into the hated rich class, marveling somewhat as he went. (*Milwaukee Sentinel*, April 24, 1926)

It is easier to follow his public career than his personal life, about which there seem to be few stories. Runyon describes him as "a big, bluff, sleek looking, well tailored chap, with a large, bland, good natured face, and a considerable worldly knowledge and gift of gab." He was married; her name was Martha. I found an internet offer of the menu from their 33rd wedding anniversary, dated September 22, 1945, placing their marriage in the late summer of 1912. They stayed married until his death did them part, in 1962, but except for that I found little about her. By 1926 when Runyon made his comments the Baron was already a part owner of the U.S. Grant Hotel in San Diego and of a racetrack in Tijuana. He had become a prominent breeder of thoroughbred race horses, but he was also keenly interested in historic architecture. Runyon recounts:

> If Baron Long has any hobby other than breeding and racing horses, it is San Diego. He will walk the innocent wayfarer quite bowlegged about the streets of the city, showing him the visible marks of the city's growth, and he likes to direct the walking along about 3 o'clock in the morning, so that traffic will not impede his progress.
> He has a mania for old types of architecture. I suppose I gazed upon fifty ancient structures in the old part of the beautiful town one early morning while Baron Long expatiated on their unique attractions, and sleepy cops viewed us with some suspicion.

The Vernon Country Club

The Vernon Country Club

Long built the Vernon Country Club in 1911 on Santa Fe Avenue at 49th Street, opening in May 1912 as the first all-night club (the others closed at 1 am). Paul Vanderwood describes it as "not much more than a roadhouse set in a beet field with parking in front." Kilty says that more people came by horse and buggy than by car, and there was a steam-powered street car that ran down Santa Fe Avenue. As a sign of the times, in 1914 Jack Doyle's saloon was robbed by two cowboys who rode through the swinging doors on horseback.

The Vernon Country Club cost $20,000 to build. It took in $1,000 the first night, and the receipts the month before Prohibition were $105,000 ($1.2 million in 2012 dollars). What was new about the club was the entertainment. This would become a standard later, but the Vernon Country Club was one of the first to be more than a restaurant with drinks. Jim Heimann in *Out with the Stars: Hollywood Nightlife in the Golden Era* calls the Vernon Country Club "the birthplace for Hollywood nightlife, and the spawning ground for countless entertainers and restaurant men. . . . It was said that the Vernon introduced jazz to Southern California." And: "The integration of floor show, dancing, chorus girls, and orchestra — another Baron Long innovation — became standard for nightclubs in years to come."

All of Baron Long's establishments one way or another served alcohol, even during Prohibition, and generally promoted some form of gambling. He was only arrested once, on February 16, 1916, on a charge of illegal gambling. No doubt the Baron was shocked, shocked, to hear that gambling was going on in his establishment. The episode proved to be part of a bitter fight between Los Angeles County District Attorney Thomas Lee Woolwine and his one-time supporter, Edwin T. Earl, owner and publisher of the Los Angeles *Eve-*

ning Express. The Earl faction was also backed by then-L.A. County Supervisor Richard Norton. The story was recounted in 2007 by Roger M. Grace in the L.A.'s daily law newspaper, the *Metropolitan News-Enterprise.*

Supervisor Norton was said to have suborned the support of several of Woolwine's deputies, who began working against their boss. Woolwine fired them, including Chief Deputy District Attorney Harry Ellis Dean. Dean then went to a justice of the peace who, believing Dean still spoke for the District Attorney's office, was persuaded to issue an arrest warrant for Baron Long for alleged gambling at the Vernon Country Club. Woolwine was outraged. He appeared personally in the courtroom to demand that the charges be dismissed, saying these were harmless games of chance that had been licensed by local municipalities, and while they had very recently been prohibited, the citizens of Vernon had a right to get a warning to desist.

Woolwine then added,

> I do not propose to surrender the jurisdiction of this office to a discharged mischief-maker masquerading under the high sounding title of "Law Enforcement League," who will stoop to anything for political purposes, and who is backed by a man in this city who would do anything to cast discredit upon my administration, for the simple reason that I will not go to his newspaper office and take orders from him.

Woolwine said flatly that he meant *Evening Express* publisher E. T. Earl.

Earl retaliated by circulating a petition to have Woolwine removed from office for dropping the charges against Baron Long. He got an attorney to file charges. This ended in a courtroom in June 1916, where the judge upheld Woolwine and let the Baron off. Tempers were so high that Woolwine's lawyer, according to the June 10, 1916, *Los Angeles Examiner,* "landed two swift blows on the mouth" of the opposing counsel. The judge claimed he didn't see a thing.

Vernon Country Club orchestra

Some 2,000 people mobbed the Vernon Country Club on June 30, 1919, when at midnight the Wartime Prohibition Act went into force. The Eighteenth Amendment, the real Prohibition, had passed on January 16 of that year but had no enforcement provisions until passage of the Volstead Act on October 28, which went into effect on January 19, 1920. The Vernon Country Club closed for six months after the June 30 event, but reopened with a BYOB policy. The Baron found ways to serve his own beer and liquor throughout Prohibition, as the Volstead Act was barely enforced and there were as many as 100,000 speakeasies in the United States where alcohol was readily obtainable up to the repeal of Prohibition in 1933.

The Baron had a knack for attracting talent. Paul Whiteman, who led one of the most popular dance bands in the country in the 1920s, played the violin there. Other famous bandleaders of the following decade who played at Long's club included Gus Arnheim and Abe Lyman. Sophie Tucker sang and danced, while Mike Lyman, Abe's brother, later a prominent restaurateur, was a singing waiter.

Long expanded the club, adding the Hawaiian Village next door. Thinking he needed to find musicians to staff it, the Baron was strolling on the Venice boardwalk one day when he heard a fellow strumming on a ukulele. The musician was a young man named Buddy De Sylva. *Life* magazine tells the story:

> De Sylva looks like a Hawaiian. Long, a shrewd judge of talent, was impressed by his obvious talent for crowd-pleasing and offered him a job at $60 a week. Buddy was then faced with a weighty decision for the first time in his life. In trying to make up his mind whether to go on working his way through college so as to become a writer like Lord Dunsany or whether to sing and play in Hawaiian costume for tips in a night club so as to become a great singer like Al Jolson, he reacted characteristically. First he procrastinated. Then he chose the night club. (December 30, 1940)

Six months later Al Jolson, a frequent diner at the Vernon club, hired De Sylva, took him to New York, and arranged to have one of his songs published. De Sylva's first royalty check was for $16,000. De Sylva collaborated on songs with George Gershwin and was a major Tin Pan Alley composer in the 1920s. He co-wrote, usually the lyrics, such standards as *Stairway to Paradise, Button Up Your Overcoat, California Here I Come, Somebody Loves Me, April Showers, Best Things in Life Are Free,* and *If You Knew Suzie.* He moved on to become a producer for Paramount Pictures.

The Baron's clientele on the other side of the musicians' stage was a Who's Who of Hollywood. Regulars included Charlie Chaplin, Buster Keaton, Cecil B. De Mille, D. W. Griffith, Mary Pickford, Mack Sennett, Mary Miles Minter, Theda Bara, Lon Chaney, and Blossom Seeley. Kilty recalls, "Tom Mix was an expert at throwing dishes at some of the singing waiters, but one night Jim Lyman retaliated by throwing beer bottles back at him."

Mix also once drove his car through the front door and onto the dance floor, where he bought everyone present a drink.

Charlie Chaplin, "when he was in the mood, would perform some of the antics he was made famous for at his table." One website devoted to Mabel Normand, Charlie Chaplin's co-star, recounts that in the summer of 1916 Eddie Cantor was

> sitting in a cafe with his back to the door when suddenly someone threw a coat over his head, lifted him from his seat and took him to a car outside. Eddie found himself in a speeding car with a coat over his head and was not able to see who was with him; he was convinced he was being taken for a "ride." When the car stopped and they arrived at the destination, he was relieved to find that his kidnappers were [silent film star] Thomas Meighan and Mabel Normand.

They had taken him to Baron Long's Hawaiian Village to hear Buddy De Sylva.

One much-told story was how Baron Long hired Rudolph Valentino as an exhibition Tango dancer — and then fired him! The firing may really have happened but there are a few variants in the telling. Kilty has it that Valentino was also supposed to sing and had no voice. Paul Vanderwood says it was for stealing a sandwich in the kitchen. Jim Heimann says the Baron said he fired Valentino but Valentino claimed to have quit. This would have happened in late 1917 or 1918.

A few years after it opened, a slightly later generation of Hollywood stars joined the Vernon Country Club regulars, including Gloria Swanson, Clark Gable, and the Marx Brothers.

The Vernon Country Club was also often used as a film location when a restaurant or nightclub was needed. Anna May Wong was said to have had her first film role shot there.

South of the Border, Down Mexico Way

The period leading up to World War I was the heyday of the California Progressive Movement. If today it is mostly the Religious Right that seeks to legislate morality, then it was the Progressive Left, which led successful campaigns against alcohol, gambling, boxing, and horse racing, not to mention prostitution. As these pursuits were successively outlawed in most Southern California towns, promoters turned their eyes southward. In Tijuana just over the border, horse races were legal. They began in the late 1880s when the town did not really yet exist — the population reached 242 only in 1900 — and without a proper track. In 1907 a Mexican government decree legalized gambling in the border town, with some idiosyncratic restrictions — games of pure chance such as roulette or slot machines were prohibited, but card and dice games where some level of skill was presumed were allowed. The final impulse came when the California Progressives succeeded in passing the Walker-Otis Anti-Race Track Gambling Act in 1909, which closed the state's race tracks. Prostitution was forced outdoors by the Red Light Abatement law of 1912, which allowed buildings used as brothels to be seized by the government. That hastened the flight south.

Best known was the ABW Corporation, a partnership of Marvin Allen, Frank "Booze" Beyer, and Carl Withington, who had run bars and whorehouses in Bakersfield. They set up a big operation in Mexicali, centered on their Owl Cafe, with an outpost in Tijuana that would expand in future years (see Vanderwood's *Satan's Playground*, and Taylor, "The Wild Frontier Moves South").

In the spring of 1915 a group of promoters organized the Lower California Jockey Club and began constructing a race track in Tijuana, which then had a population of 1,000. Baron Long joined San Francisco boxing promoter "Sunny" Jim Coffroth in buying them out, with backing from San Diego sugar magnate John Spreckels. The Jockey Club quickly became a popular stopping place for visitors from across the border. Silent film stars John Gilbert and Leatrice Joy were married there. Jim Heimann writes:

> The addition of Baron Long to the investment group cemented the Hollywood connection, and those celebrities who patronized the Ship, Vernon Country Club, and other Long hotspots knew they could count on the Baron to show them a good time.

The track opened on New Year's Day 1916. Ten thousand Americans showed up for the occasion, a San Diego railroad built a special line to get them there. Many Hollywood stars attended the opening, along with Los Angeles County Sheriff J. C. Cline and the governor of Baja California, Esteban Cantù.

Some on the American side of the border took a dimmer view. Lawrence Taylor in his "Wild Frontier" article writes:

> San Diego city authorities banned attempts to advertise Tijuana races in the downtown area. Some newspapers, particularly the *Los Angeles Morning Tribune*, believed that the crowds were drawn away from the San Diego Panama-California Exposition of 1915-1916 by the "race-track gambling hell at Tijuana."

The mayor of Los Angeles sent a telegram to President Woodrow Wilson calling on him to close the border with Mexico.

In January 1917 in heavy flooding the entire track and its flimsy bleachers were washed down the Tijuana River. Paul Vanderwood in his *Juan Soldado* writes that this prompted

> San Diego preachers to praise The Lord for purging the region of horse-race gambling, but the promoters, encouraged both by their profits and by Governor Cantù, quickly reconstructed the complex, which reopened in mid-April and just three months later had to be remodeled and expanded to accommodate a rush of betting spectators.

By the Sea, By the Sea, By the Beautiful Sea!

The Baron owned two seaside nightclub-restaurants, the Ship Cafe in Venice and the Sunset Inn in Santa Monica. Venice, California, was Abbot Kinney's fantasy imitation of the Italian original, complete with canals. Kinney built the unique *Cabrillo*, the Ship Cafe, modeled on a Spanish galleon, in 1905. It was first run by Carlo Marchetti. The building was designed by architects Norman Marsh and Clarence Russell to replicate the *San Salvador*, the ship Portuguese explorer Juan Cabrillo captained on behalf of Spain when he discovered Santa Monica Bay in October 1542. Baron Long bought it in 1917, in partnership with Julius Rosenfield.

SHIP CAFE "CABRILLO" VENICE, CALIF.

Paul Tanck, online columnist for the *Venice Vanguard,* tells more. The waiters were dressed as sixteenth-century naval officers.

It was at the Ship that Valentino had his heels cooled by movie queen Nazimova, who called him a "pimp" and a "gigolo" at a private party she was throwing for coworkers at Metro. And it was Buster Keaton who, pestered by autograph hounds, jumped out of one of the restaurant's portholes in a faked escape attempt, only to find twice as many fans when he returned.

Spanish dancers Addison Fowler and Ethyle Stewart, dubbed the "Castles of the Coast" in comparison with ballroom dancers Vernon and Irene Castle, had a fifty week run at the Ship Cafe in 1918. On Sunday, January 11, 1920, the week before Prohibition went into effect, 100,000 people jammed the restaurant and pier.

The Ship Cafe was destroyed in a fire in December 1920. It was rebuilt, this time with two masts instead of three, and lying parallel to the shore instead of pointing out to sea. Baron Long abandoned his interests in the place after the fire. It lasted until 1946.

Santa Monica Public Library Image Archives

The Sunset Inn was on Colorado Avenue in next-door Santa Monica. It was built in 1911 by prominent Los Angeles architect Alfred Faist Rosenheim, who had designed the landmark Christian Science church in West Adams at Hoover and Adams Blvd., as well as oil magnate Edward Doheny's Beverly Hills mansion. At least two websites mistakenly conflate Baron Long's Sunset Inn with the nearby Cafe Nat Goodwin on Santa Monica's Bristol Pier, claiming that the Goodwin place was renamed as the Sunset Inn.

Jim Heimann's *Out with the Stars* has photographs of both buildings, which should settle the matter. Heimann says that while Baron Long owned it, the Sunset Inn "eclipsed the Ship Cafe and the Vernon Country Club in popularity." Harold Lloyd and Bebe Daniels won many dancing contests there. Baron Long bought it in 1916 but sold out a year or two later when Santa Monica went dry.

Baron Long's Tavern

Around the time he bought the Ship Cafe the Baron opened a straight nightclub in Watts, already a predominately black community. Steven Isoardi writes:

> Watts's musical legacy predates the arrival of the Collette-Mingus generation. By the end of World War I, just a few years after the city's inception, it was an important outlet for late-night, after-hours entertainment with many small clubs and one somewhat extravagant venue in Baron Long's Tavern, populated by the wealthy and Hollywood elite.

The Tavern featured many of the same performers as the Vernon Country Club, including the Fowler-Stewart Spanish dance duo and Rudolph Valentino; in fact he seems to have been hired mainly for the Watts club. In a 1926 interview in *Photoplay*, shortly before his death, Valentino recalled:

> About that time Baron Long opened the Watts Tavern, a road house near Los Angeles. He offered me thirty-five dollars a week to dance there. As my apartment cost only eight dollars a week, I figured that I could pay my rent and board and wear a clean collar now and then. So I took it. I also thought that I might attract the attention of some director, for the film people were the chief patrons of the place. My partner was Marjorie Tain, who is now working in Christie comedies, I believe.
>
> Nothing came of the engagement except that I met some very fine people from Pasadena who suggested that I try for an engagement dancing at the Hotel Maryland, one of the most exclusive hotels in Pasadena. By that time the Watts Tavern had begun to attract an undesirable crowd, and I was disgusted with the place. The Maryland engaged me to dance with Katherine Phelps. Our first exhibition was on Thanksgiving day, when we were received very nicely. A few days later the proprietor, Mr. Leonard, returned from the East and offered me a permanent engagement. But the terms were such that I couldn't accept, and I walked out. That very day, as I was walking down to the Alexandria, I met Emmet Flynn. He grabbed me by the arm. "My God, I've been trying to get hold of you for a week," he said. "Do you remember that story Hayden Talbot said he was going to write?" I said, "Yes.'" "Well, he has done it, and

he is going to produce it. Go over and see Mr. Maxwell, the supervisor of production." The part proved to be that of a "heavy" — an Italian count, and I suited the type in appearance."

But Baron Long's Tavern is best remembered for the African American musicians who played there. One group was Benjamin "Reb" Spikes' So Different Band. They played San Francisco during World War I, where Spikes was billed as "The World's Greatest Saxophonist." A 1951 interview with Spikes in the *Jazz Journal* recounts:

> "The So Different Band was the finest of its time — remember, this is back in 1915." Reb proudly displayed a huge photo of the orchestra; and continued, "Art Hickman would come over from the St. Francis Hotel to hear us play. We had the best clarinetist in the country — fellow called 'Slocum' . . . came from Martinique . . . could hardly speak English, but he did a lot of talking through his horn. Our drummer, 'Pete' (can't-think-of-his-last-name) had played with The Georgia Minstrels. The flutist, Gerald Wells, doubled on piccolo and clarinet . . . he's now president of the musician's union in Seattle, Washington. Yes, that certainly was a fine band."
>
> After gazing at the blown-up photo, he added, "Baron Long, who now owns the Biltmore Hotel here, was running a cabaret in Watts at the time. After hearing us, he cancelled an engagement with The Original Dixieland Band and hired the So Different Orchestra to play at his club."

The most famous musician on the Baron's program was Jelly Roll Morton, ragtime and jazz pianist and composer. His *Jelly Roll Blues* (1915) is thought to be the first published jazz composition. His runaway hit *The Crave* premiered at Baron Long's Tavern. For a while he was joined by three of his compatriots from his native New Orleans, trombonist Frankie Dusen, cornetist Buddy Petit, and clarinetist Wade Whaley.

Trombonist Jasper Van Pelt in an entry on his website on New Orleans trombonist Frankie Dusen writes,

> In 1917 Dusen, Buddy Petit, and Wade Whaley went to Los Angeles to join Jelly Roll Morton at Baron Long's night club in Watts. When they arrived Morton ridiculed them so much for their down home clothes and ways, that Dusen and Petit soon returned to New Orleans, angry, and swearing to kill Morton if he ever returned to the city. Whaley stayed on and went on to play with Kid Ory.

Folklorist Alan Lomax adds:

In 1917, Frank Duson, [Buddy] Petit, and Wade Whaley went to Los Angeles to play in an orchestra led by Jelly Roll Morton mainly at Baron Long's place in Watts, on the eastern outskirts of Los Angeles. Disputes arose over dress standards, eating meals on the bandstand, and sharing tips with the result that Duson and Petit departed for New Orleans. Jelly Roll explained his side of the story in this manner:

"But, man, those guys could really play. Petit was second only to Keppard on the cornet, had tremendous power in all registers and great ideas. He was a slow reader, but if the tune was played off first, he would pick up his part so fast no one knew he couldn't read. And, as for Dusen, he was the best there was at that time on trombone. So we had a very hot five-piece band and made plenty money — $75 a night and tips doubled the salaries.

"But those guys couldn't get used to all that money. They used to bring their food on the job, just like they was used to doing in the low-down honky-tonks along Perdido Street. Here they'd come every night to this Wayside Park with a bucket of red beans and rice and cook it on the job. (Man, I wish I had some of that stuff right now. The best food in the world!)

"So anyhow, Dink and me got to kidding the boys about this, be-cause, as a matter of fact, this cooking on the job made us look kind of foolish. And Buddie and Frankie blew up, threatened to kill us. Next day, they left town, without notice, and went back to New Orleans. Which shows you never fool with a New Orleans musician, as he is noted for his hot temper." (*Mister Jelly Roll*, pp. 163-64)

Joseph Crawford was Buddie Petit's real name, the renowned second genera-tion New Orleans cornet player. His playing name is given by various sources as both Buddy and Buddie.

His First Hotels

In 1917 Baron Long bought his first hotel, the Van Nuys, which he held briefly, then sold it as a stepping stone to a major acquisition in 1919, a part ownership in the U.S. Grant Hotel in San Diego. The Grant had been begun in 1905 by Ulysses S. Grant, Jr., second son of the Civil War general and U.S. President. A few years into construction he went broke. The half-finished shell sat for a few years, then he found some backers and it opened in 1910, then the most elegant hotel on the West Coast, with a portrait of his father in the lobby and a military theme in the artwork. Baron Long expanded his share to full ownership in 1927, adding a suite of rooms on the bottom floor that served as speakeasies during Prohibition. He had an antenna erected on the roof for San Diego's first radio station. They used the hotel staff, including the bellboys, as announcers, and got high school kids who could play an instrument to perform for free to fill in the air time, eventually adding live orchestra performances. Franklin Roosevelt gave a radio address from there in the late twenties, before he was President. Every U.S. President from Woodrow Wilson in 1919 to Ronald Reagan, except for Jimmy Carter, stayed there, including John Kennedy.

U.S. Grant Hotel, San Diego

U. S. Grant, Jr., died in 1929. His widow, America Workman Will Grant, lived on at the hotel until her death in 1942. Francis Merriam, a retired waitress whose time at the Grant began in 1939, remembered America Grant well:

"She went with the hotel like chattel, you know, and they used to feed her all the martinis and meals she wanted until she began thinking they were trying to poison her or something. Then she got the measles, I remember that, and she died."

The *Los Angeles Times* ran a retrospective on the Grant in 1978. The hotel in its heyday was highly formal. No sailors allowed, and everyone dressed for dinner, into the 1930s. But prices were low. Coffee was 5 cents and it came with free biscuits or cornbread.

The reporter interviewed Carleton Lichty, in 1978 the president and general manager of San Diego's prestigious Hotel Del Coronado, who had gotten his start at fourteen in 1929 as a bellboy at the U.S. Grant Hotel. Lichty got the job because his brother Eddie was an assistant manager. He recalled that Baron Long had paid for his brother's wedding reception.

In those days The Baron had firm rules. We bellboys had to stand at attention, with hands behind our backs, right in the middle of the lobby so we could see all the doors. No guest was supposed to carry their own bags. We'd get a running start, and slide across the tile right to their sides. And another thing — we all had to carry a pack of matches in our hand. When someone lifted a cigarette to their mouth, we had to slide over and light it before they could reach for their own match. It would always be men, of course. Ladies didn't smoke in public.

Lichty described the night in December 1933 when Prohibition ended:

The Baron must have gotten his hands on more beer than anyone else in town. The fire chief put the firemen's band on a wagon and they came down the street — oompa-pa, oompa-pa — and everyone was singing "Happy Days Are Here Again." We just kept hauling barrels up from the basement into the Rendezvous Club. What a Night.

Agua Caliente — The Monte Carlo of the Americas

Baron Long had been involved in Tijuana since 1915 when he and Jim Coffroth took over the Tijuana Jockey Club and built their racetrack. With the passage of Prohibition in 1920 Americans became much more interested in Tijuana night life; 64,000 crossed the border over that Fourth of July weekend. Carl Withington's ABW Corporation had built a luxury casino they pretentiously named the Monte Carlo next to Long and Coffroth's track, and invited the Baron to build an adjacent first-class restaurant and nightclub. He did so, naming it the Sunset Inn, after the place he had owned on the Santa Monica Pier. Jim Heimann writes:

To get to the border track, merrymakers had to pass the Inn, and the gambling hall made a fortune. The Gold Room, built to accommodate high rollers, specifically Universal Studio president Carl Laemmle, was also a favorite of studio head Joseph Schenck, who would motor south in his chauffeur-driven limousine . . . to drop $100,000 on a single race.

Old standbys like Charlie Chaplin, Buster Keaton, and Harold Lloyd showed up, now joined by next-generation Hollywood stars such as Mary Astor, Norma Shearer, and Gloria Swanson. Helena Rubenstein held an event at the Sunset Inn in 1923 where her guests included the president of the University of California and Cornelius Vanderbilt, Jr. Still, ABW was a shady operation that ran brothels as well as upscale resorts (although the most famous whorehouse in town, the Moulin Rouge, was owned by Soo Yasuhara, a Japanese immigrant). Carl Withington's death in 1925 set off a chain of events that brought the Baron into a more direct interest in ABW, but with a less disreputable set of partners.

The Border Barons, from left: James Crofton, John Mills
(general manager), Wirt G. Bowman, Baron Long

The catalyst was Wirt Bowman, a wealthy rancher and Democratic Party activist from Nogales, Arizona, where he also owned a bank. Bowman assumed Withington's place in the ABW Corporation, then brought in Baron Long. These two allied with one of ABW's employees, James Crofton, a one-time drifter, machinist, circus performer, and blackjack dealer. Within two years Withington's remaining partners, "Booze" Beyer and Marvin Allen, had been forced out. Bowman, Long, and Crofton then allied with Baja California Governor Abelardo Rodríguez and emerged as the Border Barons, looking to build the largest and most extravagant spa, casino, and hotel in the Western Hemisphere. The location they chose was a run-down hot springs three miles south of Tijuana called Agua Caliente. They kept the name for their resort.

In their division of labor among the Border Barons, Bowman was to run the casino, Baron Long the hotel, and Crofton the racetrack after it was added. They put Baron Long in charge of hiring an architect and designing the whole conglomerate. He had five prominent Southern California architects submit designs. The styles of the day were unrelievedly modern: high-rise steel and glass. Long rejected them all. He had a lifelong fascination and love of old architecture and ornate decoration. Agua Caliente would be shaped by that ethos. Lawrence Herzog in his book on U.S.-Mexican border architecture writes:

> But, of course, the Agua Caliente complex really dominated the city after 1927. It was the vision of Baron Long, a horse-racing promoter from Los Angeles who also owned the elegant U.S. Grant Hotel in San Diego. Long was among the many investors and builders who in 1920 fell in love with the myth of old Spain and old Mexico and wanted to "revive" their memories in the architecture of the 1920s on both sides of the border. Long . . . ordered his workers to tear down the old wooden hotel, which had been built on the site of a natural hot springs, called the Tijuana Hot Springs Hotel, where Americans suffering from tuberculosis at the end of the nineteenth century had come to seek the curative pow-ers of the earth's mineral-filled waters. When they were through yanking out the original buildings, all that was left were two sycamore trees standing at the main entrance. Now would come the palatial casino with its Arabian-like baths and swimming pool, a touch of paradise just south of the border. One of the impressive things about Agua Caliente was the natural landscaping, the rows of palm trees and other exotic tropical plants and the bright green lawns, all the work of a Mexican landscape expert, originally from Scotland, who had previously worked on one of the great urban parks in the West: Balboa Park, across the border in San Diego. This was truly a bicultural architectural achievement.

Entrance to the hotel at Agua Caliente

With his gambler's sensibility Long finally engaged a self-taught nineteen-year-old high-school dropout, Wayne McAllister. McAllister at seventeen or eighteen had gone to work as a draftsman for a one-man architectural firm, San Diego Architectural Service Bureau. His boss, P. Brainerd Hale,

McAllister later told Chris Nichols, was a dedicated womanizer, despite the fact that he "had eleven children and a wooden leg." Hale soon skipped town for Mexico with a strip tease artist, leaving McAllister as head of the near nonexistent business. Baron Long took a liking to the young man. He drove McAllister to Tijuana to the site of the hot springs, a remote spot covered with scrub brush, where the old wood-frame hotel stood, ready for demolition. *Satan's Playground* quotes him as telling McAllister he wanted the resort to appear "so a weary traveler coming across [the border] turns down this little ravine and sees a beautiful old mission, and I want you to create this mission."

McAllister and his soon-to-be-wife Corinne Fuller spent a year creating plans for a monumental Mission Revival extravaganza. With an unlimited budget, they planned a hotel, spa, and casino, with the conventional Mission Revival white stucco walls and overhanging red tile roofs, plus eclectic additions of Art Deco elements, Mediterranean gardens, Louis XV furniture, and elaborate tile and gold filigree work throughout. In Mexico in those days there were no prolonged approval processes. Wayne and Corinne would get something down on paper at night and the next morning a crew would start to build it. Vanderwood writes:

> The McAllisters somehow pulled the components together into a celebrated, world-class jewel that architectural digests singled out as unique and praised as a marvel.
>
> At the roadway entranceway to the complex stood the resort's trademark, a massive 80-foot tower of Moorish inspiration resting on an arched base through which motor vehicles passed to and from the hotel and casino.

Construction began in mid-1927. The hotel had space for 500 guests, while nearby they built fifty bungalows arranged to look like an Old World village. The site included a professional golf course, an Olympic swimming pool, a greyhound racetrack, gardens, and its own airfield to fly in guests. At the edge of the property they built a free swimming pool for Tijuana's local residents. Agua Caliente, opened on June 23, 1928. Construction costs were $10 million ($134 million in 2012 dollars). A top-of-the-line racetrack would be added in December 1929 for another $2 million.

184:—INTERIOR OF CASINO AND FAMOUS GOLD BAR.

AGUA CALIENTE, TIJUANA HOT SPRINGS, MEXICO.

Inside, the resort was opulent. *Satan's Playground* again:

A diversity of decorators and expert craftsmen were given an open checkbook to add their specialties to the interior. Close inspection revealed a hodgepodge of style and designs, but the overall impression was of Moorish royal wealth and splendor. Floors in the gaming hall were of domestic marble, as were the columns that rose to an intricate, delicate filigree ceiling. . . . Imbedded in the filigree was a large, oval painting by the Dutch muralist Anthony Hinsburgen, which added a classical touch, as did the cast bronze statuary on pillars and in niches in the main gaming room, lit by ornate fixtures finely crafted especially for the club and an immense chandelier from Milan, said to be the most exquisite and expensive in the hemisphere.

Bruce Henstell in *Sunshine and Wealth* writes;

The facilities were first class all the way. Long personally traveled to Europe to select the finest vintages for the wine cellar. Every room in the hotel had pink bathrooms and featured tortoiseshell toilet seats. The service in the hotel restaurant was gold. The track offered a total of $1,000,000 each year in purses which no track in North American could match. A 6,902-yard, par 72, championship golf course was created out of adobe. The highpoint of its year was the Agua Caliente Open with a first prize of $15,000, the largest single golf prize in the world.

The roaring twenties were still going strong, but Prohibition and a host of Progressive-inspired blue laws against drinking, gambling, and racetracks, had cast a Puritan pall over Southern California and much of the nation. Los Angeles had even passed a law making "dancing with the cheek or head touching one's partner" illegal as well as any music "suggestive of bodily contortions." Even the fox trot and tango were banned, much less the Charleston. No wonder people flocked to the new pleasure palace, led by the rich and famous but sweeping up anyone who could get across the border for a fancy dinner and a few dollars spent at the gaming tables or slot machines. Agua Caliente was promoted as the Western Hemisphere's answer to the famous European casino spas, Monte Carlo in Monaco and Deauville in France.

Agua Caliente would later be compared to Las Vegas, but those who remember it seem to feel that it was somehow different. Vanderwood in *Satan's Playground* writes:

> Today's Las Vegas palaces may exhibit their frenetic ostentations, but they lack the warmth and hospitality of an Agua Caliente. . . . Hal Rothman, who patronized both venues, compared them for the San Diego Historical Society in 1972. "In Caliente you could not go into the casino without a coat and tie," he said. "You could not go into the Gold Room unless you were in a tuxedo and evening dress. Now, in Vegas they don't care if you go in there in the nude, if you have someone to carry your money. Down there [in Agua Caliente] it was class, strictly class."

The American press had mixed responses. For years, well before the new resort, a regular refrain had been laments at the drinking, gambling, and horse racing of Tijuana. Humorist Will Rogers in a 1926 column responded:

> Americans don't want to drink and gamble. They just go over there to see the mountains, and these scheming Mexicans grab 'em and make 'em drink, and make 'em make bets, and make 'em watch those horses run for money. It seems that Americans don't know these places are over there at all, and when they get there these Mexicans spring on 'em and they have to drink or the Mexicans will kill 'em." (Andrew Grant Wood, *On the Border*)

The *L.A. Times* chose to praise Agua Caliente as a rival to Europe's great spas, saying "The loveliness and completeness of the place is beyond compare. Everything is ultramodern. Monte Carlo, Nice, Deauville have moved to the doorstep of Uncle Sam."

The Agua Caliente hotel promised a world-class chef, orchestra, and floor show. One performer was a teenage dancer, Margarita Carmen Cansino. Her father, Eduardo Cansino, was a Spanish dancer from a little town near Seville. Her mother had been in the Ziegfeld Follies. Fox film corporation executive Winfield Sheehan saw Margarita dance at Baron Long's Caliente Club and gave her a film contract under her nickname, Rita Cansino. Later the studio dyed her hair red and changed her name to Rita Hayworth.

The big money rolling in at Agua Caliente became a tempting target for criminals. *Satan's Playground* gives an account of the worst of it. On Monday, May 20, 1929, a Cadillac money car left Agua Caliente headed for a bank in San Diego, carrying the casino's weekend receipts. The casino regularly switched cars and routes to forestall a holdup, but this time an insider, never identified, tipped off a small-time crook in San Diego. He engaged two thugs, Lee Cochran and Marty Colson, to ambush the Cadillac on the Old Dike road between National City and San Diego. They were told the driver and guard were in on it and would hand over the money — they were expecting $100,000, worth more than $1.3 million today. The robbers were supposed to follow the money car, shoot out the tires, then throw red pepper in the driver's and guard's eyes to give them an alibi.

It all went wrong. The two in the money car, driver Jose Perez Borrego, a former Tijuana police chief, and guard Nemisio Rudolfo Monroy, were not in on it. When their car was forced to stop, Monroy started firing his pistol at the robbers. Cochran and Colson, armed with classic gangster Thompson submachine guns, ineptly ran up on the money car, one on each side, and sprayed it with bullets, killing both occupants. In the process Cochran shot Colson in the shoulder. The two grabbed the money pouch, which had only $6,000 in cash, the rest in nonnegotiable checks and travelers checks, and fled to the home of bootlegger Jerry Kearney, who was not in on the robbery.

Kearney got a shady doctor to treat Colson's wound, then took Cochran out on a boat to dump the guns and checks at sea. Everyone was ultimately caught. Cochran and Colson were convicted of murder and received long prison sentences. In 1932 Colson staged a daring and

Police display the home-made guns and bullets killer Marty Colson made in the Folsom Prison shop.

ingenious attempted escape from Folsom State Prison. He and another convict spent months in the prison workshop and succeeded in making, by hand, two fully functional semiautomatic pistols. They even made fifteen bullets, using the sulphur from match heads and saltpeter for gunpowder. The pair took five guards hostage, but were locked down and couldn't get to the main gate. Colson proved the high quality of his metal work by committing suicide with his homemade gun.

The next year, Ralph Sheldon, a Chicago mobster and associate of Al Capone who had moved to Lancaster, California, hatched a plan to kidnap the four Border Barons and hold them for ransom. He and his gang staged a trial run on December 20, 1930, with an armed invasion of the Hollywood home of Agua Caliente betting commissioner Zeke Caress. They forced Caress to write four checks totaling $50,000. They planned to cash them on one of the gambling ships moored off the coast in Long Beach. Leaving two gang members to guard Caress and his wife until the checks cleared, four of the gang, including Sheldon, drove to Long Beach. They evidently looked suspicious, as their car was stopped by police on the docks, and when the police asked to search it for weapons the gangsters opened fire. One cop and one mobster received near mortal wounds. Two of the gang were captured, including Sheldon. Four were tried the next spring for the shootout, the jury in April incredibly finding them not guilty, on their claim that the police fired first. Three of them were tried again, in January 1932, this time on kidnapping charges, and were convicted. Sheldon got ten years to life.

The Agua Caliente racetrack opened two months after the 1929 stock market crash. The resort's hotel and bungalows were full to capacity, with fifteen Pullman sleeper cars added on a rail siding to provide additional beds. Twenty-thousand people filled the grandstands, almost four times the rated capacity. Al Jolson was master of ceremonies. Soon, however, the Depression began to be felt, patronage fell off and investors became uneasy. In March

1932 track manager James Crofton arranged to import Phar Lap, a world famous race horse, from Australia. The superb animal won by almost three
lengths, setting a track record. King George V of England sent a telegram,
"Heartiest congratulations on great victory of Phar Lap." One well-known
racing judge declared Phar Lap better than Man O'War. After the race the
horse's owner had Phar Lap shipped to a ranch in Menlo Park near San Francisco. Phar Lap died there a few days later of arsenic poisoning.

In 1933 the Caliente track received another blow when California did an
about-face and legalized racetrack betting. Over the next few years new and
old tracks opened — Santa Anita, heavily backed by millionaire Bing Crosby,
Del Mar, and Hollywood Park in Inglewood with Jack Warner of Warner
Brothers on the governing board.

From the outset the Agua Caliente resort had close relations with the
Baja California and federal Mexican governments. By agreement, 80 percent
of its employees were Mexican; it paid high local and federal taxes; two national presidents were generously remunerated, and the Baja governors were
actually partners. Agua Caliente was the largest employer in Tijuana, and paid
wages of $25 to $30 a day, while the average in the city was only $1.50. The
1934 federal elections spelled the beginning of the end. The new president,
Lázaro Cárdenas, was a radical nationalist reformer who had little patience for
foreign-owned businesses, particularly morally questionable ones, no matter
how much money they produced. In 1935 he ordered the casino closed.

While the Mexican government now saw Agua Caliente as an infringe-
ment on their country's sovereignty for the profit of foreigners, the San Diego
press viewed it as drain on their city's wealth for the benefit of rich Mexicans.
The California-Pacific International Exposition was held in San Diego's Balboa Park from the summer of 1935 to September 1936. Baron Long, who by
then lived in San Diego, was among the Exposition's prominent backers. The
San Diego Herald flayed him in a rather tendentious editorial:

> Tijuana is reaping millions from the Exposition while San Diego
> business men and taxpayers are starving! Now we are finding out that
> [the Exposition] has been opened for the benefit of Mexico and Baron
> Long. His holdings at Agua Caliente, and the holdings of all Americans
> in Tijuana gambling are insignificant in comparison with the holdings of
> Mexicans — some of whom are bitter haters of everything American.
> When, therefore, American money goes to Baron Long he only gets part
> of it. He is only a front for rich and arrogant Mexicans who are taking
> the cream.

There were bitter and prolonged protests by Tijuana workers against the Agua
Caliente closure. Hundreds were faced with losing their jobs and taking huge

pay cuts elsewhere in the city, but Cárdenas held firm even in the face of threats of local military-scale violence. Civil war in Mexico was far from a distant memory and Tijuana had changed hands by armed clashes more than once. The closure dragged, was partial, then there was a brief three month reopening in the spring of 1937, but without the casino. This made it a losing proposition. Cárdenas expropriated Agua Caliente on December 18, 1937, and turned it into a technical school.

The Tijuana unions then opened a fierce campaign to get the federal government to pay the fired workers compensation. There were militant demonstrations and near riots. The unrest was already at a high pitch when, on February 14, 1938, eight-year-old Olga Camacho was raped and murdered. A twenty-four-year-old soldier, Juan Castillo Morales, was arrested and confessed to the horrific crime. An outraged mob burned city hall and demanded Morales' blood. The government did not hand him over, but made an exception to the national abolition of the death penalty. Employing an obsolete military custom, Morales was released in a cemetery and told to run while his barracks mates shot at him until he fell.

In a strange turnabout, visitors to Morales' grave claimed to see blood, arbitrarily interpreting such visions as a sign, with no other evidence, that Morales was innocent. Many became convinced, despite his confession, that he was some kind of holy martyr. Within months he came to be known as Juan Soldado, John the Soldier, an uncanonized saint and object of a religious folk cult. His grave became a place of pilgrimage for thousands of believers. This incredible story is told in full by Paul Vanderwood in his *Juan Soldado*.

All the Pretty Little Horses

In 1924, nine years into his part ownership of the Jockey Club in Tijuana, Baron Long decided to go into racehorse breeding on his own. He bought the Rancho el Valle de las Viejas, a spread of 1609 acres northeast of San Diego. The place was named by the first Spaniards who explored the land. Dorothy McDonald in *The Southern California Rancher* explains the odd name:

> When the winter snows lay heavy in the mountains and the hunt sometimes took them far afield, it is said to have been the Indians' custom to make an encampment for the old people and the children beside a big spring in a sheltered draw near the south end of Viejas valley. There in the big boulders by the spring are innumerable little depressions where the squaws ground their acorn meal. Such a sight, perhaps, met the eyes of the first Spaniards who entered the valley and accounted for their naming it "El Valle de las Viejas" — the Valley of the Old Women.

She adds that

> Baron Long was the last white man to own Viejas Rancho; for about
> nine years between 1924 and 1933 his white-painted paddocks enclosed
> some of the finest race horses ever bred in the west. Cherry Tree, Blind
> Baggage, Hand Grenade, Sir Lanny, Run Star, Runnymede and Iron
> Crown — the list of famous stallions that stood at his ranch included all
> these grand horses. Here, too, was raised Ervast — the horse for which
> Jack Dempsey is said to have offered $100,000.

Baron Long Ranch, 1930

Naturally this was a topic Damon Runyon couldn't resist. He devoted a column to the Valle de las Viejas.

> Little did the good Baron dream as he spread the effulgence of the
> old castor oil smile over the inmates of the Vernon Country Club that he
> would one day be monarch of vast acres o'er which he would be gallop-
> ing, clickety-click, scores of royally bred hay burners, or horses. That he
> — Baron Long — would be Hidalgo of Rancho de las Viejas, and val-
> iantly carrying on the hoss breeding glory of California. *(Chester Times,*
> December 15, 1931)

After California's racetracks were closed by law in 1909, breeding became
unprofitable. Adolph Spreckels, owner of the giant sugar company, was one
of the few rich enough to continue the avocation, and that at a loss. Baron
Long entered the field the year of Spreckels' death, and became a major figure
nationally. Runyon continues:

I doubt that the good Baron Long had any thought of ever profiting from breeding when he bought Rancho Valle de las Viejas and his haras [a stud farm] there. It was simply a bug with the Baron. Yet in 1930 he was fourth among the breeders of America for total thoroughbred winners during that year, and he is largely responsible for the return of California to the important breeding centers of the country. . . . His stallions are the old timer Runnymede, now about twenty-four years old, Hand Grenade, the good Baron's favorite, Sir Lanny, Iron Crown and Cherry Tree. Runnymede is the sire of Morvich, a Kentucky Derby winner.

The Border Barons had a custom of naming horses for each other. Long had a horse named Wirt G. Bowman, his partners had one named Crofton, and one named Norab, after the Baron's yacht. Baron Long's horses came in first in 251 races in 1931, second 199 times, and third 201 times, winning a total of $200,000.

The Baron's career as a horse breeder came to a flaming end in 1932 in the Linden Tree scandal. Long was angry at East Coast bookmakers who regularly cheated their customers by "plugging." To cut their payouts the practice was to throw in a wad of their own money at the last minute on the horses their customers had put the most money on, thereby lowering the odds. Baron Long decided to give them a payback in kind. He had two of his own horses, a lackluster pair who finished last and next to last, entered in a race at Agua Caliente on January 6, 1932, but staged his manipulation to change the odds on the favorite, the two-year-old star gelding Linden Tree. The story is famous enough to appear in several books, including Jim Gentile's *By a Nose: Gambling Tales from a Horseracing Insider.*

The odds on Linden Tree were 1/3, meaning one extra dollar would be paid on every $3 bet, the payoff being $4. Long placed a $1,000 bet on Linden Tree with an East Coast bookie too late in the day for the bookie to respond to any last minute change in the odds. Then moments before the last window closed at Agua Caliente he bet $3,500 split among every other horse in the race. This boosted the odds on Linden Tree to 9.7 to 1, or $21.40 for every $2 bet. Long won $9,700 on his $1,000 bet, losing the $3,500 he had used to change the odds, for a $6,200 profit. He called a press conference the next day to tell the world how he had put one over on the crooked bookies. The world was not amused. The Agua Caliente stewards banned him from racing on his own track. They were concerned that betting against one's own horses looked in some way unethical. The next month the Baron announced that he would quit racing, sell his breeding ranch, and devote himself to his hotel business. The stewards relented and reinstated him, but he did not change his mind.

He opened negotiations to sell the Rancho el Valle de las Viejas to the government for use as an Indian reservation. This embroiled him in a long battle between the Indian tribe and their adversaries in Washington's Bureau of Indian Affairs that dragged on until late 1934. The government was in process of building the El Capitan Reservoir to provide water for San Diego. It had ordered the removal of about 150 members of the Capitan Grande band of the Kumeyaay Indians, who lived along the banks of the San Diego River in the floodplains of the projected El Capitan Dam. The Indians by treaty had the right to select where they might be moved. They objected first at leaving their graveyard behind, but finally chose two adjacent spreads, the Barona Ranch and Baron Long's Rancho el Valle de las Viejas.

The plan almost fell apart when it was discovered that a second village along Conejos Creek would also have to be moved and the costs of the move and the Baron's land looked prohibitive. A minority of the Capitan Grande Indians selected the Barona Ranch of J. Wadham, about four times larger than Valle de las Viejas and only $75,000. Long was asking $200,000 for his smaller spread. He eventually came down to $125,000.

The government was still dubious but Historian Tanis Thorne writes that a small group of the Capitan Grande Indians and their relatives from Conejos Creek were adamant that Long's property was what they wanted.

> It had a sportsman's out-of-town clubhouse, an abundance of hay and alfalfa, and ten to twelve barns. The Paipa brothers, stock-raisers and horse-lovers, were attracted to the Baron Long property, particularly as one of their major financial assets was a large horse herd.

The Bureau of Indian Affairs tried to persuade the pro-Viejas group to settle for shares in the already-purchased Barona Ranch. They failed. Thorne writes:

> [I]n February 1933, those in Conejos joined in the petition with the Paipa group to purchase the Baron Long ranch, touting its advantages of nearly 900 acres of almost level farm land, farm machinery in good condition, barns and stables for houses and stock, electricity, and other modern conveniences.

In a final poll of the eligible Indians in August 1934, 57 voted to go to Barona, 74 still asked for the Baron Long ranch, and 23 were undecided or planned to leave the community. The graves were moved in November 1934, the Capitan Grande and Conejos Indians following immediately, though the purchase was not finally approved by Washington until May 1935. The land today is known as the Baron Long Reservation. According to Wikipedia, 289 members of the band live on the reservation. They run the Viejas Casino, which should amuse the old Baron.

The Biltmore Years

As he was extracting himself from his horse breeding ranch, Baron Long made another huge investment, taking a twenty-five year lease on Los Angeles' premier hotel, the Biltmore, facing Pershing Square in downtown. The LA hostelry was part of the exclusive chain founded by Gustav Baumann with the New York Biltmore that opened in 1914. Baumann died a few months later in a mysterious fall from his hotel's twenty-second-floor parapet. His secretary, John McEntee Bowman, took over the business and expanded it nationally, opening the Los Angeles Biltmore in October 1923.

Recent photo of the Biltmore Hotel in downtown Los Angeles

It was elegance incarnate. Designed by architects Schultze & Weaver, the eleven-story building is a melange of Spanish-Italian Renaissance Revival, Mediterranean Revival, and Beaux Arts. It's signatory angel, representing both the hotel and the City of Angels, is used liberally.

Inside there is lavish use of bas reliefs, frescos, murals, carved marble, oak paneling, crystal chandeliers, and fine tapestries. Italian artist Giovanni Smeraldi, whose work graces the Vatican and the White House, spent seven months painting the mural ceilings in the main Galleria and the Crystal Ballroom, filling it with images of Greek and Roman gods.

Bowman in turn died in October 1931, leaving his company somewhat in disarray, and the elegant Los Angeles Biltmore soon slipped into the red. Baron Long took it over in 1933.

"The Baron then proclaimed (as only he could) the Depression over, the country healed, and turned the Biltmore into a lustrous magnet for celebrities, politicians, social elites, and foreign dignitaries" (*Satan's Playground*). He had stayed in touch with Wayne McAllister, the young architect he had hired to design Agua Caliente. Earlier in 1933, as Prohibition was ending, Long and McAllister jointly founded the Balboa Brewery in San Diego. McAllister became a capable brewer and vice president of the company, which had profitable sales in San Diego and Los Angeles. When the Baron acquired the Biltmore he called in Wayne and Corinne McAllister to make a number of strategic renovations aimed an increasing profitability.

First, he had the McAllisters add a bar on every floor, careful to make them architecturally compatible with the existing building and commissioning paintings for their walls. Then he added the Rendezvous, an afternoon dance hall open from noon to 6 pm. The final touch was construction of the Biltmore Bowl restaurant and nightclub. It premiered on April 5, 1934. It was considered the world's largest nightclub, and could seat a thousand diners. The Bowl was 140 feet long and used no interior pillars. It featured a full orchestra and floor show.

Baron Long's party for his Biltmore employees, May 7, 1939

The Baron gave a party there for his employees on May 7, 1939, that filled the place. He also added a restaurant called Little Paris where he imported not only the furniture from France but the entire staff and chef as well.

Jim Heimann comments:

> With the stars in regular attendance, the society crowd wanted in, and made the Bowl the spot for their parties. The fraternities and sororities from nearby colleges virtually took it over for Friday Collegian Nights, and local radio station KFI sent out national broadcasts from the instantly popular room. The Bowl was a jump ahead in the Biltmore's silent rivalry with the Ambassador.

Baron Long (seated in beret) on his yacht the *Norab*, 1940

The Baron kept his yacht, the *Norab*. He used it while Agua Caliente survived to sail regularly from San Diego or Los Angeles to Tijuana (he also owned a plane that he sometimes used for this trip). He gave President Cárdenas a short cruise but it didn't persuade the militant reformer to back off from his plans to close Agua Caliente. In 1936 he cruised to Catalina Island with producer Irving Thalberg and Norma Shearer as guests. He held frequent parties aboard in San Diego harbor. Vanderwood in *Satan's Playground* and even the *Los Angeles Times* in Long's obituary say that when the U.S. entered World War II Long leased the *Norab* to the U.S. government for $1 a year and it was used by General Douglas MacArthur as his headquarters during the Pacific War. As so often happens in searching for the truth about the Baron's life this account is disputed. The summer 2010 issue of the *Liberty Log*, a newsletter for U.S. merchant seamen who sailed during World War II, carries an article by Ron Stahl, who served on the *Norab* in New Guinea. He writes:

> Once it was taken over by the US Army Transport Service, the beautiful staterooms were ripped out and converted into hospital wards with four tiers of bunks close together. It was intended to use it as a sea going ambulance, retrieving wounded soldiers from the front line. Once the refit was done, it set out alone and unarmed across the Pacific war zone to join the US Army Transport Service Small Ships fleet.

Shallow draft vessels were needed to penetrate the bays and inlets in New Guinea. The ships were crewed by men too old or too young for regular military service. Stahl says that the chief steward and cook were in their seventies and two crew members were only fifteen. In New Guinea the *Norab* for several months "went up seven days a week and each day brought back about 70 stretcher cases and 100 walking wounded."

Gary Cooper visited the harbor to entertain the troops, along with Red Buttons and Una Merkel. He recognized the *Norab* from his own time aboard her at the Baron's San Diego parties. He came on board for a dinner, which Stahl attended.

After the war the *Norab* lay at anchor in Sydney harbor for several years, then was sold to lobster fishermen from Tasmania, the island and Australian state off the south coast of Australia. It sank in a storm in the country's principal harbor. Stahl returned thirty years after the war on a kind of pilgrimage:

> On the sightseeing boat which took passengers around the harbour, I was amused to find that the guide was saying that "General Macarthur's yacht was sunk below." He was very disappointed when I told him that was simply not true.

Baron Long sold his interest in the U.S. Grant hotel in 1944 for $3 million. The Biltmore was sold in 1951 for $12,750,000 to a Texas syndicate, but this did not cancel Baron Long's lease and he continued as the hotel's president and operator. His twenty-five-year lease expired in 1958, and he was then made chairman of the board. He died on April 18, 1962, of a heart attack in his rooms at the Biltmore. Martha, his wife of fifty years, survived him. The *LA Times,* which had once campaigned against the evils of the Baron's Vernon Country Club, wrote that "his name was legendary in the history of hotels and horses."

After the Biltmore renovation, Long's protege Wayne McAllister was in high demand for similar work. His wife Corinne left the business in 1938 to raise their children. Wayne designed makeovers for the Hollywood Roosevelt and Town House hotels. He designed the original Bob's Big Boy and the Pig and Whistle, as well as renovations and expansions for the Brown Derby, Clifton's Cafeteria, Lawry's Prime Rib, and the layout of the kitchens and part of the design for the golden arches for McDonald's when the franchise was just beginning.

McAllister perfected the drive-in, his creations providing no seating at all, just a circular food preparation hub around which cars parked for outdoor service on trays that were hung on the car windows by carhops. His drive-ins are now long gone: Simons, Wich Stand, Roberts, Herbert's. They are recorded in *The Leisure Architecture of Wayne McAllister* by Chris Nichols and can be seen occasionally in old movies. Alan Hess in *Googie Redux* called McAllister's works "the most radically modern buildings ever constructed in the United States. No other buildings were shaped so effectively by technology — the automobile."

In the forties and fifties McAllister worked on the hotels and casinos of the newly minted Las Vegas. He and a partner built the hotel El Rancho Vegas, opening in 1941. The next year he remodeled the El Cortez Hotel for Meyer Lansky and Bugsy Siegel. In the early fifties he designed the Desert Inn, and his most famous Las Vegas construct, the Sands, which opened in 1952. He became a vice president of the Marriott hotel corporation in 1956, moving to Washington, DC, but he and Corinne returned to California around 1961, living in Pasadena, where he gave up architecture and took up ostrich farming. He died in 2000 at the age of ninety two. Corinne followed in 2001 at ninety six.

May 6, 2012

Sources

Beltran, David Jimenez. 2004. *The Agua Caliente Story: Remembering Mexico's Legendary Racetrack.* Lexington, Kentucky: Eclipse Press.

Billboard, November 15, 1980.

Chester Times, Chester, PA. December 15, 1931.

Djedje, Jennifer Cogdell, and Eddie S. Meadows, eds. 1998. *California Soul: Music of African Americans in the West (Music of the African Diaspora).* Berkeley: University of California Press.

Ellenberger, Allan R. 2005. *The Valentino Mystique: The Death and Afterlife of the Silent Film Idol.* Jefferson, North Carolina: McFarland & Company.

Evening News (San Jose, California). December 11, 1920. "What's Doing in League of Sports."

Federal Writers' Project. 1941. *Los Angeles: A Guide to the City and Its Environs*. Scholarly Press.

Frank, Rusty E. 1994. *Tap! The Greatest Tap Dance Stars and Their Stories, 1900-1955*. New York: Da Capo Press.

Gentile, Jim. 2008. *By a Nose: Gambling Tales from a Horseracing Insider*. Bloomington, Indiana: Xlibris Corp.

Grace, Roger M. May 22, 2007. "Erstwhile Supporter Seeks Woolwine's Ouster; Former Rival Defends Him." Los Angeles: *Metropolitan News-Enterprise*.

Henstell, Bruce. 1984. *Sunshine and Wealth: Los Angeles in the Twenties and Thirties*. San Francisco: Chronicle Books.

Hess, Alan. 2004. *Googie Redux: Ultramodern Roadside Architecture*. San Francisco: Chronicle Press.

Hezog, Lawrence A. 1999. *From Aztec to High Tech: Architecture and Landscape across the Mexico-United States Border*. Baltimore: The Johns Hopkins University Press.

Heimann, Jim. 1985. *Out with the Stars: Hollywood Nightlife in the Golden Era*. New York: Abbeville Press.

Isoardi, Steven Louis. 2006. *The Dark Tree: Jazz and the Community Arts in Los Angeles*. Berkeley: University of California Press.

Jazz Journal. December 1951, Vol. 4, No. 12.

Keaton, Buster, and Charles Samuels. 1960. *My Wonderful World of Slapstick*. New York: Doubleday.

Kilty, James. 1963. *Leonis of Vernon*. New York: Carlton Press.

Kipen, David. 2011. *Los Angeles in the 1930s: the WPA Guide to the City of Angels*. Berkeley: University of California Press.

Leider, Emily W. 2003. *Dark Lover: The Life and Death of Rudolph Valentino*. New York: Farrar, Straus and Giroux

Life magazine. December. 30, 1940.

Lomax, Alan. 1950. *Mister Jelly Roll*. New York: Duell, Sloan and Pearce.

Lorey, David E. 1999. *The U.S.-Mexican Border in the Twentieth Century*. New York: Rowman & Littlefield.

Los Angeles Times. June 25, 1978. "Grant Hotel: A Bittersweet Reminder of Better Days."

McDonald, Dorothy L. Circa 1946-1948. "El Valle de las Viejas." *The Southern California Rancher*.

Merrill, Dennis. 2009. *Negotiating Paradise: U.S. Tourism and Empire in Twentieth-Century Latin America*. Chapel Hill: University of North Carolina Press.

Milwaukee Sentinel, April 24, 1926.

Nichols, Chris. 2007. *The Leisure Architecture of Wayne McAllister*. Layton, Utah: Gibbs Smith.

Nierenberg, Gerard I. 1995. *The Art of Negotiating*. Lyndhurst, New Jersey: Barnes and Noble.

Pastras, Philip. 2003. *Dead Man Blues: Jelly Roll Morton Way Out West*. Berkeley: University of California Press.

Photoplay magazine. July-December 1926 issue.

Rayner, Richard. 2009. *A Bright and Guilty Place: Murder, Corruption, and L.A.'s Scandalous Coming of Age.* New York: Doubleday.

San Diego Magazine, November 2006.

St. John, Rachel. 2011. *Line in the Sand: A History of the Western U.S.-Mexico Border.* Princeton, New Jersey: Princeton University Press.

Tanck, Paul. ND. *Venice Firsts... An Historical Guide to the Uniqueness of this Intriguing Southern California City.* An Amazon Kindle ebook.

Taylor, Lawrence D. 2002. "The Wild Frontier Moves South: U.S. Entrepreneurs and the Growth of Tijuana's Vice Industry, 1908-1935." *Journal of San Diego History*, vol. 48, no. 3.

Thorne, Tanis C. "The Removal of the Indians of El Capitan to Viejas: Confrontation and Change in San Diego Indian Affairs in the 1930s." *Journal of San Diego History*, v. 56, no. 1, Spring 2010.

Vanderwood, Paul J. 2004. *Juan Soldado: Rapist, Murderer, Martyr, Saint.* Durham, North Carolina: Duke University Press.

Vanderwood, Paul J. 2010. *Satan's Playground: Mobsters and Movie Stars at America's Greatest Gaming Resort.* Durham, North Carolina: Duke University Press.

Vieira, Mark A. 2009. *Irving Thalberg: Boy Wonder to Producer Prince.* Berkeley: University of California Press.

Wood, Andrew Grant. 2004. *On the Border: Society and Culture Between the United States and Mexico.* New York: Rowman & Littlefield.

The Twilight of Industrial Society

I spent several days at the end of May 2012 on a farm in the Appalachian Mountains near Artemas, Pennsylvania. Some 180 people had gathered there for a conference billed as The Age of Limits: Conversations on the Collapse of the Global Industrial Model. Most had driven in from the Eastern seaboard, camping in little dome-shaped tents in the dense forest that fills the majority of the 165 acre Four Quarters InterFaith Sanctuary. Four Quarters is nominally a church. Scattered around the property are little altars — to the Indian elephant god Ganesh, the Buddha, and other deities. The central spiritual focus is its Circle of Standing Stones, forty-two 10,000 pound monoliths set upright in a half circle, erected with volunteer labor over the last seventeen years. They plan to complete the circle in the decade to come. The sanctuary is off the grid, provides its own electricity (shut off at night), and grows most of its own food on thirty acres of arable land. The operation's patriarch, Orren Whiddon, a fifty-five-year-old retired mechanical engineer, oversees a first-rate machine shop on the premises that makes replacement parts for people in nearby towns.

I heard of the conference from a posting on the Energy Bulletin website (http://www.resilience.org/) of the Post Carbon Institute, a think tank in Santa Rosa, California, devoted to the study of natural resource depletion, particularly of oil, climate change, and limits to economic growth. Four of the most prominent writers on peak oil and the threat it poses to the world economy were scheduled to speak: John Michael Greer, author of *The Ecotechnic Future: Envisioning a Post-Peak World*; Tom Whipple, a retired CIA analyst who is editor of the daily online Peak Oil News and the weekly Peak Oil Review, both published by the Association for the Study of Peak Oil-USA; Gail Tverberg, who writes widely under the title Gail the Actuary and maintains the website Our Finite World (www.ourfiniteworld.com); and Dmitry Orlov, a Russian-born author who witnessed the collapse of the Soviet Union and predicts a similar fate for the United States.

I read all of these people regularly and couldn't resist the chance to meet them in the flesh. The road there was a bit long — I was one of only two people from the West Coast. It involved a plane to Minneapolis, then another to Baltimore, and on in a rental car for a 125 mile drive up into the Pennsylvania Appalachians. I packed an ultralight sleeping bag in my suitcase, and reserved one of the limited spaces in the farm's bunkhouse, for a nominal $10 a night.

I should say at the outset that most people don't pay any attention to, or take seriously, the threat of declining fossil fuels, except as it shows up in prices at the gas station, which are still far from prohibitive. The idea that our society could collapse outright because oil becomes too scarce or too expensive seems like just one more of those dystopian notions the movies and science fiction are full of. The most plausible and often portrayed include nuclear war and megaplagues. Less likely are sudden drastic changes in the earth's climate, meteor strikes, alien invasions, and, at the bottom of the barrel, brain eating zombies, giant ants, and the pod people. Because most of these are improbable or impossible doesn't mean there aren't real civilization-destroying perils in our future. The most threatening arise from our uncontrolled population growth and insatiable use of natural resources on a finite planet that is reaching its limits.

Most of us know that we are in the early stages of a human-caused rise in the earth's temperature that is already producing droughts, floods, wildfires, and flooding of low-lying areas, and is likely to make large parts of the planet uninhabitable in a century or little more. Hitting the world's limits on oil production is also already in its early stages, and those scientists who follow this are inclined to think that it will hit in full force much sooner than the worst of global warming. James Hamilton, an economist at UC San Diego, in a paper for the Brookings Institute says that rising oil prices were a greater cause of the 2008 economic crash than the housing bubble.

World output of cheap oil, on which our civilization depends for transportation, lubricants, fertilizer, plastics, and many other necessary products, flatlined in 2005, acknowledged in November 2010 by the Organization for Economic Cooperation and Development's International Energy Agency, which projects that global crude oil production will never again reach its 2005 level. We are now making up the difference from extremely expensive and environmentally destructive sources — deepwater, tar sands, fracked shale for tight oil, and corn ethanol. And there are good reasons to believe that these "unconventional" sources cannot be produced in sufficient volume to make up for the growing shortfall in ordinary crude. The UK Industry Taskforce on Peak Oil and Energy Security in its 2010 report projected that world oil production would hit its peak within ten years and possibly by 2015. The Age of

Limits conference sought to look at the consequences we face and discuss our options.

What distinguished all the speakers (because of back-to-back scheduling I did not get to hear psychologist Carolyn Baker) was agreement that no foreseeable alternative energy source is on the horizon to replace fossil fuels, particularly for transportation, and that our societies would have needed to begin scaling back energy use thirty or forty years ago to prepare a soft landing. None did. John Michael Greer commented in his blog a few days after the event that "it started from the place where most other peak oil events stop, with the recognition that the decline and fall of industrial civilization is the defining fact of our time." That was certainly the case. No time was spent on hopes that technology will magically come up with something that will let us keep our cars and energy-intensive lives. The talk was all about the post-industrial future, how to prepare for it, and how to survive in the new spartan world to come.

I am going to give my account of the talks I was able to attend in a different order than they were given. The reason is that the subject is for most people an extreme one: contemplating the breakdown of our society in the relatively near future. Tom Whipple and Gail Tverberg concentrated on the immediate problems we face in fossil fuel depletion, the most pressing potential cause of such a collapse. Their evidence should come first. John Michael Greer and Dmitry Orlov focused on what comes next, so their comments should follow on.

(Gail Tverberg and Tom Whipple presented many statistics in their talks. I have checked these and they come almost entirely from the U.S. government official Energy Information Administration. The speakers refer to the beginning of the plateau in world oil production variously as 2004 and 2005. In fact, oil output was slightly higher in 2005 than at any point in 2004, but production fell off a year later to levels a little below the 2004 highs, giving both 2004 and 2005 defensible claims as the starting point of the long flatline that followed.)

Gail Tverberg: Rentier Debt and the Collapse of Debt Based Finance

"You can't have infinite growth in a finite world," Gail the Actuary began. Natural systems stay generally in balance. If there are more predators, they thin the prey population. In the next cycle some of the predators have died off and prey numbers expand, leading in the third iteration to more predators again and so on. Human societies in contrast are growth based with no effective predators except war, disease, and occasional famine.

Even when we were hunter-gatherers the small groups of humans could move to new territories and they discovered fire, tamed dogs, and invented spears. Populations increased steadily from the adoption of agriculture, then skyrocketed with the energy boost of the fossil fuel economies of coal and then oil.

"In natural systems the rule is the survival of the fittest. Human intelligence defeats this, steadily increasing the population, overcoming hostile environments."

The modern, fossil-fuel-based industrial economy is founded on perpetual growth. "More materials are steadily needed from the natural world. These have to be transformed into usable goods. And the purchasers must have a way to pay for them. This gives rise to the rentiers, enablers of debt. Debt allows people to buy things they can't pay for. This works for the federal government as well as for individuals. In 1945 at the end of an expensive war U.S. debt amounted to half, .5, of GDP. In 2008 it had grown to 2.8 times GDP. World per capita energy consumption also shot up after World War II. And better health care led to lower infant mortality and longer lives, so population shot up faster."

The current world financial system is based on debt. "Banks loan principal. Borrowers pay back the principal plus interest. You need growth to make those payments. The number one problem of the rentier system is that it is easy to repay loans in an expanding economy, but hard in a declining economy. When oil prices rise, discretionary spending slows. There are layoffs. People can't pay their debts, and don't owe as much in taxes so the government's income declines."

There is a risk of general collapse in a prolonged economic decline. "For one thing, the FDIC has only a fraction of the amount needed to fund a general run on the banks, and the major pension funds are mostly in deficit and vulnerable to any significant downturn in the stock market. The government today is paying out $1.46 for every $1 it takes in in taxes."

One person asked if a steady-state economy without growth would be an alternative to capitalist and socialist dependence on economic growth. Tverberg replied, "The population is too high for that. There are not real alternative energy sources for steady-state. Deforestation was a problem 4000 years ago. Erosion is a big issue around the world, responsible for many society collapses. Without plentiful and cheap oil there could only be a steady-state economy at a very low level. And there isn't enough land for everyone to have their own plot."

And finally, very bluntly:

"You need to get to a small enough community to gather around a general store and run a barter tab, where you bring in your stuff to get something from the store."

Gail Tverberg on Resource Depletion in General and Fossil Fuels in Particular

Tverberg began this talk with several slides, the first showing world energy use since 1820. Beginning at perhaps 10 exajoules, the total reached 100 only in 1950, then soared to about 540 in 2010. In the total mix, oil is the largest component, followed by coal, natural gas, and, at about 30 exajoules, biofuels, including wood. Nuclear and hydroelectric contribute an insignificant amount. The United States uses about 94 exajoules of energy per year. Per capita oil consumption has been declining since the price began to escalate in 1980, while natural gas, which has been widely substituted for oil in producing electricity, along with coal, has been rising rapidly.

Conventional oil, that is, ordinary crude pumped out of onshore wells, peaked in 2004 worldwide and has plateaued since then. There is other oil or oil-like substances available and included in claims of total reserves, but we must understand that these are both much more expensive and far slower to extract. In successive layers, Tverberg said, there is shallow-water liquid oil, onshore heavy oil (Venezuela), tar sands (Canada), ultradeep-water oil, polar oil, tight oil, sometimes wrongly called shale oil, and oil shale (kerogen).

"The situation is similar for all minerals. Companies extract the best and cheapest resources first. It always looks like there is plenty left, and there is, if your standards are low enough. What is left is lower quality, usually produces less energy per volume, costs much more to extract, is slower to extract, and often requires inputs, such as massive amounts of water, that must compete with other necessary uses. The bottom line is that companies will not spend more than one barrel of oil to recover one barrel of oil. At that breakeven point no matter how much is left in the ground it will stay there."

For most minerals, companies dig them out only as they are needed. Oil is different. The need is so great that it is drilled as fast as technology permits, and everywhere it can be found if the price is high enough. According to the government's Energy Information Administration, U.S. oil production peaked in 1970 at 9.6 million barrels a day. It declined until about 2008 at about 4.95 mbd. The turn to unconventional and expensive sources has pushed output up to 5.67 mbd in 2011.

European production plateaued around 1996 at around 7.2 mbd, then went into sharp decline from 2002. By 2010 output had fallen to around 4.5 mbd. World oil production rose for a long time, from around 30 mbd in 1965 to 80 mbd in 2003 but has flatlined at between 80 and 82 mbd since 2004. Production has proven to be inelastic. It hasn't responded to wide price fluctuations, contrary to the predictions of the standard economic model. The $147 a barrel price spike in the spring of 2008 didn't bring any more oil to market. The collapse to $40 later that year as the recession hit did not produce a drop in production. The new rise to over $120 a barrel early in 2011 also failed to elicit an increase. This means that producers are pumping as fast as they can and this is the supply available.

"The question gets to be: How high a price can the economy afford? High prices for oil lead to high prices for food as well. The two prices graph as a tight parallel. As prices of oil, gasoline, and food go up, people cut back on discretionary spending. Workers in discretionary sectors are laid off. Recession arrives or lingers."

Natural gas consumption has been fairly flat, Tverberg said. "The prices have seen a big slide. There is overproduction just now. Shale gas costs $6-$7 a thousand cubic feet to produce and is selling for a little over $2. This contrasts with oil, where the global production cost worldwide is around $92 a barrel."

Eventually there will be a peak in coal production as well as the two other fossil fuels, but we are not there yet. "World output has been growing rapidly, from about 2 billion tons in 1980 to more than 3.5 billion tons in 2010, mainly to fuel the growth of manufacturing in China and the rest of Asia."

In summary Tverberg said that world oil production is flat, while demand keeps increasing, meaning rising prices, which induce recessions. "U.S. production is up a little, but not enough to fix the world's problem." Natural gas is produced and traded in national markets or where contiguous land mass allows delivery by pipeline, so prices vary widely by region. "U.S. production is up but demand is not, so prices are too low. We should expect production to drop. Coal production is up worldwide, mainly for use in Asia.

Tom Whipple: the Myth of Energy Independence

Tom Whipple, white haired, genial, and closer to my age than the other speakers, also came with a PowerPoint slide show. This time I wised up and snapped photos of his slides as an

aid in following the rush of graphs and numbers. He opened with some general observations on why, even with the current heavy investment in tar sands and tight oil, the United States is not going to become independent of the stagnant world oil market.

"Peak oil is not a theory," he said. "It is a number. Kjell Aleklett, professor of Physics at Uppsala University, Sweden, and president of the Association for the Study of Peak Oil and Gas (ASPO), has a new book just coming out, *Peeking at Peak Oil*, that pulls together some of the key numbers. The most important is that conventional oil, what we call crude oil, plateaued in 2004 at 82 million barrels a day. Conventional oil rests on a column of water, which is what makes it easy to extract, compared to oil saturating rock or sand. This key source is declining by 4-6%, or 4 mbd each year. It is supplemented in the world's supply by unconventional oil. These are tar sands, Venezuelan heavy oil, tight oil extracted from shale by fracking, and deep sea oil. U.S. Energy Information Administration experts project that these sources combined can only increase to an annual 8 mbd over the next twenty-five years. In the same period conventional will have declined by 100 mbd, more than today's total annual output. If there is to be any conventional oil at all in 2037 it would depend on a very high rate of new discoveries, and we are not seeing that."

A slide now showed that in the United States the use of fossil fuels actually increased from 70% of energy use in 1975 to 80% in 2011, with renewables supplying only 9.1% in 2011. The U.S. consumed 18.8 mbd in 2009, of which it produced 7.5 mbd. (These figures, from the Energy Information Administration, include natural gas liquids; 5.36 mbd of this total was crude oil).

"There has been a great deal of hype in the media over the increase in U.S. oil from Canadian tar sands and the Bakken Shale in Montana and North

Dakota, but the amounts are not a significant part of U.S. consumption, not remotely enough to free the country from the need for imported oil. Total oil production in the U.S. from all sources, including the new unconventional ones, rose from 7.5 mbd in 2010 to a rate of 8.2 mbd in the first quarter of 2012, an increase of about 700,000 barrels a day out of a total consumption of more than 18 million barrels. Not a game changer.

"The problem with unconventional oil is not only that the production rates are low compared to our consumption, but the costs are extremely high for deep water platforms, tight oil (fracked shale oil), and tar sands. A deep water platform costs up to $1 billion. The returns have been disappointing compared to that cost. The Atlantis Platform, the third largest oil field in the Gulf of Mexico, was supposed to be rated at 200,000 barrels a day. It hit a little over 100,000 in the first half of 2008, fell to 20,000 that fall, peaked at a little under 140,000 in January 2010, and went into a slide after that, reaching 60,000 barrels a day in April 2011. The Atlantis field is claimed to sit on 600 million barrels of oil. The media frequently report discoveries of fields with 100 million barrels as though this will solve our energy problems. The oil companies won't drill for 100 million barrels in deep water. The costs are prohibitive."

Here he showed some slides of total current and projected U.S. oil production. It had been in a steep slide from a high of 9.6 mbd in 1970 to about 4.95 in 2008. Alaskan production is in a downward slide expected to continue without improvement through 2035. There was a slight upturn after 2008 in U.S. onshore production from tight shale oil, and a sharper one in offshore, but the total production still did not reach more than 5.7 mbd (now we are talking about crude oil only), and it is projected to plateau at 6 mbd all the way through 2035. Because of the lingering recession current consumption has fallen to 14.6 mbd, the gap of 8.9 mbd made up by imports.

"The much ballyhooed shale oil has produced only 860,000 barrels a day since 2008, 6.5% of total consumption, and these plays have a huge decline rate, as much as 35% a year. It costs $10 million to drill a shale well. It is 5,000 feet down, then maybe a mile more horizontal. It is not clear that the oil companies will see this experiment as a real paying proposition when the well will be exhausted in as little as three years.

"Then there is the hype about the kerogen in Utah. There are supposed to be 1.7 trillion barrels of the stuff. Kerogen is a mixture of various organic materials a few million years short of being cooked into oil. The problem is that nobody knows how to make it usable in any potentially commercial way. The stuff in the Bakken Shale in North Dakota is actually oil. The stuff called oil shale in Utah is not. It is a solid. It has to be heated to release a vapor that is to be turned into a liquid fuel, with a high grade field producing only 25 or 30 gallons per ton of rock, and a fuel that is not suitable for gasoline, only diesel and jet fuel, with a vast input of water to process. So far there is no commercial production from this source."

The Bakken Shale mostly demonstrates the inability of this source to meet a significant part of U.S. energy needs. "The are more than 3,500 producing wells in the Bakken Shale in North Dakota. But the average well, which costs $11.5 million to drill, is producing only 114 barrels of oil per day. The total output of these thousands of wells is about 479,000 barrels a day. And the wells in the Bakken are seeing a 38% decline rate. Just to keep the rather small 479,000 flowing, the oil companies have to find 182,000 new barrels a day each year. This would need 1,488 new wells every year at a cost of $17 billion. In the last year only 1,130 wells were added, a shortfall of 25%, just to stay even with the board. Even with very high prices shale oil is not likely to exceed 2 mbd. It will not make America oil independent. We will have to consume much less to do that."

Here Whipple turned to the availability of imported oil. "The press has made a misleading issue of the fact that the U.S. exports oil products. This is mainly refined gasoline, as our refining capacity is currently greater than domestic consumption. In January 2012 the U.S. imported 10.9 mbd of crude oil. It re-exported 2.8 mbd in oil products. That left net imports at 8.1 mbd. It is not optimistic that this volume will be available indefinitely. In 2002 global net exports of the top 33 exporters was 39.1 mbd. This grew to 45.5 mbd in 2005. At that rate of growth it should have grown to 58.2 mbd in 2010, but instead it declined to 42.6 mbd. In part this is a decline in supply, in part the exporting countries are using more of their oil at home. The top 5 exporters were running at 15 mbd in 1990. This rose to 24 mbd in 2004, 53% of the global total, but is dropping to 21 mbd in 2012, and is projected to fall to zero by 2028.

"Then we have to factor in growing demand. If we extend the 2005 to 2010 rate of increase out to 2020, including China and India, and allow for only a 1% annual decline in exports by the top 33 exporting countries, the countries other than China and India would see a 60% decline in available supplies, from 40 mbd to only 16 mbd."

Natural gas displays a different trajectory from oil. At first glance it seems to promise a way out from the declining availability and increasing price of oil and gasoline. Natural gas is currently abundant and remarkably cheap. "Right now natural gas is being overproduced and is in a glut, selling below its production cost," Tom Whipple said. "In the U.S. it is around $2.25 per thousand cubic feet at the wellhead. In Japan the price is $20. Unlike oil, natural gas is difficult and expensive to transport except by pipeline, so national prices diverge sharply."

U.S. natural gas production has seen a big increase from fracking shale, the same process used to extract oil in North Dakota. Tom Whipple took as his example the Haynesville Shale, a 9,000 square mile deposit under large parts of southwestern Arkansas, northwest Louisiana, and East Texas. The natural gas bearing shale is a seam 200 to 300 feet thick found at a depth of 10,500 to 13,000 feet below the surface.

"This one deposit accounts for 11% of the total U.S. supply. The decline rate is astronomical, at best about 53% a year, or 3.8 billion cubic feet of gas that needs to be replaced annually. It is more likely that the decline rate per well is as much as 100% per year. There are already significant announcements of cancelations in plans for dry-gas drilling. At this time the natural gas companies are losing money. Most analysts forecast that natural gas will be abundant and cheap for decades. This is prompting investment in liquefied natural gas. Cars can run on either compressed or liquefied, but liquefied provides 600 times the energy of compressed. As a consequence, liquefied natural gas installations are going in across the country. My own view is that there is about a twenty-year supply of natural gas once the price goes up to make production profitable, especially if it is used more widely to fuel vehicles."

He added that he expected that "by 2020 about 40% of the world's oil supply will come from deep water wells," and that China will probably be able to outbid the United States for the available supply, mainly because their economy is smaller and a similar amount of oil would play a larger part in their operation and would be worth more than in an economy with such already extensive uses as the United States.

Tom Whipple gave a second talk Sunday morning, on the seven forces defining the twenty-first century. This, I thought, was thin compared to his presentation on oil and gas. He did draw some conclusions, however. Fossil fuels, he said, are going away. "Politicians compete," he said, "on claims of how much growth they can foster. But the price of oil permeates everything. It's going to be very hard to get the economy going again as the price of oil keeps going up. There will be some fossil fuels available for 1,000 years. It may be allocated by price. But there will not be sufficient oil to run cars." He added that the emerging scarcities include water and most other minerals as well as oil.

* * *

On the second day, I was sitting at a stone table outside when Tom Whipple sat down next to me. I started to quiz him about oil prices. West Texas Intermediate, the main U.S. price, had fallen from about $110 a barrel in January to $90 on the day we were meeting, while the European Brent price had gone from $125 early in the year to $107 (they have fallen further since, to WTI $81 and Brent $98). Whipple responded that prices had been inflated in 2011 because of disruptions in Libya, and in the spring of 2012 over Iran's threats to close the Straits of Hormuz. Now they were dropping, first to normal, and then somewhat below as the economic crisis in Europe feeds expectations of lower demand. There was also the unusual spread between WTI and Brent prices, which for years had varied by only a dollar or so. This, as I knew, was caused by storage bottlenecks in the main U.S. facility, in Cushing, Oklahoma, where Canadian tar sand oil is piling up, causing especially low prices for gasoline in the Midwest.

Whipple added, "There is a pipeline running from Cushing to the Gulf Coast, the Seaway pipeline. It is set to pump north to Cushing. To relieve the glut the pumps are being reversed. Even then they are too small to handle the volume. By a year from now they plan to install larger pumps, at which time WTI and Brent prices should reconverge and gas prices go up in the Midwest. There are other markets besides WTI and Brent. The Canadian market is going now for $72 a barrel because they can't get their product to market.

"The long-term picture is much less optimistic," he said. "World demand is going up on an annual rate by 1 million barrels a day, while the decline in production in existing wells is running at 4. That means that new discoveries need to hit the equivalent of 4 million barrels a day just to stay even and 5 to keep up with demand. I don't see that happening, and that means that prices will start to go up again unless the recession gets a whole lot worse."

John Michael Greer on Spirituality for an Age of Limits

John Michael Greer in person is charming, charismatic, and quick witted. A big burly man of fifty with a full beard, he appeared in casual clothes. Seeing him first at the opening dinner on Friday night it had taken me a moment to recognize him, as in most of his internet photos he is wearing a long white robe. That is because, in addition to his books and blogging on resource depletion and our de-industrialized future, he is also the leader of the Ancient Order of Druids in America. He has written twenty-one books, only three of which are about resource depletion. The rest explore polytheism, Renaissance magic, Kabbalah, divination, the other such topics. He was trained in the ritual magic of the Hermetic Order of the Golden Dawn, the occult lodge made famous in the last century by William Butler Yeats and Aleister Crowley. His sessions were the best attended in the heavy agenda of the three-day conference.

Saturday opened with Greer speaking on spirituality. He started before the assigned time, relaxed, speaking fluently without notes, offering advice for life in a post-oil landscape:

"You don't need to move out into the country," he told people. "Adapt in place. Deal!" He quoted wildlife author and scouting pioneer Ernest Thompson Seton, "Where you are, with what you have, right now." Greer was born in Bremerton, Washington, and lived for a long time in Ashland, Oregon. He moved a few years ago to Cumberland, Maryland, a few miles down the road from the Four Quarters InterFaith Sanctuary. The town had 37,000 people in 1950 and just 20,000 today. Greer said he picked it because it had already gone through de-industrialization and was close to farming areas.

"Brew beer," Greer advised. It could always be traded for something in a barter economy. "Japan in 1750 had almost no energy," he said. "Yet the Tokugawa period saw a great flowering of culture and the arts. It was based on rice and human labor. You have to build the skills that will be needed as energy winds down. Barter with your neighbors. There are a certain small number of places, like Manhattan, where the only option will be to get out. Even when the Greenland ice cap melts, Manhattan will still be a source of metal." He added Boston and Los Angeles to the list of unsalvageable megalopolises.

"Ten thousand years from now there will be legends about the lost cities of the desert — Las Vegas. If you are unlikely to have your own water supply, get out. Much of the suburbs used to be chicken farms, dairy farms. As the cities downsize, the suburbs can revert to what they were. Stop worrying about death. Take a risk. There is a 100 percent risk of death."

By this time the last of the audience had filtered onto the open sided roofed platform and Greer began the scheduled address.

"When people want to know about spirituality and peak oil, they usually want to hear of some supernatural force that is going to make it safe. 'Why aren't you talking about the space brothers, who are going to bring a new energy source?' Another refrain is the fantasy of the Rapture. Saint Scottie is going to beam them up to the S.S. Christ Enterprise. It's the same as the UFO fantasy except that Jesus is at the controls of the space ship."

Greer added futurist and computer guru Ray Kurtzweil, who has predicted exponential growth in computing power and in technical innovation that will solve the energy problem along with many others. "Greer's first law of exponential functions: Any exponential function taken far enough ends in absurdity. Kurtzweil predicts that we will upload our minds into robot bodies and achieve immortality. These are just glorified Rapture bodies.

"There are whole industries focused on telling us that we don't have to have the future that we have made. We can't fix it. We could have fixed it in the 1970s and we didn't. We need to stop thinking that marching around blaming the 1% will fix it. If you make $34,000 a year you are part of the global 1%."

Greer sought to distill a common element in the world's major religious traditions. "They deal with the relation between humans and gods. Gods signify that there is an order to the cosmos and it is not subject to your druthers. Every now and then the humans are off building utopia. The gods go away for a while, and return to find a smoking ruin. They ask, how is that utopia working out for you?

"Humans are pretty good at building civilizations. All start with some sense of the order of the cosmos. Over time the civilization becomes rich, lazy, and from there to the smoking rubble is not a great distance. There is a concept of order in many schools of thought: in Hinduism, in Buddhism, in the Chinese Dao. Our fossil fuel utopia ignores every scrap of the concept of order. Pride commeth before a what?

"Peak oil is not something that is going to happen in the distant future. It is happening now. Oil plateaued in 2005. Now we are scraping the bottom of the barrel for any scrap that can run a car."

Back in the 1970s, he said, after the Arab oil embargo, "There were ideas of doing more with less and establishing an ecologically stable society. Then it wilted and people dropped it. We saw the way the human ego works. It was not a satanic laugh but a whiny weaseling thing where most people decided to make more money and ignore the future. We live in the shadow of an immense moral failure. The U.S. was the leader in green technology. It could have been done. We didn't. And we will all pay the price. The universe doesn't care if it looks fair to us.

"Spiritual traditions say that the pursuit of making money is not necessarily a good thing. I want to talk about the spirituality, the holiness, of limits. You cannot not have limits. Industrial society has tried to free itself of all limits. The spiritual place is the place of limits. Social collapse is followed by spiritual focus. Today's Republican platform has a surprising number of parallels to the Satanic Bible of Anton Szandor LaVey, not to the New Testament."

In the question period he was asked how he explained the Religious Right. "Religions with high ethical standards," he replied, "morph into their opposites because of the difficulty of living the doctrine. Today salvation is a consumer product. This is not Christian except in a purely nominal sense. The Fundamentalists in the early twentieth century formed an alliance with the Ku Klux Klan. In 1924 the Rev. E. F. Stanton published a book entitled *Christ and Other Klansmen*. Christianity was mostly a liberal force in the 1960s, but the Devil worshippers who call themselves Christians today have given Christianity a bad name."

Still, when someone, most likely a Marxist, in the audience, asked if Greer thought religion was merely invented by rulers to pacify their subjects, the Druid leader responded, "Religion is born not because someone made it up for crowd control, but because people ran smack into the brick wall of transcendent experience."

Asked to predict the pace of social collapse, Greer compared it to the decline of Rome and suggested from 100 to 300 years overall. Long before we are far into that process, he said, our retirement funds will be worthless.

John Michael Greer on How Civilizations Fall

We reconvened in the afternoon for another session with John Michael Greer. "It is common for empires to claim they are eternal just before they collapse," he began. "Rome, Byzantium, Russia, which called itself the Third Rome. Civilizations have a recognizable life cycle. Joseph Tainter, in his *The Collapse of Complex Societies*, pointed to a buildup of layers of complexity. His list took from 100 to 300 years to fall, not a few decades. In 2005 I wrote an article, 'How Civilizations Fall: A Theory of Catabolic Collapse.' There I argued that there is a fixation on overnight collapse, taken from Christian mythology. This is the idea of the apocalypse — when evil reaches its peak, God will smash the crap out of it. Just think of Harold Camping.

"Our society thinks in straight lines — to the apocalypse, then everything will be rebuilt perfectly, and last forever. We don't look like we will dodge collapse, but it is likely to last one to three centuries, slipping down a notch, stabilizing for a while, then down another notch. The apocalyptic model competes with the progress model, where we keep getting better and better forever."

He then turned to America's connections with the broader world. "We don't like calling ourselves an empire. We are just exporting democracy, to countries that have either oil or drugs. The empire requires that we maintain our stuff. People are very reluctant to give up our stuff. But maintenance costs are unaffordable. Our money system requires immense maintenance. Imperialist extraction of resources becomes very expensive. As pieces fall off, your costs go down. When we strip New York City to the ground we will have a lot of cheap metal. In decline you can cannibalize your infrastructure."

Greer suggested that the history of other empires showed that three deep crises were typical in ending a civilization. "People respond, We are different. We have science and democracy, etc. This pattern has worked equally to end large and small civilizations. You are living in the civilization with the highest energy level and probably the highest population the world will ever see. The second Mayan crisis wiped out 90 percent of the population. But some Mayan cities continued for two hundred years. We probably will go through a dark age within the 100 to 300 years ahead. We are in the early stages now.

"The British Empire owned a quarter of the entire world. The American empire is really pretty limp in comparison. This was in a world in the first stage of catabolic collapse. We are heading into the second round of world catabolic collapse. The broad trends don't dictate the features of the unfolding crises, but the first round unfolded between 1914 and 1954." He dated the beginning of the first stage of the crisis for the United States from 1974-75 with the first oil shock and the American defeat in Vietnam.

So what should people do? "All the people talking about survival lifeboats or ecofarms who don't really take up farming make the advocates feel like they are doing something, while not doing anything. Think about it this way. What can you do now that would have helped you if you were living in Poland at the outbreak of World War II? Start from the assumption that what will happen to us will be fairly similar to what happened when earlier civilizations collapsed. It could come quickly. If the money value collapsed, many people's savings and pensions would disappear. I think of it as a stair-step model where periods of stability are punctuated by sudden lurches to lower levels."

He did not see protest as very effective:

"There are limits to what protest can accomplish. Most Occupy protestors would settle if they got a good middle class job. But those jobs are gone forever. People are clinging to the fantasy of endless progress and infinite wealth. Most of the jobs a hundred years from now are going to be as small farmers. There's a lot of expectations of entitlement, of feeling we deserve our high standard of living. No, we don't, and it won't be there. I know this is wildly unpopular, but I don't think so. Better to prepare for the world to come, not stake on getting concessions from the existing government and the rich. As the collapse progresses, the remaining fossil fuel technology will be protected by the military. None of us may see a drop of fossil fuel. I would expect an economy I call scarcity industrialism, very militaristic, top down.

"All of us are going to be poor. Most of us will die sooner than we otherwise would. But there would be the exhilaration of taking on the challenge of trying to navigate through the end of a civilization and working to found a new, if poorer, one."

Dmitry Orlov: Progressing Towards Collapse

I had read less of Dmitry Orlov's work than of the previous speakers. He was born in Leningrad in 1962, making him, at fifty, the same age as John Michael Greer. His family emigrated to the United States when he was twelve. He holds a degree in computer science and has been trained as an engineer. He spent extended time back in the Soviet Union just prior to and after the breakdown of Communism in 1990, and has written extensively on parallels he perceives between the sudden Russian implosion and similar trends in the United States. Having experienced the very sudden collapse in the USSR, Orlov more than any of the other speakers was ready to put a very short lead time on the demise of the American system.

"I have been predicting that America would collapse for some time," he opened. "What's holding it up is a really good question. You can't predict when exactly it will collapse, but you can track the rate of deterioration. If you drive over a structurally deficient bridge you are gambling with your life, but it's not a game. Risk can only be assessed with accuracy in an artificial setup, like a game. The one rule is that you should never risk what you can't afford to lose. Though not predictable, the timing of great events is not random."

All empires eventually collapse, he said. "The timing is more difficult to anticipate. Some sciences have real experts — physics, medicine. Economics is a pseudoscience. Nobody could predict the Soviet collapse or know now why it happened that year. I saw it coming a year beforehand."

Orlov pointed to ever growing debt as a major factor in undermining the American system. "The U.S. borrows about $100 billion a month in new debt.

There has been a lot of activity lately about China. Hilary Clinton and Geithner went to China. The news was about the blind Chinese activist. The Chinese had little reaction to his escape. What was the smoke screen hiding? Reuters revealed on May 21 that the U.S. government set up a secret deal with China a year ago to allow China to buy U.S. Treasury bonds directly from the Treasury, the only government in the world allowed to do that. Everyone else goes through brokerage houses. China has also now been approved to be allowed to buy U.S. banks. The U.S. is on the road to becoming a fully owned subsidiary of China. This is very different from the historical pattern."

He pointed to Facebook millionaire Eduardo Saverin leaving the country and taking his money with him, saying Saverin was not alone. "That happened in the last days of the Soviet Union. J.P. Morgan just lost $2 billion. It seems they can't understand the difference between hedging, betting, and gambling. No one goes to jail for any of this."

On the political front, "The government has been taking away rights. Congress is in process of passing a bill that would allow the IRS to take away people's passports if they owe a large amount of taxes, turning the country into a debt prison. The politicians make sure none of their banker friends go to jail, as they would lose their subsidies. I saw this in the USSR, as the political system was hollowed out for private interest."

As the collapse got underway in the USSR, trade reverted to barter. "In 1990 people were refusing to take money. They wanted real goods. People with money were leaving. In the USA the idea is to print money and buy oil and consumer goods with it. Very little is still made here. The assumption is that transportation costs don't matter. But they are not negligible. They are like a large hidden tax on everyone's income."

Orlov said we should expect an oil crisis, followed by a new economic downturn, "a stair-step downward." A major risk factor has been the growth of unproductive sectors of the economy, including its bureaucratic/administrative portion, which he estimated at about 30 percent. Very high debt and a weak productive sector, he said, amplify the effects of high oil prices and create a different and more dangerous curve than the curve of peak oil itself. "Peak oil is a bell shaped curve. The curve for economic collapse is lopsided, broad rise, sharp drop off. It is shaped by a number of progressions: the move of industry to China. Most spare parts come from China today. Small shops have been replaced by Walmart. They open a store, sell Chinese goods, local stores go out of business. Then Walmart leaves. Today they are more interested in opening stores in China. The pattern is that things get bigger, then things go away.

"We used to have lots of small ships. Now we have mega-container ships. Because of rising fuel prices they have to slow down to save fuel, running at 10 knots, slower than Clipper ships. Slow steaming will be followed by no steaming.

"Internet retail only works because of UPS and Fed Ex. When the big medical complexes fold we will have Web MD."

The U.S. is showing many symptoms of decline. "It has some of the most expensive cell phones in the world. But Internet speeds are slower than most of Europe and Asia. Cell phones are used for internet in rural areas. This is like Vietnam and Cambodia. The electric grid is aging and not kept in good repair. The transformers are not made in the United States. We are seeing more frequent blackouts. The nuclear plants are not being maintained. Bridges are not being maintained. The incidence of power outages has been doubling every year (according to a report by Goldman-Sachs). Countries without a reliable electric grid rely on gasoline or diesel generators. One example is Nigeria. It is now common for diesel generators to be used for local city electric power."

Two-thirds of the oil the U.S. uses, he said, is imported on credit.

Next he turned to our food supply. "A vast part of our food supply depends on Monsanto corn. It is used to feed livestock, and for the corn syrup that shows up in so many food products. There are only a few very similar varieties of corn, which are at risk of a poison-resistant pest. This could be like the Irish potato famine, where people are too dependant on a single crop. We even have exploding pigs."

This last refers to the appearance over the last few years of a mysterious foam at one in every four pig farms. The gelatinous foam seals in volatile methane gas in manure dumps on the farms. Four explosions have taken place killing thousands of pigs. "Most people are not paying attention," Orlov added.

Dmitry Orlov expects the crash to come very soon. Not in decades, and probably not even in years, but possibly in months. He offered some advice, based on his Soviet experience.

"We have far too much disposable trash. Mend, don't buy. Don't let fashion dictate technology. Strive for fewer possessions but better quality. Get another passport. Rely on local groups. Avoid debt slavery. People may be forced to make payments against debts that will go on to the end of their lives. You don't know if institutions will remain solvent. Your savings may become just some gold and silver coins for special occasions. Retirement will go away. Everyone will have to work as long as they are physically able to do so.

"It is better to give something away than to throw it away. People will stay close to home. Do household production to minimize the need for money. Wealth will be other people you can rely on. Mexicans have decamped to their own country, thinking it has a better chance than here."

In the question period Orlov was asked if he anticipated civil wars between neighboring states. "Not by state militias," he responded. "But law and order in some of the cities will be impossible. Expect tribal gangs and communal violence."

Asked if the pending collapse was a plot by the government, the rich, or the oil companies, he replied, "I try not to think there are conspiracies where mere stupidity will explain it."

At the end of the conference I picked up a copy of Dmitry Orlov's book, the revised edition of *Reinventing Collapse: The Soviet Experience and American Prospects*. He makes a convincing argument that the USSR and the USA mark the extremes of collectivism and of free market among the major powers, and that these ideological extremes make their systems more brittle than the states that have adopted a more balanced mixture of state and private institutions. It may come as a surprise in light of the Soviet Union's well known police state and impoverished citizenry that their system gave their citizens a far better chance to weather the collapse than the American system does. In the USSR no one owned their own home. Everyone lived in government owned apartments. When the collapse came there was hyperinflation, wiping out savings, and very large numbers lost their jobs and had no income. But no one lost their homes. They just kept on living in their shabby apartments rent free. In the United States, as the 2008 recession previewed, loss of job, pension, or income means eviction and homelessness. There were very few homeless in post-collapse Russia, mostly ethnic Russians expelled from the breakaway Soviet client states.

Further, for many reasons the Soviet planners did not like urban sprawl. Services were too expensive to provide, they did not want so many automobiles, for both cost and security reasons. The result was that most urbanites lived in closely packed apartment houses served by extensive mass transit. The trains and trolley cars kept running all through the worst period of the downturn. If oil and gasoline prices go through the roof here, and people lose their jobs, suburbanites and most city dwellers are going to simply be stranded. Unless the government remains more intact than seems likely we will see many more deaths from malnutrition or outright starvation here than in Russia.

July 1, 2012

The Radicalization of the Republican Party and the Current State of America

There are certain moments in history where many different and amorphous threads coalesce into a hitherto unanticipated shape. The accession of Augustus Caesar in 27 BC ended the 482-year-old Roman Republic and ushered in the Empire. A similarly historic metamorphosis seems to be taking shape in the United States, though it marks the decline of an empire rather than its inauguration. One symptom of that transition, both as outcome and mover, is the disturbing evolution of the Republican Party into an engine of obstruction within the American government as well as an increasingly extreme and belligerent theocratic combatant on sexual mores.

This marks a sharp reversal of the widely shared communitarian attitudes that shaped American politics in the first half of the twentieth century. The dominant ethos was the Progressive movement. It campaigned for women's suffrage, instituted the ill-considered Prohibition, sought to curb the power of the large corporations, regulate banking, prohibit child labor, promote the right of workers to unionize, impose government-backed workplace health and safety standards, and institute a social safety net through unemployment insurance, minimum wages laws, and a government-run pension system. Republicans, though generally anti-union (not nearly so strongly as they are today), were almost as likely as Democrats to share the rest of these goals. Insofar as religion was part of the motivation it was the social service ideals of the mainstream Christian churches, drawing on the Sermon on the Mount rather than the gospel of self-enrichment preached by the televangelists.

Contrast today's Republicans with their ancestors in the 1950s. Back then the party's leaders were eminently conventional Northern industrialists, not casino and hedge fund managers or talk radio and cable TV shock jocks.

Party ranks were filled with the respectable middle class, especially in small towns: stodgy neighborhood bankers, real estate promoters, farmers, small business owners, members of the Kiwanis and Rotary clubs. They were fiscal conservatives who dutifully went on Sundays to hear soporific sermons at conventional churches — Episcopalians, Methodists, Presbyterians, Catholics. Babbitts and boosters.

When Eisenhower's Secretary of Defense, Charles E. Wilson, the former head of General Motors, was widely misquoted as saying "What's good for General Motors is good for the country," though the Left saw this as corporate arrogance, most people shrugged and probably agreed with the sentiment. Asked to imagine a Republican woman would most likely elicit a picture of Betty Crocker, not a harridan like Ann Coulter. If anything could excite them it was the fight against Communism, and Communism, while the crusade against it in the United States went overboard and birthed its own evils, was an evil system.

Bipartisanship was central to the functioning of the American Congress. This was possible because the country by the 1950s faced no serious economic or social threat other than its low key Cold War. The two ruling parties had more in common than the issues that divided them. Dwight Eisenhower in 1952 was offered the presidential nomination by both parties. The Republicans had a strong Progressive tradition. This went back to the Radical Republicans who carried out Reconstruction in the South after the Civil War, and the trust busting of Teddy Roosevelt. In 1960, Nelson Rockefeller, a very moderate Republican who had served under Franklin Roosevelt and Harry Truman, was governor of New York. Prescott Bush, George W.'s grandfather, was the Republican U.S. senator from Connecticut. He was a strong supporter of Planned Parenthood, backed civil rights, donated to the United Negro College Fund, and attended the Episcopal Church. Henry Cabot Lodge, Jr., former Republican U.S. senator from Massachusetts, was American ambassador to the United Nations, of which he was a stout defender. Nixon's VP running mate in 1960, Lodge was shunned by Southerners for pledging, without Nixon's approval, that if his party won the presidency they would appoint an African American to the cabinet. In 1963 George Romney, Mitt's father, was elected governor of Michigan. He publicly backed the civil rights movement, resisting sharp criticism from the Mormon hierarchy, and refused to endorse Barry Goldwater in 1964 because of Goldwater's outreach to Southern segregationists. He had excellent relations with the state's powerful union movement.

The Democrats, in contrast, were a more mixed bag. The party had emerged from the Civil War as an unholy coalition between Northern big city governments with their working class constituencies and the defeated slave-holders, who held millions of poor whites in thrall and fostered a segregationist system that disfranchised blacks from voting and excluded them from public schools, with white-only restrictions pervasive throughout society. The pro-segregationist Southern Democrats put a brake on the progressive and labor forces in the party and shifted it to the right. The Democratic Party contained within it forces considerably both to the right and to the left of the more homogeneous Republicans. As these canceled each other out, the Democrats came to rest only slightly left of center, under the impetus of Franklin Roosevelt's New Deal reforms, instituted to use governmental power to lift the country out of the Depression of the 1930s.

Of course, for both parties this was a virtually all white political system, and patriarchal to boot. The 1960s and demographics changed that.

The sixties, more accurately the decade between 1965 and 1975, shattered this, in retrospect, almost bucolic pattern. As a precursor, the civil rights movement began with the Montgomery Bus Boycott in 1955-56, expanding in the Freedom Rides in 1961, winning a layer of white as well as black youth who were radicalized in the fight for school integration and voting rights in the South. President Johnson's huge escalation of American troops in Vietnam in 1965 provoked a wave of revulsion at home, magnified by the military draft that touched millions of young men. The veterans of the civil rights movement waded into the antiwar struggle, over the next seven or eight years winning the approval of a large majority of the country's population.

The black civil rights movement in the South faced a more openly hostile white population than in Northern cities, but its goals involved fairly simple legal changes: to prohibit segregation of schools, restaurants, and movie theaters, and win the right to vote. There were no comparable legal solutions for the low wages, substandard housing, and job discrimination in the minority ghettos of the Northern metropolises. When protest erupted there it was volcanic and indiscriminate. The Watts riot in Los Angeles in 1965 was the first, in which 34 people were killed. The assassination of Martin Luther King in April 1968 sparked uprisings in 110 cities. Crowds of up to 20,000 burned large sections of Washington, DC, where the government responded with the most massive mobilization of federal troops in any American city since the Civil War.

Not finished, the radical decade plowed on with the women's movement, challenging male supremacy in the home and the work place, then came the Stonewall Riots, heralding the emergence of the gay liberation movement.

This social turmoil was capped by ominous international signs of U.S. decline. The Arab oil embargo of 1973-74 quadrupled the price of oil to the then devastating but now laughable $12 a barrel, boosting gas prices to an unheard of 55 cents a gallon. Thousands of gas stations closed and those that remained mostly shut on weekends. There were block-long lines and three-hour waits. Many stations would sell only 5 or 10 gallons per customer. The event revealed American vulnerability and dependence on foreign governments it could not control.

Then in 1975 came the U.S. defeat in Vietnam, vindicating the millions who had opposed the war, but deeply wounding its supporters. A small Asian nation had beaten the colossus, an unprecedented sign of American weakness.

The end of the sixties revealed a different populace from the one that had existed in 1964. The institutions of government never recovered the level of respect and trust they had enjoyed in the 1950s. On the left there now existed an amorphous but quite large layer of people who had come to look on the federal government as an evil empire, large corporations as a sinister force in American politics, and all U.S. influence in other countries — diplomatic, commercial, or military — as predatory. These veterans of the sixties radicalization shared with a still larger group a constellation of progressive social views, starting with those inherited from traditional American liberalism: for progressive taxation to fund a strong social safety net, for universal health-care, these now expanded to add support to feminism and gay rights, antiracism, for the right of abortion. Never much attracted to socialism, whatever sympathy there was in that direction evaporated with the collapse of Communism in 1990, Tea Party claims to the contrary notwithstanding. What remained was a very moderate leftism similar to European liberals and social democrats.

The mirror evolution on the right was in some ways more complex. In 1968 Richard Nixon institutionalized the Southern Strategy, appealing to seg-regationist whites, terrified by the black uprisings earlier that year and angry at the young radicals who had undermined the U.S. war in Asia. The shift of the white South from Democrats to Republicans was prolonged, beginning with the conservative upper class and encompassing the majority of white workers only in the 1990s, but essentially consolidated with Ronald Reagan's victory in 1980. Two Democratic presidents were elected in the last half of the century, both Southerners — Jimmy Carter, on the wave of anti-Republican sentiment after Watergate, and Bill Clinton, on bad economic news that disenchanted voters with George H. W. Bush. But since 2000 the white South has been militantly Republican. Obama in 2008 lost the white Southern working class vote by 18 percent.

The fraught consequence of the realignment in the South was to give the political map a clear territorial division that had not been present since the

Civil War. The much circulated maps of red and blue states overlay with chilling precision the country's division on the eve of the firing on Fort Sumter. Today's Republicans command the whole of the Confederacy plus the Midwest, which in 1864 were territories contested between free and slave states. The Republican hostility to the federal government echoes the secessionist sentiments of the Old South, occasionally voiced openly today, as in a speech by failed Republican presidential candidate and Texas governor Rick Perry in April 2009 to a Tea Party crowd, where he threatened his state's withdrawal from the Union.

2004 US Presidential Election Results

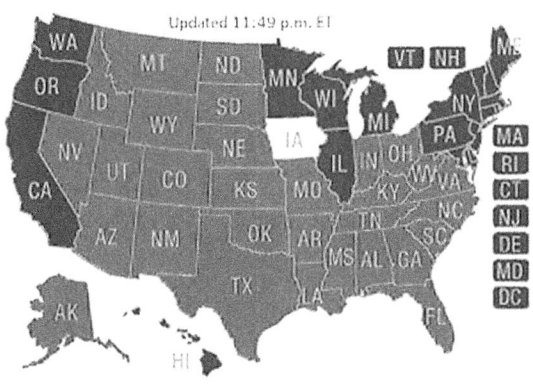

■Kerry ■Bush □Undeclared

Pre-Civil War Free vs. Slave States

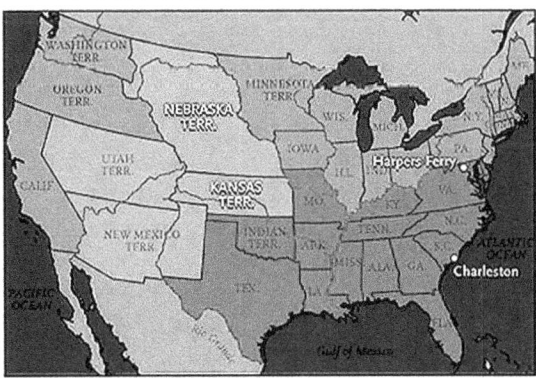

▨ - FREE STATES AND TERRITORIES
▧ - SLAVE STATES
▫ - TERRITORIES OPEN TO SLAVERY

Not only the geography but the demographics tell us we are looking at differences that have festered and metastasized since the nineteenth century. The Republican base is overwhelmingly older whites, heavily rural or Southern. The U.S. Census Bureau projects that by 2050 non-Hispanic whites will decline to 46.3% of the population. This, along with many symptoms of national decline, domestic and foreign, stoke existential fears in much of this aging white population.

Public Trust in U.S. Government

Pew Research Center

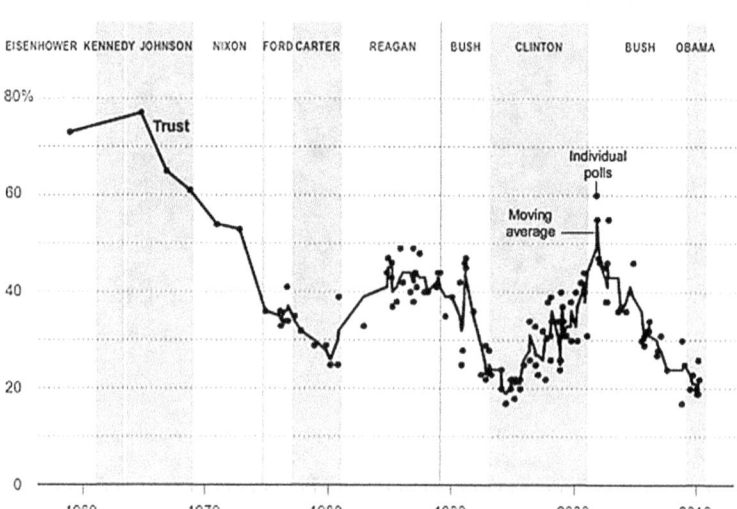

The result of the sixties was that both Left and Right came to distrust their government. Survey data from the Pew Research Center shows that in the period since 1958, public trust in the U.S. government peaked at about 77% in 1965, with a surge of patriotism at the first large-scale escalation of the Vietnam War. It plummeted almost immediately, crashing to about 26% after Jimmy Carter's failed effort to rescue the American hostages in Iran. There was a slight revival under Reagan and the first Bush administration, but it never reached 50%. 9/11 fostered a brief spark and then tobogganed steadily downward to a historic low in 2010 of 18% who would say they trusted the government.

These numbers are for both parties. They are not remarkably different between them, Republicans going up a bit when their party holds the presidency, Democrats for their side. The polarization is somewhat greater for the

Obama government. But while all sectors of the population have radically lost their faith in Washington, Republicans uniquely in the same period also changed their religion, abandoning the mainstream Protestant churches in droves and flocking to the hitherto fringe fundamentalist, Pentecostal, Evangelical, and Charismatic sects. These are spread among innumerable individual churches and vary among themselves in their specific set of beliefs, but most tend to expect the imminent second coming of Christ, stress Bible literalism, often including Young Earth Creationism, reject biological evolution and global warming, and look forward to the Rapture. The Rapture was invented in 1827 by English clergyman John Nelson Darby, based on a rather strained interpretation of 1 Thessalonians 4:16, claiming that Jesus will come back not once but twice, the first time to whisk the true believers to heaven while leaving the majority of the human race behind to suffer under the lash of the Anti-Christ until Jesus comes back again to carry out the last judgment. Catholics and mainstream Protestants do not accept this idea. It is hard not to see the Rapture as a narcissistic invention of people who imagine they are vastly superior to the rest of humanity and even to the great majority of Christians.

This trend fostered a rise in magical thinking. If these vast supernatural events are at hand, the normal rules of nature and fact are to be overwritten by the miraculous. Such an outlook depreciates the significance of facts, and of science, a method that fails to acknowledge the most important fact of all, the imminence of Armageddon, proclaimed by prophecy in thousands of church sanctuaries every Sunday. As a sign of the times, the sixteen Christian apocalyptic novels of the *Left Behind* series by Tim LaHaye and Jerry Jenkins — which began publication in 1998, in which the true Christians are Raptured to heaven and the Anti-Christ takes over the world in preparation for the final battle with Christ and his Angelic legions — sold upwards of 65 million copies.

The point here is that for the Republican Right, in large part under the influence of its Southern branch, the response to social turmoil and international decline shattered faith in government and replaced it with an embrace of apocalyptic supernaturalism, churches that look to the imminent end times rather than to the conventional homilies and modest reform efforts of the previously dominant Protestant denominations. These churches generally reject the mainstream Christian commitment to charity and aid to the poor, seeing salvation as a plan for their own members to jump into the Jesus lifeboat and escape the sinking ship, leaving the majority, who have somewhat different views, to drown. This prioritizing of saving one's own skin and letting the rest hang permeates the contemporary Republican attitude toward the poor in the here and now — particularly if they happen to be black or Latino, a rather traditional attitude of white Southern churches. Government intervention, apart from a strong military and expansive prison system, is to be focused on enforcing religious sexual mores, not on such irrelevancies as healthcare, food stamps, or unemployment insurance for the undeserving. Of course these are sociological generalizations, not descriptions of individuals. Every mass movement sweeps up its share of innocents. In 1976 it looked as though the whole of China contained nothing but fanatics. Polls show that a fair portion of the Republican voting bloc are more moderate than their leaders in Congress and in state houses, particularly younger voters. But it is the leadership and the more militant that set the agenda.

Mainline Protestants were the large majority of American believers until the U.S. defeat in Vietnam. These churches were socially liberal, committed to public service, support to government, and proponents of a strong social safety net for the poor. Fundamentalists rejected all of these views, but throughout much of the last century largely withdrew from the world. The conservative Evangelical churches that boomed after 1975 shared most of the Fundamentalists' attitudes but sought to energetically proselytize their views and to contest with other currents in the political arena. They grew rapidly as trust in government waned, becoming the new focus of self-identification for millions. In 1979 Jerry Fallwell founded the Moral Majority, the genesis of the Christian Right, that aimed at capturing the Republican Party and ultimately imposing a conservative Christian regime on the country.

The mainstream Protestant denominations were revealed by the Pew 2010 U.S. Religious Landscape Survey to have fallen to only 18.1% of the population. The conservative Evangelical churches in contrast have grown to 26.3%. Even these figures don't tell the whole story. Catholics are 23.9% and in recent years there has emerged a substantial current within American Catholicism similar to the Evangelicals. The membership in the militant Evangelical churches are far more active, somewhat younger, and have more children than their liberal rivals. The congregations of the Evangelical churches are heavily invested in the Republican Party, where they champion opposition to abortion, rejection of gay rights, disbelief in evolution, advocacy of school prayer, and, less obviously derived from any Christian religious grounds, rolling back government provision of old age pensions, medical care, or aid to the poor, the disabled, and the elderly — as well as lower taxes for the rich.

The Evangelical churches, of which the Southern Baptists are the largest single example, are largely an export of the Deep South, which, once persuaded to switch to the Republican Party, has since captured that organization and driven it far to the right of mainstream American politics.

Colin Woodard writes in the July 5, 2012, *Washington Monthly*,

The radicalization of the Republican Party in recent years has a lot to do with it having been taken over by Deep Southerners like Trent Lott and Newt Gingrich, Dick Armey and George W. Bush, Haley Barbour and Jim DeMint. The central policy goals of Tea Party Republicanism mirror those of the Deep Southern elite: rollback federal power, environmental, labor, and consumer protection laws, and taxes on capital and the wealthy. It's a program one never would have seen in the days when the GOP was run by Yankee — read "Greater New Englander" — figures like Teddy Roosevelt or George Bush the senior.

We could add to the Southern coterie Senator Mitch McConnell of Kentucky. This conservative magnet has drawn to it a few Northern ideologues such as Michelle Bachmann of Minnesota and budget slasher Paul Ryan of Wisconsin. John Boehner of Ohio as House Speaker has tried to toe the Tea Party line but has been humiliated several times by his own caucus when he supported some minor compromise with Obama.

As could be surmised, the Deep South takeover of the Republicans was possible only because the party was essentially all white. The Pew Trends in American Values 1987-2012 surveys, released June 5, 2012, show that the Republican Party is 87% white, 2% Black, and 6% Hispanic, this last heavily composed of Cubans, whose history of exile from the Castro government and automatic legalization on arriving in the United States place them far to the right of immigrants from Mexico and Central America. In contrast the Democratic Party is 55% white, 24% black, and 13% Hispanic. The most dramatic findings in these extensive surveys are the fall in Republican agreement that the government should take care of those unable to take care of themselves, from 62% in 1987 to only 40% in 2012, and the collapse of its agreement that the environment must be protected. In 1987 the two parties differed by only 5% in support to environment protection. In 2012 the gap was 39 percentage points, due to the Republican reversal. There is nearly as great a change in the Republican attitude toward unions. Never very favorable, there was a 20% difference between the parties in 1987; this has grown to 37 percentage points in 2012.

As the country has polarized into gridlock along sharp geographical as well as political lines there is the impression that the problem is simply the stubborn irreconcilability of counterposed ideologies. That is not so. Virtually all studies show that the Democrats have moved only marginally leftward, essentially being slightly center left on social issues and centrist or center right on economic ones. In contrast the Republicans have moved from center and center right to far right across the board. Worse, they have for years adopted a policy of delegitimizing the American government, using the many available procedural rules of the House and Senate to paralyze and discredit the institution. This is well documented in Thomas E. Mann and Norman J. Ornstein's recent book, *It's Even Worse Than It Looks: How the American Constitutional System Collided with the New Politics of Extremism.*

Mann and Ornstein have been involved in the professional study of Washington politics since 1969, Mann as a resident scholar at the Brookings Institution, Ornstein at the conservative American Enterprise Institute. In 1978 the two founded the Congress Project, affiliated to the American Enterprise Institute. Its purpose was to closely track changes in the American Congress. Their first program at AEI was to meet with a group of incoming freshmen representatives. These included first-term Newt Gingrich from Georgia's 6th Congressional District.

Democrats had long held majorities in the House and Senate. At Mann and Ornstein's 1978 dinners with

Where Partisan Divisions Are Largest

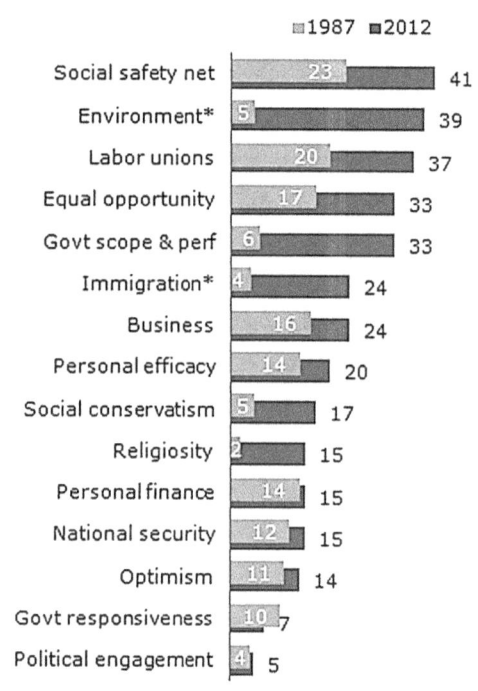

PEW RESEARCH CENTER 2012 Values Study. Bars show the differences between Republicans and Democrats across 15 values indices based on related survey questions.
* Environment index began in 1992, immigration index in 2002.

newly elected House members Gingrich presented his radical plan to discredit the Democrats and bring the Republicans to power:

> The core strategy was to destroy the institution in order to save it, to so intensify public hatred of Congress that voters would buy into the notion of the need for sweeping change and throw the majority bums out. His method? To unite his Republicans in refusing to cooperate with Democrats in committee and on the floor, while publicly attacking them as

a permanent majority presiding over and benefiting from a thoroughly corrupt institution.

Republicans as well as Democrats present were shocked. Of those around the dinner table there was one man who agreed with Gingrich. His name was Dick Cheney. One of Gingrich's first tactics was to reserve time for Republican speakers on the House floor in the evenings. C-SPAN cameras were fixed on the podium. Gingrich and some of his colleagues

> attacked Democrats for opposing school prayer, being soft on Communism, and being corrupt. . . . In the favored technique, the lawmaker speaking turned as if he were addressing Democrats in the chamber, and the lack of response made it appear as if those in the audience either accepted the charges or were unwilling or unable to counter them.

In fact there was nobody in the audience.

The Gingrich strategy of delegitimizing the American government was adopted wholesale by the Republicans following their 1994 capture of the House of Representatives in their stunning 54-seat victory, ending forty years of Democratic control. In November and December 1995 Republican intransigence in demanding budget cuts shut down the government for 28 days. Tens of thousands of federal workers were sent home. According to a 2010 Congressional Research service report, health services for military veterans were cut, the Centers for Disease Control and Prevention virtually shut down, and toxic waste clean-up was stopped at 609 sites.

This was a pale preview of Republican tactics against the Obama presidency. Mann and Ornstein write:

"Republicans greeted the new president with a unified strategy of opposing, obstructing, discrediting, and nullifying every one of his important initiatives." This went to such extremes that on January 26, 2010, six Republican senators voted against a bill of which they were themselves cosponsors — a measure to create a deficit reduction task force — when President Obama endorsed it. This kind of obstruction increased tenfold when Republicans won control of the House in 2010.

> What followed was an appalling spectacle of hostage taking — most importantly, the debt ceiling crisis — that threatened a government shutdown and public default, led to a downgrading of the country's credit, and blocked constructive action to nurture an economic recovery or deal with looming problems of deficits and debt.

By October 2011 the Republican strategy of gridlock and delegitimization had plunged public approval of the institution of Congress to a historic low of 9 percent. This was a party that seems never to have heard the maxim, Don't spit in the well from which we all must drink.

Mann and Ornstein, the latter with impeccable conservative credentials, place the blame squarely on the Republicans, declaring that

> the Republican Party has become an insurgent outlier — ideologically extreme; contemptuous of the inherited social and economic policy regime; scornful of compromise; unpersuaded by conventional understanding of facts, evidence, and science; and dismissive of the legitimacy of its political opposition. When one party moves this far from the center of American politics, it is extremely difficult to enact policy responsive to the country's most pressing challenges.

Mann and Ornstein are particularly upset by the Republican threat to have the government default on its debts that was the centerpiece of the spurious debate in the fall of 2011 over the normally routine vote to raise the federal debt limit. The debt limit was raised seventy-eight times between 1960 and 2011. These actions are taken not to authorize new spending but to cover outlays that have already taken place. To vote not to raise the limit to cover such obligations has nothing to do with preventing new government spending but is like deciding not to pay your credit card bill. Mann and Ornstein object that the Republicans "frequently mischaracterized a vote to lift the debt ceiling as a vote to add more debt."

It has been Republican presidents who have driven the country into the deep debt it faces today. According to FactCheck.org, the national debt rose 190% under Ronald Reagan, 52% under George H. W. Bush, 37% under Bill Clinton, and 86% under George W. Bush. Obama, inheriting an economy that fell into a depression almost as deep as the Great Depression from Bush Jr.'s unfunded wars and extravagant tax cuts, married to a rampant and unregulated financial sector that promoted the housing bubble with billions in subprime mortgages, raised the debt by a surprisingly low 45%, much of which went to recovery efforts. With revenue desperately needed to keep people working and stoke demand to restore businesses, total Republican intransigence in refusing even the tiniest tax increase — while taxes are at historic lows not seen since the 1950s — is a form of sabotage. They often candidly admit this with their slogan "Starve the beast." Anti-tax guru Grover Norquist, whose pledge never to raise taxes under any circumstances has been signed by virtually every Republican in Congress, famously laid out his envisioned endgame for the American government: "My goal is to cut government in half in twenty-five years, to get it down to the size where we can drown it in the bathtub." The Republicans have harped on the notion that the Democrats "tax and spend." The record shows that the Republicans spend far more — on credit.

Much has been written about the Imperial Presidency, largely because the Congress, since U.S. entry into the Korean War in 1950, has abdicated to the executive branch its authority to declare war, leaving the president with exceptional control over military and federal police powers. This was notably expanded under the George W. Bush administration in pursuit of the so-called War on Terrorism. The American government nevertheless remains a tripartite system of checks and balances, which depends for its functionality on mutual respect between branches. The Congress operates under rules in which a determined minority can veto the decisions of the majority and bring government to a standstill.

Two of the most powerful tools of a hostile minority party are the Senate hold and the filibuster. Senate rules peculiarly require unanimous consent to bring a bill to the floor for a vote. Any senator can anonymously place a hold on any piece of legislation, preventing it from coming to a vote. Intended to allow a senator to ask for time to study a bill strongly affecting his home state or committee, the hold was rarely used until the 1970s. Today it is routinely and repeatedly used by Republicans to block almost all legislation supported by the Obama administration.

Mann and Ornstein recount how Republican Senator Larry Craig of Idaho, best remembered for being arrested for indecent conduct in 2007 while playing footsie under a restroom partition in the Minneapolis-St. Paul airport, used anonymous holds in 2003 to block all Air Force promotions for months, trying to blackmail the Air Force into stationing some cargo planes in his state. Richard Shelby, Republican senator from Alabama and chair of the Senate Committee on Housing, Banking, and Urban Affairs, in February 2010 put a blanket hold on all White House nominations for executive positions — more than seventy then pending — to get two earmarks for his state. They conclude: "[T]he minority party's sharply expanded use of the hold as a political tactic to delay and block action by the majority has transformed the Senate, especially over the past four years."

Twenty-eight-year congressional Republican staffer Mike Lofgren offers a devastating survey of the Republican evolution in a widely circulated September 3, 2011, article, "Goodbye to All That: Reflections of a GOP Operative Who Left the Cult." Commenting on the debt ceiling standoff then still in progress he wrote:

> Everyone knows that in a hostage situation, the reckless and amoral actor has the negotiating upper hand over the cautious and responsible

actor because the latter is actually concerned about the life of the hostage, while the former does not care. This fact, which ought to be obvious, has nevertheless caused confusion among the professional pundit class, which is mostly still stuck in the Bob Dole era in terms of its orientation. . . . It should have been evident to clear-eyed observers that the Republican Party is becoming less and less like a traditional political party in a representative democracy and becoming more like an apocalyptic cult, or one of the intensely ideological authoritarian parties of 20th century Europe.

He excoriates the deliberate Republican misuse of congressional procedural rules to hamstring the government:

> The only thing that can keep the Senate functioning is collegiality and good faith. During periods of political consensus, for instance, the World War II and early post-war eras, the Senate was a "high functioning" institution: filibusters were rare and the body was legislatively productive. Now, one can no more picture the current Senate producing the original Medicare Act than the old Supreme Soviet having legislated the Bill of Rights.
>
> Far from being a rarity, virtually every bill, every nominee for Senate confirmation and every routine procedural motion is now subject to a Republican filibuster. Under the circumstances, it is no wonder that Washington is gridlocked: legislating has now become war minus the shooting, something one could have observed 80 years ago in the Reichstag of the Weimar Republic. As Hannah Arendt observed, a disciplined minority of totalitarians can use the instruments of democratic government to undermine democracy itself.

And finally:

"Undermining Americans' belief in their own institutions of self-government remains a prime GOP electoral strategy."

The filibuster, the right of any senator to speak as long as they wish, entered Senate procedure not in the Constitution but in an apparent error in rewriting Senate rules ordered by then-Vice President Aaron Burr in 1805. In the first half of the twentieth century it was most commonly invoked by Southern segregationists to delay or derail civil rights legislation. A filibuster can be ended only by a cloture motion, which requires 60 senators to pass. In the 1960s, there were never more than seven cloture votes in an entire Senate term; in the 110th Congress, in 2008, there were 112. Under the rules, even a successful cloture motion must be followed by thirty hours of floor debate. Republicans now routinely insist on taking the full thirty hours, mostly used for endlessly repeated roll calls that show the absence of a quorum.

One much-used tactic is to file multiple filibusters for the same piece of legislation: first for the motion to consider the bill, then for the bill itself, then for any amendment the majority may make to accommodate minority objections, each filibuster requiring debate, then a cloture vote, then thirty hours of floor time afterward. With the Democrats and their allies in the Senate down to fifty-nine, even a cloture vote is impossible, giving the minority the ability to prevent any piece of legislation from coming to the floor for consideration.

Republicans repeatedly file filibusters even against bills that they support and will eventually in their majority vote for, just as a disruption tactic. Mann and Ornstein give several recent examples. In 2009 the Obama administration sponsored H.R. 3548, a bill to extend unemployment benefits during the worst of the recession. No one openly opposed it; the bill ultimately passed on a vote of 98 to 0. But Republican senators filed two filibusters, each of which required two days of debate before cloture could be invoked, followed by thirty hours of floor time after each cloture motion. "A bill that should have zipped through in a day or two at most took four weeks, including seven days of floor time, to be enacted."

Republican filibusters were similarly invoked against H.R. 627, a bill to limit usurious interest rates and exorbitant hidden credit card charges, and the Fraud Enforcement and Recovery Act, aimed to set stiffer penalties for mortgage and securities fraud. In both cases virtually all Republicans as well as the Democrats voted for the measures, but the filibusters/cloture obstruction added weeks of congressional time. Mann and Ornstein conclude:

> One purpose is rank obstruction, to use as much precious time as possible on the floor of the Senate to retard progress on business the majority wants to conduct, and to make everything look contentious and messy so that voters will react against the majority and against the policies the senators do manage to enact.

The phony hue and cry against Obamacare is only the most egregious example of Republicans denouncing as socialist and tyrannical a policy created by Republicans themselves and in fact the hallmark achievement in Massachusetts of their chosen standard bearer in the 2012 presidential race.

The House operates more sensibly, on simple majority vote, but even there the Republican majority use their voting power to prevent the body from accomplishing anything of note. For example, the Republican House has taken the time to vote to abolish the Obama healthcare law 33 times — while it has never taken up a job creation bill.

Back in my Marxist days we would chide some of our most extreme members who took the position of advocating the worse the better for the country on the gamble that if the country fell apart our little group would be able to pick up some of the pieces. Remarkably, one of the two major American political parties now has as a whole embraced that approach, seeing a deteriorating economy and mass unemployment as a liability for Obama and therefore a plus for their side.

The Republican Party leadership and their candidate by default, Mitt Romney, have come down firmly in rejection of scientific fact when it conflicts with the shibboleths of the Religious Right on biological evolution, the causes of homosexuality, or medical understanding of fetal development. They have done the same when science disagrees with the propaganda — and lobbyist campaign contributions — of the oil industry on global warming or the risks of oil depletion. This propensity for promoting policies that have no factual basis can be seen as well in Republican economic proposals that grossly favor the rich and growing inequality over the rest of the population.

Romney has launched millions of dollars in attack ads against Obama over what should have been the noncontroversial idea that government has an important role in stabilizing the economy. Romney denies that the Recovery Act reduced unemployment, or that the bank bailouts saved the financial system, while continuing to insist that tax cuts, especially for the wealthy, produce more jobs and increase revenue for government. Economists Betsy Stevenson and Justin Wolfers in a July 23, 2012, Bloomberg post, report a nationwide poll of leading economists of all political persuasions, Republican, Democratic, and independent, conducted by the University of Chicago's Booth School of Business:

> Watching Democrats and Republicans hash out their differences in the public arena, it's easy to get the impression that there's a deep disagreement among reasonable people about how to manage the U.S. economy. Nothing could be further from the truth. In reality, there's remarkable consensus among mainstream economists, including those from the left and right, on most major macroeconomic issues. The debate in Washington about economic policy is phony. It's manufactured. And it's entirely political.

The Booth School poll showed that 92 percent of the country's forty leading economists "agreed that the stimulus succeeded in reducing the jobless rate." The economists were unanimous that the bank bailouts lowered unemployment. They were unanimous that the Republican charge that Obama's energy policies were responsible for high gas prices was false. And on tax cuts:

> How about the oft-cited Republican claim that tax cuts will boost the economy so much that they will pay for themselves? It's an idea born as

a sketch on a restaurant napkin by conservative economist Art Laffer. Perhaps when the top tax rate was 91 percent, the idea was plausible. Today, it's a fantasy. The Booth poll couldn't find a single economist who believed that cutting taxes today will lead to higher government revenue.

Stevenson and Wolfers summarize:

> The debate in Washington has become completely unmoored from the consensus, and in a particular direction. Angry Republicans have pushed their representatives to adopt positions that are at odds with the best of modern economic thinking. That may be good politics, but it's terrible policy.

The 2010 Supreme Court Citizens United vs. Federal Election Commission decision overturned a century of precedent for restricting the amount of money that can be pumped into election campaigns. The motivation in the peculiar ruling that corporations have the same First Amendment rights as actual people was supposed to be the even-handed empowerment of corporations on the right and trade unions on the left. This fiction ignored the vastly growing financial power of corporations in the American economy and the concomitant shrinking away of the unions, in large part from the massive deindustrialization of the United States and the off-shoring of its manufacturing sector to China and to lesser nations in the developing world.

Union membership peaked in 1954 at 32.5% of the work force. By 1984 it had fallen below 20%. In 2011 it was down to 11.8%, and even that is misleading, as it includes numbers above 30% among public employees averaged against private sector unionization of only 6.9%. The numbers have grown so small that it is little wonder that the vast majority who are not unionized don't look on the unions as the vanguard of the working class, but more as privileged job trusts, not entirely but predominately composed of older white workers.

Despite John Roberts' unexpected reprieve for the healthcare act, the nominally anti-government Right, using presidential appointments to the Supreme Court and a wrecking operation in the U.S. Congress, have leveraged their substantial electoral support into the ability to prevent the majority from governing. On the positive side, given American demographics this should promise to be a short-lived ascendency. The aging white base of this movement, no matter how militant, will be swamped in the electoral arena in a decade or two. This, of course, explains both their anxiety and their readiness to violate the norms of government. From their viewpoint their way of life is passing away, into the hands of aliens of many sorts: domestically, blacks,

Hispanic immigrants, and treacherous white liberals; internationally, increasingly powerful global competitors. This in the setting of the seemingly interminable economic crisis that began in 2007 that promises only a shrinking pie.

The Republicans respond with sabotage of the common institutions of governance, charges of tyranny where none exists, tacit support to rumor campaigns of the president's illegitimacy: that he is a secret Muslim, that his Hawaiian birth certificate is a forgery, that he is a socialist radical planning to take people's guns and give their money away to (nonwhite) freeloading loafers. Republican rallies and blogs abound in talk of Second Amendment solutions and, here and there in the old Confederacy, of secession. There is an air of desperation about all this.

The GOP has begun to speak of the vote as a privilege and not a right, seeking through new legislation in states under Republican control to prevent students from voting and demanding photo IDs, currently not possessed by many millions of American registered voters who do not drive and do not have driver's licenses. There are one million voters without such ID in Pennsylvania alone, the state where Republican State House Leader Mike Turzai admitted openly that the purpose of the state's new voter ID requirement was to suppress Democratic votes, declaring when listing the accomplishments of this year's legislative session, "Voter ID, which is gonna allow Governor Romney to win the state of Pennsylvania? Done."

The idea that there could be significant voter fraud by in-person appearance at the polls on election day is on the face of it absurd. There are virtually no examples of it in the last century anywhere in the country. To carry it off the voter would have to already exist on the voting rolls. The fraudster would have to be assured that the voter was not going to vote themselves, and would have to be intending to vote for different candidates than the real registered voter for the action to make any difference. Voter suppression is the only way to explain this sudden rush to outlaw a crime that doesn't happen at the cost of ensuring that very large numbers of legitimate voters will be barred from the polls. The old Jim Crow poll taxes, designed to exclude black voters in the South, were very small, often no more than $1 or $2. These obstructions to voting were declared unconstitutional with the passage of the 24th Amendment to the Constitution in 1964, as well as in Supreme Court rulings based on the 14th and 15th Amendments. Under most of the new Republican rules, already long-time voters must first secure a certified copy of their birth certificate — often difficult or near impossible if they were born at home in rural areas or urban slums — at a cost of from $10 to $45, then use that to apply for a state photo ID. The time and expense of this prolonged two-step process can be guaranteed to lose a large number of previous voters. In one case last March, eighty-six-year-old World War II veteran Paul Carroll was turned away from the polls in the Ohio town where he has lived and voted for forty years when the staff refused to accept his federal Veterans Administration photo ID, on the grounds that it did not have his current address (the VA by policy does not put addresses on their cards).

Not surprisingly this effort to rig elections by excluding potentially millions of already registered voters raises the question of how far the Republicans may be willing to go if they cannot win elections at all. Some on the left fear that the Republican Right may seek an authoritarian preemption of elections. The term they often use to describe this eventuality is fascism. It is difficult to tell how widespread this apprehension is. A Google search of "Republican Party fascist" returns 2.9 million hits. Many of these are stories about Republicans calling Obama a fascist, and much of the charge coming from the left is hyperbole, but there is significant speculation on a drift by the newly extremist GOP toward fascism or something like it. So far this discussion is mostly confined to the blogosphere. I would approach the subject rather gingerly, as "fascist" has mostly become a swear word, empty of content, for any political formation one disapproves of, or at best conjures images from old movies of Nazi storm troopers herding Jews onto trains bound for Auschwitz.

What is true is that crises of economic decline in the first half of the twentieth century spawned many authoritarian movements, of which those that called themselves fascist were the most widespread. Among these, Americans think principally of the German Nazis, who were the most barbaric, and who never used the word. If there was a mainstream of fascist type it was Mussolini's Italy, a police state run by black shirted thugs, but one that didn't kill very many people, didn't have mass concentration camps, didn't promote antisemitism (until their German allies insisted on it), and which had a tolerable modus vivendi with the traditional Right and the Catholic Church. What it did represent was a political party that ruled above the law, that disparaged parliamentary institutions, and that politicized its concept of moral norms and imposed them on a powerless citizenry.

I don't think I would worry too much that the Republicans are headed in that direction if I thought the present economic slump would soon be over and prosperity would return. It is the substantial decline in American fortunes since 1975 that has pushed the GOP as far as it has gone to date. If national decline deepens in the future there is reason to consider that we have not yet seen the limits to which the Deep South-dominated Republicans may go.

People have been trying since the 1930s to understands what fascism was really about. It is worth looking at that discussion, as we are well into a

period that poses somewhat similar social stresses of the 1930s. The old
Marxist notion that fascism was a conspiracy of the big capitalists to head off
a workers' revolution has long been discredited. Particularly to be distrusted
are definitions contrived recently, specifically to indict the Republicans. A
handful of scholars have emerged as the ranking authorities on this kind of
movement, people far removed from the debates in contemporary American
politics. Stanley G. Payne, Roger Griffin, Richard Wolin, Michael Mann, and
Robert O. Paxton are among the most distinguished. Paxton in his *The Anat-
o*my of Fascism offers a brief snapshot of the fascist phenomena:

> Fascism may be defined as a form of political behavior marked by
> obsessive preoccupation with community decline, humiliation, or vic-
> timhood and by compensatory cults of unity, energy, and purity, in
> which a mass-based party of committed nationalist militants, working in
> uneasy but effective collaboration with traditional elites, abandons dem-
> ocratic liberties and pursues with redemptive violence and without ethi-
> cal or legal restraints goals of internal cleansing and external expansion.

What is interesting here is that those who have studied these authoritarian
movements find that they arise not from ruling class conspiracies but from
within a broad community that sees itself in decline and unjustly victimized
by others, even if this is sometimes only in their imagination, as with the
Germans who believed that they were the victims of a world Jewish conspiracy. Certainly there is something of this in the situation facing the older conservative whites, who see their domination slipping away.

The talking points of Republican politicians and their promoters at Fox
News brim with victimhood. They claim to be suffering a thousand indigni-
ties, from a tyrannical federal government that is trying to shackle businesses
with crippling regulations, a hostile "lamestream" media, Christian-hating
officials who want to ban Christmas, a swarm of shiftless "takers" who use
the government to redistribute income from honest job creators to themselves,
illegal aliens who arrive by the truckload to drop anchor babies to qualify for
American welfare, black imposters who show up at voting booths impersonat-
ing actual voters who they happen to know have stayed home that day,
schools that inculcate anti-Christian beliefs that humans did not really walk
together with the dinosaurs, which really died off because they wouldn't fit on
Noah's Ark, not to mention the proponents of un-Biblical marriage in which
men marry men and women marry women, when everyone knows that the
Bible requires that marriage must be between one man and one woman, except perhaps for Solomon, who had four hundred wives.

We may all be going down, but plainly the Republican conservatives feel they are especially put upon, and that this justifies their short-circuiting the rules of democratic governance. At least so far, advocates of violent internal cleansing and external expansion are mostly found only in the blogosphere and in fringe groups, tolerated but not mainstreamed in the Republican movement.

The risk is in the gathering threats of further economic deterioration. The prosperity of the last two decades, which mostly benefitted the super rich but at least let the living standards of the rest stagnate rather than fall, was heavily based on mounting debt. For individuals and families this was unpaid credit card balances and serial home loans, speculating on an ever rising spiral of home prices. For the finance-dominated economy it was the vast sale of securitized risky mortgages. For the government it was the sale of Treasury bonds, which must be paid off with interest as they come due. Because of the Bush tax cuts, income from taxes is the lowest as a percentage of GDP it has been since 1950, and likely to stay that way given Republican intransigence. At the same time government expenses skyrocketed, with two wars, followed by the economic implosion of 2007. The result has been that Washington's income in recent years has fallen far short of its basic obligations. The government in consequence has been borrowing between 36 and 40 cents of every dollar it spends.

The almost jobless recovery has been anemic and continually threatened with relapse, as none of the three sectors can sufficiently fund new economic growth by resuming or increasing borrowing to the degree of the recent past. And in a period of world recession, export markets are not coming to the rescue. The debt crisis in southern Europe, particularly in Greece, threatens the fragile recovery. Europe remains America's largest export market, where a deepening European downturn can push the U.S. back into recession. In addition, if the Euro is devalued it would give European exporters an advantage over exports denominated in dollars going to countries like China and Brazil.

Then there are the ecological threats. Global warming, no matter who denies its existence, is already here, ravaging the Midwest and South and cutting deeply into our country's vaunted food production. And the damage done by drought, wildfires, and floods is mounting year by year.

A related potentially devastating crisis is depletion of essential energy and mineral resources, especially oil. There is a vigorous debate now in progress over the threat of peak oil. Both the European governmental International Energy Agency and the U.S. government's Energy Information Administration have concluded that ordinary crude oil has hit its global peak and is now in a plateau that will soon turn to steady decline. Historic price rises since the turn of the millennium have put a strain on the whole of the world economy. At the moment supply and demand are narrowly in balance, holding prices to the still very steep $90 a barrel for U.S. and $106 for European oil, this last used in California and much of the U.S. East Coast.

The precarious balance depends on two factors: a decline in world demand due to the recession, and a small increase in the supply of newly added "unconventional" oil: Canadian tar sands, fracking to release oil from shale deposits, deep sea drilling, very heavy oil, mostly from Venezuela, and conversion of natural gas to a liquid.

Even optimists and most knowledgeable Republicans, despite the simplistic "Drill, baby, drill!" slogan, generally concede that conventional crude oil has peaked and the days of cheap energy are over. Their hope is that the expensive and difficult-to-extract unconventional substitutes will save the day. Time will tell if they are right. A paper by Leonardo Maugeri, an Italian oil executive and visiting scholar at Harvard's Belfer Center for Science and International Affairs, goes so far as claiming that projects, now in their early stages, by 2015 will have guaranteed a sufficient oil supply to meet projected world needs through 2020, supplies being so plentiful that prices will see a dramatic fall.

Global oil output in 2011 was 83 million barrels a day (mbd) according to the Energy Information Administration. They project that unconventional oil will grow to only about 9.5 mbd by 2035. The Bakken deposit of shale oil in North Dakota, which Maugeri cites as the most important source for U.S. unconventional oil, to date is producing only 800,000 barrels a day out of American total consumption of 18 million. Stephen Sorrell, senior lecturer in Science and Technology Policy Research, Sussex Energy Group, in a post to the July 11, 2012, OilDrum website says that Maugeri's estimates are based on decline rates for existing conventional oil fields that are far lower than those of the U.S. government:

> [H]e uses an average annual decline rate for all fields of 1.6% over this period, which is less than half of the IEA [International Energy Administration] and CERA [Cambridge Energy Research Associates] estimates for 2008 (4.1%/year and 4.5%/year respectively). The discrepancy is even greater since the IEA and other analysts project an increase in average decline rates over the 2011-20 period.

If the IEA and CERA estimates are correct, even the most optimistic hopes for unconventional oil will not come close to making up the shortfall. This would have a very serious effect on the U.S. and world economy.

All of the above causes pose severe risks for the future of the American economy. The geometrically expanding world population can only be fed, housed, and provided meaningful work with some level of ongoing economic growth, a prospect that becomes more and more unsustainable. It is reasonable to expect that, with some ups and downs, the trajectory of our future economy is on a downward slope. This will generate blame for anyone holding government office and encourage extremist movements of the right and left. And here the Republicans are well ahead of any left-of-center reaction, as most liberals are simply defending the status quo.

The particular racial and sexual fears of the elderly whites who have flocked to the transformed GOP are their unique problem, above and beyond the real problems that we all share. But for those who find becoming a minority to Hispanics, blacks, and Asians intolerable, or who cannot accept radically different concepts of marriage, including gay marriage, or who refuse to abandon traditional patriarchal power over women's reproductive organs, these fears are highly motivating. They would not be the first group that, finding it impossible to rule by majority consent, seek to rule without it.

July 29, 2012

Symptoms of U.S. Decline

In his State of the Union address this year President Obama declared, "Anyone who tells you that America is in decline, or that our influence has waned, doesn't know what they're talking about."

Mitt Romney says the same thing, excepting a few admissions of slippage he feels he can blame on Obama, harping on America's "exceptionalism" and the supposedly pending new "American Century," the last one, proclaimed by *Time* magazine's founder Henry Luce in 1941, having run a bit shorter than planned.

The counter argument was voiced by Jeff Daniels as the fictional news anchor in HBO's new series *The Newsroom*, in a clip widely circulated on YouTube. Asked why America is the greatest country in the world he responds, "It's not the greatest country in the world. We lead the world in only three categories: number of incarcerated citizens per capita, number of adults who believe angels are real, and defense spending, where we spend more than the next twenty-six countries combined, twenty-five of whom are allies."

In graduate school twenty-five years ago we learned that people in different occupations will turn conversation to define status to their benefit. Stock brokers tell how much money they make, artists about galleries where their work is displayed. The discussion of whether the United States is doing well or badly runs the same way. Conservative historian Victor Davis Hanson in an April 26, 2012, post to National Review Online assures us that "Never in the last 70 years has the U.S. military been so lethal." He defines the symptoms of apparent decline quite narrowly: the large federal deficit, high oil prices, and self-pitying claims of poverty ("The underclass suffers more from obesity than malnutrition") from people who by world (or at least Third World?) standards have adequate housing and medical care. The deficit can be cured by "a new tax code, simple reforms to entitlements, and reasonable trimming of bloated public salaries and pensions," while oil prices can be lowered by drilling off both coasts and in Alaska.

We could quibble about how deep the cuts would have to be to eliminate the deficit, given Republican calls for more big tax cuts for the rich, or whether all the oil in and around the United States could free the country from its current 8 million barrels a day import habit or change the international price, or whether the problems of the American under class can be reduced to bad eating habits. I would start somewhere else entirely, as Hanson, like the hypothetical stock broker we heard of in graduate school, wants to define decline solely by issues for which his party has neat talking points.

To suggest the broader terms of the problem here is *Time* magazine editor Fareed Zakaria:

> The U.S. remains the world's largest economy, and we have the largest military by far, the most dynamic technology companies and a highly entrepreneurial climate. But these are snapshots of where we are right now. The decisions that created today's growth — decisions about education, infrastructure and the like — were made decades ago. What we see today is an American economy that has boomed because of policies and developments of the 1950s and '60s: the interstate-highway system, massive funding for science and technology, a public-education system that was the envy of the world and generous immigration policies. Look at some underlying measures today, and you will wonder about the future.
>
> The following rankings come from various lists, but they all tell the same story. According to the Organisation for Economic Co-operation and Development (OECD), our 15-year-olds rank 17th in the world in science and 25th in math. We rank 12th among developed countries in college graduation (down from No. 1 for decades). We come in 79th in elementary-school enrollment. Our infrastructure is ranked 23rd in the world, well behind that of every other major advanced economy. American health numbers are stunning for a rich country: based on studies by the OECD and the World Health Organization, we're 27th in life expectancy, 18th in diabetes and first in obesity. Only a few decades ago, the U.S. stood tall in such rankings. No more. There are some areas in which we are still clearly No. 1, but they're not ones we usually brag about. We have the most guns. We have the most crime among rich countries. And, of course, we have by far the largest amount of debt in the world.[1]

These suggestions of a downhill slide have various causes. In some cases other countries are making investments in education, health, and infrastructure that the United States has cut back on. The promotion of extreme inequality in the United States compared to other advanced countries has had an impact on a wide range of measures of productivity and well-being of the lower quintiles

---

[1] *Time* magazine, March 3, 2011.

of the population. Offshoring much of American industry has driven down domestic wages, which in turn affects the sales of businesses, including the ones saving on wages by doing the offshoring. The severe distrust in government by both Left and Right that set in at the end of the sixties spills over into attitudes toward public education, religious on the part of the Right, which tries to defund "anti-Christian" public education and remove its children to parochial schools or home study. Some negatives result from the financialization of the American economy in the 1990s, the long debt bubble, followed by the economic collapse of 2007. The Republican strategy of gridlocking and discrediting the federal government has for some years stalled government attention to a range of at least partial potential fixes. And still other negative statistics result from the growing global scarcity of cheap oil and many metallic ores that have driven prices relentlessly upward since around 2000, affecting most countries.

Let's look at some of the parameters.

Education

On the bright side, the United States still ranks number one internationally in the quality of its universities. When it comes to graduation rates, however, the U.S. shows dramatic slippage. According to a November 2011 report by the Council of Graduate Schools:

> In 2009, the United States ranked third among OECD countries in the percentage of 55-64 year-olds who had attained tertiary [college] education. In the U.S., 41% of individuals in this age group had attained tertiary education in 2009, trailing only behind the Russian Federation (44%) and Israel (45%), and considerably higher than the OECD average of 22%. Among 25-34 year-olds, however, the United States ranked 16th in the percentage who had attained tertiary education, indicating that educational attainment is increasing faster in other OECD countries than in the United States. In the U.S., 41% of 25-34 year-olds had attained tertiary education in 2009, higher than the 37% OECD average, but considerably lower than top-ranked South Korea (63%). Canada (56%), Japan (56%), and the Russian Federation (55%) also had educational attainment rates for 25-34 year-olds that were considerably higher than the rate in the U.S.[2]

The other countries with substantially higher percentage of college graduates among 25-34 year olds were Ireland, Norway, New Zealand, Luxembourg, United Kingdom, Australia, Denmark, France, Israel, Belgium, and Sweden.

---

[2] http://www.cgsnet.org/ckfinder/userfiles/files/comm_2011_11.pdf

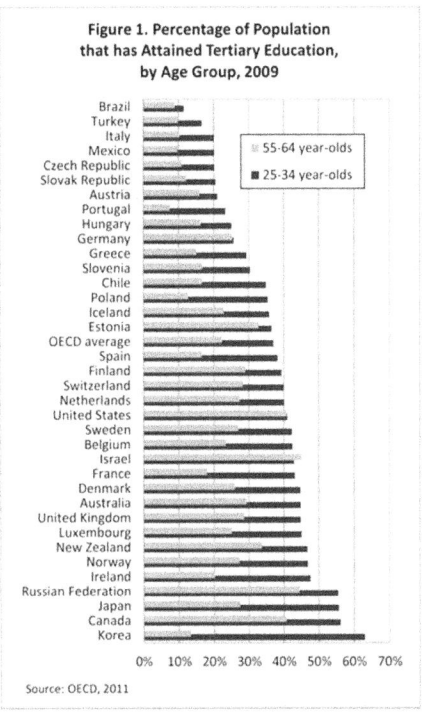

Figure 1. Percentage of Population that has Attained Tertiary Education, by Age Group, 2009

Source: OECD, 2011

When we turn to K-12 the picture is even worse. The OECD international test scores for fifteen-year-olds for 2009[3], where the U.S. came in 27th in math and 22nd in science, showed the U.S. below even the OECD average in both subjects, out-performed not only by Western Europe and Japan but by most of Eastern Europe and a formerly Third World country like South Korea. A few samples: In math, South Korea scored 547, the Czech Republic 510, Poland 495, the U.S. 474. In science: Finland 563, South Korea 522, the Czech Republic 513, Hungary 504, the U.S. 489.

A March 2012 Council on Foreign Relations report on "US Education Reform and National Security"[4] prepared by Joel I. Klein, former head of New York City public schools, and Condoleezza Rice, former U.S. secretary of state, warned, "Educational failure puts the United States' future economic prosperity, global position, and physical safety at risk." The report noted that "More than 25 percent of students fail to graduate from high school in four years; for African-American and Hispanic students, this number is approach-

---

[3] http://www.geographic.org/country_ranks/educational_score_performance_ country _ranks_ 2009_oecd.html
[4] http://www.cfr.org/united-states/us-education-reform-national-security/p27618

ing 40 percent." And "only 22 percent of U.S. high school students met 'college ready' standards in all of their core subjects; these figures are even lower for African-American and Hispanic students."[5]

The Global Innovation Index, an annual international study by the INSEAD Graduate Business School and the World Intellectual Property Organization, in its 2012 rankings placed the United States 31st out of 125 countries in education overall and 46th for its low per capita expenditure compared to GDP. On pupil-to-teacher ratio in secondary education, at 13.8:1, the U.S. ranked 61st. In higher education, the U.S. ranked second in enrollment, but 74th in students graduating with science and engineering degrees.[6]

Then we have Fareed Zakaria again:

> In 2008, the U.S. high school graduation rate was lower than the rates of the United Kingdom, Switzerland, Norway, South Korea, Japan, Italy, Ireland, Germany, Finland and Denmark. That same year, the U.S. was the only developed nation where a higher percent of 55- to 64-year-olds than 25- to 34-year-olds had graduated from high school.[7]

Not surprisingly the slackening of educational standards and participation is reflected in a shocking level of ignorance by our country's adult population. The Christian Science Monitor reports: "Only one-third of Americans can name all three branches of government; another third cannot name any. The United States ranks 120th out of 169 democracies in voter turnout."[8]

A 2008 survey by the Intercollegiate Studies Institute found that among elected officials, "43% do not know the Electoral College is a constitutionally mandated assembly that elects the president. One in five thinks it 'trains those aspiring for higher office' or 'was established to supervise the first televised presidential debates.'"[9]

A Marist Institute for Public Opinion poll of American adults found that 26 percent did not know that the United States won its independence from Great Britain. Six percent named a different country, including France, China, Japan, Mexico and Spain. Twenty percent said they weren't sure.[10]

Another survey, by the American Revolution Center, devoted to the study of the American Revolution, found that more than a third of American adults "did not know the century in which the American Revolution took

---

[5] http://www.cfr.org/united-states/us-education-reform-national-security/p27618
[6] http://www.globalinnovationindex.org/gii/main/fullreport/index.html
[7] Fareed Zakaria, CNNWorld, November 3, 2011.
[8] *Christian Science Monitor*, July 16, 2012
[9] Reported by *USA Today*, November 21, 2008.
[10] *Washington Post*, July 3, 2010.

place, and half of respondents believed that either the Civil War, the Emancipation Proclamation or the War of 1812 occurred before the American Revolution."[11]

These kinds of gaps are discouraging enough, but when we come to science things quickly get worse. Jeff Daniels quips that one of the three measures in which America leads the world is the number of people who believe that angels are real. That is not a joke. An Associated Press-GfK poll at the end of 2011 found that 77 percent of American adults believe angels are real, a number that rises to 95 percent among Evangelical Christians.[12]

There is an inverse connection between this religion-based world view and knowledge of science, and, like the social and economic effects of the dominance of Islam in Muslim countries, it does not bode well for a nation in a highly technological and competitive world.

A Gallup poll in June 2012 found that when asked to choose whether humans are the product of evolution from lower animals, the product of such evolution guided by God, or if God created humans as they now exist within the last 10,000 years, 46 percent of Americans chose the 10,000-year version, a world view held by most peasants in the Middle Ages.[13] If the Earth is less than 10,000 years old, virtually everything known by biology, paleontology, geology, astronomy, and physics is impossible. Is it any wonder then that the United States is 74th among nations in the percentage of science and engineering degrees?

While I am not particularly fond of scriptural religions I would add here that both mainstream liberal Protestantism and most of the Catholic Church would choose evolution guided by God, a viewpoint that carefully avoids a clash with the known facts of science.

A national survey commissioned by the California Academy of Sciences and conducted by Harris Interactive in 2009 found that 47% of American adults did not know how long it takes the Earth to go around the sun, and 41% believed that humans lived at the same time as the dinosaurs.[14]

---

[11] *The Atlantic Wire*, June 3, 2010.

[12] CBS News online, December 23, 2011.

[13] MinnPost 6-01-2012 http://www.minnpost.com/eric-black-ink/2012/06/ almost-half-us- dont-believe-evolution.

[14] *Science Daily*, March 13, 2009.

*Which of the following statements comes closest to your views on the origin and
development of human beings?*

1) Human beings have developed over millions of years from less advanced forms of life, but God guided
this process, 2) Human beings have developed over millions of years from less advanced forms of life,
but God had no part in this process, 3) God created human beings pretty much in their present form at
one time within the last 10,000 years or so

■ % Humans evolved, with God guiding   ▨ % Humans evolved, but God had no part in process

▨ % God created humans in present form

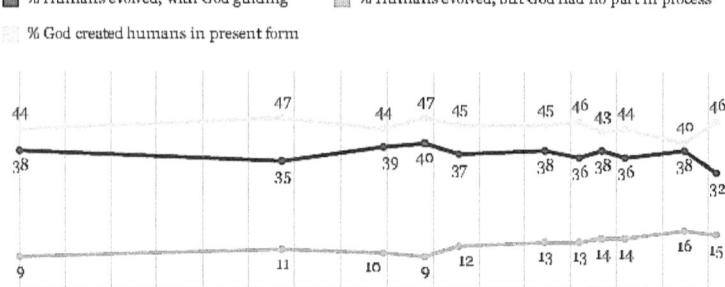

1982 1984 1986 1988 1990 1992 1994 1996 1998 2000 2002 2004 2006 2008 2010 2012

GALLUP

Our national ignorance of science, exacerbated by religion and right-wing politicians, has huge consequences in preparing for our future. A 2010 Yale University study found that "more than two-thirds of those surveyed believe that reducing toxic waste or banning aerosol spray cans will curb climate change. And 43 percent believe that 'if we stopped punching holes in the ozone layer with rockets, it would reduce global warming.'" Just 1 in 10 of those surveyed said they were "very well informed' about climate change and 45 percent said they were not very worried or not at all worried about it.[15]

In contrast, an August 2012 survey in Canada found that only 2 percent of Canadians deny climate change and only 9 percent deny human actions as a major cause.[16]

Finally on this point, UCLA scientist Jared Diamond, in an August 1, 2012, response to Mitt Romney's misunderstandings of Diamond's book *Guns, Germs, and Steel*, disputed Romney's one-dimensional pronouncements that culture determines national success:

> We Americans fail to provide superior education and economic incentives to much of our population. India, China and other countries that have not been world leaders are investing heavily in education, technology and infrastructure. They're offering economic opportunities to more and more of their citizens. That's part of the reason jobs are moving

---

[15] *New York Times*, October 1, 2010.
[16] CBC News, Calgary, August 15, 2012.

overseas. Our geography won't keep us rich and powerful if we can't get a good education, can't afford health care and can't count on our hard work's being rewarded by good jobs and rising incomes. Mitt Romney may become our next president. Will he continue to espouse one-factor explanations for multicausal problems, and fail to understand history and the modern world? If so, he will preside over a declining nation squandering its advantages of location and history.[17]

Infrastructure

The United States was once a world leader in its highway system, network of bridges, advanced telecommunications. This is not true today.

According to a University of Virginia study,

> America's infrastructure is in grave disrepair. Analysts have determined that one-third of the nation's roads are in poor or mediocre condition, and the Federal Highway Administration recently estimated that one out of every four bridges is either structurally deficient or functionally obsolete. Every infrastructure sector, from rail, air and seaways, to water supply, sewage and irrigation, to energy pipelines and the electric grid, are in need of significant capital.[18]

This decline can't be explained as typical of the developed world. World Economic Forum rankings for 2011 place the United States 23rd out of 139 countries on measures of transportation, telephony, and energy, tied with Spain, noticeably behind the major European countries, but also Singapore, the United Arab Emirates, South Korea, and Portugal, and even a bit below Barbados and Taiwan.[19]

The Urban Land Institute in a May 2011 report said that the United States has underfunded infrastructure over the last thirty years, while international competitors China, India, and Brazil have been heavily investing in theirs. The American Society of Civil Engineers has estimated that the U.S. would need to spend some $2 trillion just to repair deteriorating infrastructure networks and maintain roads, bridges, water lines, sewage treatment plants, dams and other infrastructure.[20]

Former Pennsylvania Governor Ed Rendell recounts that when he came into office in 2003 his state had 5,600 structurally deficient or obsolete

---

[17] *New York Times*, August 1, 2012.
[18] University of Virginia, Miller Center, http://millercenter.org/public/ debates/ infrastructure, accessed August 17, 2012.
[19] http://www.photius.com/rankings/infrastructure_quality_ country_ rank ings_ 2011.html
[20] Knowledge Center, The Council of State Governments, May 23, 2011

bridges. He tripled his capital budget, from $200 million to $700 million a year, plus a special appropriation of $200 million for each of the next four years. By 2008 the number of deficient bridges had gone from 5,600 to 6,000.[21]

American waterways, on which a vast amount of material is transported, are in even worse shape. As an example, the main lock on the Ohio River near Warsaw, Kentucky, broke in July 2011. This jumped the delay for ship and barge traffic from 40 minutes to 20 hours. The lock is supposed to reopen in August 2012, more than a year later. Fourteen major locks are rated to fail between now and 2020, at a repair cost of billions. Freight bottlenecks from faulty locks, too-narrow-highways, and other congestion are costing a minimum of $200 billion a year, with the conservative U.S. Chamber of Commerce putting the estimate at $1 trillion.[22]

The same article gives as another example an 83-year-old lock on the Ohio River near Olmsted, Illinois:

> Congress set aside $775 million to replace it and another nearby lock in 1988. The project began in 1993 and was scheduled to be finished by 2009 but still isn't complete [in May 2012], in part because of engineering modifications intended to save $60 million. Now, the cost has ballooned to $3.1 billion, and the new lock won't be ready until 2020 or later.

The president-elect of the American Society of Civil Engineers in June 2012 confirmed that the organization will probably repeat their near-failing "D" grade in its next report on U.S. infrastructure projects such as roads, railways, and airports due in 2013 A group of municipal bond experts were polled on this and shared this opinion.[23]

Another aspect of infrastructure is communications. On cell phones, the U.S. ranks third in the world with 327 million, topped only by China with a billion and India with 934 million. The U.S. has slightly more phones out there than it has people, at 103.9% of population. That would seem to be enough, but perhaps this includes old units that no longer work. In any case many countries have far more cell phones per capita. America is 34th, after such unexpected rivals as Indonesia, Malaysia, Ukraine, and Guatemala. Bra-

---

[21] *New York Times*, February 15, 2010.
[22] *USA Today*, May 20, 2012.
[23] Bloomberg, June 13, 2012.

zil has phones for 132% of its population, and the United Arab Emirates for 197 percent.[24]

A quarter of the world's 584 million Internet addresses in 2011 were in the United States. At the same time, neither the private companies that control access to the net nor the federal government have kept up with world standards in Internet speed. The United States ranks 14th, with an average connection speed of 5.6 megabits per second, compared to South Korea at 14.4, Hong Kong at 9.2, and Japan at 8.1. Other countries ahead of the U.S. here include Romania, Czech Republic, Latvia, and Ireland.[25]

Our space program saw a high profile advance with the Curiosity rover's landing on Mars August 6, 2012. Less well known is the drastic decline of the U.S. orbital satellite system, which began in the mid-1990s. The satellites are used to track storms, contain oil spills, monitor flooding, forecast weather, measure the strength of hurricanes, manage fisheries, and check security in shipping lanes. A new study from the National Academies of Science says that the U.S. has lost all of its wind sensors and no longer has any sensors capable of measuring ocean currents. The *Christian Science Monitor* summarizes:

> the number of in-orbit and planned NASA and NOAA [National Oceanic and Atmospheric Administration] Earth observing missions will decline from 23 in 2012 to only six in 2020. And the number of Earth observing instruments mounted on such satellites will fall from about 110 in 2011 to fewer than 30 in 2020.[26]

While the American space program is being sharply cut back, the *Monitor* reports that

> China, India, Russia, South Korea, Japan, European nations, and several other countries are aggressively developing oceanographic satellite sensors. . . . The American science community is often told by NASA managers to go look elsewhere for information and to use the foreign sensors if they can get the data.

The problem is compounded by the Republican Party's bizarre decision to oppose federal efforts to repair our infrastructure, apparently out of an animus

---

[24] http://en.wikipedia.org/wiki/List_of_countries_by_number_of_ mobile_ phones_ in_use.

[25] TechSpot July 26, 2011.

[26] *Christian Science Monitor*, June 8, 2012.

toward Barack Obama that outweighs their concern for the country. As *US News* reports:

> Many Republican lawmakers have in the past decried spending on infrastructure. When President Obama introduced the idea of a national infrastructure bank in September 2010, Representative Eric Cantor called it "yet another government stimulus effort" and House Speaker John Boehner called it "more of the same failed 'stimulus spending.'"[27]

Poverty and Homelessness

The United States among advanced countries has pretty much the highest poverty rate, the greatest percentage of children in poverty, and the most homeless. According to the Economic Policy Institute, based on the Census Bureau's Current Population Survey, "Poverty rates in the United States increased over the 2000s, a trend exacerbated by the Great Recession and its aftermath. By 2010, just over 46 million people fell below the U.S. Census Bureau's official poverty line." Looking at OECD data, the U.S. has a higher poverty rate than any OECD country, at 17.3%, compared to 6.1% for Denmark, or the strongest European countries, France at 7.2%, Germany, 8.9%, and the United Kingdom at 11.0%.[28]

Thinking of Victor Davis Hanson's snide dismissal of American poverty as unreal, compared, I suppose, to sub-Saharan Africa, we should note that 17.3% of Americans is 52.7 million people, while the U.S. Census Bureau draws the poverty line these millions fall at or below at an annual income of $11,702 for a single person under 65 and $22,811 for a family of four.[29] In Los Angeles it is rare to find a one bedroom apartment for less than $1,000 a month. The median price is $1,117.[30]

The graph below shows that the U.S. ranked 25th among developed countries in child poverty with even Turkey doing better.[31]

[27] US News, August 22, 2011.

[28] http://www.epi.org/publication/ib339-us-poverty-higher-safety-net-weaker/

[29] http://www.census.gov/hhes/www/poverty/data/threshld/index.html

[30] http://www.numbeo.com/cost-of-living/city_result.jsp?country=United+States& city= Los+Angeles%2C+CA

[31] Graph from Project America, http://www.project.org/info.php?recordID=467 See also Adamson, Peter. 2012. "Measuring Child Poverty: New League Tables of Child Poverty in the World's Rich Countries," UNICEF Innocenti Research Centre Report Card 10. http://www.unicef.org.uk/ Documents/Publications/RC10-measuring-child-poverty.pdf

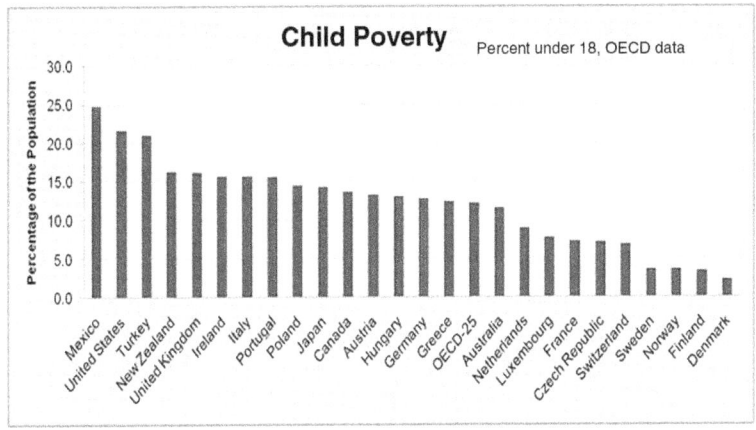

The United Nations Children's Fund (UNICEF), ranking nations by children's well-being in 20 rich countries for 2007, based on six criteria, placed the U.S. at number 19, with the UK last. The criteria were material well-being, health and safety, educational well-being, family and peer relationships, behaviors and risks, and subjective well-being. With the lower-the-score-the-better, the U.S. scored 18.0, while the Netherlands was 4.2 and Sweden 5.0. Germany was at 11.2 and France at 13.0. In this comparison the UK trailed at 18.2.[32]

Homelessness in the United States and generally in Europe is defined most narrowly as people living on the streets or in temporary emergency shelters. There are three different statistics to define this problem. The most common is "point in time," how many are, on the average, homeless on a given day. Then there is the number for how many are homeless for some part of a given year, a much larger number. And finally, there is the number for the chronic homeless, those without regular shelter for more than a year.

The most recent national survey of homelessness in the United States, "The State of Homelessness in America 2012" by the National Alliance to End Homelessness and the Homeless Research Institute, put the point-in-time daily average for 2011 at 636,017.[33] 37% of that number are in homeless families. The chronically homeless numbered 107,148. The number of homeless veterans in 2011 was 67,495.[34] All these numbers showed a slight reduction from 2009, the worst year of the recession. The declines were aided by a federal assistance program that provided aid to a million people. And while

[32] UNICEF Innocenti Research Centre http://www.photius.com/rankings/ child_well_being_in_rich_countries_2007.html
[33] http://www.endhomelessness.org/content/article/detail/4361/, p. 5 of the PDF.
[34] Ibid. p. 9.

homelessness was reduced in 26 states, it increased between 2009 and 2011 in 24 states.[35] There were huge increases in the northern "Red" states: Montana, Wyoming, Idaho, North Dakota, and Utah.

Only the point-in-time statistics are comprehensive, but a standard extrapolation of how many people are homeless for part of each year is approximately four times the point-in-time number, or about 2.5 million for the United States.

The report adds:

> A majority of homeless people counted were in emergency shelters or transitional housing programs, but nearly 4 in 10 were unsheltered, living on the streets, or in cars, abandoned buildings, or other places not intended for human habitation. The unsheltered population increased by 2 percent from 239,759 in 2009 to 243,701 in 2011.[36]

How does America's homeless problem compare with other rich countries? Statistics on this are not widely available, so I will limit the comparison to Germany, France, and the UK.

All four countries have somewhat comparable numbers of homeless people: Germany, with a population of 81.8 million has 272,000 homeless; France at 65.4 million has 133,364, and the United Kingdom with 62.3 million has 86,781. As a percentage of total population, homeless on a given day, in the U.S. and France are .002%, Germany .003, and the UK .001.[37]

If the gross numbers are similar, there the comparison ends. The British report cited above adds:

> England is highly unusual in providing, for some homeless groups, a legally-enforceable right to "suitable" temporary accommodation which lasts, in most cases, until "settled" housing becomes available. However, legislation has recently been passed by the French Parliament (March 2007) which attempts to establish a legally-enforceable right to housing for those who have experienced "an abnormally long delay" in being allocated social housing."[38]

In the United States, 38% of its homeless population, 243,701 on an average night in 2011, live on the streets.[39] In Germany it is only18,000, 6% of the

---

[35] Ibid., p. 16.

[36] Ibid., p. 6.

[37] http://www.communities.gov.uk/archived/publications/housing/interna=tional homelessness review.

[38] An International Review of Homelessness and Social Housing Policy p. 17.

[39] http://www.endhomelessness.org/content/article/detail/4361/, p. 21 of the PDF.

total. The rest are in temporary housing. In France, out of its 133,244, 74,000 are in hostels, 39,000 are in temporary accommodations, and the remaining 19,854 combine both those who are "roofless" and those in emergency shelters. In the UK, out of a total of 86,781 counted as homeless, 70,730 were in temporary housing on an average night in 2008, 6,286 were in hostels, 8,852 in overnight emergency shelters, and only 813 people known to be still out on the streets.

If we look at the measure of how each country has treated its homeless and how it has tried to reduce the problem, the United States is the most cold hearted and with the most severe problem.

Health

The United States is unique among advanced countries in not providing health care for all of its citizens. It consumes the highest proportion of GDP for health expenses of any country in the world, 17.2% in 2011, with the least to show for it.[40] In comparison, France spends 11.2%, Germany 10.7%, Sweden, 9.2%, and the United Kingdom 8.2%.[41] The Kaiser Family Foundation estimated that for 2010, 16% of the U.S. population, or 56.8 million people, had no health insurance.[42] The Commonwealth Fund, a health-promotion foundation created in 1918 by a Standard Oil heiress, in an April 2012 survey found that during 2011 an even more shocking 26 percent of Americans between 19 and 64 had no health insurance during all or part of the year, the increase due mainly to people losing their jobs.[43]

The World Health Organization in 2000 conducted an in-depth survey of health care in 191 countries. In its ranked list the United States came in 37th, behind such countries as Colombia, Saudi Arabia, Morocco, and Costa Rica. Standings for the major advanced countries showed France as number 1, Japan 10, United Kingdom 18, and Germany 25.

---

[40] http://www.pbs.org/newshour/rundown/2012/10/health-costs-how-the-us-compares-with-other-countries.html
[41] http://www.photius.com/rankings/total_health_expenditure_as_pecent_of_gdp_2000_to_2005.html
[42] http://facts.kff.org/chart.aspx?ch=477.
[43] http://www.commonwealthfund.org/Publications/Issue-Briefs/2012/ Apr/ Gaps-in-Health-Insurance.aspx

Health Insurance Coverage in the U.S. 2010

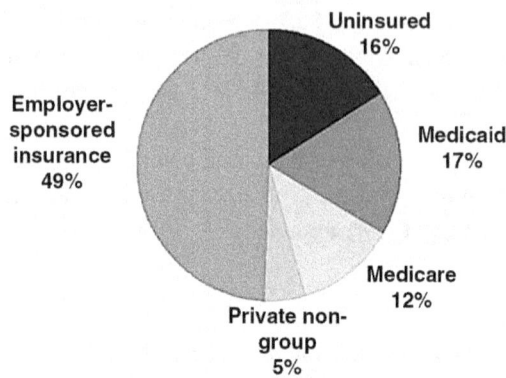

Uninsured 16%

Employer-sponsored insurance 49%

Medicaid 17%

Medicare 12%

Private non-group 5%

Total = 305.2 million

Source: KCMU/Urban Institute analysis of 2011 ASEC Supplement to the CPS.
*Medicaid also includes other publicprograms: CHIP, other state programs, military-related coverage.
Numbers may not add to 100 due to rounding.

The U.S. on one hand has the most technically advanced health facilities and technology in the world. But it fails dismally to make this available to large segments of its people. There are significant consequences for America's very large omitted population and poor delivery system. The U.S. has the highest incidence of diabetes of any advanced country, 10.3% of the whole population. Germany stands at 8.9%, France at 6.7, and the United Kingdom at the remarkably low 3.6%.[44]

According to the CIA's *World Fact Book*, the U.S. in 2012 ranks 50th among the world's countries in life expectancy, at 78.49 years, behind such similar economies as Japan, 83.91 years, Canada 81.48, France 81.46, Germany 80.19, and the United Kingdom 80.17.[45]

Infant mortality tells a similar story. The CIA's *World Fact Book* for 2012 ranks the U.S. worse than 48 other countries in infant deaths. The U.S. rate is 5.8 deaths per 1000 live births (down from 6.6 a few years earlier). The European Union rate is 4.49, but some countries are significantly better: Germany 3.51, France 3.37, Sweden 2.74, and Japan 2.21.[46]

---

[44] Figures for 2010, from UNICEF, http://www.allcountries.org/ ranks/diabetes_prevalence_country_ranks.html.html
[45] https://www.cia.gov/library/publications/the-world-factbook/rankorder/2102rank .html
[46] https://www.cia.gov/library/publications/the-world-factbook/rankorder/2091rank.ht ml

Yet another measure is the number of deaths that could have been prevented by better health care. The numbers come from a major data study by the Commonwealth Foundation in 2008 and are for 2002-2003, limited to deaths before age 74. The U.S. ranked dead last out of 14 countries studied, with 110 unnecessary deaths in every 100,000 citizens for that year, compared to only 65 for France.[47] The U.S. number adds up to 335,500 Americans who die each year because of inadequate health care. In ten years the government's savings on health care, so dear to Republican hearts, causes the unnecessary deaths of 3.35 million of our people. This compares to total U.S. military deaths in Iraq and Afghanistan up through the beginning of 2012 of 7,959.[48]

The study table compares preventable deaths in 1997-1998 to the 2002-2003 period. The authors make the following comment on the numbers from the United States:

> The decline in amenable mortality in all countries averaged 16 percent over this period. The United States was an outlier, with a decline of only 4 percent. If the United States could reduce amenable mortality to the average rate achieved in the three top-performing countries, there would have been 101,000 fewer deaths per year by the end of the study period.

The authors also write, "[I]t is difficult to disregard the observation that the slow decline in U.S. amenable mortality has coincided with an increase in the uninsured population."

Further they quote Commonwealth Fund Senior Vice President Cathy Schoen:

> It is startling to see the U.S. falling even farther behind on this crucial indicator of health system performance. By focusing on deaths amenable to health care, [researchers] Nolte and McKee strip out factors such as population and lifestyle differences that are often cited in response to international comparisons showing the U.S. lagging in health outcomes. The fact that other countries are reducing these preventable deaths more rapidly, yet spending far less, indicates that policy, goals, and efforts to improve health systems make a difference.

---

[47] "Measuring The Health Of Nations: Updating An Earlier Analysis," Ellen Nolte and C. Martin McKee, *Health Affairs*, 27, no. 1 (2008): 58-71 The ranking table was produced by Photius Coutsoukis, based on research supported by The Commonwealth Fund and published in the January/February 2008 issue of *Health Affairs*, Bethesda, MD, USA. http://www.allcountries.org/ranks/preventable_deaths_country_ranks_1997-1998_2002-2003_2008.html

[48] http://icasualties.org/

It's also worth looking at the graph below, from *The Lancet*, on the numbers and causes of violent deaths of young people, aged 10 to 24, where the United States also leads the advanced countries of the world.

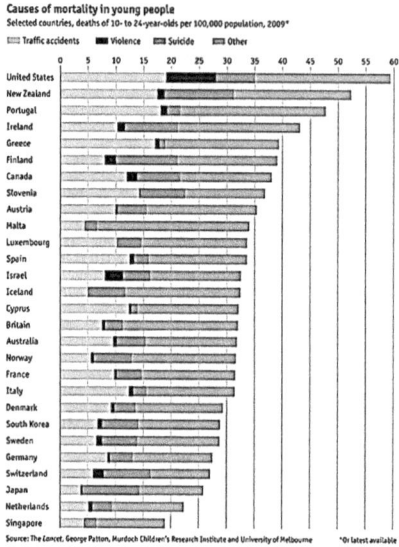

Causes of mortality in young people
Selected countries, deaths of 10- to 24-year-olds per 100,000 population, 2009*
Traffic accidents ■ Violence ▨ Suicide ▨ Other

Source: The Lancet, George Patton, Murdoch Children's Research Institute and University of Melbourne   *Or latest available

Before leaving this topic we should mention obesity in the United States. An August 1, 2012, article in the *Philadelphia Inquirer* states:

> Obesity is a uniquely urgent crisis in the United States. Americans are the fattest people in the world. The prevalence of obesity is significantly greater in America than in all the world's other wealthy nations. Americans are about twice as likely as Western Europeans or Canadians to be obese, three to four times more likely than Scandinavians, and 10 times more likely than the Japanese, who enjoy the world's greatest longevity.[49]

This problem is quantified in a 2010 report by the International Association for the Study of Obesity. It is not quite true that Americans are the fattest people in the world. In a table ranked by female obesity the U.S. comes in at number 18, behind such places as Samoa, Egypt, Saudi Arabia, and Albania. 35.5% of American females and 32.2% of males are obese. The first European country to make the list is Scotland, number 32, with 26.5% of its women and 24.9% of its men too fat. By the time we get to Germany it is 21.1 and 20.5,

---

[49] http://articles.philly.com/2012-08-01/news/32982010_1_eric-finkelstein-obesity-premature-death

France at 17.6 and 16.1, or Japan at 3.4 and 2.3. It is, after all, a cliche about declining empires that their people cease to be warriors and become fat and decadent.

The Republican argument on healthcare, as on the whole of the social safety net, is that there is no way to pay for it and that the proof is the lingering economic crisis in Europe, whose form of capitalism is based on a strong welfare state. A good example is this summation by Republican columnist David Brooks:

> [M]any Republicans have now come to the conclusion that the welfare-state model is in its death throes. Yuval Levin expressed the sentiment perfectly in a definitive essay for The Weekly Standard called "Our Age of Anxiety": "We have a sense that the economic order we knew in the second half of the 20th century may not be coming back at all — that we have entered a new era for which we have not been well prepared. ... We are, rather, on the cusp of the fiscal and institutional collapse of our welfare state, which threatens not only the future of government finances but also the future of American capitalism." To Republican eyes, the first phase of that collapse is playing out right now in Greece, Spain and Italy — cosseted economies, unmanageable debt, rising unemployment, falling living standards.[50]

If there is any truth to this idea, what should be debated is the Republican solution, of funneling vast amounts of money to the rich while abandoning the middle class and the poor. Still, we are not yet where the Republican punditocracy claim. U.S. social spending as a percentage of GDP is running at 16.2% a year. Greece, Europe's basket case, is at 21.3%. Spain, in slightly better shape, spends more, at 21.6%, and Italy, better yet, spends still more at 24.9%. But the strongest and most stable of European countries spend even more than these countries on their social safety net: Sweden, 27.3%, Germany, 25.2%, France, 28.4%. The UK falls between the U.S. and the stressed European economies, at 20.5%.[51]

Unhappily, on health as on so much else the Republican Party, while proclaiming out of one side of its mouth that we are still number 1, essentially admits the decline by insistently claiming that nothing can be done about it and funding for any government effort to try should be slashed.

Ed Kilgore writing in the online June 10, 2012, *Washington Monthly*, looks at the partisan issues in this election year debate over healthcare:

---

[50] *New York Times*, June 14, 2012.
[51] http://www.oecd-ilibrary.org/social-issues-migration-health/government-social-spending_20743904-table1.

By now we should all understand that if you put together GOP plans to repeal the Affordable Care Act and also "block-grant" Medicaid, tens of millions of Americans would quickly lose access to affordable health care. . . . There is a natural partisan-political and ideological affinity for today's Republicans to pursue this old folks versus poor folks strategy, of course. With the two parties increasingly polarized by age and race/ethnicity, GOPers have every political reason to place the vitiation of Medicare (and for that matter, Social Security) on the back burner, and treat health care for non-seniors as "welfare," designed for those improvident and/or darker people, to be devolved to the tender mercies and inflexible budgets of state governments.[52]

Opportunity, Inequality, Incarcerations

For two hundred years the great merit and attraction of America was its chance for individual advancement, endlessly contrasted to the deadening class barriers of old Europe. The era of the Robber Barons in the nineteenth century displayed uncontrolled power of the ultrarich, at the same time most of the great capitalists were examples of the promise the country offered. Standard Oil founder John D. Rockefeller's father was a traveling salesman, steel magnate Andrew Carnegie worked in a bobbin factory. Banking lord J. P. Morgan was an unusual exception, his father a wealthy banker before him. There are a few recent examples to keep hopes alive, such as Steve Jobs and Bill Gates. But the class lines have hardened in the United States while easing in Europe. As Nobel laureate in economics Joseph Stiglitz writes,

There is less equality of opportunity in the United States today than there is in Europe — or, indeed, in any advanced industrial country for which there are data. . . . America has the highest level of inequality of any of the advanced countries — and its gap with the rest has been widening. In the "recovery" of 2009-2010, the top 1 percent of US income earners captured 93 percent of the income growth. Other inequality indicators — like wealth, health, and life expectancy — are as bad or even worse. The clear trend is one of concentration of income and wealth at the top, the hollowing out of the middle, and increasing poverty at the bottom.[53]

---

[52] http://www.washingtonmonthly.com/political-animal-a/2012_06/health_care_race_to_the_bottom037852.php

[53] http://www.slate.com/articles/business/project_syndicate/2012/06/the_american_dream_is_dying_here_s_how_we_can_fix_it_.html

Stiglitz dates the freeze in upward mobility to around 1980, from the first Reagan administration. It has been marked by the dominance of rent-seeking companies such as Bain Capital at the expense of companies that actually manufacture something, the off-shoring of jobs, and the radical reduction in tax rates for the superrich. He continues:

> Many at the bottom, or even in the middle, are not living up to their potential, because the rich, needing few public services and worried that a strong government might redistribute income, use their political influence to cut taxes and curtail government spending. This leads to underinvestment in infrastructure, education, and technology, impeding the engines of growth.

A 2006 study found: "Both the United States and Great Britain have significantly less economic mobility than Canada, Finland, Sweden, Norway, and possibly Germany; and the United States may be a less economically mobile society than Great Britain."[54]

Distinguished investigative journalists Donald L. Barlett and James B. Steele in their recent book, *The Betrayal of the American Dream*, offer some figures:

> From 2002 to 2007, the income gains of the top one percent rose 62 percent, compared to just 4 percent for the bottom 90 percent of households. . . . Among the richest of the rich — individuals and families with incomes in the top one-tenth of one percent — the gains were even more astronomical: their income rose 94 percent, or $3.5 million a household.[55]

Barlett and Steele point squarely to the capture of Congress by special interests of the wealthy as the cause of rapidly advancing inequality and stagnation of the American economy:

> Over the last four decades, the elite have systematically rewritten the rules to take care of themselves at everyone else's expense. As postwar U.S. history shows, it doesn't have to be this way. For decades after World War II, personal income in the United States grew at roughly the same rate for the rich and everyone else, all except for the poorest

---

[54] Emily Beller and Michael Hout, "Intergenerational Social Mobility: The United States in Comparative Perspective," *The Future of Children* journal, Princeton-Brookings, vol. 16, no. 2, Fall 2006.

[55] *Betrayal of the American Dream*, p. 18.

Americans. During this period, the gap between the rich and the middle class remained about the same.

The rich would have you believe that high taxes are a damper on the economy, but the postwar economic boom was marked by the highest personal income tax rates on the wealthy in peacetime U.S. history. At one point in the early 1950s, the top rate was 92 percent. . . . the wealthy paid a much higher percentage in taxes than they have paid for many years since. The federal government collected that tax money and routinely reinvested it in the American people. Veterans were able to go to college, families bought homes for the first time and government invested in infrastructure projects such as the interstate highway system."[56]

Joseph Stiglitz in another article explains why our country's gross inequality is not only unfair, but is a principal cause of the miserable economy:

Those at the top spend a smaller fraction of their income than do those in the bottom and middle — who have to spend everything today just to get by. Redistribution from the bottom to the top of the kind that has been going on in the United States lowers total demand. And the weakness in the U.S. economy arises out of deficient aggregate demand.[57]

Barlett and Steele show that the top 10% of American households have an average income of $930,000 while the bottom 90% average $36,000.[58] With such huge numbers of people circling the drain toward the poverty level it shouldn't be surprising that another study has found that 46 percent of Americans die with less than $10,000 in assets. "Many of these households also have no housing wealth and rely almost entirely on Social Security benefits for support." One consequence is that those in this income bracket have no resources for more than the most minimal health expenditures, and have health quality rated at half that of people whose income is even as much as $30,000 and who have assets of $25,000 to $50,000.[59]

Economic inequality particularly affects women. On the measure of gender equality, as on so many others, the United States ranks far below the more prosperous and egalitarian north European countries — and many from other parts of the world that should surprise people. A 2008 study of 130 countries by the World Economic Forum ranked nations on women's wage

---

[56] Ibid., p. 17.
[57] http://www.washingtonpost.com/opinions/how-policy-has-contributed-to-the-great-economic-divide/2012/06/22/gJQAXTX2vV_story.html.
[58] *Betrayal of the American Dream*, p. 11.
[59] Wonkblog, *Washington Post*, August 3, 2012.

levels compared to men, female participation in the labor force, and the percentage of female legislators, officials, and technical specialists. The U.S. came in at 27. The first three places were taken by Norway, Finland, and Sweden. But other countries that treat women more equally than the United States included the Philippines, Sri Lanka, Lesotho, Mozambique, and Cuba.[60]

Even on our much vaunted freedom of the press the U.S. is a distance away from the best world examples. A 2008 ranking by Freedom House put the United States in the 9th category from the top. Rankings from 0 to 30 were rated free, 31 to 60 partly free, and 61 to 100 unfree. The best scores went to Finland and Iceland at 9. The U.S. was rated 17.[61]

While the United States does not lead the pack in positive measures it does better in some of the negative ones affecting the life chances of those at the bottom of the economic heap. According to the United Nations Development Program, with a prison population of 2,186,230 in 2007 the U.S. led the world. It was tops also in the number incarcerated per 100,000 of population, at 738, followed by Russia at 611. Cuba, a Marxist police state, came 5th, at 487, Iran, a Muslim theocracy, at 214. By the time we reach a major European country it is Spain, with incarcerations running 145 per 100,000. Germany is at 95 and France at 85; India jails only 30.[62]

And should you dodge prison and pauperization there remains the risk of simply being murdered. Among developed countries for 2000 to 2004 you would have been the safest in Greece, however bad its economy. There, fewer than one person per 100,000 (.8) faced intentional homicide. In Germany it was 1, France 1.6, the UK 2.1, but in the United States 5.6. On this measure, however, the rates are much higher in most of Latin America, Argentina at 9.5 and Mexico at 13. Russia was the worst for an advanced country, at 19.9.

Conclusion

The far Left has always described the United States as a plutocracy. It in fact became that over the last thirty years. Much of this is a consequence of policy. Manufacturing accounted for 30% of American jobs in 1950. In 2011 it was only 9%.[63] Good-paying factory jobs were replaced by minimum wage service jobs, much of this in sectors that relied on discretionary spending and

---

[60] http://www.allcountries.org/ranks/gender_gap_gender_equality_country_rankings
_2008.html.
[61] http://www.photius.com/rankings/freedom_of_the_press_2008.html.
[62] http://www.allcountries.org/ranks/prison_incarceration_rates_of_countries_2007
.html.
[63] *Betrayal of the American Dream*, p. 268.

wilted during recessions. The static or falling income of the majority shrank demand, so while companies saved on wages by moving to China, India, or Malaysia, their customers at home had less to spend. As college tuitions escalated fewer people went or graduated, reducing the quality of the country's human capital. The economy became dominated by financial speculators who created no value except numbers in computer spreadsheets. The country's politics, through the ever more right wing Republican Establishment, has mirrored the values of the old white South, which believes deeply in the morality of an aristocracy ruling over a pauperized peon class. It was a decision of the new plutocracy to defund the training of human capital at home, to encourage governmental and private debt, to allow China to become the nation's chief creditor.

Democrats have not been angels in all this. To blunt the Republican attacks they have sidled from classic welfare-state-defending liberals to centrists. And for the most part they have been unwilling to confront or try to do much about the mounting ecological threats. In their defense, in countries with large numbers of religious dogmatists democracy produces less than happy results. The overthrow of semi-secular tyrants in the Middle East more often than not opens the door to Islamic fanatics with a genuine mass base.

In the United States the militant Evangelical Christian Right with its vision of a pre-scientific theocracy commands a sizable portion of the electorate and has proven capable of setting serious limits to reform through electoral or congressional channels. That this movement, heavily composed of older racist whites, sees the poor as its enemy and our common government as an un-Christian evil, says a great deal about how far this movement has strayed from anything you might find in the New Testament outside of the bloodthirsty Book of Revelations, the favorite text of the supposed Bible literalists.

There are factors beyond policy and its woes that are shaping our dilemma. The rise of China, India, Brazil, and Russia have all promoted variants of strong-state capitalism, which is proving more able to compete in today's world than the ultra-market American variety (which hypocritically includes almost limitless corporate welfare for companies that have providentially bought ties to American politicians).

Another element is the deepening environmental crisis, composed of overpopulation, resource depletion, and the early effects of global warming. As demand for finite materials such as oil, iron ore, phosphorus, rare earth metals, potable water, and arable land come up against physical limits, prices have been escalating and scarcities looming, contributing strongly to repeated deeper and deeper world recessions and threatening governments in the less prosperous parts of the Third World, especially in the Middle East.

Oil, essential to transportation and agriculture, has escalated in price from $18.64 a barrel in 1997[64] to $97 in August 2012, with much of the country importing European oil at a current cost of $115 a barrel. Ravenous demands for many forms of metals are running ahead of world production as larger and easily mined deposits are tapped out. Prices consequently have been skyrocketing, placing heavy stresses on world economies. Here are some examples from the U.S. Geological Service of prices in 1997 compared to 2011[65]:

Iron and steel scrap: $124 a ton in 1997, in 2011, $500
Tin: $2.65/lb in 1997, in 2011, $12.60/lb
Tungsten: $66/metric ton in 1997, in 2011, $250
Copper: $108/lb in 1997, in 2011 $405

Rampant inflation of such raw materials, matched to the depressed American economy, is producing symptoms more typical of the worst of the Third World. The *Los Angeles Times* reports, "Burglars around California have torn up train tracks, carted off bleachers, nabbed park statues and helped themselves to copper wiring serving neighborhoods, hospitals and airports."[66] They even stole a 200 pound brass bell from a Catholic church. Cities are taking down and hiding their historical brass plaques. Six people have been electrocuted in the last two years stealing copper wire from street lights. The wiring from the Modesto Airport runway lights has been stolen twice. 10,000 street lights in Sacramento, the state capital, a quarter of the city's total, went dark when thieves ripped out the wiring. The other side of this Banana republic picture is that cutbacks of inspectors have been so severe that there are only two detectives in the whole of Los Angeles County to try to monitor the scores of legal and illegal metal recycling yards where the stuff is sold.

The Republican Party, while it publicly denies virtually every specific of this growing crisis, founds it whole current economic policy on their reality, promoting a vision of the future that all too much resembles the last days of Rome, when, in face of social collapse, the Senators retreated to their rural villas and abandoned the public sphere, ruling as despots over vassals who had once been citizens.

I believe the ecological crisis is real and will only get worse. Thus far the North European welfare states have met it far better than the United States. On every measure of prosperity, well-being, and fairness they come in at the

---

[64] http://inflationdata.com/inflation/Inflation_Rate/Historical_Oil_Prices_Table.asp.
[65] http://minerals.usgs.gov/minerals/pubs/commodity/.
[66] *Los Angeles Times*, August 22, 2012

top of the lists while America has fallen to the bottom. If we are going to see hard times ahead caused by objective forces such as global warming and price wars over scarce natural resources we should want to face this with a government we can trust to act in the interests of all of us, not only in the interests of an ever-richer and more arrogant minority.

August 22, 2012

The Strange Career of Ahmad Kamal and How He Helped the CIA Invite Radical Islam into Europe

A Mosque in Munich: Nazis, the CIA, and the Muslim Brotherhood in the West. Ian Johnson. Boston: Houghton Mifflin Harcourt, 2010. 318 pp.

> *Oh what a tangled web we weave,*
> *When first we practise to deceive!*
> Sir Walter Scott

Everyone is familiar with the disastrous after-effects of the American effort to mobilize radical Islam to defeat the Soviet occupation of Afghanistan in the 1980s, a project that gave birth to Al Qaeda. Ian Johnson's *A Mosque in Munich* is an account of a much older, less violent, and smaller-scale chapter in Western attempts to co-opt Islam in the battle with Communism, tracing ill-considered U.S. help to radical Islam in establishing a base in Western Europe. It opens with Nazi use of Soviet Muslim defectors and prisoners of war to try to incite revolt against Soviet rule among the Turkic peoples of Soviet Central Asia. During the war the center of this

Ahmad Kamal in 1935

operation was Berlin; in the postwar period it moved to Munich in West Germany, where, as the Cold War blossomed, both the West German government and the American CIA took over the group of aging Soviet Muslims who had fought on the Nazi side, as well as their German handlers, to use as propagandists to the world's Muslims, exposing Soviet oppression of Central Asian peoples.

Ultimately, the CIA concluded that the ex-soldiers were too compromised by their history of collaborating with the Nazis to serve as effective spokespeople. The Americans, thinking that religious zealots were just the thing to toss at the godless Russians, then turned to more authentic representatives of Islam, inviting in the radical Muslim Brotherhood, helping it to establish its first foothold in Western Europe. Communism fell but radical Islam lives on, not least in its European incarnation, from which emerged the 9/11 hijackers and, more broadly, the multi-millioned and little-integrated population of Muslim immigrants, strongly influenced by the network of extremist mosques whose first node was the one in Munich planned by ex-Nazis and the CIA as a front for anti-Soviet agitation. Unintended consequences.

Ian Johnson organizes his story around long-drawn-out plans to build the mosque in Munich as a political front. The Americans, the West Germans, and various Islamists competed for years over who would ultimately complete the building and control it. The idea came from a German ex-Nazi who had run the Muslim exile propaganda operation for Hitler during World War II. The CIA adopted the plan and was instrumental in handing it over to Islamic radicals, who in turn saw it as an instrument for expansion. Johnson writes that "Munich was the beachhead from which the Brotherhood spread into Western society."

Nothing in the thirty years of Johnson's narrative worked out for the Germans or Americans quite as they hoped. The people we meet along the way are fascinating. And in some ways the whole history is a shaggy dog story. The Nazis, and later ex-Nazis, never got very close to the mosque-building project. Even the CIA had left the scene years before ground was broken in 1967 to actually start construction. One of the most interesting characters, the American adventurer who called himself Ahmad Kamal, was never really connected to the mosque project at all, but won inclusion in the story because the West German government for several years erroneously thought he was the project's leader, an assumption apparently fostered by the CIA for its own ends.

It may seen counterintuitive that Soviet citizens, no matter their religion, would choose to fight on the side of the Nazi invaders. The brutal Stalin dictatorship in the USSR, which had killed tens of millions of its own citizens in the forced collectivizations and mass purges of the 1930s, was particularly harsh toward its non-Russian subjects. It sought to forcibly eradicate religion, most especially Islam. Large numbers of Turks, Uyghurs, Uzbeks, Tatars, Cossacks, and Caucasians went over to the Germans after Hitler invaded in June 1941. A million Soviet Muslims fought on the German side, 250,000 of them as combat soldiers, most in all-Muslim units such as the SS East Turkestani Armed Formation, which took part in crushing the Warsaw city uprising in 1944. The all-Muslim 13th Handschar Division of the Waffen SS participated in exterminating the Bosnian and Croatian Jews (*Encyclopedia of the Holocaust*, vol. 2, Israel Gutman, 1990 edition). The central leader of the Palestinians of that period, the Grand Mufti of Jerusalem, Haj Amin al-Husseini, spent the war in Berlin and recruited to the 13th Handschar SS Division. He was also closely involved with the psychological war operation directed at the Soviet Union, the precursor of the mosque project.

Throughout the war al-Husseini broadcast regularly from Berlin a profoundly antisemitic, Nazified version, of Islam that had a powerful influence on Islamic militants in North Africa and the Middle East, particularly on Hassan al-Banna, founder of the Muslim Brotherhood. This story is told elsewhere, in Paul Berman's *The Flight of the Intellectuals*. This Nazified Islam was reimported to Germany at the end of the 1950s with the help of the American government.

Palestinian leader Haj Amin al-Husseini inspecting Muslim SS troops, 1943

Hitler's effort to expand Nazi influence among Soviet Muslims was run by Gerhard von Mende, a one-time professor and former SA storm trooper, who worked for the Reich Ministry for the Occupied Eastern Territories, known as the Ostministerium, headed by Alfred Rosenberg, a Baltic German. A gifted linguist, von Mende spoke several of the Central Asian Turkic dialects as well as Arabic, in addition to German, French, English, Russian, and Swedish. Through the Ostministerium he built a staff of displaced Soviet Muslims. His first recruits came from an anti-Soviet group of Caucasus exiles called Prometheus that had been operating in Germany since 1925. Rosenberg and von Mende hoped to offer the non-Russian Central Asian peoples some form of nominal independence as an incentive to come over to the Germans. Hitler opposed this, so the Ostministerium Muslim operation never got very far. Von Mende employed Veli Kayum, a leader of the Prometheus group and a Central Asian exile, to scour prisoner of war camps to seek out talented Muslim recruits for his network.

Gerhard von Mende

Von Mende set up liaison offices for each of the major non-Russian ethnic groups from Ukraine and Central Asia. Their miniscule staffs posed as governments in exile. The Ostministerium used them to recruit to the Nazi army in territories they occupied as they moved deeper into the USSR. In the Crimea, virtually the entire able bodied male Tatar population, some 20,000, signed up, for which Stalin never forgave them. At the war's end he had the whole of the Crimean Tatars deported to Siberia.

Von Mende was high enough in the Nazi bureaucracy that he attended the 1942 conference on Lake Wannsee where the Holocaust was planned.

As the war progressed the Ostministerium set up puppet parliaments for Azerbaijanis, Volga Tatars, and Turkestanis. They needed some common glue to hold these disparate peoples together, and believed they found it in Islam. Von Mende persuaded the Palestinian Grand Mufti, Haj Amin al-Husseini, to authorize Islamic seminaries run by Nazi-approved clerics.

Gerhard von Mende survived the war. In the chaos of bombed out Germany, occupied by the USSR in the east and by the U.S., Britain, and France in the west, he managed to hide his years in the Storm Troopers and present himself as a harmless academic bureaucrat. He was soon on the payroll of British MI5, once again living well, and building his own intelligence apparatus among Soviet Muslim former soldiers and other exiles. He moved his operation to Munich, the country's most important postwar city. Soon the West German government also established a paying relationship with von Mende's intelligence group as part of their Cold War efforts to influence people and events behind the Iron Curtain.

The American consulate in Munich was said to be the second largest anywhere. It served as a listening post for all things Soviet. The Americans ran two radio stations out of Munich. The famous one was Radio Free Europe, which began broadcasting in 1949 and which still operates today from the Czech Republic. RFE was aimed at the Soviet satellite countries of Eastern Europe. It was acknowledged to be an agency of the American government. In 1951 it was supplemented by the less-well-known Radio Liberty (originally Radio Liberation), which beamed shortwave transmissions aimed at the Soviet Union itself. This posed as a civilian nonprofit, operated by the American Committee for Liberation (Amcomlib). It was chaired by former *Reader's Digest* editor Eugene Lyons. It had its headquarters at Munich's Oberwiesenfeld Airport, where, Ian Johnson writes, it commanded "more than a thousand writers, producers, technicians, accountants, and advisers." Amcomlib and its broadcasting arm were fronts for the CIA. The staff included many legitimate American journalists who chose not to be too squeamish about their secret bosses. But it needed announcers and news anchors who could speak not only Russian but the wide variety of languages of the Soviet minority peoples. Here Amcomlib recruited liberally from von Mende's Muslim operatives, who could handle the linguistic problems of translating scripts and broadcasting in multiple Turkic languages.

In addition to Radio Liberty, Amcomlib ran a think tank that published papers by its staff, and "also had an emigré relations department that recruited agents, mostly in Munich, and sent them around the world on covert propaganda missions. U.S. government involvement was carefully masked."

The Ostministerium Muslim agents were mostly able to hide their Nazi past at the end of the war by getting rid of their ID papers and claiming to be Turkish students or refugees from China's Xinjiang province. Amcomlib and its Radio Liberty aimed at the Soviet Union as a whole, so it had a Russian section and a section representing the many non-Russian peoples in the USSR. Of the latter, Johnson writes, "The people on the desks had almost all worked for von Mende in the Ostministerium." He adds: "Radio Liberty relied so heavily on Nazi collaborators that the station would have closed without them. One estimate put the proportion of Radio Liberty employees who had worked for the Nazis at 75 to 80 percent." These were no ordinary soldiers, but people trained as skilled propagandists under the Hitler regime. At least two of them were murdered by Soviet agents shortly after Radio Liberty officially went on the air in 1953.

How the CIA first located this small group of Central Asian exiles is a story that no doubt deserves a book of its own. In November 1944 in the last days of the war the CIA's predecessor, the Office of Strategic Services, sent an agent code-named "Ruppert" into Nazi-occupied France to try to find out what the Germans were planning. Ruppert headed for Berlin, where he spent five and a half months posing as a Nazi security officer. There "he recruited a group of people who would at once repulse and fascinate his American employers: Nazis eager to fight the Soviet Union. Ruppert's top recruit was von Mende." When the Third Reich collapsed, von Mende brought his cadre of Turkic Soviet exiles over to the Americans. They were debriefed by the OSS at a safe house in Frankfurt.

The downside of becoming dependent on ex-Nazi collaborators was two-fold. First, the Soviet Union quickly discovered who they were, and relentlessly exposed them. Second, aiming their propaganda at a milieu where the common denominator was devout Islam, these were people who had grown up in the USSR where religion was banned and had then lived in Nazi Germany, so their knowledge of Islam and credentials for piety were more than thin. The CIA struggled with this problem for a number of years. Finally it gave up and sought out more authentic Islamists.

The most immediate issue within Amcomlib was hostility between the Russian staff and the Muslims. The latter, no matter how tenuous their religious training, were deeply hostile to the Slavs. Several times the CIA brought in von Mende himself for consultation. His advice, Johnson writes, was to "support the Soviet minorities — and forget about the Russians." By this time von Mende was running his own network and was principally working as a contractor for the West German government in Bonn, out of upscale offices in Dusseldorf. Von Mende maintained his own moles inside Amcomlib who kept him up to date on the Americans' problems.

The CIA agents were Russophiles, which made von Mende's recommendation hard to stomach. But they did send two of their Muslim employees, Rusi Nasar and Hamid Raschid, on the 1954 Hajj to Mecca. Actually Soviet defectors, they pretended to be Turks. They harassed Soviet Muslim pilgrims, even throwing tomatoes at them, shouting "You serve the Moscow atheists!"

Time magazine and the *New York Times* reported the incident as an example of spontaneous opposition to Soviet oppression.

The CIA next sent Rusi Nasar to the Bandung nonaligned nations conference in Indonesia in April 1955, as a representative of the National Turkestani Unity Committee, a front group run by von Mende's henchman Veli Kayum. The Soviet press denounced Nasar as a "U.S. agent sent from West Germany." Many years later Rusi Nasar became a respected leader of the Uzbek community in the United States. He was interviewed by Ian Johnson in 2006, at the age of eighty-nine. Nasar acknowledged that he had fought on the German side in World War II, saying it was his way to break the Russian hold over his people. He denied he had ever been an employee of Amcomlib, saying that Isaac Don Levine, author of *The Mind of an Assassin,* an account of Trotsky's assassination, had tried to recruit him but he had refused.

By 1956 the CIA began to focus on how to employ a wider range of Muslims in the West. It sent an agent to Turkey to meet with Muslim refugees from the USSR to see if it could broaden its stable, to get away from that taint of men who had fought on the Nazi side. The West Germans were still committed to von Mende's crew. They had their minister for refugee affairs, Theodor Oberländer, contact von Mende to see if his network of Muslim exiles could put any weight in the scales in Germany's effort to regain East Germany and territories it had lost to Poland after World War II. Oberländer went way back in the Nazi party, even participating in Hitler's beer hall putsch in 1923. He had helped plan the extermination of Jews in Eastern Europe. His get-out-of-jail-free card was that he had supported the Ostministerium plan to establish puppet governments for the USSR's non-Russian minorities, which put him afoul of the SS, which favored outright slavery. This gave him just enough credentials as a critic of Hitler to return to the government, in 1953.

Von Mende proposed that the government unify Germany's Muslims by selecting a chief imam to lead them. His candidate was hard-core Nazi Nurredin Namangani, who had just arrived in Munich in March 1956. Namangani had been arrested by the Soviets in Turkestan before the war. He was freed by the German invasion and became the imam of the SS East Turkistani Armed Formation. The United States had kept him in a prisoner of war camp for two years.

The West German government embraced this plan. Von Mende had a group of his Muslim exiles, all of whom had worked for the Ostministerium, stage a meeting in a beer hall in March 1958, where they formed the Ecclesiastical Administration of Moslem Refugees in the German Federal Republic.

They elected Namangani its head. It was then funded by Oberländer's ministry for refugees.

Namangani began to collect funding to build a mosque in Munich. His first significant backer was former SS Major Wilhelm Hintersatz, who had commanded the SS Muslim unit in which Namangani had served as chief imam. Hintersatz had himself converted to Islam after World War I and changed his name to Harun el-Raschid. The plan to build the mosque was announced at a meeting of the Ecclesiastical Administration in December 1958. A Mosque Construction Commission was formed with Namangani as chairman.

The American government meanwhile was looking elsewhere in the Islamic world for potential allies against Communism. In 1957 the interagency Operations Coordinating Board for U.S. covert intelligence activities set up an Ad Hoc Working Group on Islam. This body decided its best candidates were the more militant "reform" currents within Islam, most notably the Muslim Brotherhood. That same year the CIA dispatched Robert Dreher to run Amcomlib in Munich. Dreher soon began to cultivate a newly arrived Muslim personality: Said Ramadan. Ramadan was the son-in-law and former secretary of Hassan al-Banna, the Egyptian founder in 1928 of the Muslim Brotherhood. Al-Banna had close ties with the pro-Nazi Grand Mufti. In 1937 and 1938 the Brotherhood attacked

Robert Dreher

Jewish shops in Cairo and became a channel for Nazi antisemitic propaganda, still circulated by the Brotherhood today. In 1948, at the announcement of Israel's founding, the Grand Mufti appealed to the Brotherhood to raise soldiers for the Arab armies that were launched against the new Jewish state. Hassan al-Banna entrusted that task to Said Ramadan.

The Americans first came in contact with Ramadan when he attended a ten-day Princeton University conference on Islam in 1953. He came as an official delegate of the Muslim Brotherhood. Ian Johnson cites a CIA report on the conference that made the assessment "Ramadan seems to be a Fascist."

Fascist or not, in those years the Muslim Brotherhood regarded Communism as a greater evil than Western capitalism, because the USSR prohibited religion outright. That was good enough for Washington.

By the end of 1958, Ramadan was in Munich attending meetings of Mosque Construction Commission, where he made grandiose claims about big donations he could command from Saudis and other rich Arabs. Johnson says that by this time Ramadan was working closely with Dreher of the CIA.

Said Ramadan

Von Mende was angry that his associate, Namangani, was being outmaneuvered by the Americans. In 1960, when the Mosque Construction Commission registered with the government as an official nonprofit, Ramadan, not Namangani, was listed as chairman. Johnson writes:

"Ramadan was suddenly at the helm of the legal entity charged with building the mosque." Von Mende responded by secretly asking the Bavarian ministry to raise bureaucratic obstacles to halt the mosque project. According to Ian Johnson, the Americans countered by moving one of their assets to Munich to simulate a broad Muslim clamor to see the mosque project move ahead. Ahmad Kamal showed up in town with a small staff, claiming to represent a major world Muslim charity called Jami'at al Islam (this had no connection to the radical Pakistani Islamic group with a similar name). "Within less than a year," Johnson writes, "Jami'at was so successful that the local media assumed it was running the mosque project," including printing a photo of a Jami'at official inspecting plans for the mosque. The government caved in and withdrew its objections.

Here I stopped cold. I had not heard of von Mende or Said Ramadan, but Ahmad Kamal was a different matter entirely. Back in 1979, when I was still a member of a small Marxist organization, I had moved on party assignment from New York to Virginia, Minnesota, up on the Mesabi Iron Range, to look for a job in the iron mines. Virginia was a tough little town of 12,000 sixty miles north of Duluth, closer to Canada than to Minneapolis. Its one bookstore was a disappointing B. Dalton. I discovered that once a year a women's group in Hibbing, thirty miles away, would have an outdoor book sale on a few tables. Desperate for something new to read, I went each of the three years I lived on the Range. One year I picked up Ahmad Kamal's 1940 *Land Without Laughter*.

It was one of those fascinating, slightly archaic, off-beat adventure books set in that mysterious region, Chinese Turkestan. It has a place on my bookshelves next to the romantic *To Lhasa in Disguise* of William Montgomery McGovern (1924), William Seabrook's *Adventures in Arabia: Among the Bedouins, Druses, Whirling Dervishes, & Yezidee Devil Worshippers* (1927), and *Beasts, Men and Gods* by Ferdinand Ossendowski (1921). A Pole of Lithuanian Tatar descent, Ossendowski's book chronicles his 1918-1920 flight from the Bolshevik Revolution, eastward across Siberia and Mongolia, including his failed efforts to reach Tibet. All of this literature verges into the fantastic. Ossendowski became famous in occult circles as a principal source of the legend of the King of the World and the underground kingdom of Agharti. He recounts meetings with Tibetan lamas and Mongolian princes who tell him of an underground kingdom of wise priest scientists who secretly guide the world's affairs and predict that their ruler, the King of the World, will emerge after a series of devastating world wars to establish a reign of peace and spiritual advancement.

Though Ahmad Kamal's role in the Munich mosque history was transitory, lasting from 1960 to 1962, he is the most interesting character in Ian Johnson's book, and Johnson provides the most detailed biography currently available of this strange man. First of all, Ahmad Kamal was an American, and probably a convert to Islam. Johnson under the Freedom of Information Act retrieved Kamal's FBI file, which states that he was born on February 2, 1914, in Arvada, Colorado. His name was Cimarron Hathaway. His mother was Caroline Grossmann Hathaway, his father, James Worth Hathaway. According to an interview Johnson obtained with a daughter, James was a stepfather and Cimarron's biological father was Qara Yusuf, a Uyghur from Turkestan who was much older than Caroline — he was sixty-four and she sixteen when they married. Yusuf had other wives in his homeland, to which he returned when Cimarron was very young.

Johnson suggests *Land Without Laughter* was a novel, in part by pointing to several obvious falsehoods in the back cover text of the 2000 paperback reprint edition, prepared by Ahmad Kamal's son, such as the claim that Kamal "commanded" the Basmaci rebellion against the Soviets, which ended when he was ten years old. The version published in 1940 when Kamal was alive makes no such claim. The Kirkus review when it was first published treats it as nonfiction. It is true that, despite the plethora of authentic sounding detail, *Land Without Laughter* rates an extremely high score on the improbability index.

The book lists its author and protagonist as Ahmad Kamal and includes no suggestion that it is fiction. It makes no mention of the name Cimarron Hathaway. "Ahmad Kamal" says his father died when he was an infant and that he was raised on Indian reservations, where his mother, never named, was writing histories of the various tribes. While living in Houston, Texas, his mother had him home schooled, hiring a "disinherited son of a Prussian nobleman," Lothar von Richter, as his tutor. Von Richter happened to be a student of ancient Turkish and fortuitously taught the young "Ahmad" this obscure language, as well as military tactics. The family moved on to Tucson, Arizona, where his next tutor was one Musa Jan, a Muslim scholar from Kazan, who continued his education in the same vein.

Coming of age knowing nothing but military tactics, the Uyghur language, Islam, and the history of Tartary, Ahmad finds himself unfit for anything but a military career in Sinkiang (Chinese Turkestan, present-day Xinjiang). So in late 1935 he sets sail from the Los Angeles port at San Pedro for India, landing first in Bombay. According to his FBI file he had turned twenty-one earlier that year. In his book he claims he was twenty-three. From Bombay he treks across the subcontinent to Delhi, then northwest into what is now Pakistan, and finally to Kashmir. Here, as he tells it, he hires several servants and horses, and, defying a prohibition by the British authorities, sets off in the dead of winter to cross the Himalayan passes into Tibet.

He finds the high passes littered with the corpses of dead pack animals and human travelers, some frozen to death, others killed and stripped by bandits. After many hardships his small party emerges into western Tibet. They travel on by horse and mule into Xinjiang. His goal was to connect with the Chinese Muslim garrison that controlled most of southern Xinjiang from their fortress in the town of Khotan (now Hotan).

Even today Xinjiang's Muslim people maintain a tumultuous opposition to Han Chinese rule, staging frequent riots, bombings, and acts of sabotage against the Beijing government. In the 1930s the situation was far more chaotic and complex. China was weakly governed by the corrupt Kuomintang (KMT) of Chiang Kai-shek. Mao Zedong's Long March (1934-1935) established the Communists permanently in Shaanxi in north central China. The northwest provinces of Gansu and Qinghai were ruled by Muslims, three families of Hui (Muslim) Chinese known by their enemies as the Ma Clique (Ma is the Chinese rendering of Muhammad). The Mas offered ostensible allegiance to the Kuomintang. Adjacent Xinjiang to the west was ruled until 1928 by an independent warlord. After his assassination he was succeeded first by Jin Shuren (1928-1933), then Sheng Shicai (1933-1944). Though nominally representing the KMT, both Jin and Sheng were de facto puppets of the Soviet Union.

Chiang Kai-shek in 1933 authorized the formation of the 36th Division of his national army, an all-Muslim corps in Gansu, to invade Xinjiang to overthrow Jin Shuren. The unit was commanded by Ma Zhongying, seconded by his half brother, Ma Hushan. As these troops entered Xinjiang, a Muslim Tatar uprising broke out in the south, known as the Kumul Rebellion. Jin's main troops were White Russians who had settled in north Xinjiang to escape the Russian Revolution. In a bizarre turn, Stalin sent regular Soviet troops in disguise to secretly join the White Russian units to reinforce Jin Shuren's position. Ma's forces defeated Jin Shuren in a series of pitched battles in 1933 and early 1934, culminating in Ma's capture of Kashgar in February 1934. The USSR responded with a full-scale invasion.

Ma Zhongying retreated into Xinjiang's southern prefectures, where he confronted the First East Turkestan Republic, the product of the Kumul Rebellion, a breakaway effort by the local Turkic people to establish an independent state. The locals made a sharp distinction between Turkic Muslims and the Hui Chinese Muslims. Ma mercilessly crushed his fellow religionists and established his own stable base at Khotan in the far south. Then, inexplicitly, Ma Zhongying is said to have defected to the Soviet Union, after having battled the Russian troops for more than a year. He was never seen again. The Khotan base was thereafter commanded by Ma Zhongying's half brother, Ma Hushan.

This was the situation when Ahmad Kamal, as I should now call him, rode into town in 1936, eight months after he left Los Angeles. Ahmad for some reason refers to Ma Hushan as Ma Hsi Jung, but it is clear from everything in his text, including a specific identification of the two names in an appendix, that it is Ma Hushan he claims to have met. (He says he was first told the general's name by a Mongol in Ladakh on the Indian side of the Himalayas, and that may have permanently tainted his sonic spelling. Alternatively, many Chinese have multiple given names bestowed at different times in their lives and used in different contexts.)

Ahmad Kamal claims that at their first meeting "Ma Hsi Jung" appointed him an officer in the Tungan (Chinese Muslim) 36th Division army. Almost immediately he was dispatched with a squad of thirty-five men to capture or kill a group of 181 deserters. Two battles with machine guns, rifles, and grenades ensued, in which Kamal's second-in-command was killed along with several others of his unit. A few days later he took part in the storming of Kizil Kurgan, a fortress two hundred miles southeast of Khotan that had been occupied by the Russians and their Chinese allies. This involved storming the walls on siege ladders and hand-to-hand combat with scimitars.

A few weeks after this encounter, Ma Hsi Jung meets with Kamal, telling him he is appointing him to go back to America to buy airplanes for the Tungan army. When the planes arrive, General Ma says, he "will take all of Sinkiang. First, Kashgar, then north to Urumchi, and when he is ruler of all of Sinkiang, he will conquer Kansu and Tibet. And then the balance of Asia!" No megalomaniac he! But his ambition did not stop at the borders of Asia. He dreamed the same dream as Gerhard von Mende and the American CIA, of calling forth a rising of the oppressed Turkic peoples of Soviet Central Asia, and still more broadly, the old Muslim goal of submitting the entire world to Islam. General Ma imagined, erroneously as it turned out, that he held in his hands the match that could set off the Second World War, which fit nicely into his plans of conquest:

"While the bulk of the Russian army would be occupied with the millions of Muslim fighting men besieging their frontiers, other governments would probably take advantage of the moment to throw an army into the field. Ten of every hundred men in Siberia and Russian Turkistan could be relied upon to revolt against the Soviet regime . . . Then, God willing, Ma Hsi Jung would march into the Kremlin!"

In fulfillment of these fantasies Ma Hushan sends Ahmad Kamal up the northern string of towns in western Xinjiang to begin a journey back to America to purchase his air force. Ahmad got as far as Aksu (Aqsu) before being arrested. Jailed under appalling conditions, he was eventually transferred to Urumqi, Sheng Shicai's capital. There he spent four months in a dungeon, where he lost forty-three pounds. His three traveling companions, casual acquaintances, were executed, apparently solely because they could testify that the pro-Russian government was holding an American citizen. Finally he was ordered released. On his way out of the city a counter order was received when some spy had discovered Kamal was in fact working for Ma Hushan. The telegram was garbled and Kamal succeeded in convincing the commandant that it didn't apply to him. He was out of the province before the truth caught up with him.

Ahmad Kamal crossed the Gobi desert, Mongolia, then China, and finally returned to the United States. He hints in closing that he intends to secretly purchase the aircraft he had been commissioned to buy.

Ma Hushan staged a new offensive in June 1937. He captured Kashgar and held it until October. Defeated, he fled to British India. In 1939 he returned to China. In his native Gansu he fought alongside the Chinese Communists against the Japanese invaders. Then, in 1950, he led an uprising in

Xinjiang against the new Chinese Communist government. This lasted until 1954, when the redoubtable general was captured. He was executed by the Chinese at Lanzhou. He never marched in glory into Moscow's Red Square at the head of a Tatar host.

How much, if any, of Cimarron Hathaway's swashbuckling tale is true? It is filled with images of barbaric cruelty: floggings, beheadings, rapes. He says he is speaking mainly in Uyghur, which may or may not explain why every conversation comes through as flowery and stilted. His companions — soldiers, merchants, travelers — quote more quaint proverbs than Sancho Panza. And his own bravery often seems over the top, from cutting off men at the ankles with his scimitar from the top of a scaling ladder to throwing a bowl of slops he had been given to eat back in a guard's face or tossing a cup of hot tea into the face of an interrogator who could easily order him shot.

Ian Johnson cites Hathaway's FBI file, which confirms that he did go to Central Asia in 1935, and that he was arrested by the Chinese authorities in Xinjiang and escaped. It also states that he was married while in Xinjiang and his seventeen-year-old wife died of some act of violence during the turbulence there. In *Land Without Laughter* one of the author's soldier companions without his knowledge negotiates an arranged marriage for him, but it is with a fourteen-year-old and he manages to get out of it the same night, unconsummated, returning the girl to her parents. Whatever passport he was carrying in that adventure would have borne the name Cimarron Hathaway, as he did not officially change his name to Ahmad Kamal until he was back in the United States, in a Hollywood court in 1938.

In 1941, Ahmad Kamal returned to China. There he did marry a Tatar woman named Amina, who had worked as a linguist and correspondent for Russian newspapers. They were both imprisoned by the Japanese in the Weihsien internment camp in Shandong, where they spent almost four years. On their return to the United States after Liberation the *Los Angeles Times* ran an article with their pictures. Kamal said he had gone back to Chinese Turkestan to retrieve his notebooks from his 1935-36 trip. He told the *Times* that at the time he and Amina were detained by the Japanese he had three manuscripts, a novel, a history, and a political study. Prohibited from keeping anything but a Bible, he and Amina transcribed the three manuscripts into ornate Turkic script and passed them off to the Japanese guards as a copy of the Koran. (*LA Times*, November 11, 1945)

There is yet another curious side tale here that Ian Johnson did not pick up. This one involves the mystery of Amelia Earhart, the famed woman pilot who during an around-the-world flight disappeared over the Pacific in July 1937 with her copilot Fred Noonan,. One theory was that she had been spying for the United States and was captured by the Japanese. On August 21, 1945, as the Weihsien camp was shutting down, a radiogram was sent from there to Earhart's husband, the publisher George Putnam, in North Hollywood, California. The telegram read:

"Camp liberated; all well. Volumes to tell. Love to mother."

It was unsigned. Forty-two years later, on June 28, 1987, the *Los Angeles Times* reported that a State Department employee had found a copy of this message in the Earhart files in the National Archive. This sparked a renewal of the theory that Earhart had been captured by the Japanese and interned in the Weihsien camp. "Love to Mother" was widely assumed to be some kind of secret code, and the conspiracy literature soon abounded with the abbreviation for it: LTM.

A recent post by Ron Bright and Laurie McLaughlin clears up the mystery. The sender of the mysterious unsigned message was our Ahmad Kamal. It seems that one more of the improbable claims about Cimarron Hathaway that appear on the back cover of the 2000 edition of *Land Without Laughter* was true, or partly so. This was the claim that he had been a combat pilot. Ron Bright and Laurie McLaughlin in 2001 located his son, who confirmed that Ahmad Kamal had been a licensed pilot and that he kept a plane at the Burbank airport, also used by Amelia Earhart. The son added that Kamal knew both Earhart and her husband, George Putnam, and that when he left for his trip to China in 1941 he had asked Putnam to regularly look in on his mother, who lived nearby. Beyond these facts this account is full of misinformation, claiming, for example, that Ahmad Kamal served as a guide for the famous dinosaur hunter Roy Chapman Andrews, the purported model for Indiana Jones. But Andrews' expeditions in the Gobi Desert and Central Asia took place between 1922 and 1930, when Cimarron Hathaway was still a boy. It appears that Kamal's son has a thin grasp of his father's history and has expanded his legend into myth. (http://tighar.org/Projects/Earhart/Archives/ Forum/FAQs/ltm.htm)

There is always something uncertain surrounding everything claimed about Cimarron Hathaway/Ahmad Kamal. His Jami'at al-Islam charity, which he invented while living in Indonesia in the 1950s, issued brochures claiming it had been founded in Turkestan in 1868-69 to promote revolution against tsarist Russia. Ahmad's son, the source of the information about Amelia Earhart, was born in 1950 so events in 1937 took place long before he was around. Cimarron had left for Xinjiang the first time when he was only twenty-one. He had been back in the United States only a few months when Amelia Earhart left on her fatal flight. Surely he was not a licensed pilot then, much less with his own plane in a hangar at the Burbank airport. In the years after her disappearance he became an author and sought out contacts with various publishers, including Scribners, who published his *Land Without Laughter* in 1940. Earhart's husband, George Putnam, was also a publisher. As the Weihsien camp was shutting down in 1945, Kamal sent two messages, not just one. The second was to Maxwell Perkins at Scribners.

Ahmad Kamal lived in Los Angele between 1945 and 1951. During that period he wrote and published three novels: *Full Fathom Five*, about Greek sponge divers in Florida, *One-Dog Man* about a boy and his dog, and *The Excommunicated*, a romance thriller set in pre-Communist Shanghai. He marketed a number of short stories and worked in Hollywood as a screen writer. Then he abandoned literary work and turned to Islam in a serious way, publishing *The Sacred Journey: A Pilgrimage to Mecca* in Arabic. Thereafter his life was bound up with intelligence work for the United States on behalf of Islamic, and in particular, Turkestani causes.

In the early 1950s he moved to Indonesia, where he lived in Bandung. The U.S. government lent him the money for his passage, and Johnson says that Kamal told a friend he would be working for the U.S. government. Kamal established the world headquarters for his Jami'at charity in Jakarta. Von Mende's files claim Kamal was working for the Americans in providing support to an anticommunist minister in the Indonesian government. After two assassination attempts Kamal fled to Barcelona. Von Mende's files also record that Ahmad Kamal refused to work for the CIA, because he claimed it was heavily infiltrated by Soviet spies. Instead he was paid by the National Security Council, at the personal request of Richard Nixon, then Eisenhower's Vice President. Kamal tried to have the famous 1955 Bandung nonaligned nations conference canceled, and when that failed he returned from Spain to attend for a day, but left for fear of a physical attack. Throughout all of this his primary goal remained what it had been in Xinjiang in 1936: to inspire Islamic opposition to Communist rule.

There were unproven claims that Kamal's Jami'at charity supplied funding for arms for Islamic insurgencies, including the Algerian revolution for independence from France and the Palestinians in Jordan, from which the Jami'at offices were expelled in 1961. Then in October 1961, at a conference at the New York Sheraton hotel, the Jami'at began to fall apart. It issued a declaration that it was withdrawing its pledge to refrain from "extreme methods" because of the failure of Western governments to support the Islamic cause. It also fired its principal representative in Munich, Ahmet Balagija, who, like von Mende's operatives, was a former Muslim soldier in the Wehrmacht.

The Americans now regarded Ahmad Kamal as too troublesome. They retaliated by ordering an audit of the funds they had been supplying to the Jami'at charity. Jami'at was being paid to care for some 4,000 refugees. On inspection it proved there were only 400 and the money was being used for its general propaganda work. In March 1962 Jami'at al-Islam International, to use its full name, announced that it was leaving Germany to do work in sub-Saharan Africa. It was never heard of again.

According to Johnson, "A few years later, Kamal would move back to California to continue his covert work." He is said to have traveled extensively in Burma. Johnson adds, "In 1969, he offered the Burmese opposition leader U Nu $2 million if he would depose the country's dictator, Ne Win." The back cover text of the 2000 edition of *Land Without Laughter*, repeated in reprints of his three novels, says that Ahmad Kamal was the "commanding General of the Muslim liberation forces of the Union of Burma into the 1980's." Searches trying to confirm this turn up only the back covers of the reprint editions of his books. Ahmad Kamal died on October 13, 1989, in Santa Barbara, California.

The mosque project continued without him. Now safe from the threatened government prohibition, a decisive meeting was held on November 26, 1961, where the young students from the Muslim Brothers, with support from the CIA, backed Said Ramadan to head the project while von Mende's old soldiers supported one of their own, the half-blind Ali Kantemir. Kantemir won a majority, but Ramadan, who was the incumbent, won the day when a German bureaucrat pointed out that the group's charter required a two-thirds majority for such a decision. Ramadan held on to his position.

With his American backing and his beachhead in Germany secure, Said Ramadan in May 1962 went to Mecca to help create the Muslim World League, still today one of the most important international Islamic organizations. Ramadan's agenda was to make the group sharply political, in particular to declare itself the enemy of Israel.

It didn't take long for the Americans to discover that when they bought Ramadan they didn't get what they had bargained for. Johnson writes:

"The Germans and the Americans had the same idea: control the mosque, control the local Muslims, and then use them to fight communism. The local Muslims were still in Munich and to that extent could still be used for covert propaganda purposes, but . . . it seems that Ramadan hadn't cared about uniting Muslims to fight communism."

Ramadan wanted instead to promote the Muslim Brotherhood's version of militant Islam, focused on a world revolution to impose Islam and Sharia law not only on the Communist lands but everywhere. And for that he had no use for the old Nazi soldiers. He wanted young, impressionable disciples. As Johnson puts it, "He didn't want an umbrella group; he wanted a cell.

By 1962, as Holocaust studies began to cast light on ex-Nazis still active in German political life, von Mende was snubbed by being refused an invitation to a major Washington conference on Islam and the Soviet Union. He died in December 1963. From 1964 on, Amcomlib and its Radio Liberty concentrated on broadcasting and abandoned trying to manipulate Germany's Muslims through their religious leaders. In the 1970s, when it was exposed as a CIA front, Radio Liberty was merged with Radio Free Europe.

The Mosque in Munich

The Islamic Center of Munich opened to the faithful on August 24, 1973. By this time control had passed to an alliance between Saudi Arabia's militant Wahabis and the Saudi branch of the Muslim Brotherhood. Said Ramadan, an Egyptian, was squeezed out in 1966. Acting on a well-financed, expansionist vision, over the next twenty years the Islamic Center established branches throughout Germany, promoting the Brotherhood's version of Islam. It recruited fighters for jihad in Bosnia and inspired Islamic militancy in other world hot spots.

Figures intimately associated with the Munich mosque's operation such as Youssef Nada and Ahmed Totonji helped to spread the Brotherhood to the United States. Totonji was a central founder of the Muslim Student Organization in 1962, which Johnson writes is "widely regarded as the first Brotherhood organization in the United States."

That the radical Muslim Brotherhood got there first in establishing its network of religious houses of worship has had an incalculable effect as Europe's Muslim population has mushroomed over the last three or four decades. According to Ian Johnson's figures (circa 2009-2010) there were fifteen to twenty million Muslims living in Western Europe; of these, 3.5 million were in Germany, as many as 6 million in France, and just under 2 million in Britain.

Evidence that the Munich mosque has ties to actual terrorism is thin. A regular worshipper in the 1980s was Mahmoud Abouhalima, later convicted in the attempt to blow up the World Trade Center in 1993. Mamdouh Mahmud Salim, believed to be Al Qaeda's finance chief, sought spiritual counseling at the mosque before being extradited to the United States in 1998. Somewhat less clear are long-standing accusations that two central figures of the mosque helped finance terrorism. These are directed at Ghaleb Himmat, the mosque's chief imam for twenty-nine years, and the mosque's principal financial figure, Youssef Nada. They concern the al-Tarqwa Bank, of which Nada was a co-founder and Himmat served as a director. There is little dispute that the bank is a Muslim Brotherhood enterprise, or that the Brotherhood supports terrorism at least in Iraq against the government and its American supporters and against Israel.

The bank's European functionaries include some very unsavory characters. Headquartered in Switzerland, its officers include Swiss Islamic convert Ahmed Huber, an enthusiastic admirer of Hitler, and François Genoud, a central manager of Nazi assets in the years after World War II. Jordan accused the bank of funding Musab al-Zarqawi, the since-deceased head of Al Qaeda in Iraq, while the United States insists they laundered money for Osama bin Laden and Hamas. The UN joined the U.S. in declaring the bank and its officers terrorist financers, though the UN withdrew the designation in 2010. Nada denies the charges, but Himmat was forced to resign from his long-held position at the mosque in 2002.

More indisputable is the role of the mosque and its siblings in other cities in spreading antisemitism and promoting a version of Islam that rejects integration in European societies and aspires to replace secular regimes with Islamic Sharia law governments. This has created a huge existential problem for Western Europe and generated a large anguished literature on the subject, to mention only Robert S. Keiken's *Europe's Angry Muslims* and Walter Laqueur's *The Last Days of Europe* and *After the Fall.*

One creation of the Munich mosque is the European Council for Fatwa and Research, said to be the most influential body in setting the norms of Islamic attitudes in Europe. Johnson cites a 2004 meeting of this body where German Muslim scientist Mohammad Hawari received no objection when in a lecture he explained that the Jews are responsible for the sexual revolution, with the aim of destroying the morals of Islamic youths in order to take over the world. He cited as his authority for this claim the notorious Russian tsarist forgery *The Protocols of the Elders of Zion,* a mainstay of Nazi anti-Jewish propaganda and today widely reprinted in Arabic throughout the Middle East.

Johnson adds:

"Far from setting up rules to govern a fringe group, the fatwa council issues guidelines aimed at tens of millions of European citizens and residents — members of Europe's second-biggest religion." The head of this organization, Mahdi Akef, is a past head of the Munich mosque, the Islamic Center of Munich. He calls the Holocaust a myth and is a public sympathizer of Iran's Mahmoud Ahmadinejad.

So where have we arrived? This tale is something like Rashomon, being able to see the same events from opposite and irreconcilable points of view. During World War II two evil totalitarian systems were locked in a death struggle, each looking for any weakness in the other that would let it get a grip on its opponent's throat. The captive Turkic peoples of Soviet Central Asia had their own aspirations for independence, which the Nazis exploited. The majority of these Muslim nations finally won their goal, not with the help of Nazi Germany or even the American CIA, but only with the collapse of the Soviet Union in 1990. The Muslim peoples of China's Xinjiang province, the central concern of Ahmad Kamal's life, are the exception. They remain under the domination of an alien people. In that story Ahmad Kamal is an admirable outsider, bridging American and Turkic Muslim cultures, devoted to a people that were by birth, or perhaps only in his vivid imagination, his forebears and blood kin. If he invented many details about his life and history, enough is true to validate him as a patriot to the Muslims of Xinjiang.

At the same time, in the broader world beyond Chinese Turkestan, Islamic radicalism is a declared enemy of most of the essential values of the advanced democracies. Islam as a whole does not accept the separation of church and state essential to maintain harmony among peoples of different creeds and sects. It stands where Christianity did in the fifteenth century. Moderate and reform-minded Muslims are in a decided minority, while a more militant minority at the other end of the spectrum enforces its view by violence. Giving one of the more extreme variants of this authoritarian and intolerant current a hand up in establishing itself in Western Europe ahead of the flood of Islamic immigrants that followed, and came under its influence, was a disastrous mistake for which we will pay for generations to come. Part of how that story will unfold is being written now in Egypt, where the Muslim Brotherhood finally has governmental power, and is proving to have within it some more moderate elements. One wing is seemingly willing to work with the West, to extend toleration to Egypt's Coptic Christian minority — who long predate the invasion of Islam — and to retain the peace treaty with Israel. Others hew to the traditional view of Hassan al-Banna and Sayyid Qutb, that the whole of the world that is not under strict Sharia law is jahiliyyah, degenerate barbarians, who must be forced to submit to Islam, while the Jews are fit only for extermination. Much rides on how this contest plays out.

September 26, 2012

Edmond Kovacs, 1924-2010

I FIRST MET Edmond Kovacs in the fall of 1961. I was then nineteen and he thirty-seven. He was teaching a class for the Los Angeles chapter of the Young Socialist Alliance, the youth group of the Trotskyist Socialist Workers Party. He was the SWP's Southern California Chairman, introduced under his party name, Theodore Edwards. Most of us in those days had nommes de guerre, fake names that we rather optimistically hoped the FBI wouldn't figure out. It was only years later that I got in the habit of calling him Edmond.

His subject, of all things, was Hegelian dialectics, a bit abstruse for most of our little group. Edmond explained changes of quantity into quality, the growth of new things within the shell of the old, concluding that Hegel's key insight was the idea of becoming, to keep your eyes on what was emergent rather than what already existed. It was clear that he had a wide education in European history and the history of ideas.

On November 22, 1963, Edmond was scheduled to speak for our YSA group at UCLA. I met him in the student union, moments after John Kennedy was assassinated. Together we listened to radio broadcasts piped over the public address system, saying that a pro-Castro Marxist had killed the president. This gave us more of a turn than just the assassination. Edmond and I were both Marxists and we were both local officials of the Fair Play for Cuba Committee.

I got to know Edmond better the next summer, when he served as SWP branch organizer while I was assistant organizer.

Resistance Fighter

Edmond Kovacs was born in Vienna into a socialist family. His mother was Czech; his father, Max, a nonreligious Polish Jew. Max was a member of the Social Democratic Party and of its armed militia, the Schutzbund. The city of Vienna had a socialist government but the national Austrian state was rightist.

In February 1934, threatened with seizure of their weapons, the Schutzbund staged an armed uprising. Edmond, who was not quite ten years old, carried messages during the fighting. He remembered all his life the corpses lying in the streets, the bullets flying, and the artillery shells striking the Karl Marx Hof, a large workers' housing complex.

Edmond, who was an athlete in his youth, was in training for the Austrian swim team for the 1940 Olympics, but the team was disbanded when the Nazis invaded and annexed Austria in the 1938 Anschluss. The Olympics itself was canceled because of the outbreak of World War II and not resumed until 1948.

With the Nazis in power his father lost his job and went underground for a while. Max got a visa to the United States but his American relatives refused to sponsor his wife and son. They stayed behind. Mother and son finally got American visas only on August 8, 1939, just three and a half weeks before the invasion of Poland started World War II and they would have been trapped. He and his mother went by train through Switzerland to Paris and got on the last ship to leave France for the United States before the war began.

In America the family lived first in Cleveland, then in Buffalo, New York, where Edmond went to high school. There he first encountered the Trotskyist movement through a classmate, Cynthia Copeland. She was the sister of Vince Copeland, then in the SWP but later a leader of the Workers World Party. Cynthia later married Bert Cochran, an SWP trade union activist until a split in the party in 1953.

After high school Edmond spent two years at a Catholic college, then, in 1944, was given a choice of joining the army or being interned as an enemy alien. He took basic training, then volunteered for the 10th Mountain Infantry Division, an elite ski troop unit. He had done a lot of skiing and mountaineering as a teenager in Austria, so he qualified. Interviewed half a century later, in 1998, by a historian for the 10th Mountain Division, he was asked if he had wanted to join the army. Yes, he replied, "I supported the war against Hitler. I thought that Nazi Germany was a menace to the world with its racism."

Wartime Experience

While he was in training, his parents in Buffalo were contacted by Eric Barash, a classical pianist and son of the owner of the hotel they had worked at in Vienna. Barash had also come to the United States. He had changed his name to Barrett and married Altina Schinasi, a Jewish designer, artist and Turkish tobacco heiress, whom everybody called Tina. They were moving to Los Angeles and wanted Edmond's parents to live with them as their house-hold staff and have Max manage Tina's business interests.

Edmond visited them in L.A. just before shipping out. Tina for some reason had bought an open-topped Cadillac limousine that had been built for the pope, with a throne-like seat in the back. His father chauffeured Edmond, riding on the throne, around Los Angeles the week before he left for the front.

(In an odd coincidence, I came to know Tina very well a decade later. Barash died young of tuberculosis and she married a family friend of mine, Charles Carey, so I spent a lot of time at their house while growing up and lived there for months at a time in the early 1960s. I had known Edmond for twenty years before we discovered this mutual connection.)

The 10th Mountain Division was shipped to Italy in the last months of the war. Edmond took part in the historic battle of Riva Ridge in February 1945 that broke German Field Marshal Kesselring's Gothic Line in the coun-try's north. The Germans were entrenched at the top of the Apennine moun-tain chain that crosses Italy from the Mediterranean to the Adriatic Sea not far from the French border.   .

The 10th Mountaineers staged a night assault, climbing a thousand feet up a sheer, ice-shrouded cliff on ropes tied to steel pitons they drove into the rock face as they went, using padded hammers to maintain silence. The Ger-mans were surprised, but they did have machine guns. Half of Edmond's unit were killed in the assault.

Edmond, who spoke Italian as well as English and German, was then as-signed as a liaison to the Italian partisans, engaged in mopping up isolated German units. He witnessed the execution of Mussolini and his mistress by the partisans.

Once in the 1960s, shortly after the Los Angeles SWP headquarters had been firebombed by anti-Castro Cubans, a suspicious clay-like substance was found pressed against the base of the building. Edmond was called and pro-nounced it plastique explosive. Asked how he could be sure he replied, "I planted enough of that stuff in Italy during the war."

After Riva Ridge he worked interrogating German officers suspected of committing war crimes, then was transferred to Vienna because of his fluency in German.

There is a story Edmond liked to tell about an incident right after they established a foothold at the top of Riva Ridge. The Germans were still holding a town a few miles north of them, while a bit closer there was a small hut. Edmond saw a wisp of smoke coming out of the hut's chimney and, taking no chances, fired a mortar shell at the structure. Amazingly, the shell went right down the chimney and the hut went up in flames.

Some months later in Vienna he took part in a big family reunion. One of his cousins, Heini, had served in the German army and walked in with a bad limp. Edmond asked him how he was wounded. It turned out his unit had been assigned to forward duty on the top of Riva Ridge. "We were stationed in a little hut," Heini said, "when some son of a bitch dropped a mortar shell down the chimney!"

Party Activist

On the GI Bill Edmond took a degree in chemistry at USC and went to work in the oil refineries. It was while he was at USC in 1948 that he met and fell in love with Shirley Slipokoff Morris. They moved in together that year and married in 1950. They remained together until Shirley's death in 2009.

Edmond joined the Socialist Workers Party in 1947. His chemist job lasted only a few years, until the McCarthy witch-hunt. One day he was called into the front office, where two FBI agents asked if he knew Myra Tanner Weiss, the SWP's vice presidential candidate in the 1952 elections and a leader of the Los Angeles party branch. "Myron Tanner who?" he bluffed, but they forcibly escorted him off the property.

From that point forward he was blacklisted in industry. His parents had moved to Watts, where Max worked as a watchmaker and owned a little jewelry shop. Edmond learned the trade from his father and they worked together until Max died in 1959, after which Edmond ran the business alone.

During the 1950s and 1960s he wrote regularly for the SWP's theoretical magazine the *International Socialist Review*: on the Hungarian Revolution of 1956, on Nixon's ill-fated trip to Latin America in 1958, on the United Nations, and on the early stages of the Vietnam War. The party's *Bulletin of Marxist Studies* published a nine-lecture course he gave under the title "The Soviet Union: What It Is and Where It Is Going." [The *ISR* of that period is not connected to the magazine of that name published currently by the International Socialist Organization. The name is inspired by the revolutionary magazine of the pre-World War I Socialist Party — ed.[1]]

---

[1] Insertion by the editor of *Against the Current*, where this piece first appeared.

In August 1961 I attended a big meeting at the First Unitarian Church where Edmond debated Earl Browder, former head of the Communist Party, on the topic "America's Road to Socialism: Revolution or Reform?"

Eight years later he had another notable debate, with Blase Bonpane, the former Maryknoll priest, advocate of Liberation Theology, and tireless human rights activist in Central America. The text was published as a pamphlet under the title *Marxism and Christianity: Are They Compatible?* It is still available on the Internet.

From 1965 to 1973 he had a weekly commentary show on Pacifica's KPFK radio station, under the name Theodore Edwards.

By the end of the 1960s, as people of my generation took over the New York leadership, Edmond was largely sidelined. In part this was due to the ambitions of the young people around Jack Barnes, the rising leader, who tended to discount what we called the middle generation, those in their forties, younger than the central leaders of the party's national office in New York, Farrell Dobbs and Tom Kerry, but a decade or so older than we were.

Factional Battles

Edmond faced a double obstacle. He was well past forty and also life-long friends with Myra Tanner Weiss and her husband Murray. Edmond would later write Myra's obituary for Solidarity's journal *Against the Current* when she died in 1997. There was a long-simmering semisecret fight in the party between the Dobbs-Kerry leadership and the party's founder, James P. Cannon, who lived out in Los Angeles. Cannon regarded New York as abstentionist from work with other forces, ingrown, intolerant of differences, and locked into self-generated activities like forums and subscription drives.

Murray and Myra Weiss supported Cannon. The so-called "Weissites" in consequence became a target. Edmond, without question, was a Weissite. He had some protection while Cannon, Murray, and Myra were active in the leadership, but Murray had a debilitating stroke in 1961 and Myra dropped out of activity a few years later. Most of the former Weiss group were then to one degree or another isolated, restricted to low-level assignments, or encouraged to quit the party.

Edmond got as high as an alternate member of the party's National Committee but never made the full list and was eventually dropped altogether. He finally became stereotyped as nothing more than a local branch educator.

In his private life Edmond made his living as his father had, as a watchmaker with a small jewelry store. Initially it had been in Watts, where his parents lived. But jewelry stores were a frequent target for armed robbers and Edmond, with his military training, vowed he would never just give in. He kept a gun under the counter and a couple of times shot it out, successfully, with the thieves.

After the Watts riots of 1964 he moved his store to mostly white Glendale to reduce the risk of such confrontations taking on a racial overtone. On July 21, 1981, three men entered his store near closing time. One pulled a sawed-off shotgun from under his coat; the other two had pistols.

Edmond pulled out his own gun. Later he told the press, "He was right-handed, and I kept moving to his left — keeping his body between me and the shotgun...he never could get off a shot. I got off five." He killed the man with the shotgun and wounded one of the others. He held the third until the police came.

What Edmond didn't know was that Jack Barnes, the party's national secretary, had decided to break from the world Trotskyist movement and make a bid to Fidel Castro for the Cubans' American franchise. Knowing many of the older party members would never go along with this, Barnes made up a secret hit list of about 150 party members who would have to be expelled.

Edmond's name came first. He was brought up on charges of contributing to law-and-order vigilantism and expelled from the party in 1982. His was the first of many bizarre trials, where twenty- and thirty-year party veterans were pilloried on frame-up charges and thrown out.

The whole episode is summed up nicely if unexpectedly by an ad I noticed the other day from a San Francisco bookstore. They were selling an old 1982 SWP internal bulletin giving the party leadership's version of the first wave of trials. The bookstore describes their item as a "Case study of how an organization performs a frontal-lobotomy on itself," They add, "This document contains summaries of a series of purge trials. Cases range from a straight frame-up in the case of Asher Harer in San Francisco, to an assortment of local purge trial summaries, the expulsion (or resignation according to Barnes) of Peter Camejo, and even the Dirty Harry style case of Edmund Kovacs (a.k.a. Theodore Edwards, one of the more interesting Party intellectuals) in Los Angeles."

Edmond went on to take part in the founding of Socialist Action, and then of Solidarity, of which he remained a member until his death. In his later years he regularly sent out emails to his friends with articles from the press about American and world politics. He and Shirley went to Italy numerous times to attend reunions of the 10th Mountain Division. He was an avid bicyclist, going on frequent 100-mile Saturday group rides, until late in his 60s when asthma made him stop.

Declining Health

Edmond outlived many of his friends and was in only occasional touch with the others. In recent years I saw him more often at his home than anyone else except his immediate neighbors. We had drifted apart politically but almost fifty years of friendship overrode that. Edmond remained intensely interested in politics to the end.

He could be opinionated and irascible. Those tendencies grew more pronounced in his last year. He became more and more distrustful of doctors, mostly refusing to see them; as Shirley's health declined a number of his old comrades, particularly women, became very angry at him over his bullying her to not go to the doctor. When Shirley had a serious fall in March 2009 I contacted the Kaiser HMO, which assigned a social worker and sent Shirley a visiting nurse. Shirley died that October after a second fall that broke her hip.

By that time Edmond's health was poor. He was gasping for breath, and showing signs that I took to be the beginnings of dementia. In the winter his breathing grew alarmingly worse, but he refused to see a doctor.

Finally, on Tuesday, January 12, 2010, he felt bad enough to drive himself to the Kaiser hospital. An x-ray revealed that he had undiagnosed advanced throat cancer blocking his airway, which he had mistaken for asthma. The next morning he lapsed into a coma. On Friday, January 15, his doctor told me that it was inoperable and hopeless. As his executor I told them to shut down the life support. He was three months short of his eighty-sixth birthday.

I was not blind to his faults, but there was, nevertheless, an enduring affection. He was unique and in his way irreplaceable.

Against the Current, September-October 2010

The Left and the Jews

From Ambivalence to Betrayal: The Left, the Jews, and Israel. Robert S. Wistrich. University of Nebraska Press, 2012. 625 pp.

> *Mr Deasy to Stephen Dedalus: "Ireland, they say, has the honour of*
> *being the only country which never persecuted the Jews.*
> *Do you know that? No. And do you know why?"*
>
> "Why, sir?" Stephen asked, beginning to smile.
>
> "Because she never let them in," Mr Deasy said solemnly.
> A coughball of laughter leaped from his throat
> dragging after it a rattling chain of phlegm.
>
> -James Joyce, *Ulysses*

I first had to think much of anything about Israel, the Arab states on its borders, and the subset of Arabs who were beginning to be called Palestinians in June 1967 during the Six Day War. I was living in New York at the time, a member and staff writer for the Socialist Workers Party, the largest of the American Trotskyist groups, revolutionary Marxists who revered Lenin as well as Leon Trotsky. On June 5 war erupted between Israel and Egypt, Jordan, and Syria, three of the four countries on its borders, all vastly larger. Fighting on three fronts, the Israeli Jews in a few days defeated the massive Arab armies thrown against them.

The SWP leadership declared the party firmly on the Arab side, not shrinking from unreservedly endorsing the declared Arab war aims of destroying the Jewish state altogether. There were twenty-two Arab states and a single Jewish one. Forty-six years later the population of the Arab states stands at 350 million; Israel's is 8 million, of whom only 6 million are Jews.

131

What were the reasons my Trotskyist party advanced for exterminating this one tiny country, the only country in the world against which it raised such a draconian demand? Israel was, after all, composed of a historic Middle Eastern people, some of whom were refugees from a prolonged European exile but a majority were native Middle Easterners who had been driven out of Arab states after 1945? The grounds were summarized a few years later in a resolution entitled "Israel and the Arab Revolution" adopted by overwhelming vote at a party convention attended by more than 1,000 members and supporters.[1] It is worth examining, as its arguments have become the stock in trade of a large section of the Left, in both the United States and Europe, in the years since, as well as nearly universal in the Muslim world.

The resolution asserted that Israel could have been created "only at the expense of the indigenous peoples of the area," and that it could have "come into existence . . . only by relying upon imperialism." It affirmed that the "struggle of the Palestinian people against their oppression and for self-determination has taken the form of a struggle to destroy the state of Israel," a goal to which the SWP declared "unconditional support."

To defend itself against the likely charge that this position was anti-semitic, the resolution assured its readers that "It is not justifiable to assume that a likely development of the Arab revolution will be the future oppression of the Israeli Jews." It advocated a Democratic Secular Palestine in which, after the Arab armies had smashed the Israeli state and imposed an Arab majority, the Jewish population would be guaranteed full civil, religious, and human rights. That this was not true in any of the existing Arab states did not phase my Marxist leaders. They added that while they defended the right of national self-determination for all Middle Eastern peoples, this did not apply to Jews, who should be content with the rights that the conquering Arabs would certainly be pleased to give them.

There were many essential falsehoods in this document, which were and remain typical of the progressive view of Israel. It is true that Britain, a major imperialist power, in the Balfour Declaration of 1917 promised to support the creation of a Jewish homeland in Palestine. This was drafted during World War I, in which the Ottoman Empire, which had ruled Palestine as an undifferentiated part of its territory for five hundred years, was fighting on the German side. There was at that time a large Jewish population that had been under Ottoman rule since the Turkish Muslim conquest. Some of these Jews

---

[1] http://www.marxists.org/history/etol/document/swp-us/24thconvention/zionism.htm. As this is mainly a book review I am primarily footnoting sources other than Robert Wistrich's book. In some cases where readers are likely to be particularly interested in his source I have included that in the notes.

lived in what became Palestine; others lived in the various pieces of Ottoman land that the Western governments carved into Iraq, Jordan, Lebanon, and Syria, as well as in Egypt, which was an Ottoman colony. Still others lived in the Arab states of North Africa, mainly Algeria, which had been an Ottoman regency from 1525 to the French invasion in 1830, and Morocco. With the Ottoman collapse at the war's end, Palestine in 1920, only at this time separated from Syria, became a British Mandate, which status lasted until 1948.

The borders, drawn artificially by the European and American victors after World War I, on the whole fatally ignored deep ethnic differences, not only between Jews, a historically oppressed people in Muslim lands, and Arabs, but on a larger scale within Islam, between Sunnis and Shi'ites, as well as splitting the non-Arab Muslim Kurdish population between four separate states. In Iraq a Sunni minority dominated a Shi'ite majority; in Syria this was reversed, with an Alawite Shi'ite minority tyrannizing a Sunni population. And then there was the totally unworkable Lebanon with its incendiary tripartite mix of Christians, Sunnis, and Shi'ites. The whole construct has proven ever since to be in a permanent state of crisis and internecine slaughter. All of these states have at one time or another allied themselves with "imperialists" — Britain, France, the United States, or another European power — or, before its collapse, with the repressive government of the Soviet Union, or both sequentially. Why, then, single out the Jews in particular as illegitimate and worthy of expulsion from their homeland?

Britain soon came to see the Arabs as a more important constituency than the Jews and reneged on the Balfour promise. During and after World War II it forcibly halted and turned back ships carrying refugees from Germany, condemning thousands to their deaths. The Jews in Palestine established their state, not with the help of imperialism but in a long armed struggle against British troops, an anti-imperialist struggle.

Further, on the declaration of the state of Israel in 1948, the Jewish area was invaded by five Arab states, by then established nations with large standing armies: Egypt, Lebanon, Jordan, Syria, and Iraq. No imperialist power came to the aid of the Jews. They won this extraordinarily unequal battle mainly with weapons from Communist Czechoslovakia. Nor did any "imperialist" power come to Israel's aid in the Six Day War of 1967.

Did the Palestinians or the Arab states more broadly endorse the promises about human and civil rights for Jews the SWP made for them in New York? On May 27, Nasser stated, "Our basic objective will be the destruction of Israel."[2]

---

[2] There are various sources for this quote. I am taking it from the BBC's "On This Day," its retrospective for each day of the year, for June 5. http://news.bbc.co.uk/on

The Palestine Liberation Organization charter of 1964 declared that only those Jews who could prove that their ancestry in Palestine dated to "the beginning of the Zionist invasion" would be considered to be Palestinians. No date is attached to this clause, but in the later Hamas charter the date of 1917 is given, along with the pledge that all Jews who cannot date their ancestry in Palestine to 1917 will be expelled. Under this rule the Democratic Secular Palestine was going to be an almost purely Arab state, if there were any Jews in it at all.

There were more than 800,000 native Jews living in the Arab states in 1948. By 2008 there were barely 6,000, fewer than 100 each in the major states of Egypt, Syria, Lebanon, and Iraq, where the great majority were expelled. Two hundred thousand more were expelled from Turkey and Iran.[3] There was no sign in any Arab country of tolerating even the existence of Jews, much less granting them equal civil and human rights with Muslims. The planned fate of the Jews, who had been concentrated from throughout the Muslim world into tiny Israel, was to be different only in being more final. Ahmad Shukeiri, the first chairman of the Palestine Liberation Organization, on June 1, 1967, rather than promising Israeli Jews civil rights after the expected Arab conquest said instead, "I estimate that none of them will survive."[4]

The PLO Charter expresses opinions both about Zionism, a particular movement, which it brands "fascist," despite the fact that the founders of Israel were in large part quite moderate socialists, and about Jews more broadly. Here the Charter asserts: "Judaism, being a religion, is not an independent nationality. Nor do Jews constitute a single nation with an identity of its own; they are citizens of the states to which they belong." Clearly the Arabs do not feel the same way about Islam, which aspires not merely to rule in individual

---

thisday/hi/dates/stories/june/5/newsid_2654000/2654251.stm. Retrieved March 23, 2013. A more extended discussion of Nasser's war aims is Moshe Gat's "Nasser and the Six Day War, 5 June 1967: A Premeditated Strategy or An Inexorable Drift to War?" http://www.paulbogdanor.com/israel/gat1967.pdf

[3] For a summary by country see the Wikipedia article on "Jewish Exodus from Arab and Muslim Countries" http://en.wikipedia.org/wiki/Jewish_exodus_from_Arab_and_Muslim_countries. There is also a substantial literature on this issue, such as *The Forgotten Millions: The Modern Jewish Exodus from Arab Lands*, Malka Hillel Shulewitz ed. (London: Continuum, 1999). Both the Muslim world and much of the Western Left knows and cares only about the Arab exodus from what became Israel, a double standard that obscures both the recent treatment of Jews in Muslim countries and what amounted to an exchange of populations between Arab and Jewish communities.

[4] *New York Times*, June 2, 1967. Also Theodore Draper, *Israel and World Politics: Roots of the Third Arab-Israeli War.* (New York: Viking Press, 1968).

nations but to a supranational unification of its believers in a transnational caliphate.

Today each of the states newly carved out of the Ottoman Empire in the 1920s claims distinct nationhood. The Turks had ruled Syria and Palestine since 1516. In 1948 there were a million native Jews in the Arab countries plus Turkey and Iran. In the fluidity of boundary drawing why exactly were the Ottoman Jews, whose residence predated the Arab conquest by two and a half millennia, not entitled to a small piece of land? The anti-Jewish hostility of their Muslim opponents is understandable if not supportable. It is plainly more extreme than the Jewish attitude toward Arabs, as 20 percent of the population of pre-1967 Israel is Arab. There is no comparable tolerance toward Jews in any Muslim state, Arab, Turkish, or Persian. The Arab side has most often shown itself to be racist and exterminationist toward the Jews, as witnessed by the three major invasions of Israel by its surrounding Arab states, in 1948, 1967, and 1972. The question is why the ostensibly rationalist, secular, and progressive forces in the West have, to a disturbing degree, endorsed this framing of the Arab-Jewish clash.

It should be remembered that the readiness to "unconditionally" support the call for Israel's destruction was issued by these American Marxists while the Gaza strip was still part of Egypt and the West Bank belonged to Jordan. There had been no agitation for a Palestinian state in those places. And there was no Israeli occupation of the West Bank or a cordon sanitaire around Gaza, the focal points of much leftist excoriation of Israel today. And there was no talk about a two-state solution. The Marxist Left endorsed Arab states in their military struggle to eradicate the one Jewish state outright. The reasoning behind this otherwise surprising position lies far back in the history of the relations between the socialist movement and the Jews, from the time when Jews were first gaining citizenship rights in Europe early in the nineteenth century. These were things of which I was entirely ignorant in 1967.

I voted for the party's resolution with the rest of my comrades. After all, as Lenin said, you can't make an omelet without breaking eggs. By way of disclosure, My father was Norwegian, with dashes of Irish, Scottish, and Dutch; my mother was Jewish. If she ever had any Jewish religious instruction she never mentioned it. I have never been inside a synagogue. I was raised in the New Age, semi-Christian, Church of Religious Science. My parents, insofar as they had any supernatural beliefs, were spiritualists. The only Jewish relative I ever met was my maternal grandmother, who was an evil woman who had last had any contact with my mother before I was born. She stayed with us for a few days when I was fifteen, then never spoke to any of us again.

I didn't return to these questions for many years. I left Marxism behind in the late 1980s, and began to look again at many issues I had considered settled. The Marxist attitude toward the Jews was one of them.

Over the decades since the Six Day War — and really long before that — prominent spokespeople for the Arab states and media, and, of course, among the Palestinians, fused opposition to the Israeli state with the history of Christian antisemitism in a general anathema of the Jews. A recent example is a television broadcast on Hamas's Al-Aqsa TV on November 5, 2010, by Mahmoud Al-Zahhar, a central founder of Hamas and its current foreign minister. He cites with approval and as precedent for Hamas's plans, the long series of expulsions of the Jews from Christian Europe: France in 1253, Britain in 1280, Hungary in 1360, Belgium in 1370, Germany in 1384, Austria in 1420, Holland in 1444, Spain in 1492. He adds the Russian pogroms of the 1880s and, without distinction as any worse than the others, Hitler's Nazis: "Germany expelled them once again in 1945." Merely expelled? And while the Holocaust was uniquely genocidal, the expulsions of the late Middle Ages that Al-Zahar cites with approval often included the slaughter of the entire Jewish population of cities, as many as 10,000 at a time, and the burning of hundreds at the stake in a single day.

Al-Zahhar concludes: "We have learned the lesson — there is no place for you among us, and you have no future among the nations of the world. You are headed to annihilation."[5]

We have a confluence here, of deep cultural animosity toward Jews as a group that goes back many centuries in many countries, rooted principally in religious absolutisms but resting also on ethnic and cultural differences, with present-day Arab antisemitism of an extreme kind, ending in a unique hatred, more pervasive and long-lasting than almost any other in history. While present-day leftists consider themselves unshakably anti-racist, there is a glaring exception, in their attitude toward Jewish nationalism and from there to Jews as such. Robert Wistrich puts it bluntly: "[B]y identifying with Islamist organizations like Hamas or Hezbollah which advocate and act upon an openly annihilatory form of antisemitism, radical leftists have in effect become complicit in what is a symbolic form of genocide."

A hostility to Jews as an ethnicity goes back to the very beginnings of the socialist movement, long before Zionism, much less the state of Israel, existed. It was imbibed from the societies in which the core doctrines of Marxism and other socialist leftisms were first forged. The socialist Left has been distinguished from the racist Right in one important regard: it has, gen-

---

[5] Translated by the Middle East Media Research Institute. Retrieved from their website on 2-28-2013, http://www.memritv.org/clip_transcript/en/2676.htm.

erally, been accepting of assimilationist Jews who reject any claim of a national identity for the Jewish people.

The original socialists and Marxists were, with perhaps the sole exception of the long-forgotten followers of the utopian theorist Henri de Saint Simon, openly antisemitic. Liberal political groups and parties were usually better than the socialists, because they valued the rights of all citizens, while the socialists defended only proletarians, which didn't include the Jews in enough numbers to be noticed until early in the twentieth century.

*   *   *

Robert S. Wistrich was born in 1945 to leftist Polish parents in Soviet-ruled Kazakhstan. He grew up in England, and from 1982 has taught at the Hebrew University of Jerusalem. He is one of the world's foremost authorities on the history of antisemitism, having published on the subject since 1976, most importantly his magisterial study, *A Lethal Obsession: Anti-Semitism from Antiquity to the Global Jihad,* in 2010. In a certain way the almost 700 pages of *From Ambivalence to Betrayal* is a footnote to that larger work, focusing as it does on mainly European socialists and Marxists from the 1840s to the present.

The history of religious persecution and expulsion that Mahmoud Al-Zahhar cites cast a long shadow, still strongly affecting the popular perceptions of Jews in the years socialist groups were first forming, early in the nineteenth century. During the Black Death of 1348-49 the mass of the German population blamed the Jews, accusing them of poisoning the wells, or, alternately, explaining the plague as God's punishment for allowing the Christ-killing Jews to live among Christians. The great majority of German Jews were either murdered outright or driven eastward into what is now Poland, Ukraine, Lithuania, and Romania. Over the next four hundred years some were allowed to return, but usually with severe restrictions on their rights. Many of the petty German states prohibited Jews from living in the cities. Others confined them to walled ghettos. They were often required to wear special highly identifiable clothing, the predecessor of the yellow stars of the Nazi era. Jews were barred from the professions and usually from owning land.

The consequence was that the Jews to survive gravitated into occupations that were looked on by the Germans as disreputable. Most common were horse traders, used clothes dealers, rural peddlers, grain merchants, and petty money lenders. The Jews of France were emancipated in 1791 by the French Revolution. Napoleon carried Jewish emancipation with his march into the

German states. Westphalia was the first to grant citizenship to Jews, in 1808, the North German Confederation only in 1869. (Jews in the United States were nominally given rights of citizenship in 1789, but many states continued to prohibit them from holding public office or imposed other restrictions. New Hampshire was the last state to lift the restrictions, in 1877.)

Contrary to what one might suppose today, European leftists were not at all happy about letting Jews become citizens.

Socialism in Germany

Germany had a distinct post-Enlightenment anti-Jewish tradition. The famed philosopher Johann Gottlieb Fichte in 1793, when he was an outspoken supporter of the French Revolution, wrote: "in the bosom of almost all the nations of Europe there spreads a powerful state driven by hostile feelings that is continually at war with all the others, and that in certain places terribly oppresses the citizens. I speak of Jewry." Wikipedia adds from Fichte's collected works of that period that he opposed granting civil rights to the Jews unless one managed "to cut off all their heads in one night, and to set new ones on their shoulders, which should contain not a single Jewish idea."

What was happening here, as in France of the same period, was the rise of nationalism. The forging of powerful, unifying nationalist sentiments almost invariably counterposed the ideal type true citizen against the inassimilable alien, and no group was more alien than the Jews. Marxists for generations theorized that antisemitism was a hangover from feudalism, from the once-dominant Church and from feudal landowners and peasants who had bad experiences with petty Jewish merchants. Instead, as modern states emerged, antisemitism became far stronger and was incorporated into the platforms of political parties and movements of both the Right and the Left.

Hegel (1770-1831), who had enormous influence on Marx and Marxism, explained the emergence of what we now call modernism in terms of a linear evolution in which different peoples, cultures, and religions each made a one-time contribution to the upward movement of the Absolute. Judaism for him was both inferior to Christianity but also a historical dead end whose adherents could not make any contribution to Western civilization beyond what they had done in biblical times. He supported granting civil rights to Jews on humanitarian grounds but saw no value in Jews as a group.

Marx's views on the Jews were more directly shaped by Bruno Bauer (1809-1882), the leader of the Young Hegelians. Bauer was a militant atheist but nevertheless shared Hegel's view that Judaism was inferior to Christianity. (The argument here was that Judaism supposedly bound its followers to rigid application of external laws and total subservience to God, with no concept of personal liberty, while Christianity sought through inner spirituality to raise its believers up to angelic levels.) Here nationalism of the Left raised its ugly head. Bauer opposed granting civil rights to the German Jews on the grounds that their "fossilized" beliefs and way of life made no contribution to the emerging German nation. They could be emancipated only when both Jews and Christians abandoned their religions in a new universal atheistic society. He added that this self-emancipation would be more difficult for Jews than for Christians because of his view of their negative way of life. The Jews, he said, "have nestled in the pores of civil society and taken advantage of the victims produced by the elements of insecurity in that society."

Marx largely agreed with Bauer's negative assessment of the Jews, but disagreed on how Jewish emancipation should take place. He spelled out his views in his 1843 "On the Jewish Question."[6] He begins by pointing to France and the United States to show that Bauer was wrong to suppose that granting the Jews civil rights must be deferred to the creation of a socialist future. However, while democratic France and America were an improvement on absolutist systems such as in Prussia, civil rights still allowed freedom of religion instead of outlawing it, and the right to property instead of abolishing it. I will resist the temptation to digress here on how efforts to do those two things have produced systems far worse than Prussia's of the 1840s.

Marx viewed as idealist Bauer's contention that Judaism persisted because of Jews' religious beliefs. He instead presented a "materialist" explanation. He writes:

"We are trying to break with the theological formulation of the question. For us, the question of the Jew's capacity for emancipation becomes the question: What particular *social* element has to be overcome in order to abolish Judaism?" The goal has suddenly shifted from ending the persecution of the Jews and their exclusion from even the limited civil rights enjoyed by German Christians to abolishing Judaism itself. Simple. If the Jews would just agree to abandon any distinguishing beliefs or culture they would be treated like everyone else. This in fact has been the core Marxist position on the Jews ever since.

Marx then explains what it is that characterizes the Jewish group if it is not their religion or culture:

Let us not look for the secret of the Jew in his religion, but let us look for the secret of his religion in the real Jew. What is the secular basis of Judaism? *Practical* need, *self-interest*. What is the worldly religion of the Jew? *Huckstering*. What is his worldly God? *Money*. . . . An organi-

---

[6] http://www.marxists.org/archive/marx/works/1844/jewish-question/.

zation of society which would abolish the preconditions for huckstering, and therefore the possibility of huckstering, would make the Jew impossible. His religious consciousness would be dissipated like a thin haze in the real, vital air of society. (Emphasis in original.)

He goes on:

> We recognize in Judaism, therefore, a general *anti-social* element of the *present time*, an element which through historical development — to which in this harmful respect the Jews have zealously contributed — has been brought to its present high level, at which it must necessarily begin to disintegrate. In the final analysis, the *emancipation of the Jews* is the emancipation of mankind from *Judaism*. (Emphasis in original.)

Marx's high economic theorizing here is just the retailing of the antisemitic tropes of the German nationalists. Other such gems from this same essay include: "Money is the jealous god of Israel, in face of which no other god may exist." For Jews, "even the lavatory [is] an object of divine law." And still more sweeping:

> Contempt for theory, art, history, and for man as an end in himself, which is contained in an abstract form in the Jewish religion, is the real, conscious standpoint, the virtue of the man of money. . . . The *chimerical* nationality of the Jew is the nationality of the merchant, of the man of money in general. The groundless law of the Jew is only a religious caricature of groundless morality and right in general, of the purely formal rites with which the world of self-interest surrounds itself.

Marx's hostility to Jews as a group persisted throughout his life. At best it can be said that he did not join in the racial theories of the right-wing antisemites. Instead he characterized the whole of the Jewish people as social parasites who, he believed, had invented capitalism and corrupted the Christian world with it. That situation could only be ended by Jews disappearing entirely, by renouncing anything distinctive about themselves. In an article on "The Russian Loan" of January 4, 1856, he wrote:

> Thus we find every tyrant backed by a Jew, as is every Pope by a Jesuit. In truth, the cravings of oppressors would be hopeless and the practicability of war out of the question, if there were not an army of Jesuits to smother thought and a handful of Jews to ransack pockets.

Thinking about this, there are far more tyrants than Popes, and their actions are far more oppressive than the limited power of the Pope, and Jesuits are a tiny fraction of the Catholic Church, who chose this role in life, while being a Jew is something one is born to. The apparent equivalence here is very lop-sided indeed.

Marx was still more outspoken in his correspondence with Engels. In a letter of July 30, 1862, he said of Ferdinand Lassalle, one of the central lead-ers of German socialism,

> as the shape of his head and the growth of his hair indicate, he is de-scended from the negroes who joined in the flight of Moses from Egypt (unless his mother or grandmother on his father's side was crossed with a nigger). Now this union of Jewishness with Germanness on a negro ba-sis was bound to produce an extraordinary hybrid. The importunity of the fellow is also niggerlike.[7]

Engels described Lassalle as a "greasy Jew, disguised under brilliantine and flashy jewels."[8]

But wasn't Marx himself a Jew? Genetically and by ancestry, yes. His father, to escape antisemitism, had converted to Lutheranism before Karl was born. Throughout the history of the Jewish Diaspora, particularly after the consolidation of absolutist Christian states that carried out organized persecu-tions and expulsions of the Jews, there were always a certain number of Jews who sought to escape ostracism by rejecting their fellows, often vociferously, a phenomenon we see down to our own day in figures like Noam Chomsky.

For the record, the Lassallean socialists were even worse than the Marx-ists, notwithstanding their leader's Jewish descent, which Lassalle rejected. His General German Workers Association (Allgemeiner Deutscher Arbeiter Verein), founded in 1863, regularly attacked the Marxist Social Democratic Workers Party for their (assimilated) Jewish members. The editor of the Las-sallcans' main newspaper, the *New Social Democrat,* Wilhelm Hasselmann, claimed that only his party truly represented the workers, while its socialist rivals, "spawned by the overheated imagination of arrogant Jew-boys and other mischief-makers, are falling apart." (September 18, 1872)

In an editorial against newspapers owned by Jewish publishers Hassel-mann called for their elimination and that the workers should "lead the Jews altogether, with a few exceptions, not through, but into, the Red Sea."

For Marx and the Young Hegelians there was also their vision of a class-less world government of the future that led them to, nominally, oppose na-

---

[7] This is Wistrich's translation. For the full text in a different translation see http://www.marxists.org/archive/marx/works/1862/letters/62_07_30a.htm.
[8] Engels to Marx, March 7, 1856, in Engels: *Selected Writings*, edited by W.O. Hen-derson (London, 1967), pp. 129-30, cited by Wistrich, p. 89.

tionalist and ethnic self-identities. The *Communist Manifesto* in 1848 famously declared "The working men have no country." This has proven in the hundred and sixty-five years since it was written to have been one of the greatest miscalculations of the Marxist credo. But even Marx and Engels did not mean this literally for their own time but as an expectation for some fairly distant future. The Manifesto in the same paragraph says:

> Since the proletariat must first of all acquire political supremacy, must constitute itself the nation, it is, so far, itself national, though not in the bourgeois sense of the word. . . . United action, of the leading civilised countries at least, is one of the first conditions for the emancipation of the proletariat.

This was the opening through which the rising German nationalism, which in real life was fused with a profound antisemitism, reinvaded the Marxist prospect through the back door. For Marx and Engels this reliance on the "leading civilized countries" to spark the move toward world government led them to condemn the lesser countries, which were not powerful enough to undertake such a mission. As it happened, these, along with the Jews, were the hated enemies of the German nationalists. This was developed extensively by Engels in his articles for the *Neue Rheinische Zeitung* during the revolutionary period of 1848-49. Wistrich summarizes:

> [B]oth Marx and Engels displayed a revolutionary Pan-Germanist contempt for the backward peasant peoples of Eastern Europe and the Balkans. Engels in particular denied the capacity of Slavs to create a viable State or achieve national independence, dismissing them as "ethnic trash" destined for the rubbish bin of history. In contrast to the "revolutionary" Germans, Magyars, and Poles, Engels considered the Czechs and South Slavs as "counter-revolutionary" tools of Russian and Pan-Slavist ambitions. They were "historyless peoples" (a concept later adopted by Otto Bauer) whose "mission" was simply to disappear in the future revolutionary holocaust that would sweep them away along with other "waste products" such as the Bretons, Basques, and Scottish Highlanders.[9]

Engels was particularly negative toward the Polish Jews, the "dirtiest of all races" whose essence was "huckstering, sordidness and filth."[10] In his later years he refrained from these kinds of sweeping characterizations, but held

---

[9] Wistrich, p. 90.
[10] Wistrich cites for these quotes the Marx-Engels *Gesamtausgabe*, the definitive edition of their collected works, vol 1, 7:29, 165, 176, and 291.

firm to the view that under communism Jews would have to disappear as an identifiable group.

One prominent exception to this view was Marx's close associate Moses Hess (1812-1875), who had converted Marx to communism. An assimilated Jew and Young Hegelian, in the 1840s he shared the hostility toward religious and ethnically identified Jews promoted by Hegel and Ludwig Feuerbach. He wrote on the subject himself, before Marx did, and helped formulate the ideas that found expression in Marx's "On the Jewish Question." By the 1860s Hess rethought these matters and came to reject the idea that assimilation would solve the Jewish problem or that the cohesion and persistence of Judaism lay, as the Marxists believed, in the Jews' commercial activities. It derived, he said, in a national consciousness and this could be resolved only by the self-emancipation of the Jewish people, retaining their identity. This made Hess one of the first theorists of Zionism. Wistrich writes:

> Antisemitism, [Hess] would later conclude, was an enigma for patriotic German Jews only because they insisted on denying their own nationality. Hence they had failed to understand that German nationalism with its endemic racialist features was fundamentally incapable of assimilating "alien" groups. This unsparing analysis, published in 1862, condemning the new racist antisemitism, was to prove remarkably prescient.

The real history of the world that has unfolded since 1862 has seen class struggle as a highly subordinate phenomenon. The center of the stage has been firmly held by forces the Marxist movement expected to rapidly fade away even under bourgeois rule: nationalism and religion. This was an evil omen for the stateless Jews. Hess warned:

> The beautiful phrases about humanity and enlightenment which he [the modern Jew] uses so freely to cloak his treason, his fear of being identified with his unfortunate brethren, will not ultimately protect him from the judgment of public opinion.

Beginning in the 1880s antisemitism became a major issue in German electoral politics, promoted by the Christian-Social movement of Protestant preacher Adolf Stoecker. Initially the German Marxists, organized in the Social-Democratic Party (SPD), which was then proscribed and operating underground, fought back, as attacks by the Christian-Social supporters and the government were directed at the socialists as well as the Jews. This became complicated in the 1890s, when a new brand of antisemitism arose in the form of anti-Christian left populism. This new movement was anti-government and anticapitalist as well as antisemitic.

The antisocialist laws were repealed in 1890 and the SPD was now a large legal party. The party opposed antisemitism, but wrongly theorized that it was based in soon-to-be-extinct peasant and semifeudal remnants and was not a serious problem. Worse, the Marxists viewed the anticapitalism of the antisemitic movement as a progressive step on the road to socialism.

August Bebel, the central leader of the SPD, crafted the party's long-term policy toward the antisemites and the Jews at the party's 1893 congress in Cologne. Unlike earlier Marxist writings, Bebel forthrightly described the European Jews as an oppressed people. He was opposed to attacks on the Jews, though he explained anti-Jewish prejudice as in large part a consequence of the role of some Jews in the "huckstering" trades, particularly buying and selling agricultural produce and lending small amounts of money. Bebel is famous in the Marxist movement for his declaration that "antisemitism is the socialism of fools." I have had that quoted to me in the last few months by an anti-Israel Marxist as proof that Marxists have always been total opponents of Jew hatred. This misses the meaning of this declaration in the context of its own time. It did not mean that antisemitism was a totally reactionary political view. It meant, rather, that in opposing principally Jewish capitalism it was only part way to opposing capitalism as a whole. This was spelled out in the resolution Bebel submitted to the congress, which was duly adopted, and said in part:

> Social-democracy fights antisemitism as a movement which is directed against the natural development of society but which, despite its reactionary character and against its will, ultimately must become revolutionary. This is bound to happen because the petty-bourgeois and small peasant strata, which are being whipped up by antisemitism against the Jewish capitalists, will finally realize that not merely the Jewish capitalist, but the capitalist class as a whole is its enemy.[11]

This decision, to meet the antisemites halfway and view them as inevitably a revolutionary force against capitalism, was a disastrous misreading, rooted in the Marxist dismissal of the importance of nationalism and the reduction of opposition to Jews by German nationalists to purely economic grievances. As the Nazis would demonstrate, the base of antisemitism was not at all confined to peasants and semifeudal landlords who had unhappy dealings with Jewish usurers. A very large part of the urban German working class voted for and

---

[11] Protokoll, Cologne, 22-29 October 1893 (Berlin 1891), p. 224, cited by Wistrich, p. 119.

supported the National Socialist movement, validating Bebel's prediction but in a horrific manner. There were in fact many elements of socialism in Hitler's program, a leftist populism that was an intensified version of the movement of the 1890s, fused with an exclusive, organic nationalism that in principle rejected any human rights to those who did not fit its racialist definition of the nation. Jewish capitalism, contrary to the Marxist theory, had nothing to do with this.

Through their false, reductionist theory, even as the German Marxists attempted to argue against the populist antisemites their insistence that capitalism was in essence "Jewish," but broader than only the Jews, played into the hands of the Jew haters. The SPD quoted Marx's declaration from "On the Jewish Question," that the "emancipation of the Jews was the emancipation of society from Judaism."[12] The antisemites were happy to oblige. Or here, from the SPD's main newspaper:

> Our solution consists in saying, that the so-called "Jewish spirit" is the spirit of capitalism. Certainly not every Jew is a capitalist but every capitalist is a Jew — and therefore the emancipation of the Jews and the rest of mankind coincides with the emancipation of humanity from Jewish — and other capitalism.[13]

They even tried to argue that persecuting the Jews by prohibiting them from owning land or belonging to the professions was counterproductive because it concentrated the Jews in occupations dealing with money and thus allowed them to gain mastery over Germans:

> Behold, the oppressed [the Jews] have become the lords of this world, a powerful part of the dominant bourgeoisie, impregnated with the same spirit. The irony of history has turned everything upside down and punishment has brought its reward. It has made servants out of the persecutors and master out of the persecuted.[14]

The vast majority of German Jews were impoverished and stood below the lower middle class. This image of the alien Jews as "lords of this world" and "masters" over Germans was taken from the stock in trade of the antisemites and would be a central part of Nazi propaganda a few years later. Saying you opposed antisemitism was fatally undercut by incorporating essential

---

[12] *Vorwarts*, March 24, 1893. All quotes from the SPD's *Vorwarts* are taken from Wistrich in his chapter "German Social Democrats on the Volkisch Movement."
[13] *Vorwarts*, December 9, 1893.
[14] *Vorwarts*, December 8, 1892, cited by Wistrich, p. 123.

antisemitic stereotypes into your argument, just reaffirming the beliefs of the Jew haters. The SPD's neutral position on antisemitism in the 1890s was far worse than it had been in the 1880s when Jew-baiting came from the far right and was combined with hostility to socialism. They went so far as to write that in the task of winning over the rural masses to socialism that "here Antisemitism has prepared the way. It has performed what should have been the task of the bourgeois democracy."[15] In the same period the liberals called for legal prosecution of the antisemites. The SPD in contrast publicly in an effort to discredit the liberals declared, "The progress of antisemitism is therefore not at all unwelcome to us. On the contrary, we know that we can only reap success from it."[16]

Very few of the German Marxist leaders dissented from this conciliatory view. Principally they amounted to Engels, living in England, who late in life had moved away from the anti-Jewish prejudices of his early and middle years, Edward Bernstein, the fountainhead of revisionist socialism, and Karl Kautsky. Kautsky, however, believed that antisemitism had no real deep roots but was just a tactic by politicians to distract the workers from more fundamental class issues. Engels, in his old age now firmly opposed to antisemitism, utterly misunderstand its source. In a widely reprinted letter of March 21, 1890, he affirmed:

> Antisemitism, therefore, is nothing but the reaction of the medieval, decadent strata of society against modern society, which essentially consists of wage-earners and capitalists. . . . If it is possible in a country, that is a sign that there is not yet enough capital in that country.

Only a few years later, antisemitism would see its greatest flowering in the most advanced capitalist country of Europe, under the National Socialists, who both viewed themselves and were objectively one variant of the most determined antifeudal modernism, one of whose attributes has been ultranationalism. Engels, and the Marxist movement in his wake, supposed antisemitism to be essentially based on economic grievances, just as they imagined Jews to be defined as a particular economic entity. One did not need to wait for Hitler and the Nazis to prove this whole theoretical edifice to be hollow. The Dreyfus Affair in France just a few years later stirred a torrent of anti-Jewish hatred from all ranks of patriotic citizens, this in the homeland of the French Revolution, the leading edge of bourgeois modernism.

---

[15] *Vorwarts*, August 29, 1893.
[16] *Vorwarts*, June 17, 1893.

The narrow economic-determinist schema was compounded by the expectation that the whole of the middle class and the peasant farmers were doomed to imminent dissolution into the proletariat, and therefore the Marxist movement should reject any support to their needs or demands. Engels wrote:

> If these peasants want a guarantee for the continuance of their businesses, we absolutely cannot offer it to them. Their place is with the antisemites, the Farmers' Unions and similar parties who take pleasure in promising everything and keeping to nothing. [17]

The underlying prediction, that the farmers and the middle class would disappear into a huge proletariat, essential to the Marxist project, never happened. Like the Physiocrats before them, who believed that agricultural labor was the key to human progress, the Marxist substitution of the industrial working class proved to be one more intermediate stage in social development in which advances in productivity first radically reduced the number of farmers and has since substantially reduced the number of industrial workers. This has in turn invalidated the promise that the "Jewish question" could wait to be resolved until the Jews disappeared as an identifiable group into the mass of a world socialist proletariat.

In the meantime the spread of nationalist modernism was escalating attacks on Jews. Wistrich cites

> the pogroms in Russia, Romania, and Algeria, the election of the Christian-Social Judeophobe Karl Lueger as Mayor of Vienna in 1897, the virulent plebeian antisemitism in Germany, the Dreyfus Affair in France, and the anti-alien agitation in Great Britain.

In response, the SPD, and most particularly its Jewish members and leaders, shrank from confronting the antisemites for fear that the party would be branded a Jewish defense group. Edward Bernstein, one of the few who saw the consequences of such a response, in 1894 castigated party members who

> are the most frequently on hand with declarations against "philo-semitism" — namely comrades of Jewish descent, who, precisely because of their origins, consider it their special duty to keep the party free of any suspicion of favoring Jewish interests.

A particular offender here was Franz Mehring (1846-1919), the authoritative biographer of Karl Marx, a central leader of the German SPD, and a founder

---

[17] *Neue Zeit* 1 (1894-1895: 303, cited by Wistrich, p. 138.

with Rosa Luxemburg and Karl Liebknecht of the German Communist Party, originally called the Spartacus League. Not himself Jewish, Mehring became the SPD's expert on the Jewish Question. He had been an antisemite before he became a socialist. As a leader of the SPD he warmly supported the hostile writings on the Jews by the nationalist historian Heinrich von Treitschke, who had written that "the Jews are our misfortune." Wistrich writes that Mehring "was openly contemptuous of those critics who accused Heinrich von Treitschke of antisemitism when he had simply ventilated the 'deep animosity against the Jewish character; felt in all cultivated circles of Berlin society.'"

In 1902 Mehring wrote:

> We have lived through enough examples during the last fifty years and still experience it every day, that Jewish fellow-citizens, whom we have even admired as unshakable flagbearers of bourgeois democracy, become corrupt reactionaries if the result of civil legislation harms any specifically Jewish interest. This phenomenon is as old as the participation of Jewry in political struggles.[18]

Mehring repeatedly insisted that philosemitism was a greater danger in Germany than antisemitism, going so far as to write:

> In considering the brutalities which antisemitism with words rather than deeds commits against the Jews, one should not overlook the brutalities which philosemitism with deeds rather than words is committing against everyone, be he Jew or Turk, Christian or pagan, who opposes capitalism.[19]

Edward Bernstein tried unsuccessfully to have the party reconsider this attitude, pointing out that "philosemitism" was being used in the same way by both socialists and antisemites, equating opposition to persecution of the Jews or defending their civil rights with being procapitalist. Mehring ominously responded that the worst choice the SPD could make would be to support the liberal parties against the antisemites, because the antisemites were objectively anticapitalist while the liberals were not.

The SPD hailed the victories by the populist antisemitic parties in 1893 as a victory for socialism against the dominant capitalist parties. Heinrich Braun, a leader of the Austrian socialists, interpreted the big vote for the antisemites thus:

---

[18] In Mehring's *Aus dem literarischen Nachlass von Karl Marx, Friedrich Engels und Ferdinand Lassalle* (Stuttgart, 1902), 1: 354-55, cited by Wistrich, p.163.

[19] Mehring, "Anti- und Philosemitisches," *Die Neue Zeit* 2 (1890-1891), cited by Wistrich, p. 164.

Its rapid growth is not unlike that of Social Democracy ... there can be no doubt that in antisemitism we are faced with a strong social movement and that together with the attacks upon Jewry a radical anti-capitalist trend of a general kind is more and more openly and consciously seeking to affirm itself.[20]

Wistrich concludes his discussion of Franz Mehring:

[H]e tended to regard German Jewry not as an oppressed group but rather as the embodiment of the worst features of capitalist behavior. From the young Marx to Mehring (and beyond), this anti-Jewish stereotype has continued to haunt the socialist movement like a ghostly specter.

The main difference between traditional antisemitism, which was based in religion — the refusal to accept Jesus as God — and the several modern forms is that these are all secular. They begin with the original Young Hegelian "economic" form of hostility to the Jews. This insisted that Jews as a group were economic exploiters and that this was so intrinsic to Judaism that it could end only when Jews ceased to be Jews. This diverged to the later, still more modern, cutting edge "scientific" theories that commandeered the new Darwinism to claim an inassimilable racial difference between Jews and Aryans. Economic behavior could be changed by dispersing the group that practiced it. Unacceptable inbred racial differences could be expunged only by separation or extermination. Bruno Bauer, the leftist leader of the Young Hegelians who first persuaded Karl Marx that Jews were an anti-social people-class, himself by the 1860s made the transition to the more modern theory, that they were racially incompatible with true Germans. Notably, Marx's sharp criticism of Bruno Bauer in the 1840s did not dissent from Bauer's position on the Jews, his own writings quoted earlier being even more disparaging.

At the Second Congress of the Socialist International in Brussels in 1891 an American Jewish delegate asked for a resolution condemning anti-Jewish pogroms in Russia. This was opposed most strongly by Victor Adler, the central leader of the Austrian Marxists and himself a highly assimilated Jew with a strong admiration for German culture. The conference instead passed a resolution condemning equally "anti- and philosemitic outbursts" as "one of the means by which the capitalist class and reactionary government seek to divert

---

[20] *Archiv fur Soziale Gesetzbegung und Statistik* (1893): 513-14, cited by Wistrich, p. 166.

the Socialist movement and divide the workers."[21] This ambivalence toward populist antisemitism infected such solid Marxists as Wilhelm Liebknecht, who in 1893 wrote, "Yes, the antisemites plough and sow, and we Social Democrats will reap. Their successes are therefore not at all unwelcome to us."

The German-speaking socialists generally ignored the class division within the Jewish mass and simply repeated Marx's formulation that "Jew" was a synonym for capitalists. The premise underlying Wilhelm Liebknecht's comment, Wistrich explains, ran:

> They argued that since the *Judengeist* (Jewish spirit) was identical with the "spirit of capitalism," it followed that a consistent antisemite should ultimately wish to join the only party (the Social Democrats) that was determined in both theory *and* practice to eliminate capitalism as a whole. Using this theory, the Austrian party leadership tried to appeal to an antisemitic mass constituency — presenting themselves as the most rigorous adversaries of "Jewish" (and Gentile) capital.

If even the most radical opponents of antisemitism proclaimed regularly that the Jews (undifferentiated) were the same as capitalist oppressors this validated what the antisemites were saying.

By the eve of World War I in Germany, and especially in Russia, secular Jews who had broken their ties with the Jewish community were welcomed into the socialist movement. This acceptance of assimilated Jews still went hand-in-hand with a strong reluctance to defend Jews as such from public hostility, particularly in the German-speaking lands. Wistrich writes:

> Thus in Austria the Socialists took a more opportunist position than in Imperial Germany, not infrequently exploiting Judeophobic nuances in their attacks on liberalism and even branding their Christian-Social rivals as "agents of Jewish capital." Efforts at Jewish self-defense were stigmatized as an attempt to justify the financial power of the Rothschilds.

The Austrian Marxists even tried to discredit the antisemite leadership by alleging that they were secretly pro-Jewish because of their commercial relations with Jewish businesses. On one hand this amounted to claiming that their opponents were hypocrites, but at the same time conceding there was something shameful about dealing with Jews. A particular target of this self-defeating tactic was Karl Lueger, the violently antisemitic mayor of Vienna elected in 1897. The Vienna *Arbeiterzeitung*, founded by Victor Adler, on

---

[21] Wistrich, p. 213.

March 11, 1910, wrote: "If there is anyone to whom one can apply the word 'Judaized' (*verjudet*) it is to the Viennese mayor." The Austrian Marxists continued to claim that the antisemitic parties and movements were really puppets of the rich Jews until Hitler came to power in 1933. A mirror image of this kind of stupidity are Marxist idiots who repeatedly try to prove that the Jewish Zionists in Germany who negotiated with the German government in the 1930s to get as many Jews out of the country as possible were on that account really agents of the Nazis. Walter Laqueur has dubbed this slander "The Anti-Zionism of Fools."[22]

Otto Bauer (1881-1938), the principal theorist of Austro-Marxism, by the turn of the twentieth century had already seen the rise of strong nationalism among the disdained "historyless" peoples and largely abandoned the concept, with the notable exception of the Jews. Writing in a virulently antisemitic German culture, he faced powerful pressure to have nothing positive to say about Jews. Drawing on this old theory of Marx, that had to be abandoned for virtually every other ethnicity, Bauer branded the Jews alone as unable to constitute a nation. Wistrich quotes from Bauer's 1907 *The National Question and Socialism:*

> Imagine Jewish children being taught in Yiddish in their independent schools! There the children will be taught the culture of a nation without a history, the culture of a people totally isolated from the mainstream of European civilization, a people held together by the heritage of an outmoded system of thought and by the dead weight of observances transmitted from generation to generation.

The massive redrawing of the borders of Europe by World War I largely put an end to the "historyless peoples" theory, with the sole exception of the Jews. A very few prominent socialist leaders objected to this exclusion. Notable among them was Engelbert Pernerstorfer, a close associate of Victor Adler in the Austrian party. In a 1916 article for Martin Buber's journal *Der Jude* he argued that there were twelve or fourteen million Jews with a currently productive literature of their own in Yiddish and Hebrew. "Let us not lose sight of the fact that they are indeed a nation," he wrote, "a nation of outstanding intellectual endowment, like every internally coherent and civilized people. They have a right to exist as a nation." He pointed to rising Polish nationalism which was becoming more consciously hostile to the three million Jews in their midst, and made the simple point that the European Jews did not want to

---

[22] Walter Laqueur, "The Anti-Semitism of Fools," *The New Republic*, November 2, 1987. This excellent essay used to be available on the net but has become very difficult to find.

become Poles or Romanians or Germans, and those peoples did not want them to either. The natural consequence was the emergence of the Zionist movement as the voice of Jews who opted to seek to found a state of their own. It was opposed by the Marxist movements of the major countries, as they themselves wanted uncontested control over the working class. Jewish national aspirations were received sympathetically, however, by the socialists of other oppressed nationalities, mainly the Ukrainians, Croatians, and Slovenians.

The principal early twentieth century Marxist theorist of the Jewish Question was Karl Kautsky. And even when most of his writings had been repudiated by Lenin and the Communists after Kautsky, prophetically, criticized the totalitarianism of the Bolshevik Revolution, his formulations on Jewish nationalism were retained by the Comintern. In essence it was that antisemitism would be ended by having the Jews disappear into the population of the larger nations. No Jews, no antisemitism. It specified further that Zionism was counter-revolutionary because it warned Jews that they could not trust their German and Russian Gentile comrades. The Third Reich, and to a lesser extent the turn to anti-Jewish purges by the Stalin regime in Russia, should have definitively answered the validity of that judgment.

Kautsky, like Otto Bauer in Austria, discarded Marx's theory of the historyless peoples, doomed to national extinction, to be swallowed up by larger and more progressive ethnicities, again excepting the Jews. Even here, it was evident that the projected assimilation was taking place only in Western Europe, in Germany, Austria, and France, however false that assimilation would soon prove to be. There was no comparable process taking place in Russia and Poland. Kautsky propounded the theory that Jews were not a true ethnicity or nationality but a caste, differing from their surrounding populace only by their social-economic role, hypothesizing that it is "among the castes of India that we find phenomena which correspond to the status of the Jewish community as it has been constituted since the destruction of Jerusalem and the advent of Christianity."[23]

This reductionist notion, that Jews share nothing but a now- or soon-to-be outmoded economic role, originated with Marx and was carried forward after Otto Bauer and Kautsky by the Jewish Trotskyist Abram Leon (1918-1944) in his posthumous *The Jewish Question: A Marxist Interpretation*, still considered canonical by most present-day Trotskyist groups. Leon uses the term "people-class" rather than Kautsky's far-fetched Indian caste analogy. There is, of course, some truth to this as one element in Jewish cohesion. Modern sociology uses the term "middleman minority" for ethnic groups that

---

[23] *Die Neue Zeit*, January 18, 1908, cited by Wistrich, p. 304.

occupy a distinct economic role in another ethnicity's country. Examples include Overseas Chinese in Southeast Asia and Indians in South Africa. But no one except these Marxist doctrinaires would argue that such Chinese or Indians have no attachment to others of their ethnicity in other countries, some preservation of their heritage languages, and strong cultural links to the long history of their peoples. To deny these factors to Jews, coming from theorists immersed in dominant states with strong and growing anti-Jewish prejudice, speaks for itself.

Viewed through this Marxist prism, Jews were and are divided into two groups: those who embrace revolutionary Marxism and reject all elements of Jewish identity, who are rated progressive, and those who do not do so, who are ranked among the reactionaries. As Kautsky put it in 1914:

"We have not completely emerged from the Middle Ages as long as Judaism still exists among us. The sooner it disappears, the better it will be for society as well as for the Jews themselves."[24] This unconscionable prejudice was the gold standard of the Marxist movement long before there was a state of Israel to hang it on. And think about what Kautsky is saying here about the Jews of his own country, that the only acceptable and progressive thing for them to do is — to become Germans! After Hitler came to power many of Kautsky's Marxist comrades switched sides and helped to murder their fellow socialist Jews who had followed Kautsky's advice. It did not help that Kautsky, and the socialists and leftists who have followed in his footsteps, from Lenin to much of today's anti-imperialist and antiglobalist Left, did not and do not regard themselves as antisemites. They are perfectly ready to accept without qualm Jews who have repudiated Jewish ethnic identity, or in today's parlance, who are anti-Zionist.

What can be said is that the expectation of the nineteenth and early twentieth century Marxists, that an imminent world socialist revolution would quickly lead to the collapse of nationalism and with it of ethnic prejudice, simply did not happen. Nationalism is stronger than ever, and, objectively, Jewish nationalism is just one more, not something special that must be done away with.

Interestingly, Rosa Luxemburg, herself a highly assimilated Jew, despite her defense of democratic rights against the repression exercised by Lenin's government, was the most extreme of the Marxist leaders of her generation in rejecting not only nationalism but the consequent right of self-determination. Not only the Jews were not entitled to a state of their own but neither were the Poles, Ukrainians, Lithuanians, Czechs, and Yugoslavs. In 1916 she casti-

---

[24] *Die Neue Zeit*, October 30, 1914. Cited by Wistrich.

gated "the rotting corpses" trying to "climb out of century-old graves" trying to form new nations.[25]

A further Marxist argument against Jewish nationalism was that the Zionist prospect for Palestine allowed for the Jewish state to include capitalists. That may have seemed decisive to the early Communist movement, but in today's world only two states are not ruled by capitalists: Cuba and North Korea. And North Korea is by fairly general agreement ranked as the most repressive government on the planet. Of all those capitalist states, only the Jewish one faces calls for its destruction from the Left because of its capitalist leadership. It was much later that European Marxists thought to champion Arab nationalism against Jewish nationalism.

Socialism in Russia

In Russia, Mikhail Bakunin (1814-1876), the father of the anarchist movement, was a bitter enemy of the Jews. He and his followers joined the First International in 1868, where they contested with the Marxists for a more decentralized form of socialism. His supporters had a powerful influence in Russia in the Narodnik movement and in the Spanish workers' movement through the end of the Spanish Civil War in the 1930s. He called the Jews "an exploiting sect, a blood sucking people, a unique devouring parasite, tightly and intimately organized . . . cutting across all the differences in political opinion. . . . "[26] His followers among the Narodnaya Volya (People's Will) in 1881 publicly appealed for a pogrom against "the Tsar, the nobles and the Jews," contributing to a tradition that echoes on the Left to our own day as consigning the alien Jew to the camp of the oppressors and presenting a struggle to destroy them as serving human emancipation and progress. The continuity here with medieval Jew hatred sponsored by the Church, Orthodox as well as Catholic, hardly needs to be elaborated. The executive committee of Narodnaya Volya on August 30, 1881, issued a proclamation:

> The damned police beat you, the landowners devour you, the kikes, the dirty Judases, rob you. People in the Ukraine suffer most of all from the kikes. . . . Wherever you look, whatever you touch, everywhere the kikes. The kike curses the peasant, cheats him, drinks his blood.[27]

---

[25] Cited by Wistrich, p. 363, from the German edition of her collected works.
[26] Cited by George Lichtheim, "Socialism and the Jews," in his *Collected Essays* (New York: The Viking Press, 1974), p. 427.
[27] Wistrich, p. 188.

The Russian Marxists from the last days of the nineteenth century recruited large numbers of disaffected secular Jews, but at the same time strongly opposed any national rights for the five million Jews in Tsarist Russia. This view was shared in common by Bolsheviks and Mensheviks and endorsed by Kautsky in Germany. They denied that Jews were what we would call today an ethnicity but were only a caste, easily dispersed into society if the peculiar conditions of Tsarist and Polish persecution were removed. In his "Critical Remarks on the National Question" written in October-December 1913, Lenin wrote:

> Whoever, directly or indirectly, puts forward the slogan of Jewish "national culture" is (whatever his good intentions may be) an enemy of the proletariat, a supporter of all that is *outmoded* and connected with *caste* among the Jewish people; he is an accomplice of the rabbis and the bourgeoisie.[28]

To be clear, Lenin had no objection to Jews contributing to any country's culture. His categorical objection here rests on his denial that Jews, especially those of Russia and Poland, constituted a national minority, even in the Austrian sense, where dispersed ethnic groups without a defined territory were granted rights as national minorities.

Trotsky agreed with this position at the time, but by the 1930s, when National Socialism had been firmly established in Germany, changed his mind. I will return to that later.

Once in power, the Bolsheviks soon had to confront the fact that they had inherited millions of Jews in the Pale of Settlement. Established by Catherine the Great in 1791, it comprised parts of Western Russia, Ukraine, and Poland (under Russian rule until the end of World War I). Jews were only allowed permanent residence in the Pale, and prohibited even there from living in large cities or in agricultural areas. The Pale was dissolved only by the Kerensky government in April 1917. The Bolsheviks in power changed their position, officially recognizing a Jewish nationality along with all the other ethnicities in the proverbial Tsarist prison house of nations. There was a flowering of Communist Party controlled and censored Jewish newspapers and theatres. Under conditions of one-party rule and total party control of the press, this was a culture heavily bent toward endorsing Communist orthodoxy. But it was not antisemitic. The Bolsheviks in power tried hard to suppress anti-Jewish activity by other parts of the population.

The Congress of the People of the East held in Baku in September 1920, in the aftermath of the failed revolutions in Germany and Hungary at the end

---

[28] Lenin, *Collected Works*, 1972, vol. 20.

of the war, marked the beginning of the Communist strategy of falling back on the colonial and undeveloped world as a force that could to some degree compensate for Communist weakness in the proletariat of the advanced countries. At the congress Zinoviev called for jihad by Middle Eastern Muslims against the European powers. Not until 1979 with the Islamic Revolution in Iran would it become clear that Islamic radicals have their own goals and agenda, based on extremely conservative and religious values that reject virtually all of the goals of progressive Western leftists, Communists included.

By the late 1920s much of the Soviet Jewish cultural activity was curtailed. In March 1928 the government adopted a decree to establish a territory for Soviet Jews. But instead of in the historic Jewish lands of western Russia, the new Jewish Autonomous Oblast was to be placed in the remotest part of Siberia near the Korean border. Known as Birobidzhan from its principal town, this place of exile, a frozen waste in the winter and a mosquito infested swamp in the summers, never had more than 30,000 Jews living there. In the 2010 census there were 1,628 ethnic Jews, 1% of the population.

During World War II, in seeking Western support against Hitler, the Soviet government took another turn, now endorsing Zionism and the effort to establish a Jewish state in Palestine. At home it established the Jewish Anti-fascist Committee, headed by the prominent Jewish actor and theatre director Solomon Mikhoels. The Stalin regime supported the establishment of Israel in 1948, while becoming increasingly distrustful of Russian Jews at home, who, Stalin feared, might out of sympathy for Israel dissent from other Soviet policies.

Internationally, the USSR had no allies in the Middle East. The central leader of the Palestinians, the Grand Mufti of Jerusalem, Haj Amin al-Husseini, had spent World War II in Berlin broadcasting Nazi propaganda to his people. At the war's end Egypt became, along with Latin America, one of the main destinations for Nazi war criminals fleeing prosecution. Additionally, one of the USSR's aims was to force Britain and France out of the Mandates they had held since the Versailles Conference. Support to the Israeli Jews in their guerilla war against the British fit well with this option. Later, with the rise of Arab nationalism, better options appeared to which the Middle Eastern Jews were happily sacrificed.

In January 1948 Stalin had Mikhoels murdered. That November he shut down the JAC. On August 12, 1952, five Yiddish writers and ten others associated with the JAC were secretly executed in the basement of Moscow's Lubyanka Prison.[29] This opened an era in the USSR and its then-East Euro-

---

[29] Joshua Rubenstein, "The Night of the Murdered Poets," *The New Republic*, August 25, 1997.

pean satellites of public and virulent antisemitism. Jews, most of whom were loyal Stalinists, were purged from the professions and the sciences. Many Jewish writers were killed, and Holocaust denial became common despite the Great Patriotic War against Hitler. In November 1952 the leadership of the Czechoslovak Communist Party was purged on orders from Moscow. Rudolph Slánský, the party's head, and thirteen others, eleven of them Jews, were put on trial on trumped up charges that they were Zionists and Trotskyist spies. In January 1953 six prominent Russian Jewish doctors were arrested and accused of being part of a wide-ranging Jewish conspiracy to assassinate Soviet leaders. The purge was called short only by Stalin's death. In Poland after the 1967 Israel-Arab war, the Communist Party purged virtually the entirety of its remaining Jewish membership. All Jews in Poland were declared Zionists and prohibited from teaching in public schools or universities. Many had their Polish citizenship revoked. There were by that time, of the millions before the Holocaust, only 40,000 Jews left in Poland. Between 1968 and 1971, 14,000 of these fled the country or were expelled. The official campaign was supported by the Soviet Union.

Under Khrushchev, the USSR became a major military supplier of Nasser's Egypt and routinely denounced Israel as a "puppet" of the United States. A pattern emerged here that has been widespread in the self-proclaimed antiimperialist Left after the fall of the Soviet Union. This was to support Third World dictators who had made some show of opposition to Europe or the United States, while at the same time withholding support or even information about the dictators' repressions of democratic movements or even Communist parties. Domestically Khrushchev had any kind of Jewish protest denounced as Zionist. Notable was the 1963 publication of *Judaism Unembellished* by Trofim Kichko, endorsed by the Ukrainian Academy of Sciences. This rehash of traditional anti-Jewish canards was so extreme that even foreign Communist parties demanded it be withdrawn. The protesters included Gus Hall, head of the near-moribund American CP. The March 22, 1964, issue of the CP's then-daily Yiddish language *Morgen Freiheit* quoted Hall as saying:

> I have not read or seen the pamphlet. I have seen only reproductions of portions of it in papers and magazines. Nor do I have any way of knowing whether the copies circulating in this country are forgeries or not. There is no doubt in my mind, however, about the anti-Semitic character of what I have seen. Such stereotyped, slanderous caricatures of the Jewish people must be unequivocally condemned, whatever their source.[30]

---

[30] http://antimatrix.org/Convert/Books/Jews_in_Eastern_Europe/Jews_in_Eastern_Europe.htm

At the time of the Six Day War in 1967 the Soviet press trumpeted the line that the Israeli Jews were the same as the Nazis. Brezhnev himself while the war was still in progress in a speech to military graduates said:

"The Israeli aggressors are the worst of bandits. In their arrogance against the Arab Population, it seems they want to copy the crimes of the Hitler invaders."[31]

From 1967 it became obligatory in the Soviet press to refer to the Israelis as fascists and Nazis. One only has to look at an Israeli election and the difficulty of forming a government afterwards among its many quarreling parties to see how ludicrous is the charge that this is a fascist state. The Soviet authorities, like Hamas today, soon began to claim as rightful precedent for their animosity for Israel the whole history of European persecution of the Jews. In 1975 in response to a Central Committee directive, large state editions were issued of *The Creeping Counterrevolution*, published the year before in Minsk by Vladimir Begun. This described the Torah as "an unsurpassed textbook of blood-thirstiness, hypocrisy, treason, perfidy and moral degeneracy — all the lowest human qualities." The Jewish religion as such, it said, calls for the enslavement of non-Jews and it is these teachings that have historically "brought calamity on the adherents of Judaism." Finally, "Zionist gangsterism," Begun wrote, was a loyal reflection of the Torah, and the synagogue everywhere "remains a potential basis for subversive activity."[32]

Wistrich comments on this period and its wide influence in the Western Left: "Twenty years after the collapse of Soviet Communism, this antisemitic trope still lives on, mutating into the lowest common denominator of contemporary left-wing hostility towards Israel and the Jews."

Articles in major Soviet periodicals appeared with titles such as "Zionist Heirs of the Gestapo."[33] And fantasies of Jewish world domination little different from the 1903 Tsarist forgery, *The Protocols of the Elders of Zion* (still a best seller in the Muslim world), became common in the land of Communism. Lev Korneyev in the official organ of the Komsomol youth organization claimed that Zionism rested on vast wealth

being pumped out from the gold, diamond and uranium mines of South Africa, the workshops and industrial plants of Europe, America and Australia. Zionists are trying to infiltrate into all the spheres of public life, into ideology, science, commerce. Even "Levi's" jeans are part of their operation; the profits from selling the pants are used to help the Zionists. Most of the major monopolies producing arms are controlled by Jewish

---

[31] *Pravda*, July 7, 1967, cited by Wistrich.
[32] Quotations are cited in *Israel Yearbook on Human Rights*, vol 17 (1987), p. 138.
[33] *Za Rubezhom*, October 3, 1973. Cited by Wistrich.

bankers. The business built on blood grants them huge profits. . . . Piles of dollars multiply in the safes of the Lehmans and Guggenheims while bandits in Afghanistan poison schoolchildren with gasses. It is understandable that peace in the world is the main enemy for Zionism.[34]

At the Soviet Writers' Congress in December 1990, Wistrich recounts,

> one could find a large number of copies of Hitler's *Mein Kampf*, and the *Protocols*, and various antisemitic speakers publicly appealed to the Army and the Communists to save what was left of a disintegrating Soviet Union that was sinking into oblivion under the sheer weight of a new "Jewish-Zionist yoke." (p. 442)

He was in Moscow that year and says he saw a great deal of this kind of thing.

The Communist Party of Russia after the collapse of the Soviet Union has become an openly antisemitic organization, using "Jew" and "Zionist" interchangeably. An Agence France Presse dispatch of December 23, 1998, reported:

> Russian Communist party leader Gennady Zyuganov lashed out Wednesday at Russian Jews, accusing them of benefiting from privatization and controlling the audiovisual media. . . . In an open letter to the head of the presidential staff, Zyuganov attacked the "aggressive and destructive role of Zionist capital in the collapse of the Russian economy and the looting of the people's goods."
>
> He said the Russian people were asking "a legitimate question: how the key positions in certain economic areas were essentially given to the people of a single nationality."

Zyuganov is further quoted as saying "Our people are not blind, they cannot but notice that the Zionisation of power in Russia has been one of the causes of its current catastrophic condition, its massive impoverishment and the extinction of its people." Agence France Press added:

> His comments follow earlier virulently anti-Semitic remarks by party deputies Viktor Ilyukhin and General Albert Makashov. Ilyukhin drew fire last week when he said: "There are too many Jews in President Boris Yeltsin's entourage," calling for quotas of national groups – including Jews – in government offices. In October, Makashov had issued a similar call for such quotas, saying there were "at least a dozen kikes, shylocks and bloodsuckers" he would like to "ship off to another world."[35]

---

[34] *Pionerskaia Pravda*, October 10, 1980, cited by Wistrich, pp. 437-38.
[35] http://www.paulbogdanor.com/antisemitism/zyuganov.html.

Zyuganov finished second in the 1996 Russian presidential elections. In 2005 the American Communist Party strongly disavowed the Communist Party of the Russian Federation for its antisemitism, writing in its West Coast newspaper *The People's World*:

> In January 2005, some 500 prominent Russians calling themselves "Orthodox Christian patriots" signed a letter calling on the Russian prosecutor general to launch proceedings to ban all religious and ethnic Jewish organizations as "extremist." Among the signatories to the letter were six members of the Russian parliament from the Communist Party of the Russian Federation.[36]

In 2006 thugs from the Russian CP attacked a gay pride demonstration in Moscow.

Socialism in France

The socialist movement, and its close cousin, anarcho-syndicalism, which rejected political action in preference for trade unions and the general strike, began in France and Germany. The Enlightenment was supposed to have replaced religious intolerance with Reason, but the old attitude toward Jews persisted. A leftist tradition of antisemitism was fueled by Voltaire, the paragon of the French philosophes of the eighteenth century, who declared the Jews "an ignorant and barbarous people who have long united the most sordid avarice with the most detestable superstition," and that Jews were motivated "by the most invincible hatred for every people by whom they are tolerated and enriched."

Charles Fourier (1772-1837), with Henri de Saint Simon one of the two most prominent initiators of the socialist tradition in France, inspired socialist experiments in both his native France and in the United States, where the best known were Utopia, Ohio, and Brook Farm in Massachusetts. He was a bitter opponent of emancipating the Jews, declaring it "doubly impolitic in that it opens the door to parasites and unproductive people, all of whom are devoted to trade and not to agriculture. An enlightened policy would have excluded these people as a social contagion." He proposed that the Jews be bound to the land as agricultural workers and only one family in fifty be permitted to enter commerce.[37]

---

[36] "CPUSA condemns anti-Semitism," *The People's World*, March 18, 2005. From the online edition: http://transitional.pww.org/cpusa-condemns-anti-semitism/.
[37] Nicholas Valentine Riasanovsky, *The Teaching of Charles Fourier* (Berkeley: University of California Press, 1969), p. 167.

Pierre-Joseph Proudhon (1809-1865) is more central to the European socialist tradition. He was the most influential thinker of French leftism and the
labor movement of his day. Son of a brewer and barrel maker, Proudhon had
no formal education. He was a self-taught worker in the printing trades who
eventually owned several small unsuccessful print shops before turning to
journalism after the revolution of 1848. Declaring himself both an anarchist
and a socialist, he was the effective father of the French socialist movement.
He championed local workers' control in opposition to both capitalism and the
state control advocated by the Marxists. But he shared with the whole of the
far left a hostility to political democracy. Marx both admired Proudhon and
disputed his economic theories, writing *The Poverty of Philosophy* as a critique of Proudhon's *The Philosophy of Poverty*. On the Jews, Proudhon in
December 1847 in his diaries wrote:

> Jews — Write an article against this race which poisons everything,
> by meddling everywhere without ever joining itself to another people —
> Demand their expulsion from France, with the exception of individuals
> married to Frenchwomen — Abolish the synagogues; don't admit them
> to any kind of employment; pursue finally the abolition of this cult.
>
> It is not for nothing that the Christians call them deicides. The Jew is
> the enemy of the human race. One must send this race back to Asia or
> exterminate it. . . . By fire or fusion, or by expulsion, the Jew must dis-
> appear.[38]

These views propagated through the French socialist movement for generations. Proudhon's antisemitism was championed by central leaders who were
his disciples, notably Alphonse Toussenel (1803-1885) and Pierre Leroux
(1797-1871). A signal account of this history can be found in George Lichtheim's "Socialism and the Jews" in the December 1968 *Dissent* and included
in his *Collected Essays*.

Toussenel, Lichtheim writes, "became the pioneer of a literature which
linked the medieval image of the Jew as usurer to the populism of a society
suddenly plunged into the maelstrom of early capitalism." In his pamphlet *Les
Juifs rois de l'epoque* (The Jews, Kings of the Epoch, 1845 and 1847) Toussenel declared, "Europe is entailed to the domination of Israel. This universal
domination, of which so many conquerors have dreamed, the Jews have in
their hands."

Leroux was more complex. A lifelong socialist, he died during the Paris
Commune and was buried by the Communards with high honors. A devout
Christian, he studied Hebrew and admired the Jews of the Old Testament, but

---

[38] Wistrich, pp. 186-87, quoted from *Notebooks of P. J. Proudhon*.

promoted the opinion that contemporary Jews had become possessed of "a spirit of greed and cupidity" and that as a group they lived by the exploitation of others.

In 1869 Proudhon's pupil George Duchene was to write of the Russian pogroms:

> Citizens when you hear it said that in a notoriously barbarous country the population treats the Jews roughly, do not believe one treacherous word. What you have is simply a case of honest people chasing rascals, usurers, exploiters of labor; religion has nothing to do with this act of high justice.[39]

Louis Auguste Blanqui (1805-1881) became famous for the theory — and practice — of the revolutionary putsch. He took part in the July revolution of 1830, was imprisoned, released just in time to take part in the revolution of 1848. Imprisoned again, he sent a letter from prison to London social democrats that was published with an introduction by Karl Marx. While in prison again he was elected, in absentia, president of the Paris Commune of 1871. He spent half of his long life in prison. Despite these inspiring credentials, Blanqui and his followers were the ones to introduce the new racial antisemitism into the French labor movement. Blanqui's chief lieutenant, Gutave Tridon, in his *Du Molochisme juif* (On Jewish Molochisme), written in 1868 but published only posthumously, in 1884, branded the Jews the "evil genius of the world" and, in Wistrich's summary, accused them of "cannibalism, ritual murder, and human sacrifice."[40] He called on the "Indo-Aryan race" to do battle with the Semites. The Blanquists strongly opposed support to Dreyfus during his long fight for justice, which lasted from 1894 into the early years of the twentieth century.

The first Marxist party in France was the Parti Ouvrier Français (French Workers' Party), formed in 1880 by Jules Guesde and Paul Lafargue. Socialist groups to both its right and left held openly antisemitic views. On the left there were the putchist Blanquists, on the right the moderate socialist Benoit Malon with his *Revue Socialiste*. Malon was a good friend of Edouard Drumont, a leftist who soon became the country's most militant Jew hater. Drumont published his scurrilous pamphlet denouncing the Jews, *La France juive,* in 1886. Lichtheim writes:

"Thus when Malon introduced Drumont to Parisian workingmen, he followed a consistent line, just as he did in throwing his *Revue socialiste* open to

---

[39] Cited by Lichtheim, *Collected Essays*, p. 426.
[40] Wistrich, p. 197. He gives as source Tridon's *Du Molochisme juif* (Paris, 1884), p. 5.

the notorious anti-Semite Auguste Chirac." It is wrong to assume that this can be excused as just the general prejudices of the day. Open antisemitism was strong on both the Left and the conservative Right, but, as Lichtheim says, "Respectable bourgeois liberalism . . . had always been immune to the noisier and more vulgar forms of anti-Semitism."[41]

The French socialist Left was generally indifferent to or tolerant of antisemitism. It was compelled to take a position by the Dreyfus Affair, which broke out in 1894 and was not concluded until 1906. Captain Alfred Dreyfus, a Jewish artillery officer, was convicted of treason for allegedly handing French military secrets to the Germans. He was sentenced to life in prison on Devil's Island. In 1898 new evidence showed that Dreyfus had been falsely accused and this then covered up by the military high command through a series of palpably forged documents intended to incriminate him. The main Marxist wing of the French Workers Party, led by Jules Guesde, took the position that the antisemitism in the case existed but was irrelevant and that the workers' movement had no interest in Dreyfus. A strong majority of the party took this view, some of their parliamentary delegation even supporting Dreyfus' conviction. The minority was led by Jean Jaurès, who campaigned with the Dreyfusards, those who declared Dreyfus innocent and demanded justice. The proletarians in the party mostly sided with Guesde, while, as Lichtheim writes, "Jaurès acquired a larger following among schoolteachers and students than among manual workers."

Even those socialists (and anarchists, who were still a sizable current in late nineteenth century France) who campaigned for Dreyfus's release carefully skirted the issue of his Jewishness. Lichtheim explains their consideration:

> So far as the Jews belonged to any stratum of French society, it was primarily the middle or lower-middle class. To that extent the Jewish problem was of no particular concern to the labor movement. The way out of the dilemma was that adopted by the Anarchists in 1898-1900, when (after some soul-searching) they sided with the Dreyfusards in the name of liberty, while refusing to pay special attention to the Jewish issue.[42]

That is, even the best of the French socialists could only bring themselves to join with Dreyfus's defenders on the grounds of abstract justice, and shrank from taking the unpopular step of insisting that Jews should not be persecuted because they are Jews.

---

[41] Lichtheim, *Collected Essays*, pp. 429-30.
[42] Ibid, p. 433.

Wistrich devotes an entire chapter to the French Jewish anarchist Bernard Lazare (1865-1903). As a strongly assimilationist Jew, in his youth Lazare wrote harsh articles distinguishing the Jews who had long resided in France and absorbed its culture, who he called Israelites, from the more recent Jewish immigrants from Poland and Russia, declaring:

> Russian usurers, Galician tavern-keepers and money-lenders, second-hand peddlers from Prague, Polish horse-dealers, money-merchants from Frankfurt, what do they mean to me, a French Israelite? In the name of what supposed fraternity should I care about measures taken by the Tsar against subjects who appear to him as harmful?

He was even friends with Edouard Drumont, the self-proclaimed leftist whose populist, left-seeming antisemitism was later perfected by Hitler.

Lazare was changed profoundly by the Dreyfus Affair. He became an early and prominent defender of the prisoner on Devil's Island. He concluded that the leftist demand for total assimilation and the dissolution of ties between Jews as a group simply reaffirmed the prejudices of the antisemites. Jews couldn't be any good if even the far Left wanted them to disappear. Further, assimilation disarmed the Jews, as the antisemites didn't care if the Jew they hated was religious or not, part of a Jewish community or an isolated secular individual. If, because he was assimilated and had no community ties, all the easier to strike him down.

In contrast to the socialists, of whom at least a significant minority defended Dreyfus, the anarcho-syndicalists, for whom Georges Sorel (1847-1922) was the principal ideologist, strongly opposed his acquittal, and explicitly *because* he was a Jew. After it was over, they called a mass meeting in Paris in April 1911 advertised as "a great anti-Jewish and anti-Masonic demonstration." Sorel, an iconic advocate of political violence, late in life was an outspoken admirer of both Lenin and Mussolini. His followers were a crossover current between trade union leftism and fascism. Wistrich writes of him:

> Between 1908 and 1914 he was one of the driving forces of the Cercle Proudhon which attacked democracy as a "Jewish" invention that had substituted "the laws of gold for the laws of blood." Like the integral nationalists and monarchists of Action Français, the anarcho-syndicalist Sorel blamed Jews for the decomposition of traditional European culture, linking them to the nefarious impact of liberalism, capitalism, and rationalism.

It would be a mistake to think that the stereotypical Jew-hating views that proliferated in the Soviet Union and its satellite countries of Eastern Europe from the end of World War II were confined to the declining Soviet Empire. The French Communist Party, a loyal channel for Moscow propaganda, emerged from the war with 500,000 members. By 1959 it became the largest party in the country, with 26.2% of the vote and 159 seats in the National Assembly. Even in decline it remained in many ways dominant in the French Left, and still won 15% of the vote in the 1981 presidential elections. Hatred of Israel and uncritical endorsement of the Arab cause was and is virtually obligatory for any French progressive. In 2009 the French CP at an event where they were distributing face masks to protect against swine flu had the masks stamped "State of Israel.Criminal State"; 600,000 people attended the event.[43]

And on September 16, 2012, the director of the French CP's newspaper *L'Humanité*, Patrick Le Hyaric, in his closing speech to Fête de l'Huma, described the crude anti-Islam film ridiculing Muhammad, against which Muslim demonstrations had already cost many lives, as "produced by an Israeli fundamentalist." In fact it was produced by an Egyptian Coptic Christian. Bernard-Henri Lévy in the Huffington Post asks of Hyaric,

> isn't he also participating in the stigmatization that allows angry demonstrators to come to shout "death to the Jews" in front of an embassy in Paris? Fighting the new antisemitism entails demanding an apology from Le Hyaric, the deputy, and beyond him, from the French Communist Party.[44]

Lévy makes it clear that this is not just a matter of words, as mounting physical attacks on French Jews, mainly by Muslim immigrants, have turned "synagogues, kosher grocery stores, Jewish schools . . . not only in Paris but throughout Europe" into "entrenched camps."

The Contemporary Left

I am dating the contemporary Left from the 1960s with the emergence of the New Left and of the various Maoist sects and a revival of Trotskyist groups that coalesced in that period, as well as fairly broad currents in Europe and the United States influenced by these tendencies, often without attribution. The most extreme of these various currents share what Wistrich calls Holocaust inversion, that is, referring to Israelis as Nazis, circulating cartoons

---

[43] Reported in *European Jewish Press*, September 15, 2009. Online: http://www.ejpress.org/article/38977

[44] http://www.huffingtonpost.com/bernardhenri-levy/confronting-the-black-tide_b_1971165.html

in which swastikas have been painted on Israeli flags or political figures, and a preference for Hamas and Hezbollah, which fight for the eradication of Israel, in preference to the now more conciliatory Palestine Liberation Organization, which supports a two-state solution.

In the 1967 war it was the Arab side that threatened genocide, the Jews who fought a defensive war against multiple states whose stated aim was their destruction. Most analogies with Nazis are false, but this one is particularly vicious. For anyone who knows anything about the Nazis, even from watching old movies, they are distinguished from other repressive regimes above all other things by the Holocaust, the state organized murder of six million Jews. Any comparison to them implies that the target is guilty of committing or preparing to commit mass murder on a genocidal scale.

Even before the Holocaust, Nazi treatment of the German Jews went far beyond anything Israel has done to the Palestinians, even in Gaza. There were the Nuremburg Laws of 1935, which made it a crime for a Jew to marry a Gentile, which specified prison for a Jew having sex with a Gentile ("defilement of blood"). This was later changed to the death penalty. Jews were barred from employment as lawyers, doctors, or journalists, and prohibited from using state hospitals or entering a public park, library, or beach. It was illegal for Jews to be educated in a state school past the age of fourteen. Then there was Kristallnacht in November 1938 in which Jewish stores where smashed and 30,000 Jews were arrested and deported to concentration camps. From 1939 all Jews were required to wear the yellow star.

In the real world today, Jews, beyond a miniscule token number, are prohibited from living in any Arab Muslim state. That is not Nazism, but this *Judenrein* policy is closer to it in its racialist spirit than the legal system and practice of the Israeli Jews. And the attitude of the Arab states toward Jews has historically been shared to an even greater degree by the Palestinian groups. In Israel, 20 percent of the population, close to two millions, are Palestinians. There is some discrimination against them, but nothing to the degree of the treatment of Jews in the Arab countries, much less the treatment of the Jews by the Nazis in the 1930s, before the Holocaust. The Israeli Palestinians have their own newspapers, political parties, businesses, and elected members of the Knesset, the parliament. Even the Palestinians of the occupied territories, that were the outcome of the Arab attempt to destroy Israel in 1967, have their own businesses, schools and universities, mass media, choose their occupations freely, and have mutually consensual sex with whom they wish including with Jews.

As long as Yasser Arafat lived, which was until November 2004, thirty-seven years into the Israeli occupation of the West Bank and Gaza, the official goal of the PLO, in Arabic if not always in English, was to destroy Israel and expel the Jews. Even the most liberal of the Jewish politicians in Israel, who were prepared to trade land for peace, had as a minimum that placing the West Bank and Gaza, for the first time in history, under Palestinian control, had to be in exchange for an agreement to leave the Jewish territory alone, not for this to be the first step in yet another Arab attempt at conquest.

Destruction of Israel and expulsion of virtually all the Jews remains the stated goal of Hamas in Gaza and of several of the lesser Palestinian organizations, such as Islamic Jihad, joined by Hezbollah on Israel's northern border, and Iran, as well as a great many authoritative political and religious figures even in the two Arab states that have peace treaties with Israel — Egypt and Jordan — not to mention Saudi Arabia, Syria, and elsewhere in the Muslim world.

Polls show that majorities of both Israelis and Palestinians support a peaceful settlement in the creation of two separate states. A Gallup poll published on March 21, 2013, found that 52% of Jewish Israelis, 70% of West Bank Palestinians, and 48% of Gaza Palestinians favored "a situation in which an independent Palestinian State existed alongside an independent state of Israel." Among non-Jewish Israelis, the two million Israeli Palestinians inside the 1967 borders, support ran to 85%.[45]

Why, then, doesn't it happen? While the status quo continues, the Palestinians have by far the worst of it, with checkpoints and restrictions in the West Bank and the far more severe embargo in Gaza. The two sides have come very close several times, starting with the Oslo Accords back in 1993. Once or twice the differences were almost as small as territory the size of a football field. On the Israeli side there is a right-wing minority, overly represented in the government, that still aspires to have Israel retain all or most of the West Bank. In part this is for religious reasons, looking back to biblical Israel, but also because 1967 Israel was only ten miles wide at its narrowest point, easily split in half by a concerted military drive from the West Bank.

On the Palestinian side the Fatah leadership even in the days of Oslo cherished the hope that if it waited long enough its allies in the Arab states would become strong enough to make one more assault and win for the Palestinians the whole of the land, from the river to the sea as they liked to put it.

Today the most promising sign has been the moderation of Fatah, its renunciation of armed struggle and its commitment to the two-state perspective. The problem on the Palestinian side is the split with Hamas. In the 2006 Palestinian municipal elections, an extreme rarity in Palestinian political life,

---

[45] http://www.gallup.com/poll/161456/israelis-palestinians-pro-peace-process-not-hopeful.aspx.

Hamas won 76 seats to Fatah's 43. Hamas in its election manifesto offered Israel a ten-year truce, a *hudna* in Islamic parlance, after which it pledged to resume the armed struggle to destroy it. When in June 2007 Hamas seized control of Gaza the unity government with Fatah collapsed. The joint parliament has not met since, and Mahmoud Abbas's term as Palestinian Authority president has long since expired. Hamas resumed its rocket and mortar shelling of Israel shortly after it took power in Gaza, rendering void the election pledges it had made. This makes it completely unclear what the future leadership of the Palestinians will look like.

Plainly the occupation is intolerable. The problem with Gaza from the Israeli perspective is equally so. If an end to the embargo would result in peace with Hamas, far more Israelis would support it than do now. Even under the embargo, Hamas and the still more radical Islamic groups to its right, used Gaza as a base for a steady rain of missiles — more than 3,000 had been fired by the time Israel invaded Gaza in 2009. Hamas remains pledged to armed struggle against Israel as a whole and would presumably use a lifting of the embargo to stockpile even more destructive weapons into the impoverished enclave. Then all of Israel's options would be bad ones.

A similar situation existed in Sri Lanka, where a twenty-five-year civil war was fought between the majority Sinhalese Buddhists and the minority ethnic Tamil Hindus, who were demanding independence. Like the Jewish-Palestinian dispute, religion inflamed the conflict and made it irresolvable except by the total crushing of the weaker combatant. Like the Palestinians, the Tamil Tigers used suicide bombers, and more than 100,000 people were killed in the course of the civil war, which reached its conclusion in the spring of 2009, just a few months after Israel's invasion of Gaza.

The Sinhalese dared to do what the Israelis did not. The Tigers in January 2009 were pushed back into a small area on the northeast coast around the town of Mullaittivu. They took with them some 300,000 of their followers. The government called on the Tamil civilians to leave and go to designated "no fire" zones. Once they had separated the civilians from the Tamil combatants they shelled the civilian camps mercilessly, while barring journalists from the area, denying humanitarian aid, and even shelling hospitals. The UN estimated that 40,000 civilians were killed in the shelling. Then the Sinhalese army sent in 100,000 soldiers to kill all the combatants.[46] That put an end to the ceaseless military strikes by the Tamils.

I give this example not to show that there are governments that commit worse atrocities than the Israelis, but to show that in a conflict between rival

---

[46] *Washington Post*, April 21, 2011. http://articles.washingtonpost.com/2011-04-21/world/35262099_1_ethnic-tamil-civilians-tamil-tigers-vanni-region.

ethnicities in which the weaker combatant insists that it will fight to the death, even so famously pacifistic a people as the Buddhists finally end the combat on the terms set by their opponent.

Israel held back, far back, from this kind of action when it invaded Gaza in 2009 to end the missile strikes. Hamas's demands are infinitely more far reaching than the Tamils, who did not demand the whole of the island of Sri Lanka and the expulsion of the Sinhalese.

The world was briefly shocked at the inhuman brutality of the Sinhalese. Left groups, if they noticed it at all, devoted to it an article or two, then went back to their unrelenting condemnation of every action taken by the Israelis against Palestinian militants, while presenting as heroic resistance armed actions by what Palestinians continue to undertake them. Awful as the Gaza embargo is, Israel is trying to escape being faced with the options that faced the Sinhalese. Enabling the free importation of heavier armament into Gaza is likely to set the stage for a much bloodier confrontation than the one that took place in 2009. The best hope here, which would then shift the responsibility for the blockade clearly to the Israeli side, would be if Hamas would renounce its goal of establishing a Muslim state in what is now Israel.

Abbas is a very old man plainly near the end of his service as PA president. He lacks the credibility to negotiate a definitive peace with Israel, which unfortunately encourages Netanyahu's right-wing government to make no effort to try, while continuing to construct settlements in the West Bank that can only be an obstacle to peace efforts in the future.

I deplore the Israeli occupation and strongly support the creation of a Palestinian state and the removal of the settler enclaves (except for the few very close to Israel that the PA has already agreed to permit in exchange for land swaps elsewhere). But the failure to reach an agreement, as was the case in Sri Lanka, has many causes and both sides bear responsibility. While Fatah is a secular organization and can treat the conflict as one over land, for the religious Islamists of Hamas and their cothinkers in Hezbollah, in Iran, among the Wahabi fundamentalists of Saudi Arabia, and the Muslim Brotherhood throughout the region, it is a theological dispute in which loyalty to Allah does not allow for compromise.

Wistrich traces the Zionism-equals-Nazism claim to the Prague show trial of 1952. The defendants, the large majority lifelong Communist activists and anti-Zionist Jews, in traditional Stalinist frame-up scenarios were accused of being Israeli agents. One of them who survived, Eugen Lobl, afterward said that the Soviet advisor, Likhatchev, told him:

[Y]ou are not a Czechoslovak. You are a dirty Jew, that's what you are. Israel is your only real fatherland and you have sold out Socialism to

your bosses, the Zionist imperialist leaders of world Jewry. Let me tell
you the time is fast approaching when we'll have to exterminate all your
kind.[47]

Part of the frame-up indictment was to brand the Jewish defendants "Gestapo
agents." And in a theme that became prominent in Left circles later, the officials declared:

> When the [Czech] nation raised its voice against Zionism, they cried
> "anti-Semitism" in order to cover the help they were giving to the class
> interests of the Jewish bourgeoisie and their ties with the imperialists
> through World Zionism.

Wistrich comments: "The Prague trial set a precedent which has had countless
imitators on the Left and in the Muslim-Arab world ever since."

The Soviet Union on October 14, 1965, formally tabled a motion in the
United Nations stating that Zionism, Nazism, and neo-Nazism, *in that order*,
were "racial crimes."[48] After the Six Day War, Soviet propaganda regularly
referred to Israel as the "successor state" to the Third Reich. This view radi-
ated from the official Communist parties into New Left, Trotskyist, and Maoist groups to their left, and seeped from there widely into progressive circles.

The short-lived anarcho-communist Black Rats/Tupamaros in West
Germany on the anniversary of Kristallnacht in 1969 carried out the bombing
of a Jewish communal hall in West Berlin, justifying it afterward by calling
for an "explicit and unequivocal identification with the fighting Fedayin" and
to go beyond verbal support to the Palestinians to "pitilessly combat the combination of Fascism and Israeli Zionism."[49]

In December 1972 during the trial of leftist attorney Horst Mahler, a
founder of the Red Army Faction, originally known as the Baader-Meinhof
Group, he praised the murder of Israeli athletes at the Munich Olympic Games
by Palestinian terrorists. He read a declaration that said in part, "Israel weeps
crocodile tears. It has burned up its sportsmen like the Nazis did the Jews —
incendiary material for the imperialist extermination policy." Mahler had been
an attorney for the famed German student leader Rudi Dutschke. He was on
trial for bank robbery and aiding a prison escape. The Red Army Faction re-

---

[47] Wistrich, p. 449. He cites Meir Cotic, *The Prague Trial: The First Anti-Zionist Show
Trial in the Communist Bloc* (New York, 1987), p. 219.
[48] Wistrich, p. 455. He cites Ze'ev Ben-Shlomo, "Soviets and Zionism," *Wiener
Library Bulletin* 20, nos. 1 and 2 (Winter 1965-66), pp. 7-9.
[49] Wistrich p. 467. Also discussed in "Anti-Semitism on the Left," August 3, 2006, in
the online *Workers Liberty, http://www.workersliberty.org/node/6705.*

vived the old Marxist position that antisemitism was the first stage of anticapitalism.

Another, better-known, founder of the Red Army Faction, Ulrike Meinhof, also in prison, testified during Mahler's trial. Asked about her view of antisemitism, she said it "used the hatred of the people, of their dependence on money as a medium of exchange, their longing for communism. Auschwitz means that six million Jews were murdered and carted on to the rubbish dumps of Europe for being that which was maintained of them – Money-Jews."[50]

Mahler, after serving a long prison term, became a neo-Nazi.

Two former members of the Baader-Meinhof Gang, Wilfried Bose and Brigitte Kuhlmann, who had gone on to form the Revolutionary Cells, were, along with two Palestinians, the hijackers in June 1976 of Air France flight 139 from Tel Aviv to Paris, diverting it to Entebbe airport in Uganda. Significantly, these German radicals released all the non-Jewish hostages, but kept and threatened to kill all those who were Jewish, whether they were Israelis or not.

This Holocaust inversion and the obsession with pillorying or destroying Israel is not restricted to Muslim theocrats and fringe leftists. Following are a small sample of headlines a Google search of "Israel Nazi" turns up:

> Israel is much closer to Nazi Germany than Iran is
> U.N.-Sponsored Meeting Equates Israelis with Nazis
> Now Israel is 'more loathsome' than the Nazis
> [Israel] The Nazis of our time
> Norwegian Envoy: "Israel", Nazis the Same (from the Hezbollah
>   website)
> Yes, they are vs. Yes, of course. Are Israel Nazis? (The only two
>   choices, each with a Star of David with a swastika inside it; 88%
>   had voted for the "Yes, of course" choice)
> British MP compares Jewish treatment of Palestinians to Nazis
> Professor's comparison of Israelis to Nazis stirs furor (at UC Santa
>   Barbara)
> Syrian president sticks by Israeli "Nazism" comment
> Nazi Germany Then And Zionist Israel Today (a YouTube video)
> Not So Cool Facts About Nazi Israel (a YouTube video)
> Glenda Jackson: calling Israelis Nazis is not hate speech
> Israel Follows In Nazi Footsteps
> Stop Holocaust of Palestinians by Israeli Nazis
> Israel — The new Nazi State

---

[50] From the Wikipedia article on Ulrike Meinhof,
http://en.wikipedia.org/wiki/Ulrike_Meinhof, retrieved March 20, 2013.

Roseanne Barr blasts Israel as 'Nazi state'
ISRAEL — The NAZI TERROR STATE (YouTube video)
In Norway, 38% believe Israel treats Palestinians like how Nazis
    treated Jews
Jewish MP exposes Israel crimes worse than Nazis (YouTube video)
Guardian readers and their inalienable right to make Israel-Nazi analo-
    gies (a criticism of the London *Guardian*)
What are some similarities between Nazi Germany and modern day Is-
    rael? (A Yahoo Ask question)
Israeli Persecution of Palestinians Exceeded Nazi Germany Persecu-
    tion of Jews in Time and Severity (opinion piece in Al-Jazeera,
    under the section on Cross-Cultural Understanding, December 3,
    2011)
Rachel Corrie Lawyer: Israel worse than Nazi Germany
UN investigator stands by Israel 'Nazi' comparison
Noam Chomsky on Nazi Israel (YouTube video)
How to end Israel's Nazi-inspired crimes?
UK Judge reprimanded for Israel-Nazi remarks during landmark trial
Chavez equates Israel invasion of Lebanon and occupation of Palestine
    with Nazi oppression of Jews
Sinn Fein hurls Nazi smear at Shatter and Israeli ambassador (Alan
    Shatter is the only Jewish member of the Irish parliament)
José Saramago compares Israel with Nazis (this one is older than the
    others, from 2002, when the Portuguese Nobel Laureate novelist
    and poet, and former Communist Party activist, compared Israel's
    treatment of the Palestinians with Auschwitz)

There is a nice discussion of this mass phenomena in an interview with British
academic David Hirsh. He points out that what was distinctive and abhorrent
about the Nazis was their conceiving and carrying out the deliberate physical
extermination of millions of people, mostly Jews. There has been nothing like
that in the Israel-Palestine conflict. Wikipedia's detailed summary of Palestinian deaths from just after the 1948 war to March 2012 come to about 12,000
that can be attributed to Israeli armed forces. And during almost all of this
period the Palestinians were led by armed groups that tried to seize power in
Jordan, took over southern Lebanon, and had running battles with Egyptian
forces in addition to attacks on Israelis. In the same period as many as 5,000
Palestinians were killed by the Egyptian army, 20,000 by the Jordanian army
(in 1970-71), and more than 10,000 by Lebanese Arab forces. This places the
total dead at roughly 12,000 Palestinians killed in conflict with Israel over the
whole of sixty-three years, but 35,000 killed by Arab armies.[51] Compare this
to Saddam Hussein's Iraq, where Saddam murdered some 250,000 of his own

---

[51] http://en.wikipedia.org/wiki/Palestinian_casualties_of_war.

people and killed a million in his war against Iran, with hardly a murmur from the humanitarian Left. The Palestinians during these years were not acting like the Jews of Germany, who never were trying with guns and bombs to destroy the German state. This hardly qualifies Israel as exterminationist Nazis. Hirsh comments on why this false label has stuck so widely and been repeated so regularly by leftist and more mainstream critics.

> It seems to me that one of the reasons people raise that as an analogy is because they think it has a particular effect on Jews when it is said that the Jews or Israelis have become similar to those who persecuted them. And of course it does have a particular effect on Jews. It has an effect of upsetting Jews. I think that that's really the point of it, the point of it isn't to come out with a serious [analysis]. There are all sorts of serious historical analogies for the rise of Jewish and Palestinian nationalism in the Middle East. One can look at Europe in the 19th century, one can look at the breakdown of the Ottoman Empire, one can look at the Balkans, one can look at many, many things. It's not similar to Nazism. Why do people say it's similar to Nazism? They say it's similar to Nazism in order to wind up the Jews, so actually the charge that the Israelis are the new Nazis is a kind of Jew-baiting.[52]

The European Union Agency for Fundamental Rights in the definition of antisemitism it adopted in 2005 included "Drawing comparisons of contemporary Israeli policy to that of the Nazis" as a specific example of antisemitism. Also specified was "Denying the Jewish people their right to self-determination, e.g., by claiming that the existence of the State of Israel is a racist endeavor."[53]

Of course, for every reasonable thing the United Nations does, in some other part of its rambling structure it does the opposite. The UN, after all, is a haven for Third World ideologues and despots. The January 29, 2013, *Jerusalem Post* reports,

> The UN Human Rights Council has a permanent agenda of 10 items, one reserved for condemning Israel and one for considering all other 192 UN members. Almost 40 percent of all Council resolutions condemning specific countries have been directed at Israel alone. There have been more special sessions on Israel than any other country. Israel is the only

---

[52] "Chip Berlet interviews David Hirsh on Contemporary Antisemitism and Conspiracy Theory." An interview taken on June 29, 2009, but first published September 6, 2012, by *Engage*. http://engageonline.wordpress.com/2012/09/06/chip-berlet-interviews-david-hirsh-on-contemporary-antisemitism-and-conspiracy-theory/
[53] http://www.european-forum-on-antisemitism.org/working-definition-of-antisemitism/.

UN state excluded from full membership in any of the UN's regional groups, where key negotiations and information-sharing occurs.[54]

And this is the new, improved model. The previous iteration, the United Nations Commission on Human Rights, was disbanded in 2006 for its obsession with Israel and its ignoring far greater human rights violations in other countries. The old commission had as members at one time or another Zimbabwe, Libya, Syria, Pakistan, Saudi Arabia, and, the final straw that led to its dissolution, Sudan, there to point the finger at Israel while absolving itself of the massacres in Darfur.

Wistrich cites, almost in passing, the attack on a Paris synagogue in 1980, the machine-gun assault on a Jewish restaurant there in 1982, Palestinian terror attacks on Jews in Frankfurt, Brussels, Antwerp, and Vienna in the early 1980s, the murder of a pro-Israel Socialist municipal councilor in Vienna in 1981, the regular beatings of Jewish school children by Muslim immigrants today, especially in France, demonstrations in the United States in 2009 where Israeli flags were burned and banners linking the swastika with the Star of David were displayed, or where demonstrators shouted things like "Go back to the ovens!" And one should really not leave out the various bombings by Al Qaeda affiliates in Spain, England, and elsewhere in Europe, claimed to be striking a blow against Crusaders and Zionists.

Toward the end of his long presentation, in the penultimate chapter, Wistrich steps back and summarizes his case. He points again to the million Jews expelled from the Arab, Turkic, and Iranian Muslim states:

> This forced mass exodus of Jews from Arab lands after 1945 has been erased by those left-wing ideologues who brand Zionism with the stigma of being a *Western* colonialist movement. While endlessly evoking the "injustice" towards the Palestinian Arabs, they studiously *ignore* the ethnic cleansing of Middle Eastern Jews from Arab states. Post-1945 Zionism is as much a Middle Eastern as a European phenomenon. It is no less a product of the Muslim intolerance towards non-Muslims than it is of Christian or Nazi persecution of the Jews. Along with the Russian pogroms and the Nazi mass murder, the mob assaults of Arabs against "Oriental" Jews contributed a great deal to forging the "Zionist" consciousness of what is today half of the Israeli Jewish population.

And while Israel's enemies misrepresent the actual ethnic composition of the Israeli Jews,

---

[54] *Jerusalem Post*, January 29, 2013. http://www.jpost.com/Opinion/Op-Ed-Contributors/An-anti-Semitic-agenda-at-the-UN.

Whether the rhetoric of anti-Zionism happens to be Marxist, Muslim, Christian, Third Worldist, fascist, or openly neo-Nazi, it is replete with stereotypical notions of the perfidy and diabolical cunning of the Jews; their corrosive, manipulative will-to-power; their insatiable love of gold and intrigue, mastery of hidden forces and domination of the international financial system. The more radical anti-Zionists no less than the classical antisemites are obsessed with the ubiquity and malignant impact of the Jews on the modern world.

And finally:

Anti-Zionism in the 1970s and 1980s increasingly began to look like the leftist functional equivalent of what classical antisemitism had once represented (in the interwar period) for the fascist Right. Not only was anti-Zionism clearly the historical heir of earlier forms of antisemitism, but it was steadily emerging as the lowest common denominator between sections of the Left, the Right, and Islamist circles. This has become even more true today than it was several decades ago.

Noam Chomsky and the Holocaust Deniers

Anti-Zionism has generally been linked on the far Left with anti-Americanism, but no Left organization called for the outright destruction of America or the expulsion of its people from the land. And the accusation of being Nazis has far more often been applied to the Israeli Jews than to the United States, even by militant anti-imperialists. As always in attacks on the Jews by non-Jews, a certain number of dissident Jews play a prominent part. Notable among these has been Noam Chomsky. His unrelentingly hostile books opposing Israel and the United States rarely mention Nazi Germany without making an analogy to suggest that America is worse. Chomsky's character and his attitude toward not just Israel but Jews in general appeared most clearly in the Faurisson Affair of 1989-1991. Wistrich mentions this only briefly but it is worth a bit more attention as it reveals a great deal of the character of this icon of the far Left.

Robert Faurisson was a professor of French literature at the University of Lyon in France. He is France's best known Holocaust denier, a promoter of the claim that the *Diary of Anne Frank* was a forgery, that there were no Nazi gas chambers, and even that the Jews were more responsible for World War II than Hitler. He was tried under French law prohibiting Holocaust denial as racial incitement. In 1979 Chomsky signed a petition in support of Faurisson, nominally only on the issue of free speech, although the petition described Faurisson as "a respected professor of twentieth-century French literature and document criticism." Chomsky later wrote an essay in Faurisson's defense, which Faurisson used as a preface to one of his books, allegedly without Chomsky's permission. This essay went far beyond defending the right of a vicious bigot to have his say. In it Chomsky wrote:

> [I]s it true that Faurisson is an anti-Semite or a neo-Nazi? As noted earlier, I do not know his work very well. But from what I have read — largely as a result of the nature of the attacks on him — I find no evidence to support either conclusion. Nor do I find credible evidence in the material that I have read concerning him, either in the public record or in private correspondence. As far as I can determine, he is a relatively apolitical liberal of some sort.[55]

In the same essay, however, Chomsky said that he had read an article about Faurisson in the September 1980 issue of *Esprit*. The article referred to was by the actually respected French historian Pierre Vidal-Naquet, summarizing with detailed sources Faurisson's views, beginning with Faurisson's statement, "Never did Hitler either order or accept that anyone be killed for reason of race or religion." Vidal-Naquet then summarized the core positions proposed by Faurisson and his group:

> 1. There was no genocide and the instrument symbolsing it, the gas chamber, never existed.
> 2. The "final solution" was never anything other than the expulsion of the Jews towards eastern Europe. . . . it was never anything more than their repatriation. . .
> 3. The number of Jewish victims of Nazism is far smaller than has been claimed. . . . a few hundred thousand deaths in uniform (which is a fine demonstration of valour) and as many killed in "acts of war" (*Vérité*, p. 197). As for the death statistics for Auschwitz, they "rose to about 50,000" (ibid.).
> 4. Hitler's Germany does not bear the principal responsibility for the Second World War. It shares that responsibility, for example, with the Jews (Faurisson in *Vérité*, p. 187), or it may even not bear any responsibility at all. . . .
> 6. The genocide was an invention of Allied propaganda, which was largely Jewish, and specifically Zionist, and which may be easily explained by the Jewish propensity to give imaginary statistics, under the influence of the Talmud.[56]

---

[55] http://www.chomsky.info/articles/19801011.htm. From Chomsky's own website, retrieved March 30, 2013.
[56] Cited by Oliver Kamm, "Chomsky and Holocaust denial," http://oliverkamm. typepad.com/blog/2004/11/chomsky_and_hol.html, retrieved March 19, 2013.

Finally, to explain somewhat more of the context of Chomsky's astonishing dismissal of this kind of stuff as not antisemitic but just liberal and apolitical, it should be said that Faurisson was part of a group led by Pierre Guillaume and Serge Thion called La Vielle Taupe (The Old Mole). This was an ultraleft split off from a French Trotskyist organization called Socialism or Barbarism. They had arrived at the position, not so far distanced from Chomsky's own writing, that the United States and its allies in World War II were ultimately worse than either Hitler Germany or Stalinist Russia, and they had gone into the business of publishing Holocaust denial material of all sorts. La Vielle Taupe was Faurisson's publisher. And Chomsky's association with this bizarre sect was not limited to his essay on Faurisson's non-antisemitism. He offered the group's founder and leader, Pierre Guillaume, the rights to his book *The Political Economy of Human Rights* (coauthored by Edward Herman). Chomsky later vociferously denied this, saying that the French edition was published by J-E Halier/Albin Michel, but the book itself lists Holocaust denier Pierre Guillaume as the director of the project.[57]

Chomsky carried on a fairly extensive correspondence pursuing his defense of Faurisson, quite explicitly going beyond the mere free speech issue he generally claims was his interest. In a letter to Australian William Robinson he wrote:

> I see no anti-Semitic implications in denial of the existence of gas chambers, or even denial of the holocaust. Nor would there be anti-Semitic implications, per se, in the claim that the holocaust (whether one believes it took place or not) is being exploited, viciously so, by apologists for Israeli repression and violence. I see no hint of anti-Semitic implications in Faurisson's work.[58]

This is not Chomsky's only connection to antisemitic publishers. He permitted the openly pro-Nazi Noontide Press to publish an edition of his *The Fateful Triangle: The United States, Israel and the Palestinians*. The blogosphere is full of denials of this by his loyal followers, but the proof is not hard to find. The first edition, in 1983, was by the left-wing South End Press, but the Noontide Press edition was dated June 1, 1986. It carried the ISBN number 0317530240 and the national ISBN database retains a record of it.[59] It can

---

[57] See http://www.wernercohn.com/Chomskydocs.html for a reproduction of the data page.
[58] W. D. Robinson, "Chomsky and the Neo-Nazis," *Quadrant* (Australia), October 1981.
[59] http://isbndb.com/d/book/the_fateful_triangle_a04.html.

also be found in Google Books, and I have seen two copies for sale at exorbitant prices through Amazon UK.

For the record, Noontide Press is the publishing arm of the Institute for Historical Review. Both press and institute were founded in 1978 by Willis Carto. The Southern Poverty Law Center lists them as hate groups, while the Wikipedia describes Carto as "the leading organizer of modern American anti-Semitism." Noontide's offerings specialize in Holocaust denial but include *The Protocols of the Elders of Zion* and Hitler's *Mein Kampf*. Their current catalog includes books opposing school integration and nonwhite immigration, proving the racial inferiority of nonwhites, supporting the European New Right's denunciations of existing democratic institutions, lots of white identity politics depicting American whites as the biggest victims of the present system, and even a book by Martin Luther King's assassin, James Earl Ray, claiming he was framed by the government. They used to also feature several of Chomsky's audio cassettes against Israel, but his work no longer appears.

To be exact, Chomsky is not himself a Holocaust denier, though he has been more than evasive on this subject. What he is is an antisemitism denier. As Oliver Kamm puts it,

> His disaffection from genuinely progressive values — the values that the United States at its best effectively promotes . . . is so extreme that it leads him to see not only "no enemies on the Left" but also "no enemies amongst the enemies of my enemies" — even if it puts him alongside men who whitewash Nazi genocide.[60]

Sadly, Chomsky, this embittered left antisemite, retains his credibility with much of the far Left. He remains, for example, on the list of Advisory Editors of the American Trotskyist journal *Against the Current*, published by the Detroit-based Solidarity, which describes itself as "A socialist, feminist, antiracist organization."

Trotskyists and Anti-Zionism

I began this review with the American Socialist Workers Party's call in 1967 for the destruction of the State of Israel. For historical reasons the Trotskyists have been among the worst on the Left in their embrace of Islamic radicalism and hostility to the Jewish state. One reason for this is that, with the exception of Stalin's so-called Third Period, between 1928 and the con-

---

[60] Oliver Kamm, "Chomsky and Holocaust Denial," November 1, 2004, http://oliverkamm.typepad.com/blog/2004/11/chomsky_and_hol.html.

solidation of Hitler's power after 1933, when the Comintern expected imminent European revolution and adopted an ultraleft policy, the Trotskyists have
always characterized the official Communist parties as class-collaborationist
and conciliatory toward capitalism and imperialism. That is, the Trotskyist
groups have on virtually every issue and for some eighty years, consciously
positioned themselves to the left of the official Communist parties.

Rather than establishing true independence from Stalinism, there existed
an undercurrent of rivalry in which the official stance of the pro-Moscow Stalinists (the pro-Peking variety were, in the Mao years, too crazy to become
even a negative pole) became the starting point for a critique from further to
the left. If Moscow insisted that Israel was an illegitimate bastion of imperialism, could the Trotskyists say less? And if Moscow supported Arab nationalism, then the Trotskyists would raise them one and at least impute to Arab
militancy an inherently communist dynamic. This last had a very small plau-
sibility in the days of Nasser and secular Arab nationalism. It became an unholy alliance when secularism gave way to right-wing theocratic Islamism. At
the least it generated endless exercises among the English-speaking Trotskyists in patronizing the jihadi movement, forever insisting that they don't really
mean anything they say about the Jews, they are just an oppressed people
blindly responding to repression by Jewish agents of American imperialism.

The worst example of this has been the British Socialist Workers Party.
The principal British antiwar group, the Stop the War Coalition, was founded
and dominated by the British SWP. Like its American cousin, A.N.S.W.E.R.
(Act Now to Stop War and End Racism), founded and run by another Trotskyist splinter, the Workers World Party, the Stop the War Coalition succeeded
for some times after its creation, shortly after 9/11 back in 2001, in sponsoring
some large antiwar rallies. Both are supporters of the Sunni-Al-Qaeda insur-
gents in Iraq against the Shi'ite majority and the large Kurdish minority. The
British SWP also supports Hezbollah and calls for the destruction of Israel.

The Stop the War Coalition under SWP leadership formed a close alliance with the Muslim Association of Britain (MAB). The MAB was founded
in 1997 by Egyptian-born Muslim Brotherhood member Kamal El Helbawy,
together with former Hamas commander Mohammed Sawalha, Azam Tam-
mimi, who had worked for the Brotherhood in Jordan, and Anas Al Tikriti, the
son of the head of the Muslim Brotherhood in Iraq.[61] The MAB is not the
most radical Islamic organization in Britain, which is known for its jihadi ex-
tremists, but it is an advocate of Sharia law to replace parliamentary democracy in national government, and advocates the slogan "Zionists out of Palestine." With Sharia law, the MAB is hostile to gays and proscribes women's

---

[61] http://cifwatch.com/tag/muslim-association-of-britain/.

rights. It is perhaps not surprising that in recent months the British SWP has been in deep crisis over accusations that one of its top leaders has been raping women members, then getting himself cleared by an investigating committee of his cronies.

Here I want to digress for a moment to return to Leon Trotsky's evolution on whether Jews legitimately constitute a nationality, and if so, where to put them. In an interview with Jewish correspondents in Mexico on January 18, 1937, the old revolutionary said:

> During my youth I rather leaned toward the prognosis that the Jews of different countries would be assimilated and that the Jewish question would thus disappear in a quasi-automatic fashion. The historical development of the last quarter of a century has not confirmed this perspective. Decaying capitalism has everywhere swung over to an exacerbated nationalism, one part of which is anti-Semitism. The Jewish question has loomed largest in the most highly developed capitalist country of Europe, in Germany. . . .
>   And how, you ask me, can socialism solve this question? Once socialism has become master of our planet or at least of its most important sections, it will have unimaginable resources in all domains. Human history has witnessed the epoch of great migrations on the basis of barbarism. Socialism will open the possibility of great migrations on the basis of the most developed technique and culture. It goes without saying that what is here involved is not compulsory displacement, that is, the creation of new ghettos for certain nationalities, but displacements freely consented to, or rather demanded by certain nationalities or parts of nationalities. The dispersed Jews who would want to be reassembled in the same community will find a sufficiently extensive and rich spot under the sun. The same possibility will be opened for the Arabs, as for all other scattered nations.[62]

Trotsky was a brilliant individual who had become embedded in a system that claimed to be liberating but which left behind on its collapse, or transmogrification into a strange hybrid form of capitalism, as in China, more than a hundred million corpses, more than half of those after his death — in the USSR in Stalin's last years, in Mao's China, and, on a smaller scale, in Pol Pot's Cambodia and the Kim dynasty's North Korea. Trotsky was honest enough to see that the Jews genuinely were a nationality, not just a religion or an economic caste as the Marxists before him theorized. And he was perspicacious enough to see that reuniting any people currently dispersed among others in a single

---

[62] *Leon Trotsky on the Jewish Question* (New York: Pathfinder Press, 1970), pp. 26-27.

state or divided among several states — a condition that affects many more ethnicities than the Jews, although they are the extreme example — could be resolved only through the massive exchange of populations, to clear out one ethnicity from enough land to concentrate the one being newly established in a single territory. Where fantasy overwhelms his sense here is the idea that under socialism this would be "freely consented to." This was never true, in the Ottoman expulsion of the Greeks from what is now Turkey, although Byzantium had been there for a millennium before the Turkic tribes arrived, in Stalin's massive resettlement of entire peoples in the Soviet Union, such as the Volga Germans and Crimean Tatars, or in the religious partition of Cyprus, to mention just a few examples.

Trotsky, who had led the Soviet Red Army in the USSR's founding, certainly understood that, even under a socialist government, whole groups of people were likely to oppose losing their land to make room for others solely in response to arguments about the greater good. He confronted this directly in an interview first published in 1934 and included in the pamphlet quoted above. The interviewer asks Trotsky directly for his opinion about Palestine as a possible Jewish homeland. Trotsky responds:

> I do not know whether Jewry will be built up again as a nation. However, there can be no doubt that the material conditions for the existence of Jewry as an independent nation could be brought about only by the proletarian revolution. There is no such thing on our planet as the idea that one has more claim to land than another.
>
> The establishment of a territorial base for Jewry in Palestine or any other country is conceivable only with the migration of large human masses. Only a triumphant socialism can take upon itself such tasks. It can be foreseen that it may take place either on the basis of a mutual understanding, or with the aid of a kind of international proletarian tribunal which should take up this question and solve it.[63]

This is a remarkable statement. As we have seen, the Marxist movement of the past opposed Zionism on two grounds: first, that the Marxists disbelieved that Jews could still constitute themselves as a nation, and second, that Zionism, by establishing separate organizations for Jews in European countries and encouraging Jews to emigrate to Palestine interfered with the unitary command the Marxists tried to establish over the workers' movement. Also as we have seen, after the Russian Revolution, when the tasks at hand shifted from mobilizing an opposition to the existing government and became administering a multinational state, Lenin changed his mind and agreed that the Jews, in

---

[63] Ibid., pp. 23-24.

fact, were one of the constituent nationalities of the USSR, not just a religious denomination.

Trotsky takes this a step further here, agreeing that if the Jews should desire it, a world socialist government would allocate land for them to bring together those Jews who desired to from all over the earth, and that whatever peoples were already in the selected destination would have to move to make room. Further, that this could be done in Palestine. This plainly means the emigration of Russian, Polish, German, and other European Jews to join the existing Middle Eastern Jews dispersed among the Muslim countries, "the migration of large human masses." And when he states this, in the context of considering the migration of large human masses of Jews into Palestine, there is no mistaking his meaning when he also says "There is no such thing on our planet as the idea that one has more claim to land than another." The future socialist ubergovernment will allocate territory according to its overall plan just as it will allocate means of production, not according to the wishes of local groups. If, in the most optimistic interpretation, everything was in accord with justice in the big picture the outcome would be justified.

And he goes further here and specifies what will happen under socialism if the Arab Palestinians don't agree to move elsewhere in the Arab lands to make room for the immigrant Jews: there will be an "international proletarian tribunal" which will impose a solution to the problem. These statements by Trotsky are the polar opposite of the post-1967 Trotskyist position of uncon-ditional support to Arab nationalism and total rejection of Jewish national rights.

So we have Trotsky endorsing all the basic premises of Zionism, with the sole condition that they should wait to be carried out until the world so-cialist revolution has been completed. If, as he says, a Jewish homeland carved out of other people's land, including in Palestine out of the very exten-sive Arab land, is a just and moral outcome, then is it unjust and immoral if it is accomplished when there is no reasonable hope of the particular agency Trotsky proposed to execute this task? At root, Trotsky plainly recognizes national rights of both Arabs and Jews, and since the Arabs have infinitely more land than just Palestine, his proposal is that justice requires them to make a population shift that will accommodate creating a territory where Jew-ish national rights will be dominant. It could be added that the whole experi-ence with communism in power offers no grounds whatsoever to imagine, as Trotsky does, that a world communist government would be any more peace-ful or humane than the capitalist ones that now exist in solving nationalist confrontations. In fact, quite the opposite, from the experience of the twentieth century.

In this same interview Trotsky refuses to regard Arab attacks on Jews in Palestine as by definition some kind of justified resistance, as his followers today generally do. That was the Stalinist position. The interviewer asks:

> The official Communist Party characterized, without question, the Jewish-Arab events in 1929 in Palestine as the revolutionary uprising of the oppressed Arabian masses.[64] What is your opinion of this policy?

Trotsky replies:

> Unfortunately, I am not thoroughly familiar with the facts to venture a definite opinion. I am now studying the question. Then it will be easier to see in what proportion and in what degree there were present those elements such as national liberationists (anti-imperialists) and reactionary Mohammedans and anti-Semitic pogromists. On the surface, it seems to me that all these elements were there.[65]

Any mention of the existence of reactionary Muslims or Arab antisemitic pogromists, past or present, disappeared entirely from the press of all the major Trotskyist organizations after 1967.

A useful article tracing the American and British Trotskyists' evolution away from Trotsky's positions is Werner Cohn's "From Victim to Shylock and Oppressor: The New Image of the Jew in the Trotskyist Movement."[66] This was written in 1991, but little has changed since then.

Most of the American and British Trotskyist groups today have looked for some vehicle to go beyond just writing articles calling for Israel's destruction and try to do actual damage to Israel, its individual citizens, and Jews in other countries through boycotts of Jewish-owned businesses or other stores that carry Israeli goods, or by votes in faculty committees to bar Israeli schol-

---

[64] The Arab-Jewish clashes began in the fall of 1928 with Arab protests against Jews praying at the Wailing Wall, which is both the last remaining wall of Solomon's Temple and attached to the Al Aqsa Mosque, built on the Temple's foundations. Tensions escalated the following year. On August 15, 1929, a peaceful Jewish march was held to the Wall. The following day an Arab counterdemonstration there burned Jewish prayer books. Minor clashes took place over the next week, then, on August 23, Arab groups launched an armed attack on Jews in Jerusalem that quickly spread throughout Palestine. On August 24, between 65 and 68 unarmed Jews were murdered in Hebron. The anti-Jewish riots lasted until August 29, leaving 133 Jews dead. The understaffed British police intervened and in clashes with Arab demonstrators were mainly responsible for the 116 Arabs who were killed during the riots.

[65] *Leon Trotsky on the Jewish Question*, p. 23.

[66] http://www.wernercohn.com/Trotsky.html.

ars and artists from attending conferences in their field at major universities or perform or show their work outside of Israel.

In the United States, the currently largest Trotskyist group, the International Socialist Organization, calls for the destruction of Israel and is a strong promoter of the Palestinian Boycott, Divestment and Sanctions (BDS) movement and the U.S. Campaign for the Academic and Cultural Boycott of Israel (USACBI). That no other state, no matter how repressive, is the target of such a boycott effort should give people who consider themselves to be antiracist pause for thought. What is the aim of this boycott, that will satisfy its organizers? Is it directed at the settlers in the West Bank, or the Israeli embargo of Gaza? The ISO explains that the Academic and Cultural Boycott will not end "until the illegal Israeli occupation is ended, the 700-meter apartheid wall is torn down, and the right of Palestinian refugees to return to their homeland is honored," that is, until the Jewish state is dismantled and replaced with a Palestinian Arab one.[67]

Even Mahmoud Abbas, head of the Palestinian Authority, has conceded that the long-held Palestinian demand for the return of all Palestinian refugees and their descendents, which would create an Arab majority in Israel, is not a reasonable demand. He and the Israelis have been arguing over the reduced numbers, with the Israelis proposing 50,000 and the PA proposing 500,000. The original demand by the Palestinians, which the ISO states as the goal without which the boycott will not be satisfied, would, with the natural increase of the original 800,000 or so refugees over sixty-five years, consist of some 3.9 million Palestinians living in the West Bank and Gaza, and some 4.5 million in neighboring Arab countries, including half the population of Jordan, which is geographically vastly larger than Israel.

The ISO occasionally, tongue-in-cheek, says that the boycott movement does not call for the destruction of Israel. An article, "Standing for the Right of Return" in the January 8, 2013, issue of their newspaper *Socialist Worker* is quite insistent that they mean all of the refugees. They cite as their authority an article by a Dr. Heidar Eid of Gaza who strongly opposes the two-state solution and sharply criticizes Mahmoud Abbas for agreeing to anything less than the whole of the Palestinian population being returned to Israel proper. This would, of course, immediately mean a government dominated by Muslims if not by Hamas, which calls for the physical expulsion of the Jews.[68]

---

[67] From the ISO newspaper, *Socialist Worker*, November 21, 2012.
http://socialistworker.org/2012/11/21/time-to-divest-from-israel.
[68] http://socialistworker.org/2013/01/08/standing-for-the-right-of-return.

The much smaller, San Francisco-based, Socialist Action is also a strong supporter of the BDS (Boycott, Divestment, and Sanctions) movement,[69] frequently using analogies with Nazis and apartheid South Africa in its hostile coverage of Israel. They denounce both the Palestine Authority and surprisingly, Hamas, as capitulating to Israel, reject the two-state solution, and call for the destruction of the Jewish state.

Even the Detroit-based Solidarity, which I helped to found and which I have long considered the best of the lot, is on board with the boycott movement. A November 2012 statement for its Political Committee declared "it is overwhelmingly important for the international Boycott, Divestment and Sanctions (BDS) movement to step up its grassroots activism."[70]

There is one curious exception to this pattern. It comes from the (American) Socialist Workers Party, the granddaddy of the destroy-Israel position on the American Left. Much shrunken since its heyday in the mid-1970s, it reputedly is down to barely a hundred members. In the spring of 2009 it began to back-pedal on its Israel position. In the April 6, 2009, issue of its newspaper *The Militant* it ran an article headed "Israel boycotts and divestment serve as cover for anti-Semitism."[71]

The article specifically singles out the International Socialist Organization and the Workers World Party. It points to the "Israeli Apartheid Week," then in its fifth year, as well as the BDS campaign, writing:

"The character of these activities — aimed increasingly at Jewish-owned businesses — is part of the deepening pattern of Jew-baiting and anti-Semitism in the middle-class left worldwide. It should be opposed." The author cites as a particularly bad example the looting by a BDS group of a London Starbucks. The owner of the Starbucks chain is Jewish. *The Militant* also, remarkably, disputes the continually repeated charge that Israel is an apartheid state similar to white South Africa:

> There are sweeping differences between the apartheid regime in South Africa and the capitalist regime in Israel — in terms of organization of labor, the character of the regimes, and the historical conditions under which they emerged. The attempt to paint them as the same simply obfuscates the real social and class relations in Israel and the tasks facing the toilers there to chart a revolutionary course forward. Applied to Israel the term "apartheid" is simply an epithet, rather than a scientific description of a social structure.

---

[69] http://socialistaction.org/2012/12/revolutionary-socialist-politics-part-2/
[70] http://www.solidarity-us.org/gaza_2012.
[71] http://www.themilitant.com/2009/7313/731336.html.

It also laments the "increasingly open support for Hamas" by the ISO, illustrating what is being legitimated by the ISO's stance by quoting from the Hamas charter the claims that Jews "were behind the French Revolution, the Communist revolution . . . . World War I," and etc.

The line of reasoning in this and subsequent articles seems clear enough. In South Africa the African National Congress of Nelson Mandela sought explicitly to make a place in a post-revolutionary South Africa for the formerly dominant whites. Hamas does not have the same perspective toward the Israeli Jews, instead promoting a classical exterminationist antisemitic line. *The Militant* in several articles dares to say what most anti-Israel leftists deny, that "increasingly the term Zionist has come to mean Jew"[72]

In the April 13, 2009, *Militant* long-time SWP leader Norton Sandler writes:

> [T]he term "Zionism" — or "Zionists" — has become a synonym for "Jewish" or "Jew" no matter how much those who use it try to explain it otherwise.
>
> The leaderships of much of the petty-bourgeois left in the United States, the United Kingdom, and other countries often agree with or chose to ignore reactionary Jew-baiting remarks from the leaders of Hamas or Hezbollah, or worse, make Jew-baiting remarks of their own. It is also common for them to take the anti-working-class position that workers inside Israel who are Jewish are reactionary and can never be won to support the Palestinians' fight.

These positions are a great deal better than much of the Trotskyists and others of the antisemitic Left. The SWP still clings to the hope for its Democratic Secular Palestine in which Jews, Muslims, and Christians will happily coexist, and which would under any plausible circumstances have a Muslim majority. But it is evident that it is realistic enough to have stopped projecting these rosy intentions on the existing Palestinian leadership. And as the Democratic Secular Palestine would be a unitary state, the SWP gives the Palestine Authority no credit for its recent acceptance and work toward a two-state solution.

I don't know what caused the SWP to mellow its position on the Middle Eastern Jews. One likely possibility is Fidel Castro, who the party holds in high regard. Cuba has been pretty hard-nosed in support of the Palestinians and in befriending Third World governments that are hostile to the United States, most of which are also hostile to Israel. But Castro himself draws the line at actual antisemitism. Jeffrey Goldberg in the September 7, 2010, issue

---

[72] *The Militant*, April 13, 2009, http://www.themilitant.com/2009/7314/731465.html.

of *The Atlantic* recounts his recent lengthy interview with the old Cuban revolutionary. Castro had asked for the meeting after reading Goldberg's *Atlantic* article on Iran and Israel.

Castro told Goldberg he was concerned at the likelihood of war between the U.S. and Israel on one side and Iran on the other. But he sharply criticized Ahmadinejad for his antisemitism and Holocaust denial, a criticism that Castro asked Goldberg to deliver to Ahmadinejad through his report on their discussion. He said Israel could best guarantee its security by giving up its nuclear weapons, and that all the other nuclear powers should give up theirs as well. He said to tell Ahmadinejad that he had to understand antisemitism to understand why Israelis fear for their existence. Castro went on:

> I don't think anyone has been slandered more than the Jews. I would say much more than the Muslims. They have been slandered much more than the Muslims because they are blamed and slandered for everything. No one blames the Muslims for anything.

Further, the Jews

> were expelled from their land, persecuted and mistreated all over the world, as the ones who killed God. In my judgment here's what happened to them: Reverse selection. What's reverse selection? Over 2,000 years they were subjected to terrible persecution and then to the pogroms. One might have assumed that they would have disappeared; I think their culture and religion kept them together as a nation. . . . The Jews have lived an existence that is much harder than ours. There is nothing that compares to the Holocaust.[73]

Caudillo he may have been, and dogmatic and authoritarian. But Castro comes from a different tradition than the European Marxists, who imbibed a negative attitude toward the Jews from their national cultures, and were from the beginning hostile to Jewish national aspirations and disdaining of Jewish culture, even when they accepted assimilationist Jews into their ranks. Castro, as much a nationalist as a communist, could see the legitimacy of Jewish nationalism and from that, of Israel's right to exist, whatever bad deeds its government performs. Many governments commit bad deeds, and their peoples are not eradicated on that account.

---

[73] http://www.theatlantic.com/international/archive/2010/09/castro-no-one-has-been-slandered-more-than-the-jews/62566/.

Predictably, the hard Trotskyist Left has denounced the SWP's apostasy. An online Canadian Trotskyist journal called *Links* in its August 6, 2010, issue declared that the SWP is now "in the Zionist camp."[74] Since this type of leftist also considers "Zionist" a synonym for Nazi, make of that what you will.

April 1, 2013

---

[74] "Why the left should support the boycott of Israel — a reply to the US Socialist Workers Party" by Art Young, August 6, 2010. http://links.org.au/node/1829.

Why the Middle East Is Always in Crisis

A Peace to End All Peace: The Fall of the Ottoman Empire and the Creation of the Modern Middle East. David Fromkin. New York: Henry Holt and Company, 1989. 643 pp.

Why write about a book that is almost twenty-five-years old? The best reason is that it uncovers, layer by layer, the consequences, intentional and unintentional, of the confrontations in and after World War I that dismembered the Ottoman Empire and drew the map that built into itself the incendiary ingredients that have made the Middle East perhaps the most explosive portion of today's world. The results of the final partition of the former Ottoman lands in 1922 directly laid the groundwork for today's civil war in Syria, now spreading into Lebanon, the emergent second civil war in post-invasion Iraq, the rise of jihadi Islam, and the perennial Palestinian-Israeli conflict. Only by looking at the region as a whole, pulling back from a narrow focus on the abuses of this or that Arab dictator or the Israeli occupation in the West Bank can the underlying dynamics and its actors' motives be fully understood. David Fromkin's classic work offers a convenient peg on which to hang a look back at how the Middle East mess took its modern form and what that tells us about where we are now.

Fromkin makes two points that are helpful to place at the beginning. First, it is common on the liberal-left to frame the post-World War I creation of dependent states in the Arab portion of the Ottoman territories as simply predation by Western imperialism. It is more accurate, he argues, to see that all the major actors in the war were empires and that is how all the important states involved in the conflict conceived of international politics. In the days before the League of Nations and its successor United Nations, empires, even if internally involving colonization and inequality, were the internationally unifying entities of the day. The first world war pitted the British, French, and

Russian empires against the German, Austro-Hungarian, and Ottoman Turkish empires. All had colonies, the Turks no less than the Europeans, as all of the Arab peoples had lived under Turkish domination for five hundred years. And during the war the Germans were directly involved in command positions in the Ottoman armies. Ironically, after the Russian Revolution of 1917, Lenin's Bolsheviks, after announcing to the world that they were the militant opponents of colonialism, used the Red Army to crush independence movements among the Turkic peoples of Central Asia and imposed Russian-dominated governments over them that lasted until the fall of the Soviet Union in 1989.

Second, and this is a point that has misled latter day liberals and leftists as much as it did the British and French imperialists of the last century, the central unifying element of the Ottoman peoples, particularly the Arabs, was and remains religious rather than national. And in the case of the overwhelmingly dominant Islam, it is a creed that consists largely of an extensive legal code that regulates every aspect of human life, rejects the comparable rules of every other faith, and does not accept the separation of church and state. There is a consequent extreme intolerance of religious difference, both within Islam between its warring sects, and with other confessions, particularly Jews, but also Christians.

The victors in World War I sought to create Western style nations based on patriotic identification with a territory. The ceaseless instability and endless bloodshed of the Arab East stems from the weak attraction of this concept among the peoples on the ground. Virtually every Arab state has been a theocracy, publicly acknowledged or cloaked behind a thin veil of secularism. And among the Arabs the split between Sunnis and Shi'ites, which dates from the late seventh century, remains a blood line. As I write, Bashar al-Assad's government, nominally a secular Ba'athist regime, but dominated by the Alawite branch of Shiism, prohibits all the Sunni pilots in the air force from flying, while in adjacent Lebanon the Shi'ite Hezbollah, which supports its coreligionist in Syria, is engaged in running gun battles with Lebanese Sunnis.

Because religious homogeneity is the touchstone of stability and legitimacy in the Arab Middle East, it has been the best predictor of what states that emerged in 1922 would have relative peace and which would be forever internally torn. Fromkin ranks them in three levels. First, those states that have a very long preexisting continuity have been at least geographically stable. These are mainly Egypt and Persia. Next are those new states with a very strong rulership. He lists these as Saudi Arabia (which actually dates from 1932) and Turkey under Mustapha Kemal Pasha and his successors. He proposes that there remain a group of states whose existence in its present form remains contested. He lists these as Syria, Lebanon, Iraq, Jordan, and Israel.

In each case it is religious intolerance by the state's opponents that puts its survival in question. He cites as an analogy the long period of national consolidation that followed the collapse of the Roman Empire. This was not completed until the unification of Germany and Italy in the late nineteenth century, fifteen hundred years after the fall of Rome.

This is a book largely about British actions in the Middle East between 1914 and 1922, and reactions by Turks, Arabs, Jews, and Persians. This is reasonable, as Britain was by far the most active Western power in the region in those years. French and Russian involvement are discussed to a lesser degree. To a surprising extent, even considering that it was a long-ago pre-Internet age, British information about the peoples it was dealing with was extraordinarily skimpy. This led to the proliferation of what today would look like bizarre conspiracy theories, such as the persistent belief in high government circles that Turkey was controlled by a pro-German Jewish cabal.

The Ottoman Background

The Ottoman Empire for Britain in the late nineteenth century was seen mainly as a welcome buffer to block Russian expansion, supplementing Afghanistan in the Great Game to protect British India. Though the Ottomans were notoriously in sharp decline, British policy up to the outbreak of the first world war was to stay out and leave the Empire intact, excepting Egypt, which had come under British control in 1882.

The Liberal Party in Britain in the 1880s strongly protested their government's aid to the Ottomans, circulating reports of Islamic persecution of Christians. Disraeli, England's Jewish prime minister, a Tory, supported aid to the Islamic Caliph in Constantinople. His successor in 1880, Gladstone, a Liberal, halted it. Thereafter the Turks cultivated relations with Germany instead.

Though in decline, the Ottoman Turks, as the holders of the Islamic caliphate, had for centuries pursued Muhammad's vision of total world domination. They had acquired by colonial conquest the whole of the Arab Middle East and North Africa. Long after they lost Spain they seized most of Eastern Europe — Greece, Yugoslavia, Romania, Bulgaria, Albania, and much of Hungary. They were stopped from taking Western Europe only by being repulsed during two brutal sieges of Vienna, in 1529 and 1683. Greece broke away in 1832, Bulgaria in 1878, and the last of the Ottoman Balkan colonies gained independence only in the Balkan wars of 1912-13. There were still in 1914 large Armenian and Jewish minorities as well as Coptic and Maronite Christians. Though the Empire was a theocracy, twenty-five percent of its subjects in 1900 were not Muslims and there were seventy-one sects of Muslim. The government became increasingly weak, but the Ottoman army remained formidable.

In 1908, the Young Turks, a largely secular secret society organized in the Committee of Union and Progress (CUP), staged a successful revolution, imposing a constitutional monarchy on the Sultan and restarting the Empire's moribund parliament.

If one were to say what is surprising about Fromkin's study it is how little each side knew about the other leading up to and during the war. Major decisions, particularly by the British, were based on almost hilariously wrong information. As an example we have Gerald FitzMaurice, chief assistant to the British ambassador in Constantinople. The Young Turk rebellion had broken out in Salonika, today part of Greece but then still under Ottoman rule. Because Salonika had a large Jewish population, FitzMaurice, a virulent antisemite, believed claims by their Islamist enemies that the Young Turk movement was a front for an international Jewish conspiracy. He convinced the ambassador and they developed this thesis in reports to the British government in London, which believed them because they came directly from their own people in Constantinople. This conspiracy theory became an article of faith for the British until near the end of World War I. Over the years it was further embroidered. When the Ottomans allied with the Germans in the Great War it was believed that the international Jewish power was in cahoots with Germany. Then Russia, Britain's ally, abandoned the war after the 1917 Bolshevik Revolution, in which many of the leaders were Jewish. Now high British officials concluded that the Bolsheviks were a German-Jewish front organization whose sole purpose was to stage manage Britain's defeat.

Belief in these fantastic notions played a major role in the decision to issue the Balfour Declaration. Fromkin writes:

> FitzMaurice drew an obvious conclusion from his misconception: that the world war (in which Britain was by then engaged) could be won by buying the support of this powerful group. Its support could be bought, he decided, by promising to support the establishment of a Jewish homeland in Palestine. . . . This reasoning helped to persuade the Foreign Office that it ought to pledge British support to the Zionist program — which it eventually did in 1917.

In 1913 the Young Turks took over direct control of the Ottoman government and appointed themselves as its heads. From then until the end of WWI in 1918 the principal figures in their government were Mehmed Talaat, Minister of the Interior; Enver Pasha, who headed the Ottoman military; and Djemal Pasha, Military Governor of Constantinople, and later of Syria and Palestine.

They abandoned their program of 1908, which had pledged equal civil and religious rights for all, and now concentrated dominant power in the hands of Turkish Muslims in preference to Arabs and imposed still harsher conditions on Greeks, Armenians, Kurds, Christians, and Jews.

Internationally the CUP government made its top priority securing an alliance with a major European power, to protect their Empire from the other powers. They first approached Britain. Winston Churchill, then First Lord of the Admiralty, was for it but the Foreign Office rejected the proposal. On August 1, 1914, the Young Turk government signed a secret treaty of alliance with Germany. The die was cast when two German warships, the *Goeben* and the *Breslau*, evading a British blockade in the Mediterranean, made harbor at Constantinople and were publicly welcomed by the Grand Vizier. When Britain protested, the Ottoman government issued a false claim that it had purchased the two ships, as cover inducting the German officers and crew into the Ottoman navy.

While it was still not certain that the Ottomans were really in the war on the German side, a British official met with the Ottoman ambassador in London to find out their leanings. The Turk's explanation was that they leaned toward the Germans because they feared Russia, which had tried for a century and a half to dismember them, and which was allied with Britain and France. The Ottoman government, generally called the Porte, from the gate to its central buildings, initially thought to remain neutral when the fighting started. But the stunning German victory over Russia's Second Army at the end of August 1914 led Enver Pasha to commit the Ottomans to the war on the German side in hopes of seizing Russian territory. In September the Turks mined the straits at the Dardanelles, closing off Russian access to the Mediterranean from the Black Sea, through which 50 percent of Russian exports passed. Britain declared war on the Ottomans in November.

In the war crisis Whitehall appointed Lord Herbert Kitchener as War Minister. Soon his face with its imposing moustache appeared on recruiting posters across the country, his finger pointing right at the viewer with the message in large type: "Your country needs YOU!" Kitchener had conquered Sudan for Britain, avenging the murder of General Charles George Gordon in Khartoum. He commanded successfully in the Boar War, and had served as head of the British army in India. Most recently he was governor of Egypt. He had vast and unquestioned influence with the mass of the British public. He was the first to tell the Cabinet that the war would last for years and that it would be won on the ground and not with Britain's vaunted navy. He saw the European theatre as the only one of importance and opposed any significant response to the Ottoman Empire.

It was assumed that Kitchener and his staff were expert on conditions in the Middle East. Consequently the Prime Minister and the Cabinet almost invariably deferred to him, or in practice to very junior members of his staff who were presumed to be conveying Kitchener's opinions, though this was often not the case. In fact, even those British officials on the ground in Egypt knew very little about conditions in the Arab lands. There was not at that time a single authoritative book in English on the history of the Ottoman Empire, the best thing available being a German work written in 1744. Of course, this ignorance was mutual. Little was known about British and French issues on the Turkish and Arab side.

Kitchener continued to rely heavily on his team in Khartoum and Cairo. Mainly this was Lieutenant-General Sir Francis Reginald Wingate, British Governor-General of Sudan, based in Khartoum, Wingate's Cairo deputy, Gilbert Clayton, who was also Director of Intelligence for the Egyptian army, and Kitchener's former secretary, Ronald Storrs. In London, a central figure in the Kitchener group became the young MP Mark Sykes, later coauthor of the Sykes-Picot Treaty.

Wingate and Clayton became devotees of Gerald FitzMaurice's crackpot theory that the Young Turk heads of the Porte regime were pro-German Jews. Their working hypothesis was that they should try to break the Arab colonies away from the Turkish heartland of the Ottomans. These British officials were misled here by a few self-seeking Arab radicals, who greatly exaggerated Arab discontent with Turkish rule, to imagine that liberation and then administration by a Christian power would be seen as an improvement.

This was a view fatefully promoted in London by Kitchener and his staff. They were at that time opposed by central figures in the then-Liberal Party government: Prime Minister Herbert Asquith, Foreign Secretary Sir Edward Grey, and Winston Churchill (then a Liberal) were against any acquisition of Ottoman territory by Britain.

Kitchener's reasoning ultimately shaped British war aims and from there, much of our contemporary Middle East. He grasped that Islam was the unifying element in the Muslim East, but he erroneously supposed it to be rigidly centralized. From this he concluded that whoever controlled the Muslim caliphate would command the whole of the Middle East. He believed, along with Wingate and Clayton, that the caliphate was already in the hands of pro-German Jews, and expected that even if the Allies won the war that it would then fall into the hands of the Russians, who it was plain hoped to conquer Constantinople to protect their route to the Mediterranean. Either a German or Russian Caliph would be a mortal threat to Britain's colonies in Egypt, Sudan, and India, which contained half the world's Muslims. Kitchener believed that Tsarist Russia had ambitions to conquer India. So he advocated breaking the caliphate away from the Turks and giving it back to the Arabs. His candidate was Hussein bin Ali, the Ottoman Sharif of the Hejaz.

Hussein's Hashem family, the Hashemites, were descended from Muhammad's daughter Fatimah, and had ruled the holy cities of Mecca and Medina in western Arabia since the tenth century. Under the Ottomans they held the title of Sharif and were in charge of the Hejaz, a narrow strip on the west of Arabia that ran from the Gulf of Aqaba in the north to the border of what is now Yemen in the south. Britain did not consider the alternative contender for control of Arabia, Abdulaziz ibn Saud. Kitchener on September 24, 1914, had Storrs in Cairo send a messenger to Hussein's son Abdullah asking if the Hejaz would support Britain in the war.

To the Kitchener crew in Cairo the proposal that the Hejaz ruler become the Caliph was seen as a religious and moral authority like that of the Pope in Christendom. To Hussein, in accord with Muslim tradition, the Caliph was the fully empowered political ruler as well, so the offer was taken to mean kingship over the whole of Arabia at minimum and more likely over the whole Arab world.

The British Raj in India, based at its summer capital at Simla, was appalled. They wanted to maintain the Afghanistan-Arab buffer between the British colony and the European powers, but did not want to see a unified Arab state in place of the weak and more distant Ottoman Empire. This split between British officialdom in Simla and Cairo persisted throughout the Great War. A further difference was that Simla had opened relations with Ibn Saud in eastern Arabia while Cairo was negotiating with the Hashemites of the Hejaz in the west. And while Simla opposed immediate Arab independence from the Ottomans, Kitchener's people were issuing proclamations calling for an Arab revolt.

Meanwhile in Constantinople, Enver Pasha, against the advice of his German advisers, had delusions of grandeur. In December 1914 he launched an invasion of Russia, attacking in the mountainous Caucasus in the dead of winter. After defeating Russia he planned to conquer British India. Forced to leave his artillery behind in the snow, and with inadequate food, a typhus epidemic scattered his forces, the Russians finishing off the job.

In Europe the invention of barbed wire and the machine gun, combined with greatly improved artillery, produced static trench emplacements in northern France that were almost impossible to breach. Hundreds of thousands of casualties fell in single battles. Kitchener and the rest of the War Cabinet grasped early in the fighting that this would be a long war with prodigious human costs. They began to look for some way to outflank the Germans. In

December 1914, Maurice Hankey, secretary of the War Cabinet, submitted a memorandum proposing an attack on Constantinople by breaching the straits of the Dardanelles, then, in alliance with her Balkan allies — Greece, Bulgaria, and Romania — a march on Austria-Hungary and Germany from the east. Later historians agree that this could have easily been accomplished, but the effort was bungled at several stages, leading to one of Britain's most costly defeats in the war.

Kitchener, responding to Russian appeals that the seaway from the Black Sea be reopened, approved the plan, but only on the condition that only the navy would take part. He refused to allow troops to be diverted from the Western Front. At the last minute, in February 1915, he agreed to send one British division along with new units from Australia and New Zealand. The plan still called for the navy alone to open the straits, with the troops following later. The Turks anticipated the attack, but had no plan to repel it, expecting to lose. British warships fired the first shot on February 19. The Ottomans were in such extremis that they proposed to the Germans to try to get Russia to switch sides in the war to defend them.

Fromkin gives us the oft-told tale of Britain's missteps that followed. Newly appointed Admiral John de Robeck opened the main attack on the straits on March 18, 1915. His first day was a disaster. A French ship exploded. Three of Robeck's ships struck mines, two of them sinking. He withdrew, cabling London that he would resume hostilities in a few days. In London they received intelligence reports that the Turks had run out of ammunition. Fromkin writes:

> All that stood between the British-led Allied fleet and Constantinople were a few submerged mines, and Ottoman supplies of these were so depleted that the Turks were driven to catch and re-use the mines that the Russians were using against them. Morale in Constantinople disintegrated. Amidst rumors and panic the evacuation of the city commenced.

At this juncture de Robeck lost his nerve and refused to continue. The War Cabinet decided to send in its limited army units without naval support. In the interim the defense of the Dardanelles was assumed by Mustapha Kemal, the Turkish officer who later was to rule Turkey as Kemal Ataturk. The British forces, under Sir Ian Hamilton, attacked the northern side of the straits, the Gallipoli peninsula. There was a delay of almost a month while Hamilton assembled his troops. The assault began on April 25. Taking the ridges in several places, the British lost the initiative by camping overnight. By the next day Mustapha Kemal's reinforcements had arrived. The British dug trenches as in France and the same bloody stalemate ensued. The Turks held the heights while the British were pinned down on the beaches.

Despite the fact that the army had taken over the campaign, Winston Churchill was blamed for the defeat. It had been Kitchener who had insisted that the navy go it alone and initiated the separation of the two services, but he was above reproach while Churchill had been prominent in the public eye in the lead-up to the Gallipoli landing. He was dismissed from the Admiralty on May 19. In the end there were 200,000 English, Australian, and New Zealand casualties in the Gallipoli campaign.

The vast loss of life at Gallipoli ironically led to the feeling in Britain that it had made a great investment in the Middle East and had a stake that should be pursued territorially at the war's end, as Fromkin puts it, "to give some sort of meaning to so great a sacrifice."

The public, the press, and initially the Tory critics of the Liberal prime minister, Herbert Asquith, and his second in command, who would succeed him in 1916, David Lloyd George, were convinced that Britain's setbacks, in Gallipoli and in France, were due to civilian meddling with Kitchener's military. Over time, both the leaders of the Liberal Party majority and the Tory minority came to realize that Kitchener was out of his depth and having increasing difficulty formulating a course for Britain's military. This became a closely guarded secret of the high command.

While British victory over the Ottoman Empire, as well as over Germany, now looked remote, an effort was set afoot to explore plans for a postwar Middle East. A central figure in this was Sir Mark Sykes, a young protégé of Kitchener who had spent a good deal of time in the region. The first version had a unified Arabic-speaking domain, in which religious authority would be exercised by Sherif Hussein in Mecca while temporal authority was exercised by the King of Egypt, with Kitchener to be British High Commissioner behind the throne. The British in India had some idea of administering Mesopotamia (later Iraq) from India, but opposed the consolidation of any large Arab state. They were supported by the Foreign Office, but Kitchener backed Sykes and won out. An Arab Bureau was created in December 1915, headquartered in Cairo, where it was effectively dominated by Kitchener's proteges Wingate and Clayton. A low-level functionary brought in semi-officially was T. E. Lawrence, soon to win fame as Lawrence of Arabia.

The British at that time had no definite agreement with any Arab leader or group. It seemed providential, then, when Ottoman staff officer Lieutenant Muhammed Sharif al-Faruqi presented himself, claiming to speak both for Sharif Hussein and for allegedly powerful secret Arab societies. The reality behind this was that Hussein had learned that the Porte intended to depose him. Reluctantly, he tried to interest the British, sending them a letter in the summer of 1915, expressing his understanding of what the caliphate meant, that they should make him ruler of the whole Arab-speaking realm. In making this demand he had been in contact, through his son Feisal, with Arab secret societies in Damascus who thought they could stage an insurrection with several units of the Ottoman army in which Arabs were the majority. The British did not take his demands seriously.

Al-Faruqi had been a member of one of the underground groups. By the time he approached the British in Cairo at the end of 1915 Djemal Pasha had discovered the plot and crushed the Damascus plotters. Al-Faruqi in effect tried to hoax the British by claiming he spoke for the Ottoman army officers in Damascus as well as for Sharif Hussein. He clearly knew the details of Hussein's correspondence with the Arab Bureau in Cairo, and claimed the insurrection was still ready to go. He played a role something like that of the informer Curveball in the lead-up to the American invasion of Iraq in 2003.

The British were convinced now that Sharif Hussein both wanted an alliance and that he had significant military backing from within the Ottoman army. Al-Faruqi insisted that the price of the pending revolt was a British pledge to support an independent Arab Middle East. On the basis of al-Faruqi's assurances the War Cabinet opened negotiations to try to persuade France to give up its claims to Syria.

From here unfolded the famous Arab Revolt of 1916. In a lengthy correspondence between British High Commissioner in Egypt Henry McMahon and Sharif Hussein the British used formulas that could be read to mean a vague promise of postwar Arab independence but were intended to be unenforceable, while Hussein on his part opposed conceding "a single square foot of territory" to France in what are now Syria and Lebanon. While not winning that commitment he joined the Allied side anyway, as he had few options on the Turkish side.

If the British assurances of independence were false, so were the Arab promises made by Sharif Hussein, al-Faruqi, and by Aziz Ali al-Masri, a leader of the Damascus secret societies, who also participated in the exchanges. Fromkin writes:

> Hussein had no army, and the secret societies had no visible following. Their talk of rallying tens or hundreds of thousands of Arab troops to their cause, whether or not they believed it themselves, was sheer fantasy.

The next step was London's negotiations with Paris that ended in the Sykes-Picot Agreement, signed in May 1916. François George Picot represented the hard-colonialist elements in the French government. Their war aims in Asia Minor were to directly administer the coastal cities of Syria, plus all of what became Lebanon, and to control the interior of Syria through Arab puppet rulers. They had some hopes of getting northern Mesopotamia as well, specifically the area around Mosul, now in northern Iraq. Britain was privately sympathetic to these aims, as it would provide a French buffer between British-dominated areas and Russia. The secret treaty Sykes and Picot negotiated gave France everything it asked for, while giving to Britain the provinces of Basra and Baghdad in Mesopotamia, and the loosely defined area the British called Palestine, which was based on the Ottoman vilayet called the Sanjak of Jerusalem but with larger boundaries. There was no area called Palestine under Ottoman rule. Variants of the term Palaestina appear in Herodotus among the ancient Greeks, in Roman writings, and among the Byzantine Greeks, possibly referring to the Philistines, but the term was not used by either Turks or Arabs until the British introduced it, and in British minds it was meant to signify geographically the biblical Jewish Holy Land. "Palestine" was to be placed under an as-yet undefined form of international administration, because of the Holy Land it contained, though the treaty made no mention of the Jews. The French, almost immediately after the signing, made another secret agreement with Russia, in which France, not some international body, was to control Palestine.

Sykes, who had a lifelong fear of Jews, came soon to feel, in contrast to Picot, that Britain ought to promise the Jews a place in Palestine to head off damage to the British cause this mysterious and powerful global force might be inclined to perpetrate. Around the same time, in the spring of 1916, the inveterate conspiracy enthusiast FitzMaurice persuaded a friend in the Foreign Office to submit a memo suggesting that

> if we could offer the Jews an arrangement as to Palestine which would strongly appeal to them we might conceivably be able to strike a bargain with them as to withdrawing their support from the Young Turk Government which would then automatically collapse.

In actuality, Djemal Pasha, the Young Turk administrator in Syria and Palestine, at the end of 1914 had ordered the destruction of the Jewish settlements and the expulsion of the Jews. This was partially carried out before the Germans got him to stop, for fear of pushing foreign Jews into the Allied camp. Ironically, David Ben-Gurion in 1914 offered to raise a Jewish army to defend the Ottoman Empire. He was deported to the United States, where for a few years he continued to propose his pro-Turkish force, switching to a plan for a pro-Allied Jewish army only in 1918.

No one intervened when, early in 1915, the Islamic Porte's xenophobic hostilities turned on the Armenians, far outdoing the massacres of the mid-1890s. Fully half of Ottoman Armenians were deliberately killed or died under the severe conditions of a forced-march deportation. A common figure is that the dead reached 1.5 million. The massacre did strengthen opinion in the West that the Ottomans should not be left in control of non-Islamic peoples after the war, and perhaps not even of non-Turkish Muslims.

Sykes seems to have been a rather naïve young man and believed his treaty's phraseology about independent Arab states. Picot was pleased to use such verbiage so long as France's sphere of influence was included, while Sykes' colleagues back in Cairo felt the same way about "independent" Arab regimes where Britain was to be their advisor.

The Kitchener era ended abruptly on June 5, 1916. Asquith, afraid of the public's reaction if he had the failing hero removed from command, but unwilling to allow him to continue, sent him on a long voyage to confer with their Russian allies. His ship, the *Hampshire*, struck a German mine a few hours out of port from the naval headquarters at Scapa Flow. It went down with almost all aboard. A South African Boer adventurer, Fritz Joubert Duquesne, who had tried unsuccessfully to assassinate Kitchener during the Second Boer War, later claimed that he had given the *Hampshire's* course coordinates to the Germans. During a stint in America Duquesne served as Teddy Roosevelt's trainer for big game hunting. While living in Brazil during some part of World War I he planted time bombs disguised as mineral samples that sank twenty-two Allied ships. He was finally arrested in New York in 1942 during World War II as the head of the biggest German spy ring ever discovered in America.

The Arab Revolt

Emir Hussein proclaimed his long-awaited revolt the same week that Kitchener died. Only a few thousand Bedouin tribesmen joined in, but no regulars from the Ottoman armies. The British navy guarded the Hejaz coast, while a few units of British Muslim troops from Egypt landed to support the Emir. The Arab secret societies, insofar as they existed, much as they wanted independence from the Turks were firmly opposed to British rule and did nothing. Even Hussein himself kept a diplomatic line open to the Porte, offering to change back to the Turkish side if they would guarantee his rule in the Hejaz. The British spent 11 million pounds on the revolt that fizzled (about US$886 million in 2010 dollars).

Just as it seemed that the revolt would come to nothing at all, T.E. Lawrence, then working as a translator in the Cairo headquarters, proposed to have the Emir's small force engage in a guerrilla campaign. It should be placed, he said, under the command of Hussein's son Feisal, and that Lawrence himself was the only liaison Feisal would accept. Thus Lawrence got his foot in the door of the Arab Revolt. He was five foot five inches and had been turned down by the regular army as too short. He left Cairo to join Feisal on November 25, 1916.

In the course of 1916 and 1917 all three of the Allied governments that had entered the war in 1914 fell. The Liberal government in Britain was replaced by a coalition dominated by the Unionist-Conservative Party of Andrew Bonar Law, which endorsed the Liberal Lloyd George as prime minister. Unlike Asquith, Lloyd George ranked British conquests in the Middle East very highly. And unlike his colleagues, who had been schooled in Greek and Latin, he had been raised on the Bible, and viewed the Holy Land as a coherent whole that should be placed under the protection of the Jews, its original inhabitants, though he expected a Zionist state to accept British tutelage.

In November 1917, after several earlier and inconsequential changes of government, France gave the premiership to the seventy-six-year-old Georges Clemenceau. He differed from his predecessors in being more implacably anti-German, and in being less interested in colonies or Middle East affairs, seeing Europe as the political essential. Fromkin comments:

> The fortunes of war and politics had brought into power in their respective countries the first British Prime Minister who wanted to acquire territory in the Middle East and the only French politician who did not want to do so.

And of course, there were the two Russian Revolutions of 1917, that ended with Lenin's Bolsheviks in power and Russia out of the war.

Fromkin includes an interesting account of one more element in the British high command's misinformation and conspiracy theories, in which they amalgamated Lenin and the Communist Revolution to the notion that the Ottoman Empire was controlled by a pro-German Jewish cabal. The fact that Lenin returned to Russia in the famous sealed train, provided by Berlin, and that Lenin within the year took Russia out of the war, to Germany's great advantage, convinced many of Britain's leaders that the Bolsheviks were a mere front for German policy. One figure provided what looked like solid evidence for that theory. This was Alexander Israel Helphand (1867-1924).

Helphand, a Jew born in a shtetl in what is now Belarus, became a Marxist in the late 1880s. He helped Lenin found the newspaper *Iskra*, was friends with Rosa Luxemburg, and was best known, under the name Parvus, for developing the theory of permanent revolution, which he then shared with Leon

Trotsky. He was active in the Russian Revolution of 1905, when he was arrested and imprisoned. He later made a great deal of money in various businesses. And here is how he intersects our current story. He moved to Constantinople, where from 1912 he became close to the Young Turk leaders. He became an arms dealer, where he supplied the Ottoman armies during the Balkan Wars. At the outbreak of World War I he lobbied the Turks to ally with Germany against Russia. In 1915 he went to Berlin to try to persuade the German high command to throw their support to Russian Marxist revolutionaries with the goal of getting Russia out of the war, and if possible inciting a revolution there that would dismember the Russian state. He especially told them to put their money on Lenin. The Germans assented, and gave Helphand a million marks to put his plan into operation. Trotsky and Rosa Luxemburg broke with Parvus. Lenin did so formally, but Fromkin says that Lenin's correspondence shows that he secretly received money from him "via a Polish and a Russian Social Democrat." And, most important of all, Helphand arranged the German sealed train for Lenin's return to Russia in April 1917.

The British intelligence services knew most of this and added it into the conspiracy: Here is a highly placed Jew who advises the Ottoman government, has extensive business connections with it, but is also a pro-German agent who secures German aid for the Russian Bolsheviks to undermine Britain's wartime ally. Case proved. As Fromkin writes, "British observers of the Russian revolutions in 1917 were struck by the apparent conjunction of Bolsheviks, Germans, and Jews." The Turkish angle just clinched it.

The colonial aspirations of the British and French were complicated when the United States entered the war in April 1917, in response to the sinking of American ships by German submarines. The U.S. was particularly outraged by the telegram German Foreign Secretary Arthur Zimmerman sent to his Minister in Mexico instructing him to try to get Mexico to join the German side, and in the event the U.S. entered the war, to seize Texas, Arizona, and New Mexico. The British intercepted and decoded it and turned it over to the U.S. in late February. Woodrow Wilson strongly opposed the creation of any new colonies and called for the right of nations to self-determination. This and a general climate that was emerging in which colonialism was getting a bad name, explains why at the war's end French and British administrations in the Middle East were framed as temporary Mandates rather than as colonies as would have been the case a generation earlier.

The Balfour Declaration and the British Conquest of Palestine

Interestingly, the international Zionist movement remained firmly neutral throughout World War I. A cardinal reason was fear that siding with Britain in the war would provoke the Turks into taking reprisals against the Jews of Palestine, as they had done with the Armenians. The British connection to the actual Zionist movement came through Dr. Chaim Weizmann, a noted chemist and naturalized British subject, who headed a British Zionist Federation. He held no position in the international Zionist movement and opposed their policy of neutrality. He would at the end of his life become the first president of Israel.

In early 1917 Weizmann arranged to meet Mark Sykes. Sykes was still trying to adhere to the terms of the secret Sykes-Picot agreement, so told Weizmann a Jewish state in Palestine would have to be under a joint French-English international condominium. Weizmann responded that he favored British only. As it happened, this was already Lloyd George's view and Sykes was working with a policy the highest ranks of his government had abandoned. Lloyd George eventually met with Weizmann directly and backed his mutually agreeable position. The main obstacle to a public announcement was seen to be France and its ambitions rather than either the Turks or the Arabs. In fact, figures such as Lloyd George and Mark Sykes viewed themselves as equally pro Arab and pro Jewish, thinking both would benefit from escaping from Turkish rule, and that Jewish knowhow and financial backing could rapidly raise the standard of living in Palestine, to the benefit of both peoples. This view simply failed to grasp how Islam was viewed by its faithful.

Nevertheless, Lloyd George believed he needed French agreement to issue anything formal. The problem was solved by putting forward yet another fantasy: that a pledge of a Jewish homeland in Palestine would enthuse the millions of Russian Jews sufficiently to keep Russia in the war. The negotiations with the French took place before the Bolshevik seizure of power. Nahum Sokolow, an official of the international Zionist movement, told the French government that he would undertake a mission to the Jews of Russia if they would in return make a statement of support to a Jewish Palestine. The French issued a carefully worded document that in practice promised nothing, but it was enough for the British to move ahead and have Foreign Secretary Arthur Balfour draft a statement. This was held up for several months in one of the complications typical of everything involving this issue, when several prominent British Jews, particularly Edwin Montagu, Secretary of State for India, strongly opposed it, seeing the creation of a Jewish country as a threat to Jewish acceptance in Britain and raising charges of divided loyalty.

When it was finally released, on November 2, 1917, the famous Balfour Declaration consisted of only three sentences, only one of which was substantive. It read:

> His Majesty's Government view with favour the establishment in Palestine of a national home for the Jewish people, and will use their best endeavors to facilitate the achievement of this object, it being clearly understood that nothing shall be done which may prejudice the civil and religious rights of existing non-Jewish communities in Palestine or the rights and political status enjoyed by Jews in any other country.

Britain adhered to this affirmation for a number of years, but by the late thirties had abandoned it.

*   *   *

The devastation in Europe was so extreme and the trench warfare so difficult to break through that there was little to fight for there, even though the fight could not be escaped. There were hopes of winning something in the Middle East despite the Gallipoli disaster. The new effort got off to a rocky start. Britain's Indian Army made a push toward Baghdad in late 1915, but were mauled by the Turks the following spring. Under a new general, Stanley Maude, the Anglo-Indian Army of the Tigris entered the Mesopotamian provinces in December 1916 and captured Baghdad on March 11, 1917. Close to a majority of the city's inhabitants at that time were Jews, their occupancy predating the Muslim conquest by a thousand years. The British thinking was to place the provinces of Baghdad and Basra under King Hussein, a Sunni Muslim, ignoring the fact that the two provinces as a whole were strongly Shi'ite.

Also in the spring of 1917 British forces based in Egypt set out to march north and capture Palestine. The first British commander, Sir Archibald Murray, was twice defeated in Gaza by Ottoman troops commanded by German officers. Djemal Pasha, the military governor, began a new campaign of suppression of unreliable elements. He expelled the entire Jewish and Arab populations of Jaffa, many of whom died in the process. He announced he intended to deport the whole civilian population of Jerusalem, the majority of whom were Jews. In June General Murray was replaced by General Sir Edmund Allenby, who was ordered to take Jerusalem by Christmas. He did, but by the time he got there only about a third of the Jewish population remained. Fromkin writes: "[M]ost of the rest had died of starvation or disease."

T. E. Lawrence had his first success with his Arab guerrillas in July 1917, when he accompanied a Bedouin chief who staged a daring raid, capturing Aqaba at the northern tip of the Red Sea in what is now Jordan. Lawrence showed up afterward near Cairo in Arab dress to recount the exploit. Always ready to exaggerate his own role and prone to retail fantasy for fact, Lawrence was en route to becoming a national hero.

The Aqaba battle marked the first breakout of the Hejaz forces, who had been blockaded by the Turks. Now their fighters, though not numerous, took part in guerrilla actions supporting the British drive into Palestine. Feisal was made a general in the British army to command these troops. He never had more than about 1,000 Bedouins and another 2,500 former Ottoman prisoners of war. Small as this force was, it was welcome when, after the Bolshevik Revolution and Russia's definitive exit from the war, Germany transferred most of her Eastern Front units to the west, and almost all of Allenby's troops were recalled to Europe. What saved the British in Palestine was a decision by Enver Pasha to launch a major offensive in the other direction, to try to capture for the Ottomans a big piece of Russia's Central Asian territories, mainly Azerbaijan and Turkestan, although he had megalomaniacal hopes of conquering Persia, Afghanistan, and India as well. He succeeded in occupying Baku, but was forced to evacuate his troops by the terms of the armistice as the war ended. He was dismissed as War Minister in October 1918.

*   *   *

Implementing the Balfour Declaration did not fare well on the ground. And this was not particularly because of Arab opposition, but due to anti-Jewish feeling among the British leadership in Cairo. Fromkin writes:

"Even by the standards of the time, Clayton and his colleague, Wingate, were strongly disposed to be anti-Jewish." Sykes began as an antisemite, but once he committed himself to the idea of the Jewish homeland he remained steadfast. On the whole, Clayton and Wingate sabotaged the Balfour commitment.

Early in 1918 Chaim Weizmann led an international Zionist delegation to Palestine. He met with Prince Feisal and the two got on well. Feisal above all wanted British support to become the ruler of Syria and had little interest in Palestine. He was content for the Jews to have it if it meant British backing for his own cause. Feisal followed through by a public endorsement of Zionism at the Versailles Peace Conference in 1919. Unhappily, the British remained split, with the former Kitchener people in Cairo backing the Hashemites while the Indian government was supporting Ibn Saud. How firmly to back Feisal was put to a test as Allenby approached Damascus in September 1918. In London there was division over whether the Sykes-Picot Treaty was still valid. If it was, Syria was to be ceded to France. If not, then most likely Feisal would be named king.

Allenby raised Feisal's flag over Damascus on October 2, but Feisal and his troops did not arrive until the following day and played no part in the city's capture. Allenby met with Feisal that afternoon and laid down Britain's conditions. France was to have direct control of the coastal cities, including Damascus. The Arab sector would be inland Syria, but excluding Lebanon and Palestine. Even in the Arab sector Feisal would be "under French guidance and financial backing" (from the minutes by France's representative at the meeting).

The French had very limited forces in the region. They had hoped to capture what is now Lebanon and Syria, if not Palestine as well, but lacked the troops to do so. They were able to win out in only a part of Lebanon. Allenby brought T. E. Lawrence to London to argue for rejecting all French influence in Syria. Feisal, Lawrence said, did not want French advisers but would prefer British or else, surprisingly, American Jewish Zionists. There was a heated debate on whether to set aside the Sykes-Picot Agreement, which had made the promises to France, with Sykes and the Foreign Office opposing but most of the rest of the government, including the Prime Minister, in favor.

Publicly London now advocated an independent Syria under Feisal, free of French interference. Behind the scenes they expected Britain to pull Feisal's strings.

In March 1918 Germany concluded its armistice with Lenin's Russia, touching off a race between the Germans and their erstwhile Turkish allies to seize Russian dominated Transcaucasia, consisting of Georgia, Armenia, and Azerbaijan. The area briefly declared its collective independence. Azerbaijan and its capital Baku were the main prize because of the plentiful oil. A small British force allied with a loose coalition of local ethnic and radical leftist groups briefly held Baku, but were overwhelmed by the Ottomans in September 1918. The Bolshevik Red Army invaded Azerbaijan in April 1920 and it, along with the other Transcaucasian states were incorporated into what became the Soviet Union in 1922. One of the strangest confrontations of the war took place in Turkestan, when the British and Ottomans fought together on one side against Bolsheviks joined by contingents of German and Austrian prisoners of war.

Bulgaria sued for peace on September 26, 1918, opening the way to Germany's eastern flank, within days bringing the long war to an end.

Remaking the Middle East

At the war's end Britain had 1,084,000 troops in the Middle East, and had seen 250,000 of its men killed or wounded there. The French had only a tiny force and the Americans, who had joined the war late, nothing at all. Based on its strength on the ground, Britain made large-scale demands for territory. As its troops left for home, however, and its armies on the spot rapidly dwindled away, these demands became impossible to enforce. Her position was worsened by a major domestic recession in 1920-21. Lloyd George continued as Prime Minister, and Churchill returned to the government, as Secretary of State for both War and Air, placing him in charge of the demobilization and also of whatever military moves would be made in the former Ottoman territories.

Unexpectedly, Italy, which had been on the Allied side but had nothing to do with the Middle East, laid claim to a portion of Anatolia and landed troops at Smyrna. Stories of Italian atrocities raised international outrage. The Allies, with strong American support, asked Greece, which was nearby, to send in its own forces to expel the Italians. This set up a major confrontation between the Greeks and the Turks. Smyrna had been a Greek city since the days of classical Athens, and the Anatolian Mediterranean coast was dotted with Greek towns and offshore islands that had been colonized by Greece for some 2,500 years. Lloyd George and Woodrow Wilson at the Versailles Peace Conference were sympathetic to the idea the a portion of Anatolia around Smyrna should become part of Greece. It might seem that Europe and Asia are naturally separated in that area by the Aegean Sea and the Sea of Marmara, yet in the end these natural borders didn't hold, but it was the other way around, and Turkey incorporated a portion of European Greece.

Through astute manipulation of the agenda, Lloyd George managed to keep virtually all of Britain's holdings in the Middle East off the floor at Versailles: its occupation of Mesopotamia/Iraq, its influence in Persia, its alliances in Arabia with both Hussein and Ibn Saud, and even the fate of Palestine. Only France's claim to Syria was up for debate. Woodrow Wilson spoke forcefully for national self-determination, but returned home early and the Senate refused to ratify either the Treaty of Versailles or American membership in the League of Nations. The commission on the Middle East excluded almost all the interested parties. It was initially composed of five states, then reduced to a Council of Four — the United States, Britain, France, and Italy. Italy soon withdrew, and when Wilson went home there were just Britain and France.

The details were worked out not at Versailles but in a series of succeeding conferences and treaties, concluding in a final redrawing of the Middle

Eastern map in 1922. Fromkin notes that "Lloyd George, between 1919 and 1922, attended no fewer than thirty-three international conferences." The most important ones for the Ottoman Empire were the First Conference of London (beginning February 1920), a meeting in San Remo, Italy, in April, and a treaty at Sevres near Paris signed in August 1920.

The greatest omission from the settlements were the hoped-for creation of a homeland for the Kurds, the largest ethnicity in the world that had no state of its own. The British had hoped to sponsor one or more Kurdish homelands, but when they occupied the area in 1919 the Kurds rebelled against them and the project was dropped. Today the Kurds are divided between Iraq, Turkey, Iran, and Syria, their unrealized hopes for nationhood leading to perennial clashes in all four states.

The intent of the armistice terms were to break off the Arabic-speaking territories from the Ottomans and shrink their empire to its Turkish core, under various restrictions and impositions of external control. When popular opposition arose to the limits on national sovereignty, the new sultan, Mehmed VI, who intended to cooperate with the Allies, imposed a dictatorship. Outside of Constantinople the government's authority collapsed, replaced by roving bands and local administrations. This became an international problem when Muslim bands attacked Greek villages near Samsun on the north Black Sea coast. The Sultan appointed Mustapha Kemal to suppress the unrest. Kemal set out on May 6, 1919, but his real intent was to recruit an army in the Turkish interior to resist excessive Allied demands.

As the Greeks were massing in the west at Smyrna, Mustapha Kemal revolted against the Sultan in the interior. He called a national congress at Sivas and declared Turkey independent. In February 1920 Kemal led an army of 30,000 in defeating a small French unit in southern Anatolia, providing the first indication to the Western powers that his army existed. Kemal was an exception in the region in that he was a secular nationalist, while for all the prominent Arab leaders Islam was the center of their politics.

Parallel to Kemal's uprising in Turkey, Arab resistance to the French began to stir, based in Damascus but extending into Lebanon. It was led by former Ottoman officers and pro-Ottoman land owners, now committed to Arab independence from Turkey but persisting in their hostility to the Western Christian powers. These elements were far weaker than Kemal and divided among themselves, but the British, the only serious Western military force nearby, withdrew in September 1919. That left Feisal, who was claiming to rule Syria in alliance with Britain, caught between the Arabs who wanted independence and the French who would have none of it. When Clemenceau, who had been willing to concede a good deal to Feisal to maintain relations with Britain, was defeated for the French presidency in January 1920, re-placed by hard-line colonialist Alexandre Millerand, the period of negotiations with Feisal abruptly ended.

The terms arrived at in London and San Remo in 1920 provided that the Arabic-speaking portion of the Ottoman Empire would be split off from Turkey and divided between France and Britain, under League of Nation Mandates that were nominally temporary. France would get Syria and Lebanon; Britain, Mesopotamia and Palestine. Arabia would be independent, but its kings were allied to Britain. Turkey's finances were to be administered by France, Britain, and Italy, while the Dardanelles were to be under international control. It didn't work the way it was planned.

Local unrest soon broke out throughout the British-occupied areas: Rioting in Egypt in 1919, a war in Afghanistan, anti-Jewish riots in western Palestine in the spring of 1920, and a revolt in Iraq that summer. France and Communist Russia also faced Muslim revolts. Fromkin devotes a brief chapter to each of the trouble spots that confronted the British.

In November 1918 an Egyptian delegation, led by Saad Zaghlul, a founder of the Wafd Party, had a meeting with Sir Reginald Wingate, the British High Commissioner in Cairo, asking to attend the Versailles Conference. This was refused, and when Zaghlul persisted, he was arrested and deported to Malta. Protests erupted, there were massive strikes, railroad lines were torn up. Two British officers and five soldiers were murdered. Things were brought under control only when General Allenby returned to Cairo and ordered Zaghlul's release. Fromkin writes: "The principal British fantasy about the Middle East — that it wanted to be governed by Britain, or with her assistance — ran up against a stone wall of reality." Britain continued to rule, without the consent of the governed, mainly because of its concern with control of the Suez Canal. It issued a unilateral declaration of Egypt's independence on February 22, 1922, which reduced but did not eliminate Britain's military presence. Saad Zaghlul was elected Prime Minister in 1924. The last of British influence essentially ended with the Egyptian officers' revolution in 1952, the last British troops leaving in 1954.

On February 19, 1919, Amanullah Khan, the Emir of Afghanistan, a British protectorate, issued a declaration of independence. He planned to sponsor a national anti-British uprising in India. Afghan troops crossed into India on May 3, 1919. The British won the skirmish, bombed several Afghan cities, but in August conceded complete Afghan independence.

In Arabia both monarchs were being financed by Britain, but they were engaged in a religious war against each other. The Saudi family were allied with the fanatical and puritanical Wahabi sect, which viewed all other forms of Islam as heretical. In May 1919 a Bedouin force of Wahabi militants, numbering just 1,100, armed only with swords, spears, and some antiquated rifles, completely destroyed a Hejaz force of 5,000 camped with the latest European equipment. In 1924 Ibn Saud and his Wahabi warriors totally destroyed the Hashemite system and incorporated the Hejaz into what was soon renamed Saudi Arabia.

Turkey proved the biggest surprise for the Western powers. As late as the beginning of 1919 Lloyd George was considering a plan in which Turkey would be divided between Greece, France, Italy, and the United States. By 1920 he came around to the idea of keeping the country unified, but under strictures of foreign control. In Turkey, in contrast, national elections were held late in 1919 that produced delegates quite unwilling to accept Britain's terms. The new delegates held an informal meeting at Angora (now Ankara) where they endorsed a declaration called the National Pact that proclaimed Turkey an independent Muslim state. In January 1920 when the new Chamber of Deputies formally convened in Constantinople they voted to adopt the National Pact and announced this publicly on February 17. Fromkin comments:

> If the political theme of the twentieth century is seen to be the ending of Europe's rule over its neighboring continents, then the Ottoman Chamber's declaration of independence signaled the dawn of the century.

A new war began. Mustapha Kemal delivered a smashing defeat to the French in Cilicia near the Syrian border. Then, in mid-March, the British occupied Constantinople. Prominent officials and members of the Chamber of Deputies were arrested and deported to Malta. This simply released Mustapha Kemal from any obligation to the Sultan and his government. Free members of the Chamber of Deputies made their way to Angora, where they declared a new parliament and elected Mustapha Kemal president.

The British took a while to grasp what Kemal represented. They first thought he was an agent of the Sultan. Then, when he signed a treaty with the Bolsheviks in March 1921, they thought that he was acting either for the Communists or for Enver Pasha, who had been given asylum at the end of World War I. All these assumptions were wrong. Kemal and Enver were enemies, and Kemal soon outlawed the Turkish Communist Party and had its leaders killed. The Communists ignored this and began to pump money and military supplies into Turkey on the grounds that driving out the British was more important.

Because the Ottomans had just been defeated in a long war, the British did not believe that Kemal could mount a credible opposition. This was a grave miscalculation. After a Kemalist attack on a British battalion outside of Constantinople in June 1920 London, looking for reinforcements at low cost, asked Greece to send troops. So began the Greek-Turkish war. The Greeks opened an offensive from their base at Smyrna, capturing most of Asia Minor. A second salient in mainland Greece captured Thrace, the portion of European Greece long held by the Ottomans. On August 10, 1920, the captive Sultan in Constantinople was compelled to sign the humiliating Treaty of Sevres. They were ignoring Kemal's forces deep in the interior.

The decision was cast to push further when Greek elections brought to power the pro-German leaders who had been in exile during the Great War. They were determined to try to conquer Turkey outright. France and Italy took this as a sign that they should make peace with Kemal. Churchill and most of the cabinet were opposed to war with Turkey on financial grounds. Lloyd George almost alone remained committed to defeating Mustapha Kemal.

In Syria, Feisal was still in uneasy charge. He called a General Syrian Congress on June 6, 1919. The congress demanded total independence for a Greater Syria that would include what is now Lebanon, Jordan, and Israel. Feisal, in Europe, negotiated an agreement with Clemenceau offering very minimal French oversight for Syria, but on his return to Damascus the Arab nationalists rejected this. They also issued declarations opposing British rule in Mesopotamia and Palestine. The British, in consequence, withdrew their military protection of Damascus. The French in Beirut marched on Damascus. Feisal at the end of July 1920 was sent into exile.

Now the French made one of the great mistakes for which the world is still paying. Their core concern was to protect the Maronite Christians of the Levant. With their momentary military advantage they added to what is now Syria a Great Lebanon that expanded far beyond the territory where the Maronite Christians were the majority. The Maronites had historically, for security from Muslim threats, retreated into the Mount Lebanon range that parallels the coast inland. The French now added the coastal cities of Beirut, Tripoli, Sidon, and Tyre, as well as the long Bekaa Valley, all of which had large Sunni or Shi'ite populations, making Lebanon in the long run almost ungovernable.

The British had their own problems. A main public reason for them to be in the Middle East was to support Prince Feisal, who had fought on their side in the Great War. Now Feisal, to retain his Arab following, had declared his opposition to both French and British presence in the region.

What Happened to Palestine?

Now that the French had a strongly pro-colonialist government that aimed to grab whatever it could in the Eastern Mediterranean, the generally undefined borders of Syria, Lebanon, and Palestine left open the opportunity to lay claim to the whole of it. To discredit Britain's Balfour policy they dug deep into the arsenal of French antisemitism. Fromkin quotes the Oeuvre des Ecoles d'Orient, the representative of French Catholic missionaries in the Middle East, claiming there was a world Jewish-Bolshevik conspiracy "seeking by all means at its disposal the destruction of the Christian world." The president of this organization declared, "It is inadmissible that the 'Country of Christ' should become the prey of Jewry and of Anglo-Saxon heresy. It must remain the inviolable inheritance of France and the Church."

The original Mandates for Syria to France and Palestine to Britain were issued by the San Remo conference in April 1920, pending final approval by the League of Nations. The most important decisions concerning the Palestinian portion were made at a Cairo Conference held in March 1921. These were already in place by the time the League of Nations took up the issue and confirmed the British Mandate on July 23, 1922. Throughout these three international gatherings, "Palestine" was defined consistently as the territory that today constitutes Israel, the West Bank, and Gaza, west of the Jordan River, and what is now Jordan on the east side. Though the Mandate specified that Palestine was to provide for a Jewish national home, the British, for reasons outlined below, decided at the Cairo Conference to exclude the Jews from 75 percent of Palestine, in order to set up an Arab state in what was then called Transjordan. It has been argued ever since, with some justice, that already in 1921 the Palestinian Arabs were given 75 percent of the total land of Palestine.

The eastern part of Palestine, Transjordan, posed a problem for the British after the bulk of their military had gone home. They had essentially no administration there. The French were looking for an excuse to invade Palestine and take it from the British, and the road in would certainly be through the undefended Transjordan. The British adopted a strategy of trying to get the local Arab groups to fight among themselves to divert them from staging raids over the border into Lebanon that would give the French an excuse to invade. The British saw a solution at the Cairo Conference both to put an administration in place on the east side of the Jordan and to win back the Hashemites as their main Arab allies in the Middle East. Their proposal was to offer the throne of Mesopotamia to Feisal, and to create what was supposed to be a temporary monarchy in Transjordan for Feisal's brother Abdullah. Part of the reason here was that Abdullah, with 300 Bedouin followers, had shown up in

Amman in November 1920, claiming he was on his way to attack the French in Damascus. This seemed highly improbable, but the British wanted to take no chances on provoking the French, and so tried to persuade the Hashemite prince to stay where he was. Churchill, who presided at the conference, insisted that both the terms of the Mandate and the Balfour Declaration would be met if the Arabs got the larger portion of the land, east of the Jordan, while the Jews got the 25 percent that remained west of the Jordan.

Abdullah agreed to govern Transjordan for six months on a trial basis. He ruled until July 20, 1951, when he was assassinated by a Palestinian of the clan of the pro-Nazi Grand Mufti of Jerusalem, Haj Amin al-Husseini. His descendents continue to rule Jordan today. As many as 20,000 Palestinians were killed in 1972 when they staged an unsuccessful uprising to try to overthrow the Hashemite dynasty.

On the west side of the Jordan many of the British officers, even those who publicly claimed to agree with the idea of Jewish immigration, secretly opposed it. This gave encouragement to Arab exclusionists who opposed both Jewish and Christian communities, of no matter how long standing. There were attacks on Jews by Bedouin tribesmen in the Upper Galilee in 1919. Several Jewish settlers were killed by Arab marauders in early 1920. There were three days of anti-Jewish riots in Jerusalem in April 1920 in which many Jews were killed and hundreds wounded. The British government mostly ignored the rioters but meted out long prison terms to members of Ze'ev Jabotinsky's self-defense force, which had prevented violence in the section called New Jerusalem. Local British authorities blamed the Jews for the violence, but an investigation by the head of Military Intelligence from Cairo determined that the Jewish witnesses were telling the truth. His investigation showed that a British colonel was conspiring with the Arab Mufti of Jerusalem to start further anti-Jewish riots.

It seems that there were two dominant families among Jerusalem's Arabs, the al-Husseinis and the al-Nashashibis. The former were strongly anti-British and antisemitic, the later more conciliatory and willing to live in peace with the Jews.

Priming the Iraqi Powder Keg

Submerged in the broader Ottoman matrix, the many otherwise hostile groups in the territory of Mesopotamia were held in check by the far greater power of the Empire. When the borders shrank down to the state renamed Iraq in 1920, the hostilities seemed more able to be acted on. We have seen a similar pattern since, when the Tito dictatorship ended in Yugoslavia and Saddam Hussein was overthrown in Iraq. Authoritarian regimes have for a time successfully repressed internal animosities, but when the bonds are loosened all hell breaks loose.

Britain began with the Ottoman vilayets of Basra and Baghdad, but was able to add Mosul in the north, a Kurdish enclave, desirable because of its oil. The national majority were the Shi'ites, who strongly opposed being governed by the Sunni minority. The Kurds were against any Arab ruler. And there was a large Jewish minority, especially in Baghdad, as well as Nestorian Christian refugees from the fighting in Turkey. The Jews would be expelled en masse after the founding of Israel, as part of the one million Jews driven out of the Arab, Turkish, and Persian lands between 1945 and 1960. This would sweep up virtually the entire Jewish populations of Egypt, Iraq, Iran, Turkey, Syria, Lebanon, Algeria, Libya, Tunisia, and Morocco, peoples whose unbroken residence long-predated that of the Arabs. These refugees, who became the majority in the new State of Israel, seem in the minds of many progressives and leftists in the West, who know only about the smaller number of Palestinian refugees in the mass exchange of populations of that period, to have neither existence nor a right to a place to live.

In June 1920 the British got a taste of what they were up against as revolts by a multiplicity of the mutually hostile groups became focused on driving out the Europeans. Outposts were overrun and soldiers killed, communications were cut. In August some of the rebels proclaimed an Arab provisional government. By the time order was restored Britain had 450 dead and 1,500 wounded.

Placing the Pahlavis on the Persian Throne

It is astonishing to recall just how geographically widespread was Britain's influence even after its armies had been repatriated. As World War I ended she had four small military groups in Persia. Russia had occupied northern Persia in 1911, a status disavowed by the new Bolshevik government in Moscow. In London, Lord Curzon undertook to install a postwar pro-British regime, but had little in the way of forces with which to do it. He somehow managed to get Persia to sign a treaty in August 1919 that delegated to British officers construction of a railroad and put British experts in charge of the country's national finances. Britain was to offer a loan that would cover the railroad and the staff salaries, recovering it from custom duties. He did not grasp that the Persians were no longer worried about the Russians and now looked on the British as unwelcome guests. Twenty-five of Teheran's twenty-six newspapers denounced the agreement.

On May 18, 1920, a flotilla of Bolshevik battleships attacked the Persian port of Enzeli, drove off the small contingent of British defenders, and seized a number of ships that had been taken over by the Persians from defeated anti-Bolsheviks. In the autumn London sent Major-General Edmund Ironside to see what he could do in northern Persia. He quickly concluded that only an indigenous military force could expect to remain functional as Britain retreated further. He set his eyes on the Persian Cossack Division. Originally a creation of the Russian Tsars, it served as a bodyguard for the Persian Shahs. After the Bolshevik Revolution it was financed by the British. Ironside took it over, sacked its anti-Bolshevik Russian commanders, and put Reza Khan, a tough Persian colonel, in their place.

On February 21, 1921, Reza Khan, encouraged by Ironside, marched into Teheran at the head of a small force of 3,000 men in a coup in which he appointed himself commander in chief of the Persian army. In 1925 he overthrew the Shah and named himself Reza Shah Pahlavi. He was the one to change the name of the country to Iran, in 1935. He drove out both the British and the Soviets and established a modernizing secular regime like that of Mustapha Kemal in Turkey. His son, Mohammad Reza Pahlavi was overthrown by the Ayatollah Khomeini's Shi'ite Islamic revolution in 1979, affirming, after more than half a century of secular rule, that Islamic religion remained dominant over nationalism.

Lenin's Russia in the Middle East

Despite its colonial rule in India and Egypt, Britain was fairly well regarded among Muslims before World War I because it was seen as their protector from Tsarist Russia. This changed dramatically after the war with the Ottomans and the Bolshevik Revolution. Now it was Britain that was imposing restrictive treaties in Muslim lands while the new Russia had renounced its secret treaties and publicly encouraged Kemalist Turkey and revolts in Persia and Iraq. This opened a debate in London between Lord George Curzon, former Viceroy of India and currently Secretary of State for Foreign Affairs, and the current Secretary of State for India, Edwin Montagu. Curzon viewed the Bolsheviks as a military threat and advocated a tough military presence in the Middle East. Montagu, an anti-Zionist Jew, saw Curzon's policy as making enemies of the Muslims. He opposed the division of the Ottoman Empire, and saw Soviet influence as political rather than military, proposing to counter it by support to Muslim and Arab nationalism. Montagu, Fromkin writes, held that

> It would be a mistake for Britain to maintain a military presence in the
> Middle East . . . or even a merely economic one, for it might lead native

leaders to conclude that the real threat to their independence came from London.

Montagu also called for changing India's status from a colony to a dominion as with Canada and Australia.

Montagu largely won the argument when the War Office ruled against Curzon on the grounds that there were neither the troops nor the money to mount an interventionist policy.

As for the Soviets, while in their propaganda they were anti-imperialist, in practice they used military force to subdue the Muslim peoples of Central Asia who had been colonized by the Communists' Tsarist predecessors. The first of these conquests was the seizure of Azerbaijan. This former Russian colony declared its independence in May 1918 and created a parliamentary republic. It gave women the vote, which was unique among Muslim states. It also created a modern university at Baku. The Bolshevik 11th Red Army invaded on April 28, 1920, ending the brief experiment in independence. They did the same in the Christian states of Georgia and Armenia.

Around the time of the October Revolution Muslims in Central Asia gathered in Kokand in what is today Uzbekistan and declared an autonomous government. The Bolsheviks had a Soviet of their own in nearby Tashkent, composed entirely of Russians without a single Muslim. The Red Army moved in and crushed the Kokand Muslims. Survivors, in 1919, organized the Basmachi rebellion, that fought for an independent Muslim Turkestan and saw the Bolsheviks as no better than the Tsars. Heavy fighting continued for four years, with the main Basmachi forces defeated by the Communists in 1923, but continuing on as guerrillas for another decade.

There were two existing Muslim states besides the armed efforts to create new ones. These were the former Tsarist protectorates of Khiva and Bukhara. The Red Army captured Khiva in September 1920 and executed its leaders. They lost a small war with Bukhara in 1918. A second assault with armored vehicles and aircraft overthrew the emirate and Bukhara became a People's Republic. It became a province of Uzbekistan in the 1990s after the Soviet collapse.

Our old acquaintance Enver Pasha played a role in these events. Exiled from Turkey, he went first to Germany. There he contacted his friend, General Hans von Seekt, who was interested in establishing contacts between defeated Germany and Soviet Russia. Enver contacted Communist leader Karl Radek, went to Moscow, and for a time served as director of the Soviet government's Asiatic Department. In November 1921 Lenin sent Enver to Turkestan to bolster the Communist forces fighting the Basmachis. Enver changed sides and soon rose to Basmachi supreme commander, supported by the Emir of Bukhara. He was killed in a battle with the Communists on August 4, 1922.

One consequence of Enver's negotiations on General von Seekt's behalf was the second Treaty of Rapallo, in April 1922, between Weimar Germany and the Soviet Union. A secret annex of July of that year provided for mutual military training. German factories were set up in the USSR to manufacture military aircraft, poison gas, and explosive shells. Fromkin adds that "The German army established training and academies for its tank commanders and fighter pilots on Soviet territory." Soviet officers received training in Germany as well.

The Soviets, by military force, subjugated a vast Muslim territory in Central Asia. These were organized into Soviet Republics, all of which broke away from Russia as soon as the Soviet Union collapsed in 1989. They comprise the five present-day nations of Turkmenistan, Uzbekistan, Tajikistan, Kyrgyzstan, and Kazakhstan. Fromkin writes:

> Soviet Russia's liquidation of the last of the Turkish independence movements in Central Asia completed the process by which the Bolshevik authorities revealed that they would not keep their promise to allow non-Russia peoples to secede from Russian rule. It was now evident that they intended to retain the empire and the frontiers achieved by the czars.

Finalizing the Situation in Palestine and Turkey

The final shape of the postwar Middle East took form in 1922. Foreign colonial control, masked as temporary Mandates for the British and French, and as socialist liberation by the Russians, was codified, in the establishment of the Soviet Union in December 1922, and in the final series of conferences among the Western Allies.

Winston Churchill played an outsized role in the final deliberations of the Western powers, but his views nevertheless did not prevail. He favored continuing his country's nineteenth century strategy of maintaining Turkish power intact as a buffer against Russia. Hence he called for recognizing the Mustapha Kemal government and establishing good relations with it. And now that the Arabs were separated from the Ottomans, Britain should try to stay on good terms with them as well. He was particularly opposed to the Greek military in Smyrna and their campaign against the Kemal forces. He warned that Britain could not prevail if she were enemies with the Russians, Turks, and Arabs all at once, and that Greek opinion didn't matter in the bigger picture. Though their views did not coincide, Lloyd George in January 1921 made Churchill Colonial Minister. The Indian office had finally reached agreement with Cairo to support the Mandate protectorate plan for Iraq and Palestine under the rule of Hussein's sons and not press for direct control.

T. E. Lawrence had an important influence on Churchill's conclusions. From the time of the Aqaba raid in 1917 Lawrence had persistently exaggerated the role played by Feisal and his small band of Bedouins in the British campaign in Palestine and Syria. This falsely led Churchill and others to believe that Feisal represented a powerful military force and was widely popular among the Ottoman Arabs. None of this was the case, but it underlay the ultimate decision to give Iraq to Feisal and to split off the majority of Palestine and give it to his brother Abdullah. By the early 1920s, with Britain deep in recession, the eagerness of its high officialdom to possess large tracts of the Middle East had definitely waned, and this now looked more like a useless drain on an exhausted treasury. One advantage Churchill saw in installing two Hashemite kings was that it would simplify future disagreements. Pressure on one could likely extract compliance from the other. Churchill was more ready to look to some level of force to get what he wanted from Arab leaders while Lawrence advocated the free adherence of Arab states to the British Commonwealth.

At the Cairo Conference in March 1921 the plan for Feisal to rule Iraq and Abdullah Palestine were approved. In the debate over how Britain could supply the resources to maintain its influence, Churchill proposed a scheme in which a few regional air bases backed by small military units with armored cars were to manage internal security. As this would be much cheaper than large numbers of troops it was accepted.

Feisal was made king by the Mesopotamian/Iraqi Council of Ministers on July 11. His principal opponent for the position, Sayyid Talib, who campaigned under the slogan "Iraq for the Iraqis," was conveniently deported to Ceylon just before the vote.

Abdullah in Transjordan proved to be a weak and lackadaisical ruler. Initially sorry they had chosen him, the situation was stabilized by the appointment of the competent Colonel F. G. Peake to run a Transjordan Bedouin military, consolidated in 1923 as the Arab Legion. The Legion gained fame later under its British commander, John Glubb (Glubb Pasha), 1939 to 1956.

The Cairo Conference decisions plainly ran counter to the Balfour Declaration and the understanding that underlay the League of Nations grounds for Britain's Palestine Mandate, whose draft was then under discussion and scheduled for a formal vote in 1922. Fromkin writes:

> But to maintain Abdullah — an Arabian — as ruler of Transjordan and to maintain Transjordan as an Arab preserve, in which Jews could not settle to build their homeland, was to depart from the Balfour Decla-

ration policy of fostering a Jewish National Home. If the British were indeed planning to make Palestine into a Jewish country, it was hardly auspicious to begin by forbidding Jews to settle in 75 percent of the country or by handing over local administration, not to a Jew, but to an Arabian.

Churchill responded by changing the text of the Mandate declaration to read that Britain was not required to implement the Balfour Declaration east of the Jordan River. Chaim Weizmann wrote to Churchill strongly protesting ceding Transjordan to the Arabs. He also objected to Churchill's agreement to let the French take a goodly strip of northern Palestine and incorporate it into Lebanon. A similar protest was sent by U.S. Supreme Court Justice Louis Brandeis. The Zionists were assured that the prohibition on Jewish immigration to Transjordan was likely to be purely temporary. It was not.

Putting a Hashemite in charge of Transjordan did not bring peace to the country. In 1922 Ibn Saud's Wahabi warriors staged an invasion that almost toppled Abdullah, who was saved by Churchill's airplanes and armored cars.

Fromkin concludes about this situation:

> The recurring suggestion that Palestine be partitioned between Arabs and Jews ran up against the problem that 75 percent of the country had already been given to an Arab dynasty that was not Palestinian. The newly created province of Transjordan, later to become the independent state of Jordan, gradually drifted into existence as an entity separate from the rest of Palestine; indeed, today it is often forgotten that Jordan was ever part of Palestine.

Meanwhile in western Palestine Arab violence against Jews was mounting, with the secret encouragement of sections of the British officer corps. On May Day 1921 a small demonstration of Jewish communists was met by an Arab riot in which thirty-five Jews were killed. This quickly spread to the rest of the country. A key event that would echo down the years to our own day was the selection of a new Grand Mufti of Jerusalem on the death of the existing one on March 21, 1921. Under rules that were inherited from the Ottoman Empire, a Muslim electoral college was to select three candidates and the final decision was referred to the civilian government. The winner this time was not even one of the three approved candidates. A violently antisemitic officer in the British High Command secretariat, Ernest T. Richmond, rigged the selection to give the position to Amin al-Husseini, one of the most anti-Jewish of the Arab leaders, who had been sentenced to ten years in prison for his role in the anti-Jewish riots of the previous year. Fromkin writes:

Richmond must have believed that he was striking a blow against Zionism. As time would show, he had struck a crueler, more destructive blow against Palestinian Arabs, whom the Grand Mufti was to lead into a bloody blind alley. An all-or-nothing adventurer, the Grand Mufti placed Arab lands and lives at risk by raising the stakes of the Arab-Jewish conflict such that one or another — Jews or Arabs — would be driven out or destroyed. Eventually the Grand Mufti's road was to led him to Nazi Germany and alliance with Adolph Hitler.

The Jews, for their part, tried to avoid confrontations with the Arabs by purchasing unused land from the large landowners. This rapidly inflated land prices and even those Arabs who were anti-Jewish were eager to make money selling land to the Jews. Fromkin says that at least a quarter of the elected leadership of the Arab Palestinian community sold land to Jews between 1920 and 1928. Churchill and his government supposed that the hostility toward the Jews arose from the land purchases and took at face value the publicly professed Arab complaints that the land could not support a larger population than existed at that time. Fromkin comments:

> Arab opposition to Jewish settlement was rooted in emotion, in religion, in xenophobia, in the complex of feelings that tend to overcome people when newcomers flood in to change their neighborhood. The Arabs of Palestine were defending a threatened way of life.

Arab hostility was fanned by anti-Jewish British officers who assured them that Britain would renounce the Balfour Declaration. Fromkin reports that Churchill believed "that 90 percent of the British army in Palestine was arrayed against the Balfour Declaration policy." In fact, back in London the House of Lords on June 21, 1922, passed a resolution by 60 to 29 that the Palestine Mandate and the Balfour policy were unacceptable. Churchill responded in the House of Commons with a brilliant speech in which he said that while he had no part in creating the Balfour policy that Britain was morally bound to carry out its obligations and that most of those who had voted to abandon the Jewish cause in Palestine were on record as favoring it in the past. His position was passed in the Commons by a vote of 292 to 35.

The Palestine Arab Congress sent a telegram to Churchill saying they rejected the League of Nations Mandate in its totality. The Zionists, having little choice, supported it even in the greatly reduced territory it left open to them.

Elsewhere, in the fall of 1921, the French signed a separate peace with Turkey, a major victory for the Kemalists but disconcerting to Britain and Greece. The French in the process supplied weapons to Turkey to use against Greece, which Britain was supporting, putting the two allies from World

War I on opposite sides of a new small war. Fromkin traces the roots of this disunity back to the decision of the Asquith government in 1915 agreeing to Russian demands to be given Constantinople and control the straits of the Bosphorus. So long as British policy had been to keep the rest of Europe out of the Ottoman Empire it was not a source of contention. But once opened for division, each country was staking its own territorial claims, if possible at the expense of its rivals.

This led to the last major event in remaking the Middle Eastern map: the Greek invasion of Turkey. Lloyd George at the conclusion of the London Conference in March 1921 sent a message to the Greek delegates that his country would not oppose a new Greek offensive in Turkey. The Greek troops at Smyrna opened hostilities on March 23. They reached the Anatolian plateau but were repulsed by Kemal's forces. The Greeks decided to renew the offensive in the summer. It began on July 10, 1921. Initially they met with success, capturing a major rail center at Eskishehir. Kemal asked the new assembly for, and received, dictatorial powers. He pulled back his troops to the Sakarya River, less than fifty miles from Angora, where they dug in on the hillsides on the east bank.

The Greeks succeeded in crossing the Sakarya, and even fighting their way to the top of the ridges. There, cut off from supplies and harassed by the Turkish cavalry, they abandoned the campaign on September 14 and began the long trek back to Eskishehir. The battle resumed the following year and in early September the Greek front crumbled. Athens sent an evacuation fleet. The defeat had historic consequences. The largest of the Greek settlements on the Turkish coast was Smyrna, the greatest city of Asia Minor, which had been Greek since the 11th century BC. The Turkish forces burned it to the ground, sparing only the Turkish quarter. Fromkin estimates that by the end of 1922 1.5 million Greek civilians were driven out of Turkey. The fact that their occupancy predated the arrival of the Turks by thousands of years carried no weight at all.

The expulsion of the Greeks, following on the Armenian massacre a few years before under the Ottoman government, was a clear sign of the ethnic and religious intolerance that would come to mark all of the Middle Eastern Muslim regimes, even those that, like Kemalist Turkey, tried to be secular.

An Allied occupation force still held Constantinople, but hasty negotiations in October 1922 confirmed that Turkey would have full control of the old capital, of the Dardanelles, and of the former Greek territory of eastern Thrace on the European side. In November Mustapha Kemal expelled the Sultan from Constantinople. Only then did the Ottoman Empire officially come to an end. The Greeks put their whole top leadership who had waged the war against Turkey on trial and executed six of them, including Prime Minister Gounaris. In London, Lloyd George, who had supported the Greek invasion of Turkey, resigned. Much of the British press demanded a full withdrawal from Iraq, Transjordan, and Palestine. Even Winston Churchill lost his seat in Parliament.

What Was Settled in 1922?

If 1922 ended with the map redrawn, what did the settlement amount to? First, the new Soviet Russia's southern borders were settled, while Turkey, Iran, and Afghanistan had managed to remain independent. Next, the long awaited demise of the Ottoman Empire had finally taken place. The results were recorded in not one but in a score of different agreements, treaties, and decisions by national assemblies. While the British Mandate for Palestine was signed off on by the League of Nations, the comparable status of Iraq rested on a treaty Britain concluded with Feisal, also in 1922.

The bonds between Britain and Egypt were loosened under the terms of the Allenby Declaration of 1922. The Kurds were abandoned and split among several countries, which was also a decision, if a negative one.

While a vast territory changed hands, the days of direct colonialism were already numbered. Control of new lands was being entered into shamefacedly and half-hearted. Fromkin writes:

> By the time that the war came to an end, British society was generally inclined to reject the idealistic case for imperialism (that it would extend the benefits of advanced civilization to a backward region) as quixotic, and the practical case for it (that it would be of benefit to Britain to expand her empire) as untrue. Viewing imperialism as a costly drain on a society that needed to invest all of its remaining resources in rebuilding itself, the bulk of the British press, public, and Parliament agreed to let the government commit itself to a presence in the Arab Middle East only because Winston Churchill's ingenious strategy made it seem possible to control the region inexpensively.

The British had begun in 1914-15 by viewing French claims to Syria as reasonable in the course of the World War, with the Ottomans as an enemy state. By 1918 they looked on them as a disaster. On their own side they were shackled to the Hashemites, who Kitchener had chosen for them early in the world war. By 1918, Fromkin writes,

> British officials had come to regard Hussein as a burden, who was involving them in a losing conflict with Ibn Saud. By 1922 British politi-

cians and officials had come to view Hussein's son Feisal as treacherous, and Hussein's son Abdullah as lazy and ineffective. . . . . Palestine was another case in point: in 1922 Britain accepted a League of Nations Mandate to carry out a Zionist program that she had vigorously espoused in 1917 — but for which she had lost all enthusiasm in the early 1920s . . . . *British policy-makers imposed a settlement upon the Middle East in 1922 in which, for the most part, they themselves no longer believed.* (emphasis in original)

Here Fromkin launches on a meditation about the nature of modern states, mainly to say that the Western concept of secular, territorially based states as the universal standard is not accepted in the Muslim Middle East. There religious sect remains the core of loyalties, and the states created in the Ottoman breakup drew borders that locked together peoples with historic hatreds of each other, or in the case of Palestine, consolidated within a single portion of the Empire one such people who all the Muslim sects hated.

Fromkin, writing in 1989, points to Wahabi militancy in Saudi Arabia, Islamic extremism in Afghanistan, the Muslim Brotherhood in Syria and Egypt, and the Shi'ite Islamic revolution in Iran as volcanic fault lines. He reminds us of the millennium and a half after the fall of Rome that it took to weld together the modern states of Europe out of ethnically and religiously divided smaller entities. And of course, the places where the religious divides were deepest, even in 1989, were Iraq, Jordan, Syria, Lebanon, and Israel. These states do not have settled legitimacy because legitimacy in the region is measured by adherence to particular shades of Islam. And in a 2009 afterword, David Fromkin adds that parliamentary democracy is not an accepted form of rule in the Muslim Middle East. He quotes an article from *The Economist* in 2004 that said, "The Arab League's 22 states remain the most uniformly oligarchic slice of the world. Not a single Arab leader has ever been peacefully ousted at the ballot box."

In Europe there were great wars and terrible persecutions over religious doctrines. Catholics slaughtered Albigenses, Protestants slaughtered Catholics, Protestants murdered each other as their branch of Christianity fragmented into scores of sects. The bloodletting over religious difference ended only with the abolition of state religions, when belief became a private matter. Islam does not accept that. At its core are the legal rules of the Quran and the Hadith that regulate every aspect of human life. Most of the Middle Eastern states are theocracies and those that are not, such as Turkey and Egypt, have powerful Islamic forces within them that are profoundly opposed to non-Islamic creeds. Legitimacy in that context is bought by religious agreement or acquiescence, not by legal rules about rights of free speech, religious tolerance, or respecting electoral outcomes.

This inheritance does not inspire one to believe that peace is a likely outcome in the near future, between Sunnis and Shi'ites, Turks and Kurds, Lebanese Maronites and Hezbollah, Egyptian Muslims and Coptic Christians, or, of course, in the most famous conflict of all, between Israelis and Palestinians.

June 1, 2013

Bygone Days in West Adams

My wife Jennifer and I have lived in the old West Adams section of Los Angeles, not far from the University of Southern California, for almost twenty-five years. Once, from the 1880s through World War I, this was a prized neighborhood for the affluent. It faded when Beverly Hills was opened in 1917. Despite the hundreds of architect-designed mansions, the area decayed in the Depression, when many of the grand old homes were cut up into boarding houses, with heavy-duty locks cut into the bedroom doors. When, in Shelley *v.* Kramer in 1948, the U.S. Supreme Court outlawed racial housing covenants, the area turned mostly black. The Santa Monica 10 Freeway was the white bureaucracy's revenge. Its route was chosen to slash its way through the center of the most concentrated stretch of historic two-story mansions, the pride of the black middle class. Thereafter the freeway marked the dividing line between L.A. proper and the feared South Central. In the 1990s Latino immigration again transformed West Adams, as Spanish-speakers became the plurality ethnicity.

A fascinating succession of people have lived in my neighborhood, from the early days when the city was wide open and it was still possible to rise from total poverty to become vastly wealthy, through the generations, first white, then more diverse, down to our own day. What follows is adapted from a talk I gave on November 13, 2012, on our local history and architecture to the West Adams Avenues neighborhood association in the western end of West Adams. Many of the more famous figures in West Adams history were based at the eastern end, around the intersection of Figueroa Street and Adams Blvd. I had to include a few of those, while omitting many others, to explain something about how West Adams came into being, but I concentrated on the blocks where my audience lived, between Arlington Avenue and Crenshaw, mostly just south of the 10 Freeway.

The talk consisted of very brief sketches of some of these interesting people along with their photos and pictures of a few of their streets and homes.

Judge Robert Maclay Widney (1838-1929)

Born in Piqua, Ohio, Widney left home at sixteen to wander for two years around the Rocky mountains with his rifle and backpack. He came to California in 1857, went to college, and became a mathematics professor. He moved to Los Angeles in 1867, where he opened the city's first real estate office, took a law degree, and became a judge. In 1871 in a gun fight between two Chinese, a Caucasian was accidentally killed. This touched off a lynch mob of whites and Latinos who looted every building in Chinatown and murdered nineteen Chinese. Judge Widney showed up, sent for his pistol, and helped save the other Chinese and stop the riot.

In 1871 Judge Widney became the central founder of USC. He got the land donated, wrote the articles of incorporation, and donated $100,000 ($2.3 million in today's dollars). USC opened in 1880 with 53 students and 10 professors. Its first building was Widney Hall, still in use today.

Widney Hall, USC, opened September 4, 1880

Adams Street (later Adams Blvd.) at Figueroa, around 1890

Pico and Figueroa, 1890

Western Avenue near Pico, 1895

Edward Doheny (1856-1935)

Born in Wisconsin, Doheny spent years as a drifter, prospector, fruit packer, singing waiter, and gunslinger in Mexico, New Mexico, and Texas. He came to Los Angeles in 1892 dead broke with his first wife and an ill daughter, who died at seven. They were living in a boarding house where they hadn't paid the rent when he saw a wagon driver near Westlake Park with a load of caked oil. Doheny borrowed $400 to lease a few empty lots and began digging with a sharpened tree trunk. He struck oil and soon became a millionaire.

In 1901 he moved to West Adams where he bought a palatial home at Adams and Figueroa and developed a private park on Chester Place. This is now Mt. St. Mary's College. He made an even bigger fortune on oil in Mexico, where he built railroads and whole cities and had his own private army. He became the richest man in America.

In 1921 he and a partner sent suitcases of money to Washington to bribe the Secretary of the Interior to lease them government oil land. They were all arrested in the famous Teapot Dome scandal. To try to buy back his respectability Doheny built the beautiful St. Vincent De Paul Catholic Church at the corner of Adams and Figueroa. He never served jail time.

In February 1929 at Greystone, a home in Beverly Hills Doheny had built for his son Ned, Ned and his male secretary were shot dead. The family moved the bodies and hid evidence so the true circumstances of the killings were never known.

Doheny's Chester Place mansion

Chester Place, west of Figueroa, looking from 23rd Street

St. Vincent de Paul Catholic Church, 1923

Adams Blvd. and Figueroa Street, 1926

Caroline Severance (1820-1914)

A famous Abolitionist before the Civil War, Caroline Severance was a leader of the Boston Anti-Slavery Society. Born in upstate New York, she fought slavery, was a crusader for women's rights, and was a religious free thinker. She was a founder in 1866 of the Equal Rights Association with Susan B. Anthony. She and her husband moved to Los Angeles in 1875, where she helped create the city's system of public libraries, was a founder of the Los Angeles Philharmonic, helped to found UCLA, and worked to find homes for orphans. She had a home at 806 W. Adams Blvd. It is now the site of the John Tracy Clinic, devoted to helping deaf children, founded in 1942 by Spencer Tracy and his wife Louise to honor their deaf son John Tracy.

Frederick H. Rindge (1857-1905)

Rindge was born to wealthy parents in Cambridge, Massachusetts. In his youth he traveled in Europe and America and for a while owned a sheep ranch in Colorado. He moved to Los Angeles in 1887. He founded a life insurance company, became a vice president of Union Oil, and was a director of the Edison Company. He owned a 17,000 acre ranch that included most of what is today Malibu and Topanga Canyon.

In 1903 he built the beautiful French Chateau mansion at 2263 S. Harvard Blvd., across the street from the First AME Church, but was only able to live in it for two years before he died at the age of forty-eight.

Rindge Mansion, 2263 S. Harvard Blvd.

James Taber Fitzgerald (1864-1956)

Fitzgerald came to Los Angeles in 1891, and ran a successful piano store in downtown Los Angeles. He is best remembered in West Adams as the builder in 1903 of one of our landmark houses, the 6,665 square foot Italian Gothic mansion at 3115 W. Adams Blvd., known as the Elegant Manor. By 1910 Fitzgerald and his wife had moved to Pasadena. It was owned after that successively by a part owner of a clothing store and a former opera singer who ran a downtown liquor store. In 1952 it was purchased as a clubhouse by a group of women circus performers who called themselves the Regular Associated Troupers.

In 1977 the Troupers sold the house to Arlillian Moody, daughter of a Louisiana sharecropper. Ms. Moody was a fine dressmaker who moved her business into the big old house. She also rented it out for marriages and upscale parties for the black community. Ms. Moody died in 2001 and the house passed to her son Ronald Carroll. It fell into disrepair. Carroll became a hoarder of junk vehicles, that filled the large three-lot yard. The wedding business fell off and Mr. Carroll began renting the house to street gangs for parties. In January 2004 during a party by the Black P-Stone gang, a young Latino brother and sister who asked to attend were robbed and murdered on the front steps. A zoning hearing that April revoked the Elegant Manor's conditional use permits to hold public events. In October 2004 the city removed thirty-three inoperable vehicles and twenty tons of trash from the property. Ronald Carroll eventually lost the house for nonpayment of debts. It has been empty since and has been occasionally listed for sale but is at present sitting vacant.

3115 W. Adams Blvd., the Elegant Manor, in 1909

Secundo Guasti (1859-1927)

Guasti was a farm laborer in Italy. He came to Los Angeles when he was nineteen, in 1878, and got a job as a cook in an Italian restaurant. He married the owner's daughter, and they explored the desert together near Cucamonga. They found water not far under the surface. In 1901 Guasti bought 5,000 acres of land for $3,750. He planted grapes and soon had the largest winery in California. He built a company town called Guasti and imported wine workers from Italy. In 1910 he built the Italianate Guasti Villa at 3500 W. Adams Blvd.

In 1903 a locomotive derailed and plowed into the Guasti vineyard, killing thirty-two men. The place got a reputation as haunted, and for a few years until 2005 a house at the winery site was a tourist attraction called the Haunted Vineyard.

Guasti Villa, 3500 W. Adams Blvd., in 1910

Busby Berkeley (1895-1976)

After Secundo Guasti's death his family sold his Adams Blvd. home to Hollywood choreographer Busby Berkeley. Born in Los Angeles — his real name was William Berkeley Enos — he served in World War I, where he staged camp shows for soldiers. He broke into big time stage shows as dance director for Florence Ziegfeld's production of "A Connecticut Yankee in King Arthur's Court." From there he became a dance director in the movies. He was the first choreographer to insist that he should control the cameras during a dance sequence. He became famous for fantastically elaborate dance routines using as many as 150 dancers. His heyday was between 1933 and the early 1940s. He was an alcoholic and was tried for murder in 1935 for driving drunk and killing someone on the Pacific Coast Highway. Since 1977 the Adams Blvd. mansion has been the headquarters of the Peace Theological Seminary and College of Philosophy, founded by New Age mystic John-Roger Hinkins.

Busby Berkeley production number from Footlight Parade

Wyatt Earp (1848-1929)

One of West Adams' most famous and colorful residents was the famed Western lawman Wyatt Earp and his wife Josephine Sarah Marcus. He and his brothers, Virgil and Morgan, along with Doc Holliday went into history as the winners of the gunfight at the OK Corral in Tombstone, Arizona, in October 1881. The Earps were enforcing a city ordinance prohibiting carrying guns in town. They shot and killed Billy Clanton, and Tom and Frank McLaury. Morgan Earp was later murdered by one of the Clanton gang. In later years Wyatt and Josephine mined gold in Arizona, lived in San Diego and San Francisco, and made a fortune running a saloon in Alaska during the gold rush at the end of the 1890s. They settled in Los Angeles in 1901. In the winters they worked mining claims in the Mojave Desert, and spent the summers in Los Angles. The last place they lived was a bungalow at 4004 West 17th Street, between Arlington and Crenshaw and Venice and Washington Blvd. It was demolished to build the Mount Vernon Junior High School, which is today the Johnny Cochran Middle School. One long-time resident tells me that the bungalow was actually moved to a nearby street and still exists but I have been unable to trace it.

Wyatt Earp in 1929 at
4004 W. 17th Street

Ramon Novarro (1899-1968)

Heart-throb of the silent movies, he was born in Mexico and his real name was Ramon Gil Samaniego. His family moved to Los Angeles in 1914.

Ramon Novarro with Greta Garbo
in the film *Mata Hari* (1931)

He became an actor in little theater, then in silent movies. His first big role was as Rupert of Hentzau in *The Prisoner of Zenda* in 1922, where he was still credited as Ramon Samaniegos (misspelled). For his next film, *Trifling Women*, the third of his credited films, also in 1922, the studio decided to re-name him to the simpler Navarro. A secretary misspelled that and he became Ramon Novarro ever after. His break-through role was in *Scaramouche* the next year. He made eighteen films. The most famous was the silent version of Ben-Hur in 1925. He bought a house in West Adams at 2265 W. 22nd Street, just east of Western Avenue and just south of the 10 Freeway. It has since been demolished. He made a few successful sound films, particularly *Mata Hari,* with Greta Garbo in 1932, but his career faded by the mid-1930s. He had roles on television in the 1950s and 1960s. Novarro was discreetly gay. He was murdered in 1968 by two brothers he had brought to his house, then in Laurel Canyon. They tortured him to death trying to get him to reveal the location of a nonexistent fortune they had heard was hidden in the house.

Bessie Bruington Burke (1891-1968)

Her parents came to Los Angeles from Kansas in a covered wagon in 1877. She attended Los Angeles State Normal School, a teacher college later incorporated into UCLA. In 1911 she was the first African American teacher in the Los Angeles school system, at the 51st Street elementary school (today the Holmes Avenue school). In 1918 she became the school's principal, again the first African American to hold such a post in Los Angeles. She was a leading figure in the Wilfandel Club and active in the Los Angeles NAACP. Her last school as principal before she retired in 1955 was in West Adams at the Virginia Road Elementary School, 2925 Virginia Road.

Virginia Road Elementary School, 2925 Virginia Road.
Class of 1954. Bessie Burke on left.

The Wilfandel Club

The Wilfandel Club, at 3425 W. Adams Blvd., is the oldest African American women's club in Los Angeles. It was founded in 1945 by Della Williams and Fannie Williams, and has held monthly meetings there ever since. The club raises funds for many charitable causes. The clubhouse is regularly opened to many community groups, and is rented out for weddings and receptions. My November 13 talk to the West Adams Avenues group was given there. Some mystery surrounds the house's origins. The Wilfandel Club website as well as the Wikipedia state that the house was built by Ramon Novarro in 1922 for his brother. I repeated this in my talk. Afterward one of the club members told me she had always heard that the house was older. I checked the Los Angeles Zone Information Map Access System (ZIMAS), which gave the construction date as 1912. Ramon Novarro was a child of thirteen in Mexico in 1912. He was just established in Hollywood in 1922, and perhaps he purchased the house. He was one of thirteen children and had five brothers.

The Wilfandel Club

Charles Bukowski (1920-1992)

Heavy drinking poet and novelist, Bukowski was born in Germany to a German mother and American serviceman father. The family moved to Los Angeles in 1923. They lived for some years in a house on Virginia Road in the Jefferson Park section of West Adams. He attended Virginia Road elementary school and Mt. Vernon Jr. High. He lived at 2122 S. Longwood Ave.

(between Crenshaw and La Brea and Adams and Washington Blvd., slightly west of the West Adams area) from 1931 to 1939. He spent ten years drifting around the United States, returning to Los Angeles in the early 1950s where he worked in the post office. He began to publish his poetry. He wrote a column called "Notes of a Dirty Old Man" for the *L.A. Free Press*.

Bukowski published six novels, of which the first, *Post Office* (1971) is considered the best, as well as more than forty books of his poetry and hundreds of short stories. One critic described his work as a "detailed depiction of . . . the uninhibited bachelor, slobby, anti-social, and utterly free."

2122 S. Longwood Ave. Bukowski lived here until he was 19

Hattie McDaniel (1895-1952)

She was the first African American film star to win an Oscar, for her role in *Gone With the Wind* (1939). Born in Wichita, Kansas, her father was a freed slave. She dropped out of school at fifteen to become a singer in a minstrel show. At twenty she was a singer with a traveling orchestra. She became a star in vaudeville and had high billing in major theatres until the end of the 1920s when vaudeville collapsed. She moved to Los Angeles in 1931 where

she became the star of a local radio show. She got her first film role, as a maid, in the 1932 film *The Golden West*. She was typecast by racist attitudes, and mostly played maids after that. When criticized for this by radical blacks she retorted, "I'd rather play a maid than be one." Her movie maids were not deferential to their employers but strong characters who frequently talked back. In many films she had important singing parts, as Queenie in *Showboat*, and in duets with Will Rogers and Clark Gable. In the 1940s she starred in the radio show "Beaulah," and in the first few episodes of the television version before her final illness. She led the campaign to abolish racial real estate covenants in Los Angeles that won their reversal in 1948. Her home after that was at 2203 S. Harvard Blvd., just east of Western Avenue and just south of what is now the 10 Freeway.

Hattie McDaniel's home at 2203 S. Harvard Blvd.

General Hilario Moncado (1898-1956)

This is a name little known in America but famous in the Philippines. Hilario Moncado was born in Cebu province in the Philippines. His father was a Spanish Monsignor, Fermin del Prado. Hilario was sent to school in India at the age of six, and graduated at nine from the College of Mystery and Psychics in Calcutta. He published his first book at thirteen, and claimed to be fluent in eleven languages. He lived in Los Angeles where he founded a magazine, *The Filipino Nation,* in 1924. The United States ruled the Philippines from 1902 to 1935. It granted the islands

General Hilario Camino Moncado (center) in Berlin in 1931

commonwealth status in 1935. Moncado was a delegate from Cebu to the 1935 Constitutional Convention and was commissioned Brigadier General in the new Philippine army. He founded a religious sect called the Filipino Crusaders World Army, sometimes called the Moncadistas, which advocates raw food and vegetarianism. To this day he has loyal followers in the Philippines. He spent most of his life here in Los Angeles, at his home and headquarters at 2302 W. 25th Street, at the corner of Arlington. This house is best known as the set for Fisher and Sons Mortuary in the HBO series "Six Feet Under."

2302 W. 25th Street

Joe Louis (1914-1981)

World boxing champion, 1937-1949, he was born Joseph Louis Barrow in Lexington, Alabama. His father died when Joe was four. His mother remarried and moved to Detroit. He studied cabinet making and worked in an auto plant when he took up amateur boxing. He won 50 of 54 amateur bouts and decided to go professional in 1934. He won his first 68 professional fights. His first defeat was in a match with Germany's Max Schmelling in 1936. Louis won the world championship the next year. Louis had a rematch with Schmelling in June 1939. He met with President Roosevelt before the fight, while Schmelling got a personal phone call from Adolph Hitler. Louis knocked Schmelling out in the first two minutes and four seconds of the match. He served in the Army in a segregated unit in World War II, and retired from boxing in 1948. He had a home in the Lafayette Square section of West Adams, but spent much of his time in Las Vegas. He earned some $4.6 million during his boxing career but his managers got most of it. His portion was only $800,000. He was generous to family members and started several businesses that failed, leaving him with a large and ever growing tax debt due to interest to the IRS. Max Schmelling, who was never a Nazi, sent Louis money in his later years and served as a pall bearer at Joe Louis's funeral.

Sugar Ray Robinson (1921-1989)

World welterweight boxing champion, he also held the world middleweight title five times. The Associated Press in 1999 named him the greatest boxer of the century in both weight classes. Robinson was born in Detroit. His original name was Walker Smith, Jr. His mother divorced and took her children to New York, where he joined an athletic club. Because he was underage for an amateur match he entered the contest using an older boy's ID, Ray Robinson. He kept the name afterward. He won 85 straight fights, and Sugar was added to the name. He went professional in 1940. He retired from the ring in 1952. He had fought 137 matches and been defeated only three times. Robinson then became a tap dancer and worked at high wages in Las Vegas and Europe. He returned to the ring in the 1950s where he won and lost the middleweight title several times, retiring for good in 1965. He moved to Los Angeles in 1965 with his third wife, Millie Bruce. They lived in the top story of a two story duplex at the corner of 10th Avenue and Adams Blvd.. I had photographed the corner I thought most likely, as I could not find any online verification of Robinson's address. It turned out that the

building I had chosen was the right one. Two members of my audience were old enough and had lived in the neighborhood long enough that they knew Sugar Ray and Millie Bruce and confirmed the house. The duplex was owned by Millie Bruce's uncle, Wright Fillmore, a head waiter on the Southern Pacific Railroad. Fillmore and his wife Babe lived in the downstairs, at 3930 West Adams Blvd., while Sugar Ray and Millie lived upstairs at 3932.

3930-3932 W. Adams Blvd., where Sugar Ray Robinson
and Millie Bruce lived upstairs

Ray Charles (1930-2004)

His original name was Ray Charles Robinson. He changed it so as not to be confused with Sugar Ray Robinson. He was born to a poor family in Albany, Georgia, and raised in Greenville, Florida. He went blind at the age of seven from glaucoma. He attended a school for the deaf and blind where he trained in classical music. He taught himself jazz and played with Cannonball Adderly. His mother died when he was fifteen and he went on the road. In Seattle he started making records. Signing with Atlantic Records he had a number-one hit in 1955 with his "I Got a Woman." His style was a mixture of gospel, jazz, and blues, and had a major influence on rock and roll. In the sixties he added country music to his mix. In the 1980s he recorded "Seven Spanish Angels" with Willie Nelson. He performed at Ronald Reagan's second inaugural and Bill Clinton's first inaugural. Ray Charles maintained his own recording studio, in West Adams, at 2107 W. Washington Blvd., between Normandie and Western Avenue.

Ray Charles' studio, 2107 W. Washington Blvd., West Adams

Reflections on Gnosticism

Han Solo: *Hokey religions and ancient weapons are no match*
for a good blaster at your side, kid.

Luke Skywalker: *You don't believe in the Force, do you?*

Ancient Gnosticism: Traditions and Literature. Birger A. Pearson.
Minneapolis: Fortress Press, 2007. 362 pp.

The Gnostic Bible: Gnostic Texts of Mystical Wisdom from the Ancient and
Medieval Worlds. Willis Barnstone and Marvin Meyer, eds. Boston
and London: Shambhala, 2009. 880 pp.

Voices of Gnosticism. Miguel Conner. Dublin: Bardic Press, 2011. 225 pp.

Forbidden Faith: The Gnostic Legacy, from the Gospels to the Da Vinci
Code. Richard Smoley. Harper San Francisco, 2006, 244 pp.

Gnosticism, the Hellenistic mystery religion centered in Alexandria, Egypt,
predated and then merged with Christianity, only to be rejected as heresy and
violently suppressed. Gnosis is merely the Greek for knowledge, and Gnosticism — more or less, the Knowers — was a coinage that dated only from
commentary literature in English in the seventeenth century. The Gnostics, to
begin with a single one of their characteristics, rejected the Christian idea that
salvation could be achieved by faith, as well as the Greek ideas that grew into
materialism. They instead claimed that there was a special secret knowledge
that, if sought and learned, could allow the spirit to escape the physical body
and return after death to a remote realm of nonphysical existence.

For two centuries, from roughly 100 to 300 CE, the founders of Christianity were locked in a fierce battle with the Gnostic current over who would
define Christian doctrine. For those who believe in biblical inerrancy it should
be recalled that there was no central accepted orthodoxy for centuries after the

death of Jesus. The faction that became Catholicism confronted not only the Gnostics but endless other claimants within the Christian fold, and imposed their views only when Christianity became the Roman state religion after Emperor Constantine called the Council of Nicea in 325, and the tendency within Christianity that he endorsed gained the military power to physically crush their religious rivals. The twenty-seven documents composing the New Testament were not approved as canonical until long after that. They were first even proposed in a single list by St. Athanasius, bishop of Alexandria, in 367 CE and finally approved by the Catholic church only in 1546.

That said, even the most Christianized Gnostics, apart from making a prominent place for Jesus in their pantheon, remained an essentially different religion, rejecting even the God that Christians believe created the earth and humanity. The victorious faction within Christianity burned the Gnostics' books and their churches, and sometimes the Gnostics themselves. Thereafter, in Europe, the Gnostic current went underground. Echoes of its mystical views have persisted to our own day as the Western Esoteric Tradition. Its French adherents, the Cathars, were the victims of an exterminating crusade in the thirteenth century. In the seventeenth century Rosicrucianism revived ideas of the ancient Gnostics mixed with support to the Protestant Reformation against Catholicism.

In the century beginning in 1850 an occult revival, led by figures such as Helena Petrovna Blavatsky and her Theosophical Society, explicitly looked back to Gnosticism as an alternative mystic world view to Christianity, adding elements from Buddhism. Since the end of World War II, and quickening from the 1960s, there has been a new revival of many forms of ancient mysticism. Within that ferment has been growing interest in Gnosticism, fueled by the discovery, at the village of Nag Hammadi in Egypt in 1945, of the first large collection of Gnostic writings. These only became available to American readers with the publication of translations from the Coptic as *The Nag Hammadi Library* in 1978, popularized the following year by Elaine Pagels in her book *The Gnostic Gospels*.

For some eighteen hundred years all that was known of the Gnostics derived from the voluminous hostile polemics against them by the early Church Fathers, written mainly by Irenaeus (130-202), bishop of Lugdunum in Gaul (present day Lyons in France); Hippolytus of Rome (170-235); and Tertullian of Carthage in North Africa (160-225). The first actual document written by the Gnostics themselves to resurface in the West was the *Pistis Sophia*, discovered in 1773 in a Coptic translation from the original Greek. This was translated into Latin in 1856, into German in 1905, and the first English version, by Theosophist G.R.S. Mead, made from the Latin and German versions, was published only in 1921. Beyond this there were only two known original Gnostic documents, the Bruce Codex, which also sat ignored in the British Museum for centuries, from its acquisition in 1769 to its first English publication only in 1978. Lastly, there was the Berlin Codex, four short documents in Coptic, discovered in 1896 but not translated until 1955 and not widely circulated until the 1970s.

The subject was revolutionized by the Nag Hammadi collection. These took more than thirty years to translate and publish, and the work of analyzing them and trying to understand their meaning and historical context began really in the 1980s, with major revisions of our understanding emerging only in the last ten years. Birger A. Pearson's *Ancient Gnosticism* is one of the best summaries of our current knowledge about the Gnostics. William Barnstone and Marvin Meyer in *The Gnostic Bible* offer an exhaustive collection of the known Gnostic writings, grouped for the first time by the various Gnostic schools of thought, an essential aid in disentangling this difficult subject. Miguel Conner's *Voices of Gnosticism* is a transcript of a number of radio interviews with scholars in the field, a light chatty overview. Richard Smoley's contribution is a brief glimpse at the influence of Gnosticism on European esotericism down to our own day.

My Encounters with Gnosticism

I first heard of Gnosticism at the age of sixteen back in 1958 in reading Hermann Hesse's novel *Demian*. As you can see from the above, little that was reliable was known about this set of beliefs even when I ran into them, much less when *Demian* was published, in German in 1919. In the story, shy schoolboy Emil Sinclair comes under the influence of Demian, a mysterious older schoolmate. When the story of Cain and Abel is recounted by a teacher, Demian tells Sinclair that Cain was the real hero and Abel was a weakling who deserved to die. Demian gives Sinclair a note telling him that the soul is like a bird whose aim is to fly away from the Earth to find a God named Abraxas. One of Sinclair's teachers tells him that Abraxas was, in antiquity, the name "of a godhead whose symbolic task is the uniting of godly and devilish elements." Demian ultimately reveals that he and his mother belong to an ancient secret religion that traces its lineage back to Cain and reveres the God Abraxas, who presides over both good and evil. A teacher says that people who believed this in ancient times were a sect called Cainites.

Sinclair by accident discovers Demian's secret church. There he is befriended by the organist, Pistorius. He tells Pistorius that he has dreams of flying. Pistorius replies that this is the first step in teaching his spirit how to fly beyond the Earth to reunite with Abraxas, that the secret of surviving death lies in special spiritual knowledge and training, which most people will not bother to undertake. To jump ahead to the Nag Hammadi manuscripts, some of these contain accounts of astral travel. For example, in *Zostrianos* the character of that name is visited by "the angel of knowledge" who takes him on a journey through the heavens. Birger Pearson comments:

"Zostrianos can be seen as a detailed description of the heavenly world, populated by beings we have already encountered in other Sethian texts, including the heavenly Seth, and many more besides." I will come later to who the Sethians were. *Marsanes* is another of the tractates focused on astral travel.

Coming from a family of spiritualists who believed in the Astral Plane and its many ethereal denizens, I was intrigued by this tale of the ultimate secret society that claimed to know the mystery of soul travel. I didn't much care for the notion of embracing evil on a par with good, or see anything admirable in Cain, but I did want to find out more. Only on reading Birger Pearson more than fifty years on did I discover that Hesse had been conned by the old Church Fathers. The Cainites never existed. They were the malicious concoction of an anonymous Church heresiologist known as Pseudo-Tertullian in the 220s. His invention was picked up and imaginatively amplified by Epiphanius, Bishop of Salamis in Cyprus, circa 310-403 CE.

Hesse, who had been born in Germany but raised in Switzerland, appears to have acquired his knowledge of Gnosticism from Swiss psychologist Carl Jung. Hesse underwent psychotherapy with Jung's student Josef B. Lang in 1916-1917. He finished the manuscript of *Demian* in October 1917 (see Ralph Freedman's *Hermann Hesse: Pilgrim of Crisis*). Jung in 1916 had penned his own version of a Gnostic myth, *Seven Sermons to the Dead*, in which he wrote: "Abraxas begetteth truth and lying, good and evil, light and darkness, in the same word and in the same act. Wherefore is Abraxas terrible." This was first published privately only in 1920 and circulated only to friends, but Hesse may have seen it or had discussions with Lang about its contents, as its ideas are strongly present in *Demian*.

The Core Gnostic Mythos

Around 1960 an older family friend with a large library gave me a copy of F. C. Burkitt's *Church and Gnosis*. This presented a wholly different vision from Hesse's Cainites, which I immediately abandoned. Burkitt, whose text was based on lectures given in 1931, was working with scant sources, mainly the Church heresiologists and the *Pistis Sophia*. This last was written later than most of the Gnostic texts found in 1945 and was consequently highly

Christianized, claiming to recount eleven years that the resurrected Jesus spent with his disciples in Jerusalem after his crucifixion. Even from these limited materials it was plain that there were many varieties of Gnosticism.

According to the Church heresiologists, Gnosticism was founded by Simon Magus, a Samaritan contemporary of Jesus. The Samaritans are closely related to the Jews and lived in what is now southern Syria. There is a story about Simon in the New Testament book of Acts, where he is described as a wonder worker and prophet in Samaria. It claims that he was converted to Christianity by Philip on a mission there, but then was rebuffed by Peter on a later mission to Samaria, when Simon is said to have offered money to be given the gift of healing.

Birger Pearson accepts that Simon Magus was probably the first Gnostic teacher, but regards the story in Acts as an invention to magnify the importance of Peter and dismisses the idea that Simon had anything to do with Christianity as "obviously tendentious." He points to the fact that Christian apologist Justin Martyr (100 to circa 165), himself a Samaritan, describes Simon as having moved to Rome, where he had a large following and preached his non-Christian theology.

According to this source, Simon Magus came from the village of Gitta, and had a companion named Helen, a former prostitute who Simon claimed was the reincarnation of Helen of Troy. Justin also states, mistakenly, that a statue in Rome was built in Simon's honor, inscribed in Latin "to the holy god Simon." Birger Pearson tells us that the statue was found in 1574 and the inscription actually reads "to the faithful god Semo Sanco," a figure in the Roman religion associated with Jupiter.

Simon left no writings so it is impossible to know the details of his system. The element of the fallen Helen is similar to the Gnostic myth of the fall and redemption of Sophia. According to a fourth century writing by Clement of Rome, Simon was the favorite disciple of John the Baptist. And while John is revered by Christians as the herald of Jesus as the Messiah, he is also treated as a revered authority by the Mandaeans, the only surviving Gnostic sect, who reject Jesus as a false prophet.

The two major Gnostic figures of the second century and focus of the heretic hunters were Valentinus of Rome (circa 100-160) and Basilides of Alexandria (dates unknown but he taught circa 117-138 CE). Valentinus' doctrines had strongly Christian elements. He was narrowly defeated to be the Christian bishop of Rome. Very little was known about Basilides except that he was the main Gnostic proponent of Abraxas (more commonly spelled Abrasax, a name that by numerology came out to 365, the number of days in the year). On this slim foundation I formed a lifelong dislike of Valentinus as a place-seeker in the world of conventional religion, and a great fondness for Basilides.

The Gnostic congregations were highly decentralized. Their core belief was a strong dualism: that the world of matter was deadening and inferior to a remote nonphysical home, to which an interior divine spark in most humans aspired to return after death. This led them to an absorption with the Jewish creation myths in Genesis, which they obsessively reinterpreted to formulate allegorical explanations of how humans ended up trapped in the world of matter. And they loved myth-making, each prominent teacher embroidering and changing the creation myths in ways large and small.

The basic Gnostic story, which varied in details from teacher to teacher, was this. In the beginning there was an unknowable, immaterial, and invisible God, sometimes called the Father of All and sometimes by other names. "He" was neither male nor female, and was composed of an implicitly finite amount of a living nonphysical substance. Surrounding this God was a great empty region called the Pleroma (the fullness). Beyond the Pleroma lay empty space. The God acted to fill the Pleroma through a series of emanations, a squeezing off of small portions of his/its nonphysical energetic divine material.

In most accounts there are thirty emanations in fifteen complementary pairs, each getting slightly less of the divine material and therefore being slightly weaker. The emanations are called Aeons (eternities) and are mostly named personifications in Greek of abstract ideas. Like the God, they are nonphysical light beings. They are described as androgynous or bisexual. The Aeons in turn generate large numbers of simpler entities, sometimes called angels. The first of the great emanations, according to several Gnostic groups, is named Barbelo. This is a predominately female persona. A common stipulation is that only Barbelo is able to see or communicate with the invisible Father God. Even the other nonphysical dwellers in the Pleroma have no contact with this remote entity, sometimes called the Silent God. Often there is a central trinity of Father, Mother (Barbelo), and Son.

The common outcome of the myth rests on the thirtieth emanation or Aeon, Sophia. This is both the Greek word for Wisdom and also a woman's name. Sophia becomes jealous of the power of the Father of All to create. Without permission of her consort, the other of her matching pair, she gives birth or otherwise creates an offspring. It proves to be monstrous, with the head of a lion and the body of a serpent. She names him Yaldabaoth. He is also called Saklas (in Hebrew, the fool), and Samael (the blind God).

Ashamed of her progeny, Sophia takes Yaldabaoth outside of the Pleroma and hides him in a cloud. There he matures alone, having no knowledge of his origins. Imbued from birth with a portion of the divine material he inherited from his mother, Yaldabaoth, now given the title Demiurge (Greek: craftsman), creates a dozen Archons (Commanders), and then, in a mirror image of the great emanations of the Pleroma, hundreds of lesser angels. Yaldabaoth then creates the cosmos, understood to mean, not the entire universe as in modern usage, but the known planets. These were, in the order then understood: Moon, Venus, Mercury, Sun, Mars, Jupiter, Saturn, and the zodiac of visible stars. According to the new Ptolemaic system of astronomy, all of the stars were thought to be attached to a single crystal sphere.

Yaldabaoth assigns seven of his Archons to rule over the seven planetary spheres, then creates the Earth and decides to populate it. He has his angels make Adam, each of 365 angels contributing a single part. But Yaldabaoth and his Archons find that their creature is lifeless, or at least unable to stand. By this time Sophia has discovered what her offspring has done and is horrified at the fate of the humans he is in process of creating, who will be encased in deadening matter as in mobile tombs. In one version she and her consort come down from the Pleroma and trick Yaldabaoth into breathing life into Adam and Eve, thereby giving them and their descendants greater spirit power than the Demiurge is able to retain. In another version Christ or another Illuminator comes to earth disguised by a magic helmet and imbues the near-lifeless human prototypes with tiny divine sparks.

Yaldabaoth then creates the Garden of Eden, not on Earth as in Genesis, but at the level of the stars. He cruelly tells his human captives not to eat of the tree of the knowledge of good and evil. In some versions, for example, in *The Hypostasis of the Archons* among the Nag Hammadi texts, the serpent is the agent of Sophia, urging Adam and Eve to disobey; in more Christianized accounts it is the Christ who comes to the garden to warn Adam and Eve of the Demiurge's plan to enslave them in deadening matter. As must be clear by now, Yaldabaoth is known by Jews and Christians as Jehovah, or just as God. The Gnostics frequently and ironically quote Yaldabaoth declaring that he is a jealous god, claiming in his ignorance that he is the only God.

The Gnostics similarly offer counter versions of the accounts of God's destructiveness in Genesis, where the vindictive Demiurge sends flood and fire in a vain effort to wipe out humanity, of which he has become jealous. Noah's flood is an act of blind vengeance thwarted not by Noah's ark but by entities from the Pleroma hiding the children of Seth in a cloud. Sodom and Gomorrah were holy cities destroyed out of Yaldabaoth's cruelty. In the *Apocalypse of Adam*, Abrasax is one of three angels who come from the Pleroma to save the people of Sodom and Gomorrah. In this and several other Sethian texts, so called because of the importance given to Adam's third son, it is the incorporeal Seth who provides salvation, and is called, not a savior, but an "Illuminator of knowledge." Note that unlike the God and Jesus figures of Christianity, such saving acts are not offered to individuals and are not scheduled for masses at the end of the world but are extremely rare events directed to groups of the people of Seth threatened by the Demiurge and his Archons. There are other illuminators mentioned in Gnostic texts, so its seems that Seth is primus inter pares, not the unique God figure Jesus is imagined to be, and his role, like that of lesser illuminators, is mainly to awake susceptible humans to their inner spark and prepare them for their cosmic journey.

Finally, the role of a savior, even in the later documents when this is (mostly) Jesus, is not to die for people's sins. Sin has little to do with the Gnostic vision, particularly the peculiar Christian concept of original sin borne by every human. The savior figures in Gnosticism try to wake people up from the deadening effect of being encased in matter and prepare them for the arduous nonmaterial individual flight through the cosmos after death to try to reach the Pleroma and re-merge their divine spark with the main mass located there.

In the Gnostic cosmos each of the "planets" is ruled by one of the Archons and the spirit released from matter by death must persuade the Archon to allow it to pass through that "planet's" crystalline sphere.

Burkitt has an interesting discussion of this cosmology that I have not seen reprised in the recent works. Burkitt proposes that the planetary cosmology so central to the Gnostic mythos was an effort by Jewish Christians to incorporate the latest science of their day into their belief system. It looks bizarre to us today only because the ancient science has been since discarded. The new science of the second century CE was the Ptolemaic model of the universe, the pride of Greek civilization of its day. This was the model in which the Earth was a sphere in the center of the universe. The Earth was thought to be surrounded by nested transparent crystal spheres, the "seven heavens" of proverb, one for each of the planet-type objects, which included the Sun and Moon. The eighth sphere, the ogdoad, contained all of the fixed stars. On the other side of this sphere of the zodiac were imagined various celestial locations, from Plato's realm of perfect ideas to the abode of gods, to the Christian heaven, to the Gnostic Pleroma.

That this was a wrenching ideological change was because the Hebrew scriptures, today the Old Testament, embodied the view general among not only the Jews but virtually all the surrounding peoples of the Eastern Mediterranean except the Greeks, that the world was not only the center of the universe but was flat, covered with a single hard bowl called the firmament. For example, in the book of Job, Elihu asks Job, "Can you beat out [*raqa*] the vault of the skies, as he does, hard as a mirror of cast metal?" (Job 37:18) The *Jewish Encyclopedia* expands on this:

> The Hebrews regarded the earth as a plain or a hill figured like a hemisphere, swimming on water. Over this is arched the solid vault of heaven. To this vault are fastened the lights, the stars. So slight is this elevation that birds may rise to it and fly along its expanse. (http://www.jewish encyclopedia.com/articles/4684-cosmogony#2736)

Often seen on the Internet described as a Gnostic image this is actually the Biblical-Hebrew flat earth. From Camille Flammarion, French astronomer and lithographer, in 1888 illustrating a medieval monk at the end of the flat earth looking through a hole in the hard firmament to which the stars are attached

For the ancient Jews the planets and stars were all stuck to a single hard surface over a nearly flat Earth, so close that birds could bump into the stars. One could stop here and ask our present day Evangelical believers in biblical inerrancy who are so numerous in the American Congress how the God of the universe could have been so ignorant.

F. C. Burkitt points to the difficulty this bumptious cosmology posed for Jewish Christians living in cosmopolitan, Greek-dominated Alexandria:

Towards the end of the first century of our era this new, scientific, "Ptolemaic" view of the world had come to be held by most cultivated persons in much the same sort of way as most cultivated persons now believe in "Evolution."

In both systems the Earth was the center of a relatively tiny universe. The Hebrew cosmology with its one fixed dome could not explain the motion of the planets among the fixed stars. Ptolemy envisioned a set of nested transparent spheres, each of which could rotate independently of the others. This could explain the rising of the Sun, which in the Hebrew/Biblical cosmology simply hid behind a distant mountain every night, and the wanderings of the known planets.

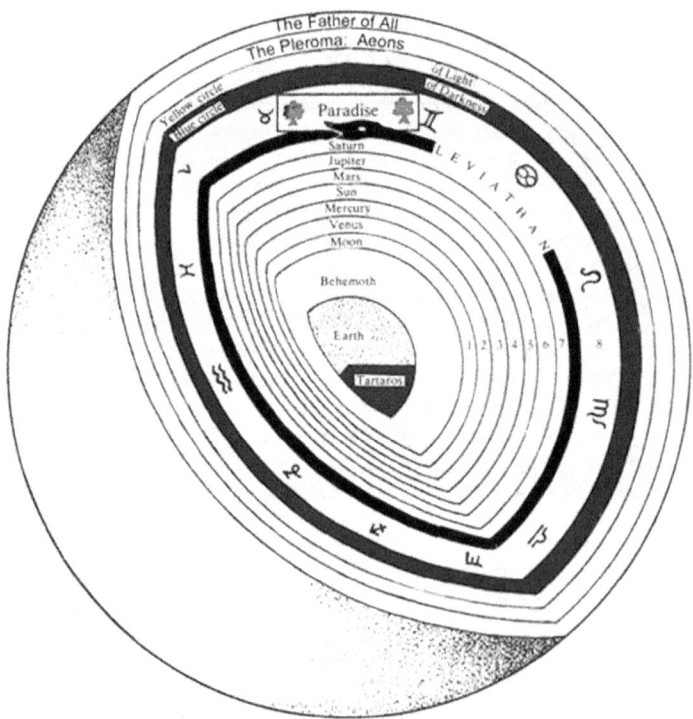

Gnostic version of the Ptolemaic system. Behemoth and Leviathan are in the book of Job. The first guards the earth, the second the seas.
In Genesis, God divides the waters between the earth and the sky so here Leviathan is guarding the sky waters.

Even a century after the heyday of ancient Gnosticism Catholic theologians were reluctant, on biblical grounds, to accept that the Earth was round, and still retained the old Jewish cosmology of a single solid sky. Saint Augustine (354–430) on the nature of the firmament wrote, "We may understand this name as given to indicate not it is motionless but that it is solid." He also ridiculed the idea that the Earth was round and people on the other side of the globe walked upside down:

> But as to the fable that there are Antipodes, that is to say, men on the opposite side of the earth, where the sun rises when it sets to us, men who walk with their feet opposite ours that is on no ground credible.

The Gnostics, then, sought to remain current with the science of their day. But in the Ptolemaic system the planets had been promoted from mere moving points of light to the central points on gigantic crystal spheres far larger than the Earth. Many of the Greeks now thought of the planets as minor gods. For the Gnostics in particular this posed the problem of how the escaping spirits were supposed to get through each of the eight transparent spheres to reach the Pleroma. Hence their concern with inventing verbal formulas and supposed passwords for the voyaging spirits to declaim to each planetary Archon or its minions to gain passage.

The Gnostics also differed from the Christians on how the material world would end. For the Christians it would come with the rise of the Anti-Christ, the battle of Armageddon, and the second coming of Jesus to hold the Last Judgment in which all of the dead would be raised at once in their physical bodies. For the Gnostics there was no general resurrection, only the departure of individual spirits, and never with their physical bodies, which the spirit was eager to escape. The material world would fade away as more and more of the divine sparks departed to rejoin the Pleroma, and would finally simply collapse when all of the divine material was gone. Humans whose spark was missing or too weak, or who lacked any consciousness of their true state and therefore made no effort to reach the Pleroma would simply be extinguished.

Insofar as Jesus is grafted onto this very different world view, the radical distinction the Gnostics made between matter and the nonphysical world made it impossible for them to accept the idea that any entity from the Pleroma was ever actually a human being, much less that any human being could possibly be a God. Their various groups found different solutions for this, all of which fall under the doctrine called Docetism, the belief that Jesus was never human and appeared on Earth as a kind of phantom. One version of this has the ghostly Jesus watching from a nearby hillside as some poor human is crucified in his place. In another the spirit of Seth "puts on" the body of Jesus like a costume or a case of spirit possession and leaves it before the crucifixion, making Jesus something of an animated puppet. In a related and nominally more Christian version the Christ of the Pleroma is the entity that enters and possesses the body of the mere human Jesus, usually at the time of Jesus' baptism, leaving it again just before the crucifixion.

In my youth I absorbed this mythos with fascination. I never took it literally, in part because the contrarian retellings of Genesis seemed so intentionally allegorical, and because of the obvious limitations of the science of the second century. I was always interested, if not quite a believer, in the possibility of realms of nonphysical entities and some kind of afterlife. I did not on that account ever become so world denying as the Gnostics. Reduced to its most minimal essentials, I read Gnosticism as resting on a few simple propositions:

1. There is no God or savior figure that answers any kind of personal prayers. The Christian conceit that they can ring up God or Jesus for an uplifting chat on that huge switchboard that can handle millions of simultaneous very personal calls, or get results by praying to improve the health of their ailing uncle, win for them the coveted promotion at work, or improve their love life, is utterly absent from the Gnostic vision.

2. Insofar as there is any survival of human personalities after death this is not guaranteed and cannot be secured by personal declarations of loyalty to any supernatural entity as Christianity maintains. But it may happen and this depends on a combination of one's innate nature, which is not changeable, modified by knowledge and concentration on that end.

3. Insofar as anyone survives death, contrary to the Christian version, they do not take their body with them, and are not instantly transported to a post-death destination such as heaven. Instead, as an incorporeal shade, they must make their way by their own wits across the visible universe to a place beyond the stars where they would become part of the plane of nonphysical, bisexual energy beings.

4. Life in one's physical body exaggerates the separation of subject and object, and even in one's most alert states of consciousness is like sleep compared to existence as a disembodied spirit.

5. There are many kinds of nonphysical entity of the types the Greeks called daimons, as on Earth there are all kinds of people

with many and complex motives. This differs from the Christian hard division of all supernatural entities into wholly good or wholly evil, angels or devils, although the Gnostics did pose an opposition between the entities from the Pleroma and those of the Demiurge, mainly on their different attitudes toward physical matter.

The Gnostic Canon Today

Birger A. Pearson, Professor Emeritus of Religious Studies at UC Santa Barbara, is a distinguished scholar of Gnosticism and one of the translators of the Nag Hammadi Codices. (A codice is something between a scroll and a book. They are leather bound sheets of handwritten text.) The Nag Hammadi discovery was of fourth-century translations into Coptic of older Greek originals. There were twelve codices or volumes, containing forty-four separate documents, called tractates, plus eight duplicates. The best guess on their origin is that they were part of the library of a Christian monastery and were buried by monks who sought to protect them from destruction during an intolerant purge by their superiors. There are by now numerous editions in English. The earlier ones simply present the whole collection. Recent scholarship has shown that the texts, as one would expect from a library collection, are from different sources, not all Gnostic, and among the Gnostic documents, from different schools. This is easier to follow in the most recent collection, *The Gnostic Bible*, compiled by Willis Barnstone and Marvin Meyer, which includes materials from other sources beyond Nag Hammadi.

Barnstone and Meyer break the texts, which appear in full, down into seven categories:

Early Wisdom Gospels, in particular *The Gospel of Thomas*, which was long thought to be a Gnostic work but in fact is a version of Christian mysticism;

The Literature of Gnostic Wisdom, which is Gnosticism proper, which they divide into four types: Sethian, Valentinian, a Thomas school, and miscellaneous others;

Hermetic Literature, the second century Egyptian writings attributed to Hermes Trismegistus, a staple of Renaissance mysticism and marked by strong Gnostic elements;

The last four sections are on independent Gnostic religions further removed from its Syrian-Egyptian origins: Mandaeanism, the only surviving

Gnostic sect, among the Marsh Arabs of southern Iraq; Iranian Manichaean-ism; Islamic mysticism; and the medieval French Cathars.

Birger Pearson provides a detailed survey of all of these sources with the exception of the Islamic and the Cathars. He critiques, summarizes, and quotes from all of the major documents. It is best to read *Ancient Gnosticism* with a copy of Barnstone and Meyer or one of the earlier Nag Hammadi collections at hand to look more closely at the full text of some of the core documents. Be aware, however, that the Barnstone and Meyer translations are much smoother and more polished than the earlier editions.

Now that the mass of writings has had time to be assimilated, a number of revisions in the Gnostic landscape emerge. First, none of the Gnostic teachers described by the Church heresiologists are mentioned. None of the tractates list an author or provide any history of the teachers or groups that produced them. At best it has been possible to distinguish Valentinian from other unnamed schools by a comparison of quotations in Irenaeus and Hippolytus to otherwise anonymous papyri. In the process a new category has emerged. These are the adherents of Seth. Barnstone and Meyer identify twelve tractates as Sethian, including the more recent separate discovery of *The Gospel of Judas*. Pearson classes thirteen of the Nag Hammadi scriptures as Sethian, which he also calls Classic Gnosticism, the school that was least Christianized and most clearly professed the Sofia myth. Nine of the others have been identified as Valentinian. Nothing of Basilides has survived except scattered fragments. And these, to my dismay, Pearson tells us, show him to have been even more militantly Christian, in the Gnostic manner, than Valentinus.

The most important of the Sethian documents is The *Apocryphon [secret book] of John*. It begins nominally with the resurrected Christ descending to Earth to instruct the Apostle John, the son of Zebedee. But the story he tells is of the invisible unknowable entity, the One. This invisible and incomprehensible entity's "thought became a reality, and she who appeared in the presence of the father in shining light came forth." This is Barbelo, "the mother-father." Barbelo asks the invisible great spirit for several qualities: foreknowledge, incorruptibility, eternal life, and truth. These all appear as separate creatures and stand beside her. She then becomes pregnant by the invisible One and bears a child, who in turn asks the invisible One to create more creature-attributes. Thence comes Mind, who in turn asks to have Will created, and then Word. The child is now referred to as the "self-created god." Four luminaries "derive" from the child-god. These are named Harmozel, Oroiael, Daveithai, and Eleleth.

Next come spirit versions of the later early mythical humans: Geradamas, the spirit of Adam, and his son, the spirit Seth.

The last of the great aeons is Sophia, "who is the wisdom of afterthought and who constitutes an eternal realm." She gives birth without the consent of her consort. "Something came out of her that was imperfect and different in appearance from her." Her progeny "changed into the figure of a snake with the face of a lion." This is Yaldabaoth, who Sophia casts outside the Pleroma and hides in a cloud. In this version, Yaldabaoth produces out of the power of his mother that is within him twelve authorities or Archons. Seven of these he stations at the seven planetary bodies, "one for each sphere of heaven." The remaining five "reign over the depth of the abyss." The twelve powers in turn create between them 365 angels.

Sophia repents her actions, which have dimmed her own powers by the share imbued in Yaldabaoth. The beings of the Pleroma have pity on her and she is restored some of her power but not allowed to return to the Pleroma, instead placed in the ninth heaven, just above the realm controlled by her son the Demiurge.

In the Gnostic cosmology there are three levels of being: matter, soul, and spirit. Soul is something intermediate between the spirit beings that inhabit the Pleroma and the physical creatures of the Earth. In later Western mysticism this is the astral body, different from the Christian idea which does not distinguish between soul and spirit. When Yaldabaoth and his Archons decide to create Adam they first make a soul body, what Barnstone and Meyer call a "psychical man with a psychical body." The 365 angels each make a part to compose the psychical Adam. The text names each of the angels and the part each was responsible for. Taphreo, for example, made the backbone while Boabel made the toes. When this psychical body is completed it remains lifeless.

In the *Apocryphon of John* it is five "luminaries" who are sent by Barbelo who trick Yaldabaoth into breathing into his inert creation. "He breathed his spirit into Adam. The spirit is the power of his mother, but he did not realize this, because he lives in ignorance. The mother's power went out of Yaldabaoth and into the psychical body that had been made to be like the one who is from the beginning." Yaldabaoth and his minions soon realize that Adam has become superior to themselves through the infusion of light energy so they throw Adam "into the lowest part of the whole material realm."

Barbelo takes pity on the divine material within Adam and sends a spirit-being to help him. This entity hides within Adam to advise him. In the earlier translations, such as the 1988 edition of *The Nag Hammadi Library*, such beings are identified by their Greek names, this one called Epinoia, which Pearson renders "reflection." Barnstone and Meyer choose to render all of the traditional Greek terms into simple English, so the Pleroma becomes just "the fullness." In some ways this makes the text more easily understood, but it tends to obscure the personifications conveyed by the Greek designations, as the texts treat these as both abstract ideas and actual beings. In Barnstone and Meyer the creature who hides inside Adam is just "afterthought."

Now the Archons mix up a batch of matter from the then-known elements — earth, air, fire, and water — and imprison Adam in a physical body, "the fetter of forgetfulness." Thus "Adam became a mortal being, the first to descend and the first to become estranged." The encased Adam is banished to "paradise," where the tree of life's branches are death and the "dwelling place of those who taste of it is the underworld." In this text it is Jesus, not the serpent, who tells Adam to eat of the tree of the knowledge of good and evil, which Yaldabaoth wanted to withhold from his creation.

The tale goes on, with Yaldabaoth creating, then raping Eve and throwing the primal couple out of paradise. Yaldabaoth, not Adam, is said to be the father of Cain and Abel. Seth, the third son, is the only true child of Adam and Eve. The consequences of Yaldabaoth's actions were to introduce sexual intercourse into the world and to make the humans forget their origins in the realm of light.

After relating this creation myth, Jesus and John discuss life after death. Jesus proposes that the spirits of light and darkness compete for influence over each soul. In those humans where the spirit of light predominates they will "be taken up to eternal rest." Those who do not know where they belong, that is, who do not have the knowledge of the origins of their divine spark, will be imprisoned by the Archons until they awaken from their forgetfulness. Some "will be made to follow another in whom the spirit of life dwells, and she is saved through that one. Then she will not be thrust into flesh again." This seems to point to the idea of reincarnation. Those who reject the light entirely will suffer eternal punishment.

The document concludes with Jesus telling John the story of Noah's flood, in which Noah is warned by the emissary of the light, but not only his family but many other of the descendants of Seth were hidden in a cloud and survived the flood. Thereafter Yaldabaoth's angels disguised themselves as women's husbands and slept with them to produce humans in whom the spirit of light was very diluted and these descendents remain in ignorance to the present day. This seems to be derived from Genesis 6:4 in which the Nephilim, described as "sons of God," have sex with Earth women and produce a race of giants, though in Genesis this takes place before the flood rather than after.

What to make of all this? Birger Pearson points out that despite the incorporation of Jesus into the frame story, "the basic myth contained in it has no Christian feature in it at all." In fact, a shorter version of this text exists in which Jesus does not appear, strongly suggesting that it has pre-Christian origins and the Jesus element was "interpolated into the text by a Christian editor." His best estimate is that the first version dates from late first century, contemporary with the drafting of the Christian gospels. Most of the other Gnostic texts are from fifty to eighty years later, and by the time one gets to the third century and the *Pistis Sophia* they are heavily Christianized, but that generally means appropriating Jesus as a spokesman for the Gnostic mythos.

Pearson points to two other Nag Hammadi tractates that display the same pattern, *Eugnostos the Blessed* and *Sophia of Jesus Christ*. Of the fourteen known Sethian texts, six incorporate no Christian element. Pearson lists these as: *Apocalypse of Adam*, *Thought of Norea*, *Three Steles of Seth*, *Zostrianos*, *Allogenes*, and *Marsanes*. The first is strongly Jewish, the last four influenced by Middle Platonism. The remaining eight have been Christianized, but to various degrees. For example, in *The Gospel of the Egyptians* it is the spirit-being Seth who "puts on" the young Jesus to manipulate his body to carry out Seth's mission of illumination.

Who Were the Gnostics?

Despite the wealth of original documentary material now available, none of it contains any account of the Gnostic groups or teachers. Any deductions about their origins, apart from the limited and not always reliable writings of their enemies, depends on contextual analysis. This is leaning away from the traditional view that they were simply Christian heretics or, more generously, one of the many varieties of early Christians. Their central focus on the Hebrew creation myths and the extensive use of Hebraic names for many of the entities that are not Greek abstractions strongly suggests a Jewish origin, despite their hostile interpretation of the God of the Torah.

Pearson suggests that the Gnostic current arose either prior to Christianity or at least parallel to it. None of the existent texts appear to date earlier than around 90 CE and most are mid to late second century. This is after the Roman war on the Jews and the destruction of Jerusalem in 70 CE, the start of the Jewish Diaspora, followed by Rome's crushing of the Bar Kokhba Revolt (132-136 CE). These events must have been more shattering for ancient Judaism than the Holocaust of the twentieth century. The evidence, then as now, that people are on their own in face of an unpredictable and commonly hostile world, was infinitely greater than the claim that a personal God is concerned with the fate of every sparrow.

One place of exile was the cosmopolitan Greek-dominated city of Alexandria, which developed a large Jewish community. There the exiled Jews would have come in contact with Plato's ideas as well as the Ptolemaic astronomy so marked in the Gnostic scriptures. Platonism is strongly evident in the concept of the Pleroma, as well as the description of its denizens as the embodiment of Greek abstractions about mental processes. Plato was a metaphysical dualist, dividing reality into a nonmaterial realm of ideal unchanging perfect forms and the lower material world of imperfect, changeable, and mortal copies. Plato in fact coined the usage of calling the creator of the material world the Demiurge ("craftsman"), often applied to Yaldabaoth, without the attendant mythology the Gnostics built onto this terminology.

Pearson concludes:

> Gnosticism is clearly dependent upon aspects of Platonist philosophy. It is also clearly dependent upon aspects of Jewish religion, most notably apocalyptically oriented Judaism. The most plausible way of explaining these dependencies is to posit a Jewish origin for Gnosticism, involving Jews who had imbibed a good deal of Greek philosophy.

While the Gnostics were disappointed in and rejecting of the Jewish God, they nevertheless based their speculations on Jewish writings and traditions. Pearson comments:

> The main difference between Gnostic eschatology [the part of theology concerned with death, judgment, and an afterlife] and biblical-Jewish eschatology is that the former is focused on the return of the individual soul to its divine origins.

Pearson regards as outmoded the view of scholars from before the Nag Hammadi publications who saw the Gnostics as anti-Jewish Christians who had incorporated Hellenistic ideas while rejecting the Jewish God and the Old Testament. Instead, Pearson maintains that the Gnostics were engaged in an extreme form of Jewish religious speculation. The obvious problem being confronted in separating the Earth and its creation from the transcendent God is the explanation for evil. Jews previously had explained it by demonic forces. And who created the demons? In Jewish literature these were angels who rebelled against God. Pearson takes the issue back one step: Why would God create angels who would rebel against him? The Gnostics conclude the speculation by surmising that the problem is not a handful of evil angels but that the creator of the world was an inferior being while the true God was too remote to pay attention.

I had always taken the Sophia myth as inspired by the Greeks or by a non-Jewish eastern Mediterranean mystery religion. In fact, as Pearson documents, it has a Jewish origin, which runs through the book of Proverbs. Here in Proverbs 3:18: "The Lord by wisdom [Sophia] founded the earth." And then Sophia (wisdom) is personified and speaks (8:22-31):

> The Lord created me at the beginning of his work,
> the first of his acts of long ago.
> Ages ago I was set up,
> at the first, before the beginning of the earth.
> When there were no depths I was brought forth,
> when there were no springs
> abounding with water.
> Before the mountains had been shaped,
> before the hills, I was brought forth —
> when he had not yet made earth and fields,
> or the world's first bits of soil.
> When he established the heavens, I was there,
> when he drew a circle on the face of the deep,
> when he made firm the skies above,
> when he established the foundations of the deep,
> when he assigned to the sea its limit,
> so that the waters might not
> transgress his command,
> when he marked out the foundations of the earth,
> then I was beside him, like a master
> worker [demiurge];
> and I was daily his delight,
> rejoicing before him always,
> rejoicing in his inhabited world
> and delighting in the human race.

(New Revised Standard Version. Note also that the skies were made "firm" and the earth had "foundations." And here in the Old Testament Sophia herself is the demiurge.)

This is clearly the material for a creation story differing from Genesis, and on which the Gnostic myths were built.

Similarly Pearson cites ambiguities in the original Hebrew of the account of Cain's birth in Genesis, where the conventional translation has Eve saying she bore Cain with the aid of YHWH but could be read "I have gotten a man, namely Yahweh." The Gnostics held that Cain's original name was Yahweh. This traces back to Rabbinic commentary where one school of Jewish thought held that Cain was fathered not by Adam but by Sammael, the Angel of Death, a name the Gnostics applied to the Demiurge along with Yaldabaoth and Saklas. Here we have another Hebraic origin of their mythological speculations.

The schools of Gnosticism are today divided into three broad categories, the Syrian-Egyptian, which we have been following, marked by the Sophia myth and including Sethians, Valentinians, and Basilidians; Hermetic, around the writings attributed to Hermes Trismegistus; and the Iranian, which encompasses Manichaeism and Mandaeanism, these last two beyond the scope of this survey. The followers of the prophet Mani were centered in Iran and powerful throughout the Roman Empire and its successor region until the seventh century. They retained many believers in south China until the seventeenth century. As a variant of the Gnostics, they professed a cosmology divided between a distant world of light and the realm of material darkness. The Mandaeans were not so widespread but are the only continually surviving Gnostic movement, limited today to southern Iraq.

Pearson ultimately views Gnosticism as a particular Jewish response to a flowering of individualism that began throughout the region in the first century BCE and ran through the third century CE, which combined both pessimism about the external world with a breaking away from communal orthodoxies and ties and a search for individual self-realization. For the Gnostics this was not only looking forward to their soul journey to the Pleroma on death but looking inward to discover the divine spark that gave them hope that such a journey was a possibility.

Miguel Conner's Interviews

Radio interviews by their brevity and absence of source material have their limitations, but this is an informative collection in adding some informal insights from specialists. Conner hosted a long-running radio show that specialized, improbably, in commentaries on Gnosticism, initially titled *Coffee, Cigarettes & Gnosis*. He captures the Gnostic ethos nicely in his introduction when he describes it as "a dualistic theme of existentialist despair yet ultimate, ecstatic liberation."

Stevan Davies, professor of Religious Studies at Misericordia College, Pennsylvania, comments on why the Gnostics were so focused on the creation story in Genesis:

When you understand how the problem arose, of the spirit being trapped in the human body in the world, then you can reverse the process. That seems to be the reason why they're so obsessed with creation mythologies. It's not for its own sake, speculating about how the world came into being, it's the idea that you would want to reverse the process and send the world back into God where it came from.

Davies himself is a nondenominational Christian and views Gnosticism from that perspective. He agrees with Birger Pearson that the *Apocryphon of John* was a work of Jewish speculation before it was Christianized, not an anti-Jewish polemic, as some scholars have concluded from its hostile attitude toward the Jewish God:

> I think that the only people in the world who really had a serious concern for the Jewish Torah were the Jewish people. So I don't envision a bunch of pagan people, or any non-Jewish people, suddenly getting obsessed with revising the Jewish scriptures. I think Jewish people worked with the Jewish scriptures.

There is a nice interview with the ever-readable Bart Ehrman on the large number of variants in the surviving manuscripts that make up the Christian New Testament, of which no copies of any of the documents can be dated earlier than the year 200, some 150 years of hand copying after they were written, and some texts survived only in copies of considerably later date. In addition, many of the ultimately rejected gospels were considered canonical by Christians as late as 400 CE. He points out that there have been found more than 200,000 variations in the surviving manuscripts of the Gospels. In one case, the story in John of the adulteress about to be stoned where Jesus says "Let he who is without sin cast the first stone," is entirely missing from the earliest version of this document and was added by some scribe only centuries later. When the Bible was translated into English they did not have access to what are now known to be the earliest versions. These facts convinced Ehrman, who began as an Evangelical fundamentalist, that the New Testament could not possibly be the inerrant word of God.

Birger Pearson, who we have already spent some time with, makes an appearance, where he takes up the cudgels against present day scholars such as Karen King who deny that Gnosticism was a separate religion but see it as simply a Christian heresy. He comments:

> This was the standard view until the nineteenth century when historians of religion were interested in the comparative study of near-eastern and middle-eastern and Indian and other traditions [and] began to look at

the bigger picture and could see that what was described at that time by the early Christian fathers as Gnosticism looked an awful lot like some of the stuff they were uncovering in ancient Babylonia or ancient Iran or ancient India.

He does say clearly in response to a question from Conner that he believes the Gnostics regarded their versions of stories about the events in Genesis as allegorical and never intended them to be taken literally.

John D. Turner, professor of Religious Studies and Classics at the University of Nebraska at Lincoln, is another specialist in Sethian Gnosticism. He affirms that Sethianism is pretty certainly the earliest form of Gnosticism and that "we have no figure that we can identify as the founder of this movement." He believes it began among dissenting Jewish priests as early as the second century BCE. He suggests that they left Jerusalem in disgust at the corrupt Temple leadership and developed in exile their radical re-interpretation of the Old Testament.

Turner complicates the picture by proposing that the *Apocryphon of John* is a fusion of the views of two distinct early Gnostic groups. The Sethian theology, he says, is marked by a dominant trinity of the Invisible God, his consort Barbelo, and the self-generated child, and in their writings it is Barbelo who acts to rectify the damage done by Sophia. A different group, the Ophites, from the word for serpent, whose writings see the serpent in paradise as a positive figure, have a pantheon of five figures rather than three, and have Sophia herself arrange to have the divine spark instilled into the original humans.

Turner is more interesting when he turns to why the Gnostics settled on the obscure Seth as their central figure, about whom little beyond his birth and list of descendants is mentioned in the Torah. He proposes that the Gnostic authors are confronting the favorable account in the Pentateuch of the creation by the God they now regard as ignorant and inferior and responsible for the deadening world of matter. The Pentateuch is credited to Moses, and Turner comments, "Moses was never in Paradise. Who was in paradise? Adam was in paradise." And his son Seth long predated Moses.

Turner elaborates this more fully in his "The Gnostic Seth" in Stone and Bergren's *Biblical Figures Outside the Bible*. Here he cites ancient Jewish sources of biblical commentary that regard Seth as the only biological child of Adam and Eve. The *Targum Pseudo-Jonathan* held that Samael, the angel of death, was the father of Cain and Abel. The *Midrash Genesis Rabbah* held that Cain and Abel were sons of the devil. Genesis lists two genealogies, the descendants of Cain and those of Seth. The sources Turner quotes regard the descendants of Seth as the righteous and those of Cain as a wicked people.

This view imbues the Gnostic Sethian writings where they regularly refer to themselves as "the seed of Seth." Turner adds that the Gnostic centrality of Seth seems to be because Seth is never credited with praising Jehovah or having any special relations with him, unlike his father Adam or figures like Moses.

Einar Thomassen, a professor of Religious Studies at the University of Bergen in Norway, was interviewed about the Valentinians. Thomassen says that it is a mistake to imagine that there was a central strong Catholic Church combating numerous small heretical Christian sects. "There wasn't really one Christian community, but a lot of Christian communities, all over the capitol [Rome], and they were all teaching their own adaptations of Christianity." Valentinus and his Gnostic variant was just one more. He sees the Valentinians as a compromise between Christianity and classic Gnosticism in that they did not think the material world all bad, believed that the remote God had some influence on the creation of the material sphere, and that there was a limited redemption possible for Yaldabaoth. He does not see a continuity between the old Gnostic trinity and the one that came to be central to Catholicism:

> I think that the trinity is actually an idea that was created in its present form in the fourth century when you have the various church councils, and so on, who have defined metaphysically the idea of a trinity. I don't think you have anything like that anywhere in the second century.

Thomassen is asked what finally happened to the Valentinians. He replies:

> You know, the last we hear of the Valentinians is very precisely dated. It's August 1, 388 C.E., where there was an incident in a village in upper Mesopotamia or eastern Syria where some of these fanatical monks — there were a lot of those in that time — were burning down the church of some Valentinians in that place. And this we know only because Bishop Ambrose tells us of the incident. He tries to persuade the emperor not to punish those monks who, in his opinion, acted quite righteously.

The Gnostic Legacy

Except for the Mandaeans in Iraq there is no proof that any Gnostic group survived continuously down to our own day. There are strong continuities mediated through Iranian Manichaeanism that re-penetrate Eastern and Western Europe over the millennium after the original Jewish-centered originators are gone. After that the connections with successive occult movements become more attenuated.

There is a substantial literature that seeks to trace Gnostic influence in Europe over the centuries. Richard Smoley's *Forbidden Faith: The Gnostic Legacy* is just one example, a brief survey that skims the surface of a large and complex topic and is not always as specific as could be desired. Smoley is not a learned scholar with command of the ancient languages but was the long-time editor of the journal *Gnosis*, which focused on Western spiritual traditions. I will skip his summary of the original Gnostics as we have covered that ground. And Manichaeanism is further afield than I care to go. The dualist doctrine of the remote god of light and the nearby one of evil who controls the world of matter returns to Europe with the Paulicians of Armenia, followers of the New Testament St. Paul, but with a Gnostic interpretation of the two rival Gods. The Paulicians flourished between 650 and 872, when Armenia was split between Persia and the Byzantine Empire.

Little is known of their doctrine except that they rejected the Old Testament, viewed the God of Earth as evil, and looked toward a good God in an afterlife. They saw Christ as a spirit being rather than a human and so did not venerate Mary.

A larger and more influential sect, the Bogomils, arose in Bulgaria around 900 CE and spread among the Balkan Slavs, remaining powerful into the early 1300s. Again, they believed in a dualism between good and evil gods. Like the original Gnostics they professed Docetism, claiming Christ was a spirit entity only. The Byzantine Empire tried to suppress them, and in the twelfth century the Orthodox Serbs drove them into Bosnia. The Bogomils won power in Bosnia in the fourteenth century. After the Muslim conquest by the Ottoman Turks in the 1450s, however, most of them converted to Islam. Smoley does not touch on this, but part of the reason for Islam's success in the Eastern Mediterranean was the widespread rejection by heterodox Christians such as the Bogomils of the Orthodox doctrine of the Trinity. Among the Gnostic-like sects the Christ was distinguished from the human Jesus, and even the Christ was viewed at most as a powerful angelic figure, not as God, while the human Jesus was mostly seen as a vessel for spirit possession.

Next in line were the Cathars, also called Albigensians, ultimately centered in Provence in southeastern France, the region whose capital is Marseille. Said to have been founded through conversions by Bogomil preachers, the Cathars first appeared in Cologne in Germany in 1143. Catholic officials had the archbishop of Cologne and his unrepentant followers, branded as Cathars, burned to death. This Gnostic Christian doctrine then took root in southern France, where it generated two somewhat different schools of thought, one that later scholars describe as "mitigated dualists," who followed the original Gnostic doctrine that the evil God had been produced from elements around the good God, and another school now called "absolute dualists" who believed good and evil principles existed separately from the beginning of eternity, which implied that the powers of the good God were limited. The two groups remained on good terms. The Cathars were also known for producing the romantic troubadours and the ideas of courtly love of the late Middle Ages.

Also informative on the Cathars are the few of their original documents to survive, reprinted in Barnstone and Meyer's *The Gnostic Bible*, as well as Willis Barnstone's introduction to that section of the anthology.

The pope declared a crusade against the Cathars in 1209, which raged for twenty years of brutal savagery. The Inquisition burned large numbers of the Cathar elite alive. The Cathars were destroyed in France with the long siege of their last fortress, at Montségur at the edge of the Pyrenees. In March 1244 more than two hundred of the leading figures from the fortress were burned alive. A small remnant fled to Italy where they survived into the fourteenth century.

The Renaissance and After

Gnosticism revives again in Europe after the Turks captured Constantinople in 1453 and many Greek scholars fled to Italy, bringing copies of ancient manuscripts with them. At the request of Cosimo de' Medici, Marsilio Ficino (1433-1499), best known for translating the whole of Plato's works into Latin, made a Latin translation of the documents known as the Corpus Hermeticum. These made a huge impact, not as a religious movement but among Renaissance intellectuals. These documents carried the authority they did because they were mistakenly attributed to an ancient Egyptian sage, thrice-great Hermes, or Hermes Trismegistus, who was identified with the Egyptian Ibis-headed god Thoth and believed to date back to the time of Moses. This was a non-Jewish, Egyptian source, actually written in the second century CE.

The first of the Hermetic texts is the *Poimandres*, the title taken from the name of the narrator, a being whose name signifies a personified attribute of God as *Nous* (intellect or intuition). Poimandres tells a disciple a creation story. As in Classic Gnosticism, "*Nous*, God, being male and female, beginning as life and light, gave birth, by the Word, to another *Nous*, the Creator of the world." (*The Way of Hermes*, p. 19). This second god, while not a negative creature like Yaldabaoth, is of a lower order. This bisexual entity creates the world of matter. And as in the Gnostic eschatology, humans contain an immaterial spark that must, after death of the body, transcend the eight spheres surrounding the Earth and make its way back to the realm of the higher God. The Hermetic writings do not include the mythology about multiple emanations and Sophia, but the general outline is very similar.

The Hermetic texts held their high position for a bit more than a century, until in 1614 the Swiss Calvinist Casaubon proved that they could be dated no earlier than the beginning of the Christian era. The use of the Ptolemaic system should have been a dead giveaway. Gilles Quispel, emeritus professor at Utrecht and Harvard, in his introduction to the text quoted above notes that two Hermetic texts were included among the Nag Hammadi tractates and one of these suggests the Hermetic writings in some form may have long predated the documents translated by Marsilio Ficino after all, though certainly not back to the eighth century BCE, which is the earliest mention of Moses.

The Corpus Hermeticum also contained materials about alchemy and astrology that prompted interests that contributed to the modern sciences of astronomy and chemistry, which in the sixteenth century were just emerging from their magical beginnings.

In the same period Jewish Kabbalah, which had absorbed Gnostic elements, attracted the interest of European intellectuals, particularly under the influence of the German scholar Johannes Reuchlin (1455-1522), who championed the teaching of Hebrew in German universities to gain access to these documents and to the Hebrew texts of the Old Testament.

The century following the publication of the Hermetic texts is a period of occult ferment in Europe. Giordano Bruno (1548-1600) called for a revival of what he thought of as the ancient Egyptian religion. He was also an early advocate of Copernicus's heliocentric theory of the solar system and, remarkably for his age, went beyond Copernicus by claiming that the Sun was just a star like all the others, drifting in an infinitely large universe filled with many other worlds. He was burned at the stake for these ideas on the order of Pope Clement VIII.

A contemporary in England was John Dee (1527-1608), Queen Elizabeth's court astrologer. Dee was a leading mathematician of his time and a prominent expert in navigation. He was influential in laying the groundwork for the British empire, but was most famous for his long experiments in communications with spirits and angels. Dee also made an expedition to Poland and to Prague, then the capital of Bohemia, where he met with rulers deeply interested in alchemy and communication with spirit beings. His interests have led scholars of today to regard him as an important predecessor to the Rosicrucian mysticism that emerged just a few years after his death. (See Nicholas Goodrick-Clarke, "The Rosicrucian Prelude: John Dee's Mission in Central Europe," in Matthews, et al., *The Rosicrucian Enlightenment Revisited.*)

A wonderful fictional account of both Bruno and Dee is contained in John Crowley's Ægypt series of novels: *The Solitudes* (originally titled *Ægypt*), *Love & Sleep, Dæmonomania,* and *Endless Things.* The distinguished literary and religious critic Harold Bloom includes the first two of this series in his expanded list of The Western Canon, several hundred European and American works beginning with Gilgamesh and extending up to its compilation in 1994. Bloom considers himself a Gnostic and develops his somewhat idiosyncratic views on this in *Omens of Millennium: The Gnosis of Angels, Dreams, and Resurrection.* Crowley's series also shows a strong influence of Gnostic themes.

The Rosicrucian Temple of the Rosy Cross, 1618

In the seventeenth century we come to the great Rosicrucian furor, begun with the publication, in 1614 and 1615 in Germany, of two anonymous manifestoes claiming to speak for a secret occult society said to have been founded by Christian Rosenkreutz, who was supposed to have been born in 1378 and died in 1484. The manifestoes, published almost a century into the Reformation, affirm a strong anti-Catholic Protestantism merged with Hermeticism.

For a long time the Rosicrucian documents were dismissed by scholars as an irrelevant hoax. No one has ever established that the secret order of the Rosy Cross existed in fact. But historian Frances Yates in her *The Rosicrucian Enlightenment* established beyond doubt that there was a lively experimentation with occult matters linked to Rosicrucianism. A key center of this was the court of Frederick V, Elector Palatine (1596-1636), the young ruler of the German principality of the Palatinate. He strongly supported occult studies and Hermetic scholars at his court at Heidelberg. A number of Rosicrucian and Hermetic treatises were published at places in the Palatinate. Invited to become king of Bohemia, which was launching a Protestant revolt against the Catholic Holy Roman Empire, Frederick and his English bride accepted. He was crowned in Prague in August 1619. This touched off the Thirty Years War. Frederick was defeated and driven into exile in November 1620, the brevity of his reign earning him the nickname "The Winter King." His exile led to the dispersal of the mystical scholars who had gathered at his courts.

Smoley continues with figures and movements that, independently of the old Gnostics, adopted views that in part echoed theirs. He includes the German mystic Jacob Böhme (1575-1624), the original Freemasons, the Bavarian Illuminati of Adam Weishaupt, proclaimed in 1776, and the Swedish Christian mystic Emanuel Swedenbourg. From there he moves on to stock characters of occult speculation such as the adventurers the Comte de St.-Germain and Count Cagliostro. These were interesting figures but seem to stray from the point.

One of the major moderns to declare for Gnosticism was the poet and artist William Blake (1757-1827), a founder of Romanticism. Subject throughout his life to visions of angels, Blake considered himself a Christian but repudiated the official churches. He maintained that each human contained a portion of godlike material, which he interpreted to mean that God was not a separate and superior being. He also, in the full Gnostic spirit, claimed that the Earth was not created by the highest God but by Elohim, a lower angel, seemingly equivalent to the Gnostic demiurge.

Smoley comes finally to the Gnostic revival in the late nineteenth century, which begins with Madame Blavatsky (1831-1891) and her Theosophical Society and is carried on by her acolyte, the indefatigable independent scholar G. R. S. Mead. Blavatsky, dismissed by mainstream academics as a crank, had an influence on the twentieth century almost as great as that of Sigmund Freud. She was the principal initiator of Western interest in Eastern religions, mainly Theravada Buddhism, and the occult revival. She paved the way for major esoteric figures of the early twentieth century such as Rudolph Steiner, George Gurdjieff, Peter Ouspensky, and Krishnamurti, and ultimately the currents that coalesced as advocates of New Age spirituality.

Madame Helena Petrovna Blavatsky with her associate Henry Steel Olcott. Olcott was a colonel in the Civil War and served on the investigating committee into the assassination of Abraham Lincoln. He lived in India from 1879 to his death in 1907. To this day he is honored in Sri Lanka for his contributions to Buddhism

The New Age covers a very diverse assortment of people and movements that have broken with conventional religion, particularly Christianity, but find scientific materialism inadequate, or incomplete, either on moral or ontological grounds. They have more than their share of insipid maundering about crystals and auras that makes it hard to take them seriously, but the countercultural spiritual movement also contains people seriously concerned with alternate states of consciousness, lucid dreaming, and, further afield, new efforts with the kind of research done a century earlier by the Society for Psychical Research. This and the preference within the New Age to rank personal empirical spiritual experience higher than received doctrine, knowledge ahead of faith, mark them as kindred to the old Gnostics. They have been unsatisfied with scriptural authority while feeling a need to explore expanded states of consciousness to see where these may lead.

Blavatsky taught a doctrine with a strong affinity for Gnosticism, depicting a cosmos whose higher levels were nonphysical consciousness and grading downward ending in its densest realm of physical matter. Individual human souls were said to be a spark that sought to unite with a remote "oversoul" in the nonphysical realm. She claimed that Gnosticism was the heart of a traditional ancient wisdom and that Christianity was "the usurper and assassin of the great master's doctrine." Smoley cites a key statement on this from Blavatsky's *Secret Doctrine*:

> It requires *a lower order of creative angels* to "create" inhabited globes — especially ours — or to deal with matter on this earthly plane. The philosophical Gnostics were the first to think so, in the historical period, and to invent various systems upon this theory. Therefore in their schemes of Creation, one always finds their *Creators* occupying a place at the very foot of the ladder of spiritual Being. With them, those who created our earth and its mortals were placed on the very limit of *mayavi* [illusory] matter, and their followers were taught to think — to the great disgust of the Church Fathers — that for the creation of those wretched races, in a spiritual and moral sense, no high divinity could be made responsible, but only angels of a *low hierarchy*, to which class they relegated the Jewish God, Jehovah. (From *The Secret Doctrine*, 1888, her emphasis.)

I was never attracted to Blavatsky, because of her pseudo histories of humanity, which posit multiple sequential racial groups from the mythical continents of Atlantis and Lemuria. Also because it was one thing for people of the second century to think in terms of what we today call Creationism, however non-Christian, but it would seem that this would need a little distancing when writing about world origins in recent decades. I had a discussion of this in May 2012 with John Michael Greer at a conference on peak oil in Pennsylvania. Greer writes widely on the threat posed to industrial civilization by the depletion of oil and other essential minerals, but he is also Grand Archdruid of the Ancient Order of Druids in America and one of the country's most prominent occultists. He insisted that Blavatsky intended her pseudo histories to be allegorical and figurative.

Which brings us down to the present. Science charts the history of the known universe from the Big Bang through the origin of life on this planet, and across the vast space of time it has taken for organic evolution to produce, pretty plainly by accident within the general framework of the rules of natural selection, we humans, who have been here for hardly a few moments of the geological timeline and seem unlikely to last a great deal longer the way we are heading. The dinosaurs lasted 165 million years. The earliest modern human appeared 43,000 years ago and agriculture goes back only 10,000 years. It is pretty difficult to have the chutzpah to claim that the Earth, much less the universe, was created by some supernatural spirit just for us.

We could add to that the effects on human personality of disease or injury to the organic brain as an obstacle to the idea that there is a personality independent of the physical body.

The Gnostics were prototypical rootless cosmopolitan Jews, eerily similar to the emancipated Jews in the late nineteenth century who, when freed from the shtetl and allowed out of the Pale of Settlement, or offered citizenship in Germany, exploded in creative speculation beyond the bounds of rabbinic commentary. In their way the Jewish Gnostics were experimenters who relied on personal experience and refused to accept either faith or reason as the ultimate arbiters of truth. Many of their writings look foolish or bizarre because they are bound up with a long-outmoded science and they chose to try to explain their ideas by making allegorical use of Jewish creation myths that all but the most extreme Evangelical Protestants and Islamic and Jewish conservatives now see as fairy stories. If they had known modern science would they have given the whole thing up? That is, is there a loophole in the evidence that makes a place like the Pleroma conceivable?

Physics today is in another period of transition as consequential as the adoption of the Ptolemaic system, confronted by numerous rival theories of the underlying reality behind our perceptions of the physical world. Some of those theories, such as proposing the actuality to be a great hologram or the universe as an information system analogous to a computer program, begin to see the universe as physically immaterial, its physicality an artifact of the informational construct, like the images on your computer screen. Does this leave an opening for the Buddhist belief that the world is an illusion, or the Gnostic reversal of the priority of matter and energy? Were these not just foolish fantasies but intuitions drawn from the immersion of the brain in the holographic or information matrix? There are even a few scientists who think so.

Religions are as powerful as ever despite the Enlightenment, and at least some of the certainties of nineteenth century materialism look narrow and dogmatic. Is the persistence of religion just a sign of incorrigible human wishful thinking, perhaps hard-wired into the brain as an inability to fully conceive personal annihilation? Or is there some possibility that buried under the ossification of doctrine, religion survives because some transcendent experience occurs often enough to enough people to keep alive a belief that there are other planes of existence? If so, the Gnostic approach seems more likely to uncover it, while the faith-based scriptural dogmas of Christianity, Islam, and Judaism mostly reinforce earthly political and ethnic prejudices.

In the end, Han Solo is probably right, that a good blaster is more useful than the Force. But, just maybe, Skywalker has it right.

December 24, 2012

Further Reading

Bloom, Harold. *Omens of Millennium: The Gnosis of Angels, Dreams, and Resurrection.* New York: Riverhead Books, 1996.

Burkitt, F. C. *Church and Gnosis: A Study of Christian Thought and Speculation in the Second Century.* London: Cambridge University Press, 1932.

Ehrman, Bart D. *Lost Christianities: The Battles for Scripture and the Faiths We Never Knew.* New York: Oxford University Press, 2003.

Goodrick-Clarke, Nicholas. *The Western Esoteric Traditions.* New York: Oxford University Press, 2008.

Hesse, Hermann. *Demian.* Translated from the German by Michael Roloff and Michael Lebeck. New York: Bantam Books, 1970. First German publication, 1919.

Matthews, John, et al. *The Rosicrucian Enlightenment Revisited.* Hudson, New York: Lindisfarne Books, 1999.

Mead, G.R.S., trans. *Pistis Sophia: The Gnostic Tradition of Mary Magdalene, Jesus, and His Disciples.* San Bernardino: SubliminalSelfHypnosis.com, 2012. This is the 1921 version based on a Latin translation from the Coptic in 1856 and a German version that appeared in 1905. Mead had done a less authoritative version in 1896 based only on the Latin.

Meyer, Marvin, ed. *The Nag Hammadi Scriptures: The Revised and Updated Translation of Sacred Gnostic Texts Complete in One Volume.* New York: Harper One, 2007.

Pagels, Elaine. *The Gnostic Gospels.* New York: Vintage Books, 1989 (originally published 1979).

Robinson, James M., ed. *The Nag Hammadi Library in English.* HarperSanFrancisco: 1988 (originally published 1978).

Rudolph, Kurt. *Gnosis: The Nature and History of Gnosticism.* Translated by Robert McLachlan Wilson. HarperSanFrancisco, 1987. First German edition, 1980.

Salaman, Clement, et al., translators. *The Way of Hermes: New Translations of The Corpus Hermeticum and The Definitions of Hermes Trismegistus to Asclepius.* Rochester, Vermont: Inner Traditions, 2000.

Segal, Robert A., ed. *The Gnostic Jung.* Princeton: Princeton University Press, 1992.

Stone, Michael E., and Theodore A. Bergren, eds. *Biblical Figures Outside the Bible*. Harrisburg, Pennsylvania: Trinity Press International, 1998.

Van den Broek, Roelof, and Wouter J. Hanegraaff, eds. *Gnosis and Hermeticism, from Antiquity to Modern Times*. Albany: State University of New York Press, 1998.

Yates, Frances A. *The Rosicrucian Enlightenment*. Routledge, 2001 (originally published, 1972).

The Hunger Ahead

The Coming Famine: The Global Food Crisis and What We Can Do to Avoid It. Julian Cribb. Berkeley: University of California Press, 2010. 248 pp.

The Race for What's Left: The Global Scramble for the World's Last Resources. Michael T. Klare. New York: Henry Holt and Company, 2012. 306 pp.

Back in 1798, Thomas Malthus published his *Essay on the Principle of Population.* He put forth the simple proposition that, land being finite, the food supply increases only arithmetically, by small percentages, while humans have multiple births that in the next generation have multiple births so that population increases geometrically and will periodically locally, and in the end globally, outrun the food supply. The premise would seem irrefutable, though the date when the ultimate bill comes due is uncertain. On the Right, Malthus was rejected on the ground that God would take care of his own. On the Left, for two centuries Malthus was dismissed with the argument that there would always be sufficient food if distribution were more equal. We are now in the endgame.

On one side of the ledger we have a human population that has just topped seven billion, headed for nine billion by 2050, with large sections of the underdeveloped world rapidly raising their standard of living. On the other we are hitting the planet's limits of arable land, potable water, mineral nutrients required for agriculture, and severe depletion of sea life by global over-fishing. All of this while global warming lights a fire under the whole kettle, most immediately reducing the snowfall and mountain ice caps that feed the world's great river systems on which a large part of world farming depend, and temperatures rise, producing historic droughts. As the days of cheap oil have departed the crisis is exacerbated as food crops are diverted to make biofuels.

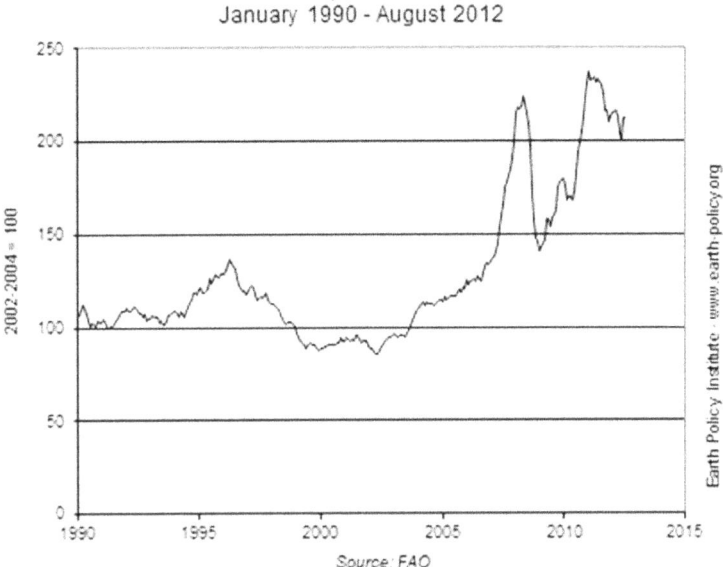

World Monthly Food Price Index,
January 1990 - August 2012

Source: FAO

Julian Cribb provides an excellent summary of what we are up against, along with many proposals that might improve our situation if governments were to act on them. Harvey Clare brings the survey two years ahead to where we are now, and offers a broader canvas on our limits, including oil and minerals. Since 2004 global food prices have more than doubled. Like oil, with which food prices run in close tandem, this has been an ascending roller coaster, with sharp rises followed by steep falls, but with the overall trajectory upward. The UN Food and Agriculture Organization's World Food Price Index stood at 100 in 2004. It hit 240 in 2008 along with the spike in oil prices to $147 a barrel, touching off food riots in a dozen countries and sparking the Arab Spring, especially in Egypt. But when prices fell in 2009 they did not get below an index of 148, almost a 50% increase over 2004. The index has been above 200 since 2010 and is currently rising from there.

In America, where food is still a small part of the budget of the employed, despite the millions on food stamps, the effects of this shockwave are still little felt. In the Third World, fifteen thousand children die each day of hunger-related disease.

World hunger was abated in the 1970s by the Green Revolution of more productive and pest resistant grains. That improvement has run its course, while population has continued to explode. Cribb reports that by 2009 a billion people were eating less than the year before.

Many currents are converging on the impending world famine. The rise in oil prices has compelled Thai rice famers to park their tractors and plow with buffalo. In China increasing meat consumption by the burgeoning middle class has led to a ten-fold growth in the need for feed grain. In eastern Australia there was a ten-year drought. Cribb writes: "This challenge is more pressing even than climate change. A climate crisis may emerge over decades. A food crisis can explode within weeks — and kill within days."

Population growth rates are declining, but not fast enough. World growth rates average at 2%, while food output is only going up by about 1%. There will be two billion more people by the time world population stabilizes at mid-century. In the meantime, as living standards rise rapidly in China, India, Brazil, and other poor countries, pressure on world food supplies are heading toward a breaking point.

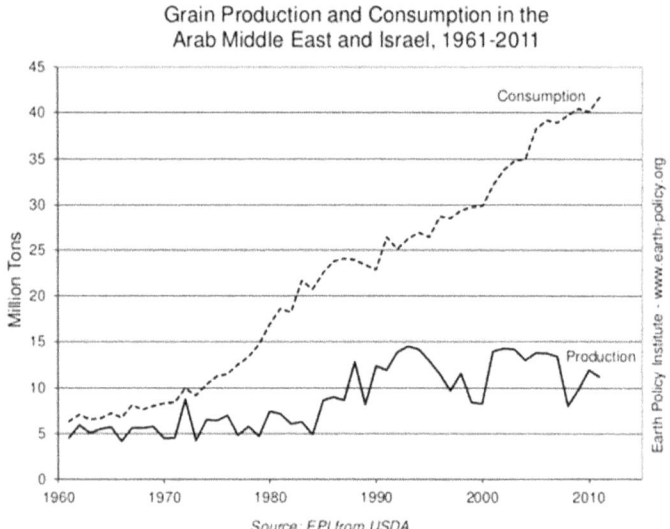

Grain Production and Consumption in the Arab Middle East and Israel, 1961-2011

Source: EPI from USDA

By 2050 total food output will have to double to meet the larger and more affluent population. This will have to be done, Cribb writes, "using far less water, less land, less energy, and less fertilizer."

Water

Drought only exacerbates a more fundamental problem. Only 2.5% of the water on earth is fresh water, usable for farming and drinking. All of that comes from rain and snowfall. The vast majority of the water that falls from the sky quickly disappears again, from evaporation and runoff to the sea. Perhaps 10% is usable by humans. Of that, today 70% is used for agricultural irrigation, power generation takes 20%, and urban water supplies take 10%. Much of the world's drinking water is contaminated. This kills 2-5 million people a year in poor countries.

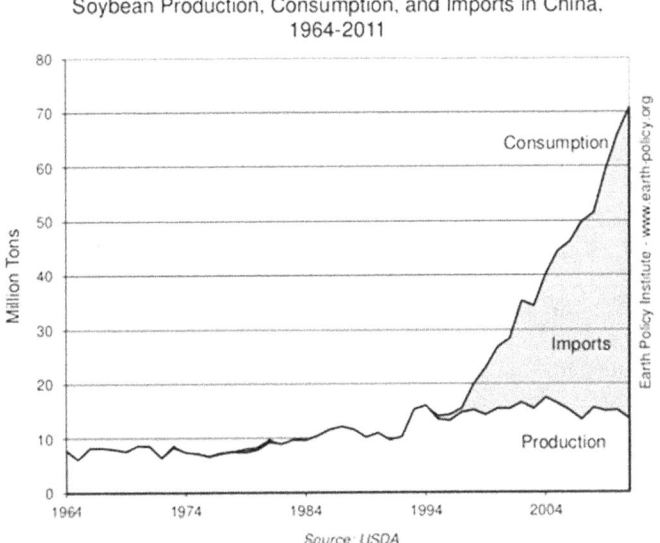

Soybean Production, Consumption, and Imports in China, 1964-2011

Source: USDA

The world's population is rapidly urbanizing, departing rural areas for the megacities. As urbanization expands, it concretes over adjacent farmland, reducing cropping area, and the urbanized people use more water. According to Cribb, "Urban demand for water may soar by as much as 150 percent by 2025 as the cities themselves burgeon."

The water needed to make our food varies hugely by what we eat. It take 7 gallons of water to grow a potato, 179 for a pound of grain, but 1,797 gallons for a pound of beef and 719 for a pound of chicken. As standards of living rise in developing countries there is more consumption of animal meats requiring far greater amounts of water in agriculture and stock raising.

At the same time, the total available amount of fresh water is rapidly de-clining. There are many causes: desertification from natural causes, climate change, or over cropping; removal of natural vegetation leading to rising sa-line groundwater or leaching of acidic soils into streams; concentration of toxins such as arsenic from humans pumping out ground water; and overuse of lake and river water for human uses that dry up reservoirs and even large rivers. Shockingly, Cribb reports, "In the last four decades of the twentieth century, the amount of fresh water available for each human being worldwide shrank by almost two-thirds. It is expected to be halved again by 2025." On a planetary scale, we have hit "peak water."

China faces one of the most serious water threats, "with 22 percent of the world's people and just 8 percent of its available freshwater. The Chinese Ministry of Water Resources has warned of a serious crisis by 2030 due to falling per capita water availability." The other areas facing the most serious shortages are the Indian subcontinent, the Middle East, North Africa, and parts of southern Africa. Lacking sufficient water to be self-sufficient in agri-culture, these regions will have to import a large part of their food, a major drain on their economies, if world food markets are even able to provide what they need.

This is not just a problem for poor people in faraway places:

> In the United States . . . groundwater supplies more than half of all drinking water and more than one-third of all agricultural water needs. The huge Ogallala aquifer, which underlies eight states in the American Midwest and is extensively used to grow food, is being depleted at ten times the rate of natural recharge, and some experts fear it could dry up completely within twenty-five years.

The situation is even worse in the arid Southwest.

Farmland

The amount of farmland per person on our planet has been in decline for fifty years. It was 1.1 acres in the 1960s. By the 2010s it had fallen almost by half, to .6 acre. It will keep heading downward as the next 2 billion people join us in the next 35 years. The margins for possible increased planting vary significantly by region. Asia already has 75% of potential land under cultiva-tion; the Middle East and North Africa, 87%. Latin America is only at 19%, but the land not turned to crops is largely the Argentine pampas and the Bra-zilian and Peruvian rain forest. Russia is in perhaps the best position, with only 44% of potential farmland under cultivation and large stretches of Siberia expected to be more amenable to agriculture as global warming advances.

Cribb tells us that Asia will have to double its food supply by 2050 but has only 25% more land to do it in. The Middle East and North Africa will need 150% more food with only 13% more land to grow it on.

But even this gloomy picture hides worse news. Most potential farmland is not in use now because it would be environmentally destructive to use it, as in Brazil, or because the soils are very poor and would need extensive fertilizer and energy to grow crops there. At the same time existing productive land is degrading faster than new lands are put in service, through erosion, exhaustion of the water tables, salinization, and loss of soil nutrients. Cribb concludes:

> [T]he arable area, which produces most of the grain, oilseeds, fruit, and vegetables we eat or feed to livestock, is growing at only one-seventh the rate of consumption and one-forty-sixth the rate of population. Thus, from 1990 to 2005, world demand for food grew fifteen times faster than the area of land available to produce it.

A truly frightening response to this dire situation has been the purchase by arable-land-scarce nations of vast tracts of farmland in other people's countries, mainly in sub-Saharan Africa. This trend set in after the food price shock of 2008, when it became clear that world grain markets could not supply demand. China, Saudi Arabia, the Arab emirates, and some other countries decided for their food security to buy large pieces of other countries. China bought 3 million acres in the Philippines and 1.7 million in Laos. The United Arab Emirates bought 2.2 million acres in Pakistan and 934,000 in Sudan. South Korea also bought large acreage in Sudan. Even Russia, which wouldn't seem to need it, is buying up farmland in Africa. This neocolonial land grab has continued apace since Cribb went to press in 2010. Harvey Klare adds more on this trend and we will come to his findings later. Corrupt governments, for a one-time payment, sell off land essential to their people's future survival, usually in the process expelling indigenous subsistence farmers who have lived there since time immemorial.

Existing farmland is degrading at a devastating rate. In 1991 a UN survey found that 15% of the planet's land was no longer bearing vegetation. In January 2008 the FAO reported its own global satellite survey, which found that 24 percent of the world's land was now denuded. Cribb estimates at that rate 1% of productive land is reduced to unusability each year. On the same principle as compound interest this "will ruin two-thirds of the world's productive land by 2050." The United States is among the world's top five countries with the worst land degradation. The others are Russia, Canada, China, and Australia, all five key grain producers in the world economy.

Salt and acidic poisoning of farmland afflicts different regions. The Indus valley that feeds both India and Pakistan suffers heavy salinity, ruining 100,000 acres of Pakistan's irrigated land per year. Acidity is a product of cutting down tropical forests, leaving behind land good for only a year or two of planting. There is a lot of this in Southeast Asia and still more in South America. This puts severe limits on replacing Brazil's rainforest with farms. Arsenic poisoning is another threat, arising from pumping out too much groundwater, which concentrates naturally found arsenic as the soil dries. This is prevalent in China, the Indian subcontinent, Southeast Asia, Iran, Argentina, and the United States. Since Cribb published we have had the revelations of the high levels of arsenic in rice, with brown rice retaining seven times the amount of arsenic legally permitted in water, and the worst of this crop coming from the American South, where the natural arsenic is compounded by the residues of arsenic-based pesticides used when the land was given over in the past to cotton.

Cities and their suburbs are mostly built on prime farmland. Bedroom suburban communities and still further outlying recreational areas eat up still more land. New York occupies 4,349 square miles, while the Boston to Washington, DC, urban mega corridor has left very little room for farmland. The land further out is often of poorer quality and less productive. There is also a grave risk in this pattern. Cribb writes:

> [M]odern cities, which once supplied quite a lot of their own food, especially in the form of fresh fruit, vegetables, and poultry — notably in Asia — have largely been planned and developed in ways that expel agriculture from within the urban perimeter. This is a piece of extraordinary blindness on the part of today's urban planners . . . which could well turn some of these giant cities into death traps in the event of serious future disruptions to food supplies.

On the same page Cribb refers without qualifiers to "the coming famine of the midcentury."

Expected sea level rise from global warming is another cause that will diminish the world's arable land. Even a modest rise, of fifteen inches, at the conservative end of predictions for the end of this century, would displace thirteen million people around the Bay of Bengal and cut Bangladesh's rice harvest by a sixth.

The Limits of Fertilizer

The Green Revolution, which staved off starvation for the last half century — while population grew from 3 billion in 1960 to 7 billion in 2012 —

depended on both new, more productive, varieties of grains, and also ample supplies of fertilizer. Commercial fertilizer is also essential to agribusiness production, the largest source of food for the American consumer. Cribb goes so far as to say that fertilizer has been "the principle cause of the human population explosion." Modern commercial fertilizer is commonly called nitrogen fertilizer after its largest ingredient. Commercial nitrogen is produced from natural gas as a feed stock, and this remains comparatively plentiful and, at least in the United States for a while, relatively cheap. Nitrogen can also be set in the soil at a smaller scale by planting legumes.

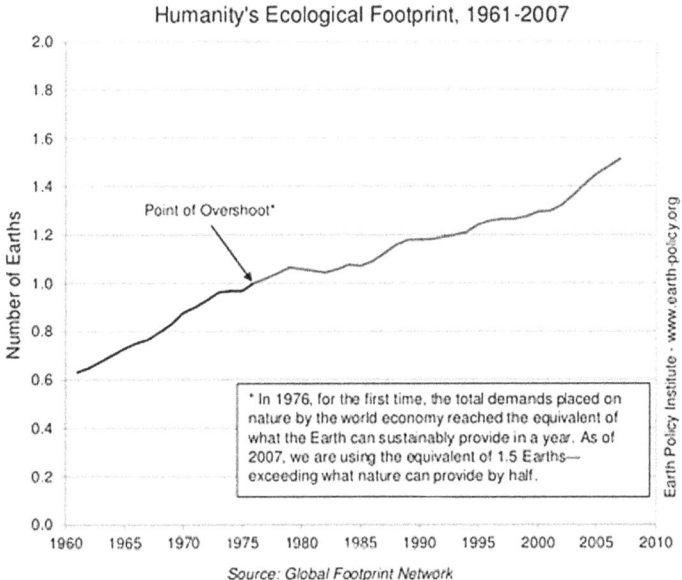

Humanity's Ecological Footprint, 1961-2007

* In 1976, for the first time, the total demands placed on nature by the world economy reached the equivalent of what the Earth can sustainably provide in a year. As of 2007, we are using the equivalent of 1.5 Earths—exceeding what nature can provide by half.

Source: Global Footprint Network

But there are three essential ingredients of functional fertilizer and the other two are more problematic: phosphorus and potassium. All three are essential. If one is missing plants are likely not to grow at all. Phosphate rock, the source of phosphorus, is the most at risk. Eighty-four percent of world phosphorous comes from only four countries: China (37 percent), Morocco and Western Sahara (32 percent), South Africa (8 percent), and the United States (7 percent). As this mineral essential to our lives becomes more scarce the price has been escalating. It sold for barely $3 a ton through the first half of the twentieth century. In 2000 it reached $44 a ton. During the oil and food spike of spring 2008 it shot up to $430 a ton. Now in late 2012 it has stabilized at about $185 a ton. Spurred by the higher price, world output, which had fallen to 120 million tons in 2009, was estimated at 186 million tons in 2010. Unlike oil, for which at least some partial substitutes are available, there is no substitute for phosphorus. "No phosphorus, no food." It seems at least unlikely that world phosphorus output can be doubled in the next thirty-eight years to feed the population expected to be here by 2050, not to mention the shift to greater meat in the diets of developing countries, necessitating vast increases in grain for feed compared to a principally vegetarian diet. Here price as well as sheer volume is an essential determinant of potential use. Already many poor farmers have been priced out of the fertilizer market by the price spiral after 2008.

Fertilizers are heavily overused, with little or no control of the runoff, which massively pollutes waterways and the broader ocean. The waterborne fertilizer provides food for algae blooms that rob the water of oxygen and can lead to mass extinction of sea life. On land, much fertilizer, to save costs, shorts the phosphorous and potassium and leans mainly on nitrogen, with the result that whatever quantity of the two shorted minerals does exist in the soil is leached away.

Cribb ranks the nutrient crisis as of similar weight to the far better known ones of climate change, peak oil, and water scarcity.

There is leeway in the system to expand food production, though the raw statistics would seem to overstate it. Some 40 percent of all food produced in the United States is thrown away. This ranges from spoilage before it can be shipped, to unsold vegetables in the markets, to canned and other goods that are tossed when they reach their sell-by date, though they are actually good for some considerable time after that. It would take a major organizational effort at many levels to improve this picture.

One option for recovering both nutrients and water is to recycle city sewage and human waste, which contain large amounts of recoverable phosphorous. This would require expensive processing, along with recycling waste water for reuse.

Cribb also advocates re-greening cities. His proposal is far more extensive than backyard and community gardens. He suggests planting foodstuffs on freeway and highway sidings, flat building roofs, and front yards, and even enveloping existing buildings in fruit-bearing vines. "It is time to recognize," he writes, "that regulations about waste disposal and urban farming, created with perfectly sound public health aims in view, threaten far more lives in the event of major food scarcities than they will save."

He cites approvingly a proposal by Japanese civil servant Makoto Murase for large-scale saving of rainwater by installing cisterns under buildings. A related idea is to replace ordinary concrete with permeable material to direct rainwater back into the water table instead of running it out to rivers or the ocean.

There Are Not So Many Good Fish in the Sea

> Worldwide, the evidence is mounting that the fish are running out. Almost one in three sea fisheries has collapsed or is in the process. . . . Most of the continental shelves have been swept clean and even miles down, in the deep ocean, the rapine is now taking its toll.

With the continental shelves nearly empty, deep-sea trawlers with vast nets scour the deeps. The ocean depths are dark and there is little food. Large predatory fish such as the cod, tuna, and orange roughy, have evolved to a long, slow existence. The orange roughy, fished to near extinction off the coast of Australia and New Zealand, lives to as much as 140 years. It doesn't reproduce until it is thirty or forty. Cleaning out one year's population can mean the fish is gone for a century, if it returns at all. Cod, once the commonest fish in the sea, is all but gone. Tuna is well on its way out. The November 3, 2006, *New York Times* reported:

> If fishing around the world continues at its present pace, more and more species will vanish, marine ecosystems will unravel and there will be "global collapse" of all species currently fished, possibly as soon as midcentury, fisheries experts and ecologists are predicting.

Disputed at the time, what can be said is that world marine fish catch plateaued at the end of the 1980s and has not risen since. Within the captured tonnage the size and value of the fish have sharply declined. Today it takes greater effort to catch many smaller fish as the larger ones are fished out. By 2004 farmed fish constituted two-fifths of the world's total harvest.

The greatest devastation has taken place off the coast of Southeast Asia, for whose people fish are a major staple. Cribb reports: "In the Gulf of Thailand, Thailand's most important fisheries location, the density of fish has declined by 86% from 1961 to 1991." In the world at large, the bigger fish, such as tuna, billfish, snappers, and dories, have become scarce and the total weight of the catch is being made up with anchovies, pilchards, and sardines. And world food consumption is supposed to double by 2050. At least for fish, it can't happen. And if land-grown meat were to be substituted for fish, the increased demand over the next 38 years would alone consume an additional volume of water "larger than all the irrigation water used worldwide in farming today." That is equally impossible.

As Cribb summarizes, even if we could continue world sea and freshwater fishing at today's level, if we could not increase that level and had to substitute land-grown meat to feed our growing population, it takes 22 pounds of grain to produce 2.2 pounds of meat. It would require a billion additional tons of grain a year, twice the current North American annual grain harvest.

But aren't farmed fish comprising an ever larger portion of the fish in our supermarkets? Yes. Farmed fish amounted to 29% of global fish consumption in 2008. But those fish have to be fed. It takes five tons of wild fish, ground into fish meal, to produce one ton of farmed fish. The only advantage is that farmed fish are easier to catch. Grain can be substituted, but on large scale this competes with all the other uses that are on the razor's edge of falling short.

There is a still greater threat to our sea life. That is the little-discussed effect on the oceans of the human-caused increase in atmospheric carbon dioxide. Cribb cites a 2005 report by Britain's Royal Society that determined that the oceans have, over the last two centuries, absorbed a full half of the carbon dioxide produced by human use of fossil fuels. This increases sea water's acidity, an effect the Royal Society says is "irreversible during our lifetimes. It will take tens of thousands of years for ocean chemistry to return to a condition similar to that occurring at preindustrial times." ("Ocean Acidification Due to Increasing Atmospheric Carbon Dioxide," Royal Society policy document, June 2005, cited by Cribb, p. 94.)

The increasing pH dissolves calcium, which is deadly to corals, algae, and plankton that draw carbonates from sea water to build their shells. These tiny organisms are the foundation of the ocean's food chain. The atmospheric level of CO_2 that halts oceanic calcification outright is 500 parts per million; we are at 450 ppm now and headed for 550 in the next thirty-five or forty years.

Julian Cribb reminds us that the greatest extinction in the history of the Earth was not the extermination of the dinosaurs sixty-five million years ago, but the Great Dying at the end of the Permian, 251 million years ago. Then 96 percent of all sea life went extinct, including almost all fish. The cause is debated but is generally believed to have been volcanic eruptions in Siberia that released large amounts of carbon dioxide into the atmosphere. As the corals and other shelled organisms died, the way was cleared for giant bacterial colonies that drained the seas of their oxygen. We are seeing something similar on a smaller scale today as human pollution creates large dead zones in the seas. The recovery time from a mass oceanic extinction, of which there have been five in the Earth's history, is about ten million years. Cribb quotes Dr. Charlie Veron, Chief Scientist of the Australian Institute of Marine Science:

"It cannot rationally be doubted that we are now at the start of an event that has the potential to become the Earth's sixth mass extinction. . . . It is a case of humans changing the environment."

What Are We Doing About It?

The Green Revolution of the 1960s and 1970s reduced world hunger from one person in three to one in eight despite population growth. Its success rested on the development of high-yield, disease-resistant wheat. American plant geneticist Norman Borlaug was the central figure in this effort, which was carried out in Mexico, jointly funded by the Mexican government and the Ford and Rockefeller Foundations.

Since the mid-1980s, funding for agricultural research in the United States has been drastically cut. It accounts now for only 1.8 cents of every science dollar. Even more serious, government policy has shifted support from public to private research, an approach almost obsessively endorsed by the Republican Party and its candidates. Julian Cribb is fully supportive of private corporate investment in improving crop yields. But there are key sides to the agrarian crisis in which food producing and marketing corporations have no involvement and to which they make no contribution. As Cribb writes:

> Public research bodies tend to select technologies to work on that deliver public good outcomes, like putting more food on the world's table, helping the poor, improving health, or curing the environmental impacts of agriculture, whereas private research tends to favor technologies that offer the greatest potential for profit to the investing company.

Corporate food production research works reasonably well with large, well-funded growers. High royalties on patented seeds and varieties that are sterile, where seeds must be repurchased from the corporation each year, are more likely to be prohibitive for small and subsistence farmers. These small fry may be marginal in the United States but remain the large majority of agrarian producers in sub-Saharan Africa and much of Asia and Latin America.

> These technologies are too costly, are unsuited to small farms, demand extensive training and high educational levels, depend heavily on scarce and expensive inputs based on fossil fuels, or else need to undergo prolonged and expensive adaptation for use in smallholder agriculture — which developing countries' national agricultural agencies rarely have the resources to carry out.

Oil for Food

Inevitably any discussion of rising food prices and impending shortages comes around to agriculture's dependence on oil and the effects of peak oil. As a fossil fuel, the world's oil is a once-in-a-lifetime treasure that, once spent, will never be there again. A sobering fact for our ever-exploding world population is that it takes 10 calories of fossil oil energy to come up with one calorie of food energy. And here we should turn to Michael Klare's *The Race for What's Left*. The central fact for our oil-dependent civilization is that crude oil, that is, oil that can be pumped out of the ground as a liquid, flatlined globally in 2005 and has not risen since, while both population and demand have continued to grow.

This essential fact has been obscured by a shift to supplement our insufficient crude output with various unconventional alternatives: Canadian tar sands, deep-sea oil, fracked "tight" oil, and corn-based ethanol. The salient point about these alternatives, as Klare explicates, is that they are all far harder to obtain, much more costly, have, with the exception of deep sea, much lower outputs per well, and in some cases lower energy content per barrel. These are the planet's dregs, after the good stuff is depleted.

As the northern polar ice melts away, a fatal consequence of fossil fuel combustion, the five nations that border the polar sea — Russia, Canada, the United States, Norway, and Greenland (administered by Denmark) — are scrambling to lay rival claims to the ocean floor. Compared to a Texas gusher of a century ago, the efforts to tap oil in the Chukchi and Beaufort Seas off the northern coasts of Alaska and Canada say much about our limited options. Oil drilling has gone on for decades in shallow offshore waters on continental shelves. This is a technology not much different from drilling on land. Deep sea drilling is a wholly other technology. BP's Deepwater Horizon rig was drilling in 5,000 feet of water and was capable of reaching combined water and under sea land to depths of 30,000 feet. The April 2010 explosion that killed eleven workers took three months to cap, released 4.9 million barrels of oil, devastating sea life and damaging the Gulf tourist industry. The leak is still seeping today.

The point is that even with major cities nearby and clear water the explosion was a historic disaster. Imagine that same explosion in the ice-filled Arctic seas inaccessible to any human habitation larger than a village. Shell Oil has been several years trying to complete a salvage ship that would have some small capacity to confront a major leak, and even then was forced to close its preliminary predrilling preparations in the Chukchi Sea in late summer 2012 as ice floes threatened the stability of its exploratory operation. Klare writes:

The pursuit of untapped oil and mineral resources in remote and haz-
ardous locations is part of a larger, more significant phenomenon: a concerted drive by governments and resource firms to gain control over
whatever remains of the world's raw materials base. Government and
corporate officials recognize that existing reserves are being depleted at
a terrifying pace and will be largely exhausted in the not-too-distant future. The only way for countries to ensure an adequate future supply of
these materials, and thereby keep their economies humming, is to ac-
quire new, undeveloped reservoirs in those few locations that have not
already been completely drained.

It is mainly oil that has companies scrabbling in the most dangerous and in-
hospitable parts of the Earth. Klare continues:

What we expropriate from these areas represents all that remains of
the planet's once abundant resource bounty. In all likelihood, we are
looking at the last oil fields, the last uranium deposits, the last copper
mines, and the last reserves of many other vital resources. These materials will not all disappear at once, of course, and some as-yet-
undeveloped reserves may prove more prolific than expected. Gradually,
though, we will see the complete disappearance of many key resources
upon which modern industrial civilization has long relied.

Central to the multifarious declines is the ravenous pace of extraction, as
population burgeoned and standards of living ate up greater and greater resources per capita. Klare offers some figures on the increase in annual production of common minerals for the fifty years from 1950 to 2000. Bauxite went
up 1,513%, copper 399%, iron ore 324%, and crude oil 618%.

The consequences are most apparent in oil. The world's top 10 oil fields
have declined from their peak output an average of 30%. Europe's International Energy Agency estimates the annual decline rate at 6.7%. New discoveries plus unconventional add-ons have kept production flat and even shown a
very small increase over the last seven years, but supply is matching demand
only because much of the world is still in a steep recession that has driven
demand downward.

Other essential materials are heading into decline as well. Klare gives
one example:

In 2005, Indonesia produced 1.1 million metric tons of copper ore,
nearly as much as the United States, the world's second leading producer
after Chile. But production has fallen substantially since then, largely as
a result of diminishing yields at Freeport-McMoRan's giant Grasberg
mine. According to the U.S. Geological Survey, Indonesia's net output

in 2008 was just 650,000 metric tons, down more than 40 percent in only three years.

Chilean copper output is stagnant despite rising world demand.

The paucity of rare earths is particularly alarming. These are elements with little public recognition: cerium, europium, lanthanum, neodymium. These are essential components in flat screen TVs and computer monitors, lasers, aero-space components, arc lighting, camera lenses, energy efficient light bulbs, catalysts for oil refineries, and high capacity magnets and batteries. They are essential for making cell phones, laptop computers, iPods, and other devices with liquid crystal screens. Michael Klare in his survey tells us that every Prius battery requires two pounds of neodymium and between twenty-two and thirty-three pounds of lanthanum. Rare earths are also used in finishing fine mirrors and glassware. More than 95 percent of commercially available rare earth elements come from China. In November 2010 China cut its rare earth exports by 35 percent, after a three-month total embargo on rare earth shipments to Japan.

Prosperity in our current economies depends on constant economic growth, and our species is still in a cycle of constant population expansion. Klare writes:

> According to a projection by the U.S. Department of Energy, world-wide GDP will grow by an estimated 3.4 percent per year between 2008 and 2035, climbing from $66 trillion to $162 trillion over the course of this period (in constant 2005 dollars). Demand for basic resources is bound to expand at a comparable pace, placing extraordinary pressure on energy and mineral producers to find and develop new sources of supply.

He adds:

> According to one estimate, global REE [rare earth elements] demand will jump from 124,000 tons in 2010 to 185,000 tons in 2015, an increase of nearly 50 percent. With consumption increasing so swiftly and Chinese output unlikely to grow, many observers expect to see a high-stakes race among potential REE suppliers around the world.

The Limitations of Unconventional Oil

The oil companies have chosen, unwisely for our future, to proclaim that their turn to unconventional oils and oil substitutes will compensate for the decline in traditional crude. They have launched a propaganda campaign centered on a wildly overoptimistic "study" by Italian oil executive Leonardo

Maugeri, a visiting scholar at Harvard, which allowed him to get Harvard's name on his product. Mitt Romney cited this study in his first debate with Barack Obama. Another hustler for the oil companies has been the ultraconservative *Wall Street Journal*, owned by Rupert Murdoch's News Corporation, which also owns the far-right-wing Fox News.

Inasmuch as most Republican politicians are Bible literalists who reject both evolution and geology in favor of Young Earth Creationism, they are disbelievers in the source of oil in the first place, as the time scales required for its production and the flora and fauna that decomposed to form oil all fall outside of their 7,000 year time frame for the age of our planet, and their reading of the Bible tells them that God would not let us run out of such an essential material. This puts them in a poor position to judge objectively the facts of this issue.

Klare's summary is as good as any, and represents the views of oil geologists and other experts in this field. Let's begin with Canadian tar sands. Saudi crude is simply pumped out of the ground. The substance up there in Alberta is not crude oil but bitumen, otherwise known as asphalt, the thick gooey material used to repair roads. It is found mixed with sand, and, in Canada's chilly climate, is firmly solid. It has to be mined like coal, or heated underground to get it to flow. This requires a large amount of external energy and creates a large amount of environmental damage.

First, the native forest has to be leveled. Then the topsoil is removed, and open pit mining begins. The chunks of asphalt and sand are trucked to a plant where they are ground up and mixed with chemical solvents to create a liquid called syncrude. The wastewater tailings ponds are toxic and kill birds that alight on them.

The alternative method, used where the deposits are too deep for open-pit mining, is to heat vast quantities of water, using steam to melt the underground deposits. The used water is toxic, from chemicals and contact with the liquefied bitumen, so must be stored somewhere indefinitely so it does not contaminate waterways and ground water. Large amounts of natural gas are used to heat the water to make steam.

Another alternative fuel, Venezuela's heavy oil, presents similar high costs and problems. Heavy oil is found as shallow deposits, formed when regular crude, far in the past, seeped up near the surface, where bacteria and weather removed the lighter components, leaving a thick, viscous material with a high proportion of sulfur and other impurities. Like bitumen, heavy oil must be heated to make it flow, then it is mixed with lighter hydrocarbons such as regular crude to allow it to be run through a pipeline to refineries. Klare adds:

"The necessary amount of such dilution can be quite substantial, with as much as one barrel of diluents required for every three or four barrels of extra-heavy oil produced."

Deep sea drilling, tar sands, and heavy oil, despite their environmental risks, high costs, and low net energy because of the energy inputs required for their extraction and processing, are known stable technologies. There are two remaining potential fossil fuel energy resources: oil shale and shale oil. The unfortunate reverse terminology can obscure the fact that these are entirely different materials. Oil shale is a name given to kerogen, a substance a few million years short of being naturally cooked into oil. There are vast deposits of this stuff in eastern Utah and western Colorado. Kerogen is a solid. It takes huge quantities of water to extract it, and it is found in mostly desert areas where that volume of water is not available. It must be heated to between 530 and 930 degrees Fahrenheit to become liquid. To date no one has found a way to do anything with it commercially.

For some reason, Klare does not spend any time on shale oil, more accurately called tight oil. This is real oil embedded in limestone shale. It is being fracked in the Bakken Shale of North Dakota and Montana, and the Eagle Ford Formation in south Texas. This source accounts for a significant but still relatively modest increase in U.S. crude output that has turned around an almost forty-year decline. It is being vastly overhyped by the media with claims that this will mean oil independence or that the United States will soon be outproducing Saudi Arabia.

Of course the addition to U.S. output is needed and welcome, but it falls far short of the hype. Total production in the Bakken, the largest shale oil play, reached 546,000 barrels per day (b/d) in January 2012, up from 187,000 b/d in 2009. The United States uses 18 million barrels of oil a day, about 40% of that imported. Oil analyst Tom Whipple comments:

> It took the production from 6,617 wells to produce North Dakota's 546,000 b/d in January. Divide the daily production by the number of wells and you get an astoundingly low 82 b/d from each well. I say "astounding" because a good new offshore well can do 50,000 b/d. BP's Macondo well which exploded in the Gulf a couple of years ago was pumping out an estimated 53,000 b/d before it was capped. (http://www.fcnp.com/commentary/national/11418-the-peak-oil-crisis-parsing-the-bakken-.html, March 21, 2012)

Not only is the output per well extraordinarily low, the depletion rate of these wells is prohibitive over time. Whipple continues:

Although a few newly fracked wells may start out producing in the vicinity of 1,000 barrels a day, this rate usually falls by 65 percent the first year; 35 percent the second; and another 15 percent the third. Within a few years most wells are producing in the vicinity of 100 b/d or less which is why the state average for January is only 82 b/d despite the addition of 1300 new wells in 2011. From here on the path ahead seems clear. We seem on course to drill another 2,000 or so in 2012. As long as the price of crude stays up, this pace can continue for a while. The drilling can spread into Montana and Canada until diminishing returns set in. While recently drilled wells may be producing well, the vast bulk of the wells will be close to depletion. While some predict that the Bakken will be producing a million b/d within a few years, it will not stay there long as depletion rates are simply too high.

Another false hope appeared in a widely reprinted October 23, 2012, Associated Press dispatch by Jonathan Fahey headed "US May Soon Become World's Top Oil Producer." It claimed America would soon be out-producing Saudi Arabia. The Saudis typically pump 11.6 million barrels of crude a day. Fahey gleefully reports that "Driven by high prices and new drilling methods, U.S. production of crude and other liquid hydrocarbons is on track to rise 7 percent this year to an average of 10.9 million barrels per day. . . . the biggest single-year gain since 1951." He adds an Energy Department forecast that U.S. output will reach 11.4 million barrels a day in 2013.

U.S. output of crude oil, including the recent upturn, is only slightly above 6 million b/d, little more than half of Saudi Arabia's average, and only amounting to a third of U.S. consumption. The rest of the current 10.9 million daily barrels are those "other" hydrocarbons. Though useful, they are not oil. They include natural gas liquids, mainly propane; biofuels, mainly ethanol; and refinery processing gains. This last doesn't add any oil; it is the fact that when refining oil into less dense gasoline the total volume increases somewhat as you thin the oil.

And while politicians, particularly Republicans, make a great issue of energy independence, with the United States consuming 25% of the world's oil it is not going to be free of significant need for imports in the foreseeable future, though it can reduce the current percentage. And oil prices, the main component of gasoline prices, are set globally, so even if we were producing all of our oil needs domestically it would not reduce the price of gasoline.

Getting a Stranglehold on Other Countries' Farmland

We return at the end here to the world food crisis. Michael Klare expands on and updates our picture of land-grabs by food-stressed countries of other people's arable land. The global leap in food prices in 2008 left Saudi Arabia at the mercy of international grain merchants, many of whom had run out and could not ship anything. Several Saudi companies, backed by the government's King Abdullah Initiative for Saudi Agricultural Investment Abroad, have bought up large foreign landholdings. Saudi Star owns 750,000 acres in Ethiopia, where it is producing rice on one 25,000 acre parcel. Hadco is growing wheat, corn, and soybeans on 22,800 acres in Sudan. Klare writes:

> The proliferation of Saudi agricultural projects in desperately poor African nations such as Sudan and Ethiopia has produced some striking scenes. Nancy Macdonald of *Maclean's*, who visited the Saudi Star pilot operation in Alwero, described guards with AK-47s protecting humidity-controlled greenhouses that are watered by computerized irrigation systems — high-tech plantations set in the middle of a country where farming is still conducted with sickles and ox-drawn plows and where millions suffer from chronic malnutrition.

Sudan has sold or leased 245,000 acres to Qatar and 700,000 to the United Arab Emirates, which also controls 100,000 acres in Egypt. The UAE's Minerals Energy Commodities Holding Company has leased 245,000 acres in Indonesia. Bigger players — China, India, and South Korea — are also buying up or leasing acreage. Klare reports that the South Korean government is providing backing to some sixty South Korean companies running farms in sixteen foreign countries. In Madagascar, the Daewoo Logistics Corporation, part of the giant Daewoo conglomerate, in 2008 secured a lease on 3.2 million acres of farmland, where it planned to grow 50 percent of South Korea's corn. This sparked a popular rebellion that forced President Marc Ravalomanana out of office in March 2009. His successor canceled the contract.

South Korea then moved on to Sudan, where its companies gained control of 1.7 million acres. Hyundai Heavy Industries Company is acquiring thousands of acres in Siberia.

> Another branch of the same conglomerate [Klare writes] is planning to buy large parcels of farmland in Brazil. With strong government support, South Korean firms aim to control a combined one million acres of foreign farmland by 2018, enabling them to supply 10 percent of the country's annual imports of corn, wheat, and soybeans.

India and China between them have 2.6 billion people and rising. India is expected to add 300 million by 2050. And the Green Revolution has reached its limits. Making any noticeable contribution to the food resources of such giants could drain many small countries dry. But India, through its state-owned

Minerals and Metals Trading Corporation of India, is buying up land across Africa: in Tanzania, Ethiopia, Kenya, Malawi, and Mozambique. One private Indian firm, Karuturi Global, based in Bangalore, has bought 770,000 acres in Ethiopia.

China has adopted a "go outward" strategy that Klare says is being carried out "on an enormous scale and with blistering speed." The state-owned Chongqing Grain Group Company is investing $2.5 billion in soybean production on 500,000 acres in Brazil. They expect to process two million tons a year. Another company is investing $7 billion in another area in Brazil. China is also pursuing large tracts of land in Africa, in Mozambique, Benin, Cameroon, Mali, Uganda, and the Democratic Republic of the Congo. They have leased 250,000 acres in Zimbabwe to grow corn. The Beidahuang Land Cultivation Group, the major agricultural power in Heilongjiang province, is making large investments in leasing or purchasing farmland in Venezuela, Zimbabwe, Australia, Brazil, Argentina, Russia, and the Philippines.

Some of the largest land transfers have taken place in the Democratic Republic of the Congo, which has ceded 7 million acres to a Chinese company; Kenya, where Canadian, British, and Qatari companies have heavy investments; Liberia, where a Malaysian company has a sixty-three-year lease on 545,000 acres; and Senegal, where the Saudis are acquiring a million acres.

Former Soviet collective farms, abandoned since the fall of communism, are also on the block to foreigners.

Private companies, including American hedge funds, are making similar investments. One securities consultant has coined the term "peak soil" to describe the world scramble for the last remaining farmland. Klare points to Susan Payne, CEO of the British giant Emergent Asset Management, which is making extensive investment in foreign croplands and holds 370,000 acres of good farmland in southern Africa:

> Payne's views on global food availability combine the nineteenth-century precepts of Thomas Malthus — who predicted that overpopulation would inevitably lead to mass starvation — with twenty-first-century statistics showing declining water levels in China and India, increasing desertification from global warming, and, of course, global population levels rising by some 80 million people per year. All of these factors, Payne explains, could lead to significant food shortages by 2020, giving anyone who controls large areas of farmland the chance to accrue colossal profits.

With 100,000 acres here and 500,000 there, the global totals of foreign cropland purchased have become enormous. A World Bank study reports that these trades were running at 10 million acres a year until 2008, then leaped to

110 million acres in 2009, an area, as Klare notes, the size of Sweden. (*Rising Global Interest in Farmland*, Klaus Deninger and Derek Byerlee. Washington, DC: The World Bank, 2011, 264 pp.)

Klare concludes:

"For all the importance and forthcoming scarcity of oil, gas, and vital minerals, perhaps the fiercest resource struggle in the coming decades will involve food and the land it is grown on."

A bitter struggle is implicit between the governments of the land hungry nations that are laying claim to other people's land, and the indigenous populations, often forced off their traditional lands by their own corrupt governments to complete these transactions. Notable here for those leftists and Marxists still living in the 1960s, the predators here are to only a small extent from the advanced "imperialist" nations. Most are slightly better off Third World countries. And these are only the trigger points of a far wider threat of famine. As population growth, water scarcity, and global warming press harder on our limited and declining resources, terrible contests, literally for survival, will be waged. Even rich America, though it may not see the worst of this, is not likely to be spared.

November 1, 2012

The Controversy over America's Oil Future

For the last decade there has been growing concern among petroleum geologists, energy specialists, the Defense Department, investors, and environmentalists over the radically rising price of oil. A 44 gallon barrel of oil that sold for $12 in 1998 is going today for $95, and that understates things, as that is the American, or West Texas Intermediate, standard. This is what many in the Midwest pay, but on both coasts and much of the South, oil is going at the European Brent price, which is now at $111 per barrel.

Unlike climate science, where the professionals have reached overwhelming consensus that global warming is caused by human use of fossil fuels, the constituencies concerned with America's energy prospects remain divided. Those who think this finite, precisely "fossil," material is running short of world demand are proponents of the peak oil thesis. They advocate strict conservation of fossil fuels and crash investment in energy efficient technologies and renewable energy sources. Their opponents call them doomsters, while the peak oilers refer to the deniers as cornicopians. The cornicopians maintain that there are large enough untapped resources still in the ground to delay indefinitely any need to change our high energy standard of living or our economy, which depends on perpetual growth. They got a huge boost last fall when the prestigious Paris-based International Energy Agency, the twenty-eight-nation consortium that reports to the Organization of Economic Cooperation and Development, on November 12 released its *World Energy Outlook for 2012*, predicting:

> By around 2020, the United States is projected to become the largest global oil producer (overtaking Saudi Arabia until the mid-2020s) and starts to see the impact of new fuel-efficiency measures in transport. The result is a continued fall in US oil imports, to the extent that North America becomes a new oil exporter around 2030.

What had changed from the long decline in American oil production since the early 1970s was the fracking boom in tight oil in North Dakota and Montana.

The *Wall Street Journal* ran an editorial headed "Saudi America," airing Republican talking points venerating fossil fuels: "This is a real energy revolution, even if it's far from the renewable energy dreamland of so many government subsidies and mandates."

These kinds of heady promises produced lots of headlines to the effect that peak oil is a dead idea for at least the next generation and possibly for a century to come. Before we abandon renewable energy and start to binge spend on the promised new oil wealth we should remember that deals that look too good to be true usually are.

What the IEA Report Did and Didn't Say

Even the most authoritative of the mainstream press made gross mistakes in what they claimed the IEA's *World Energy Outlook for 2012* said, always on the side of presenting a more positive picture of U.S. energy prospects. Richard Gilbert in the November 21, 2012, Toronto *Globe and Mail* lists several of these.

The *Wall Street Journal* said that U.S. current domestic production is about 18 million barrels per day (mbd) now, will rise by 2022 to 23 mbd, and that U.S. imports are currently 20 percent of its consumption. In fact U.S. crude oil output hit 6.5 mbd in 2012 and imports are running at 56% of consumption.

(Another set of figures come from a December 28, 2012, Dow Jones newswire. This says that U.S. crude imports in October 2012 were 8.091 mbd with domestic production at 6.820 mbd, this last an increase of 935,000 mbd from the previous year.)

The *Washington Post* said the U.S. will be almost self-sufficient and will become a new exporter by 2035. The *New York Times* had the U.S. becoming a new exporter by 2030.

The IEA actually said that North America as a whole would become a net exporter by 2030, while the United States would still be importing 30% of its oil indefinitely. And to get that close, the IEA's chief economist, Fatih Birol, at a London press conference cited by Gilbert, said that 45% of America's expected reduced imports would be the result of improved conservation, while the IEA's projected American increase in oil output by 2035 is only 14%. Gilbert calculated that to meet the energy efficiency standard the IEA is expecting "would require per-capita oil use to fall by more than 40 per cent, which would represent astonishing changes in how people and goods move in the U.S."

Kjell Aleklett, professor of physics at Sweden's Uppsala University and president of the Association for the Study of Peak Oil and Gas (ASPO), offers an excellent analysis of *World Energy Outlook 2012*, released by ASPO International November 29, 2012. He stressed that the IEA report does not say that the U.S., as opposed to Canada and Mexico, will become self-sufficient in oil. It did say that the United States would, briefly, overtake Saudi Arabia, but this claim needs some unpacking.

On one side, it rests on a drastic and ominous decline from the IEA's prior estimates of Saudi Arabia's contribution to world oil supply. In their 2004 *World Energy Outlook* the IEA had predicted the Saudi's in 2030 would be pumping 22.5 million barrels a day. Now they have scaled that back to only 12.3, and in the period between now and then, only in the high 10s. Given that total world crude output today is around 68 mbd that is an enormous setback. The year where the U.S. is supposed to out-produce the Saudis is 2020, where the IEA expects Riyadh to come up with 10.6 mbd, with the U.S. slightly ahead at 11 mbd. There is a little trick in this number, as the Saudi's are turning out real crude oil, while the projected American figure is for all liquid hydrocarbons.

Counting all hydrocarbons as "oil" misrepresents what they can be used for, but also significantly overstates the total energy content. U.S. totals include between 25 and 28% natural gas liquids (NGLs). NGLs refine into propane, butane, and similar fuels, good for heating but not usable to run automobiles except for a small number of specialty fleet vehicles. Natural gas liquids, apart from their limited uses, have only 70% of the energy content of crude oil. The same is true for ethanol.

Ted Patzek, chair of the Department of Petroleum and Geosystems Engineering at the University of Texas at Austin, breaks down U.S. hydrocarbon output as follows, using the figures for 2011 provided by the U.S. Energy Information Administration. The EIA reported that total crude oil produced by the United States for 2011 amounted to 5.7 mbd, including fracked oil from the Bakken and Eagle Ford shales. The EIA claimed a total of 10.3 mbd of all "hydrocarbons." Patzek lists the components of this 4.6 mbd of other "oil." Some 1.1 million barrels a day is refinery gains. This is a form of double counting. When crude oil is refined into gasoline, which is a much thinner liquid, it expands, like adding water to a thick soup. It doesn't increase the total amount of oil, but is counted as though it did. Next comes corn ethanol, technically not a hydrocarbon at all, which adds .9 mbd. Patzek writes:

Basically, ethanol is obtained from burning methane, coal, diesel fuel, gasoline, corn kernels, soil and environment. We destroy perhaps as many as 7 units of free energy in the environment and human economy to produce 1 unit of free energy as corn ethanol, and make a few clueless environmentalists happier and a few super rich corporations richer.

He adds that "your mileage would drop by 33% if you were to use pure ethanol as a fuel for your car." And by diverting human food to car fuel the price of corn is driven up, increasing hunger and the risk of starvation in poor countries. (http://www.theoildrum.com/node/9619)

The remaining 2.6 mbd of "other oil," 25.2% of total U.S. hydrocarbons, is natural gas plant liquids, which cannot be used for transportation fuel for ordinary cars and trucks.

Another reason the comparison is misleading is that the Saudis claim to have a reserve of about 2 mbd that can be used as an emergency source to stabilize world oil prices. The American output is not even all oil and has no such reserve. In any case the IEA sees the U.S. putative supremacy as very short lived, with the Saudi's in 2035 pumping 12.3 mbd while the United States has declined back to 9 mbd. And of that amount, Aleklett adds, "Around 50% of the USA's crude oil production in 2035 is to come from fields yet-to-be found."

Kjell Aleklett summarizes the European International Energy Agency predictions for 2035 and then critiques them. Current world liquid hydrocarbon production is 84 mbd, of which 68 mbd is crude oil, the rest NGLs, tar sands, and heavy oil from Venezuela. The IEA predicts that global crude oil will decline to 65 mbd in 2035, while overall liquid hydrocarbons will rise to 97 mbd, the 32 mbd difference made up entirely of nonconventional liquids. (Non-conventional refers to the methods of extraction and processing, not to the ultimate product. Fracking tight oil from shale produces real crude oil; heavy oil from Venezuela is not real crude and must be heavily processed to be used as such; natural gas liquids, a byproduct of fracking for both gas or oil, never becomes crude oil but ends as more limited-use hydrocarbons.)

Aleklett challenges this on several points. He is particularly dubious of their projection that crude oil will deplete by only 3 mbd. The IEA has the non-OPEC world (Europe, Asia, the Americas except for Venezuela) essentially flat through 2035, at around 50 mbd of all hydrocarbon liquids. But the mix within that amount is marked by a massive decline in crude oil, to be replaced by non-conventional liquids. The total loss is 40%, leaving the non-OPEC bloc's contribution to the world total of crude oil at only 19 mbd, a decline of 13 mbd from today's levels, and even to get the 19 will depend on large increases from current levels in Brazil and Kazakhstan. The sharp declines will come mainly from Russia, down about 2.25 mbd; China, down 2.1; the U.S. and UK down about 900,000 bd each; and slightly smaller losses from Canada, Norway, and Mexico.

So how, then, to hold the global decline to only 3 mbd and end with 65 mbd in 2035? The IEA looks to OPEC to make up for the losses from the non-OPEC states. To do so OPEC would have to hold steady on its current production and add 10 of the lost 13 mbd from the rest of the planet. This means increasing its ordinary crude from today's 36 mbd to 46 mbd in 2035. A bit more than half of the promised increase is supposed to come from Iraq, which they foresee adding 5.3 mbd in output between 2011 and 2035.

Aleklett thinks that unlikely. Iraq has not achieved the stability to count on such a large boost in output. The other half of the prediction has to come from existing fields in other OPEC countries. He points out that the majority of new oil fields discovered in recent decades have been in non-OPEC countries, where the IEA is expecting a 40% decline, while OPEC, working with old giant fields that have been in production much longer, not only are not expected to suffer from noticeable depletion but are tasked with coming up with a 28% increase. He writes:

"That we will see declining production outside OPEC and increasing production inside OPEC during the next 25 years is not logical. Once again we see the IEA telling a fairy stale about OPEC that lacks any foundation in reality."

At least one U.S. government agency, the National Intelligence Council, in its *Global Trends 2030,* released in December 2012, prophesied that oil from fracking alone would be so plentiful that by 2020 there would be "a production breakeven price as low as $44-68 per barrel depending upon the fields." This startling claim is based on some rather extraordinary expectations for tight oil output. I will return to that.

One major Wall Street firm, Bernstein Research, challenged the idea that tight oil is going to result in any lower oil prices, much less the half-price sale the National Intelligence Council is hoping for. In a 180-page September 11, 2012, report, "Global Oil Prices: At 'Base Camp' Before the Final Ascent," their analysts projected that Brent oil would hold steady at around $113 a barrel through 2015, then escalate to $158 in 2020, with U.S. West Texas Intermediate only $5 lower. A Reuters summary said "new supplies are too small to meet emerging market demand growth. By 2015, shale oil is forecast to constitute just 3.2 pct of global supply, up from 1.5 pct now." And in a direct quote from the Bernstein report:

Emerging market demand is still robust, rising with higher wealth and mobility; in developed markets the role of fuel economy in demand destruction is overstated; conventional non-OPEC supply is increasingly mature; OPEC capacity growth will likely lag its required rate.

Bernstein estimates current break-even costs for new oil wells for the 50 largest publicly traded oil companies at $92 a barrel. Canadian tar sands break-even is $100, and because of inadequate pipelines to the United States it cannot get all of its product to market and is selling at a loss. Even OPEC oil production cost is $94 a barrel and rising fast. Those are costs before refining, transportation, marketing, and distribution.

How Much Oil Can They Squeeze from the North Dakota Shale?

The IEA is bullish not only about holding world crude deliveries to a minimal decline, but even more so in their expectations for non-conventional hydrocarbons, which would have to increase by 16 mbd to meet their postulated 97 mbd global liquid totals.

The main candidate to replace declining conventional crude is tight oil. Conventional oil, by definition is found in liquid form in porous rocks from which it can be simply pumped. It has been on a plateau since 2005, and the IEA, as we have seen, expects it to decline from there.

Tight oil, as well as shale gas, is found in shale rocks from which it is unable to flow. Richard Vodra in the January 2, 2013, investor newsletter *Advisor Perspectives* describes the process:

> Shale is a very solid rock that forms numerous thin layers. When gas is present, it is found in pores barely larger than a single gas molecule. Oil engineers have combined several technologies developed over decades to drill horizontally along a shale layer, rather than vertically through it, and to apply a high-pressure mix of water, chemicals and sand through holes in the drill pipe to shatter, or fracture, the shale, allowing the gas or oil to move to the pipe and up to the surface. Fracked wells in oil country commonly produce a mixture of oil, gas, and natural gas liquids.

Given the extraordinary importance of this source in hopes for America's oil future, no one should overlook the important reservations the two principal agencies that study these matters have raised about the available data. Energy securities analyst G. Allen Brooks in a November 21, 2012, posting to Rigzone.com writes:

Fatih Birol, the IEA's chief economist, said his agency's forecasts to 2017 were based on data about existing reserves and production. He warned that the geology and reservoir performance of the oil shales were "poorly known"' and he said it was unclear whether new reserves would be found to sustain production levels, let alone grow them. This is a critical consideration that underlies all the bullish forecasts for a new petroleum age for North America.

Brooks notes the very steep decline rates of fracked gas wells compared to conventional oil and comments that

> The IEA has conducted extensive research into oilfield decline rates in the past, but we sense little of that research was brought to bear in this study. . . . there are enough qualifiers to the assumptions underlying this long-term forecast to cast doubt on how firmly to embrace the report's conclusions.

Similarly, representatives of the American branch of the Association for the Study of Peak Oil and Gas held a December 17, 2012, meeting with senior officials of the federal government's Energy Information Administration. In their December 24, 2012, *ASPO USA Peak Oil Review* they report:

> Of relevance to our concerns, we learned that the EIA information on drilling costs and other costs of oil and gas production may not be very robust. Their projection models, therefore, may grossly underestimate the significance of increasing production costs as a constraint on oil or gas supply. EIA's projection models seem to be more demand-driven than supply-driven in general. . . . Perhaps most importantly, we learned that EIA's interaction with and input from experienced experts in technical oil and gas issues may not be as regular and rigorous as it should be.

The National Intelligence Council's *Global Trends 2030* is the most optimistic projection I have seen, claiming that for oil from fracking alone, apart from ordinary crude or deep sea drilling, "Preliminary estimates for 2020 range from 5-15 million barrels per day." An accompanying graph is even more exuberant, proposing a range for tight oil output in 2020 between 12 and 19 million barrels a day, the high end more than twice Saudi Arabia's output for November 2012 of 9.5 mbd.

This kind of hype is prevalent in the press. In fact the upturn in U.S. oil output, due almost entirely to fracking tight oil, restores only a fraction of the decline that set in around 1972. Oil totals then were almost 10 mbd while today, after adding about 1.5 mbd from fracked wells, it is still at only 6.5 mbd.

US Oil Output 1920 to 2012

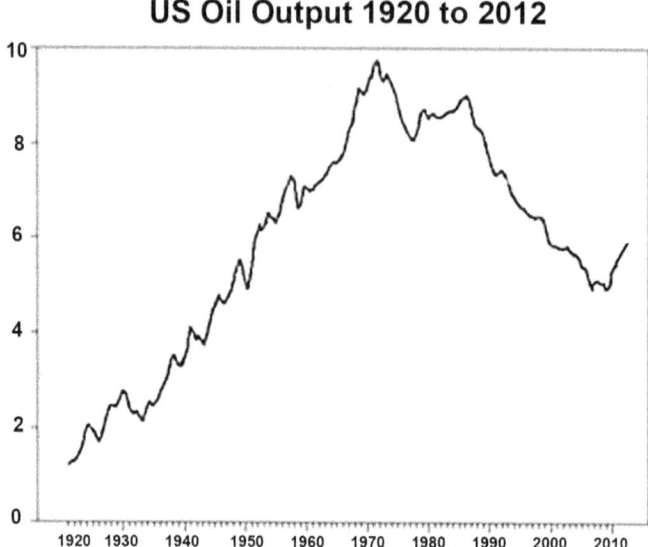

Richard Vodra, in the article cited earlier, suggests some reasons this rosy picture may be far from the mark:

> Two aspects of shale production make it radically different from conventional production. First, it takes a lot more energy (including many miles of steel tubing per well, for example) to extract energy out of these wells. Traditional wells have a ratio of energy returned on energy invested (EROI) of 10- or 20-to-one, or an energy cost factor of 5 to 10%. The EROI with fracking is in the range of 5- or 10-to-one, or a cost factor of 10 to 20%. Professor Charles Hall of the State University of New York, a recognized expert in the field, claims that modern civilization will have trouble functioning with an average EROI under 10-15, so shale oil and gas alone could not support our civilization at its current standard-of-living. EROI roughly correlates with financial cost, and the typical fracking oil well in Texas now costs over $10 million to drill, compared to less than $1 million for a conventional well.
>
> The other thing about extraction from shale is that it ends quickly. A conventional well's production declines at about 5-8% per year, and it can remain productive for decades. By contrast, the first-year decline in shale wells is over 60%, and about 90% of a well's production occurs in the first five years. That creates a "drilling treadmill," as new wells are needed simply to replace production from wells drilled a few years before.

Even the treadmill only works if there is a very large physical area in which to keep drilling the wells. The total area of the Bakken Shale in North Dakota, Montana and Saskatchewan; the Barnett and Eagle Ford plays in Texas; and the Marcellus in West Virginia, New York, and Ohio are geographically vast, but drillers are discovering that only relatively small "sweet spots" within them produce significant output. Chemist Roger Blanchard in a November 11, 2012, post on the Resilience website cites data showing that in June 2012 80.8% of total Bakken output was coming from just four of North Dakota's 53 counties, while Bakken output in adjacent Montana has been in decline since 2006. In Saskatchewan it was flat for a decade from 2000 to 2010, followed by a 2.2% rise in 2011.

Stuart Staniford, physicist and chief scientist at the web security company FireEye, writes on the Early Warning blog spot:

> I am less persuaded myself that using a thousand oil rigs to generate an extra one million barrels per day of oil is necessarily a sign of a large and long-term sustainable increase in US oil production (as opposed to, say, frenzied scraping of the bottom of the barrel). (November 12, 2012)

Tom Whipple, who writes regularly on oil issues, in his December 12, 2012, column in the *Falls Church News-Press* (Falls Church, Virginia) reports on the just-concluded annual conference of the Association for the Study of Peak Oil and Gas in Austin, Texas:

> There are now about 5,000 wells in North Dakota, one of the two major tight oil production "plays" that are pumping out an average of 143 b/d for each well or some 700,000 per day. Our speaker's well-by-well study of the first 2500 wells in the Bakken discussed at the conference, however, concluded that this production would drop by 38 percent within a year unless more wells were drilled. At these depletion rates, it will take 1,600 new wells per year just to stay even. In the most recent 12 months of drilling available some 1750 new wells came into production in the Bakken — leaving very few to increase production.
>
> If we assume that the decline characteristics are similar in other tight oil formations, then if production were ever to reach 3 million b/d, well over 1 million b/d of production would have to be replaced through new well drilling each year to maintain production. For this reason, the skeptical presenter at the Texas conference estimates that tight oil production in the U.S. will only reach 1-2 million b/d by 2020 — depending on price — as compared to the 4 million b/d forecast by the optimistic presenters.

No one but the people at the National Intelligence Council are mooting numbers past 4 or 5 mbd.

James D. Hamilton, writing in the November 15, 2012, issue of the UC San Diego Department of Economics journal *Economics in Action*, shows that for both the United States and the broader world the more or less steady rise in crude output from the mid-nineteenth century to 2005 depended overwhelmingly on the continual opening of new areas of exploration, far more than on improvements in extraction technology. The 113-year rise in total U.S. oil output from 1859 to 1972 appears on a countrywide graph as though wells were good for more than a century of increasing volume, presumably boosted by increasingly sophisticated technical innovation. This is not true. The initial wells were in Pennsylvania in the Oil Creek District. These peaked in 1874. Ohio peaked in 1896, West Virginia in 1900.

Total national output kept rising as exploration kept moving west. But even there, of the four most generously endowed states, Oklahoma peaked in 1927, Louisiana in 1971, Texas in 1972, and California in 1985. Hamilton points out that despite the new tight oil gains in North Dakota and Texas,

> oil production in 2011 was still less than 60 percent of what it was in 1970. And a key unknown is how quickly production is likely to decline after the initial surge. The North Dakota Department of Mineral Resources estimates that production from a given fracking well will decline 80 percent within two years of initial production.

Hamilton sees a similar story at the world level, where drastic declines at the end of the 1990s were temporarily offset by new finds in the North Sea and Mexico, while today "the North Sea is now only producing at about half of its 1999 level, and Mexico is down 25 percent from its peak in 2004." The current plateau, which has held steady since 2005, is now resting on finds in Central Asia, Africa, and Brazil, and after that, promises from Iraq. The rapidity with which similar large fields have depleted and the large part of the globe already in decline, combined with the far more rapid depletion rates for fracked oil, lead Hamilton to see only a short future for current output levels:

"Optimists may expect the next century and a half to look like the last. But we should also consider the possibility that it will be only the next decade that looks like the last."

So now let us look more closely at the International Energy Agency's projections for America's oil future through 2032. As their graph on the next page shows, conventional crude, at around 5.7 mbd in 2012, will decline to a bit more than 4 mbd by 2032. Some 2.2 mbd will be natural gas liquids that do not convert to gasoline, while an optimistically large portion depends on extending the current rate of increase in tight oil uninterrupted to 2020 before it begins to decline, peaking at a little under 4 mbd.

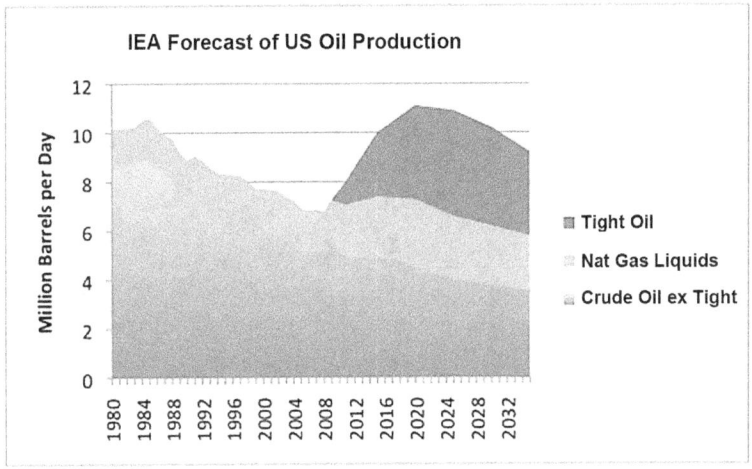

If we set aside the natural gas liquids as special purpose products, even the hoped for peak in 2020 would be just 9 mbd useful for transportation. If the IEA's admittedly uncertain numbers for tight oil prove to be high, the usable 2020 production for transport would fall to less than half of current daily consumption, any improvement over that being dependent mainly on government efforts to prod auto makers to scale up fuel efficiency.

The IEA's global figures also need to be scaled back. Apart from skepticism about volumes of tight oil, rates of decline, and other grounds to lower their estimates, the most indisputable is the *World Energy Outlook 2012*'s treatment of hydrocarbons with lower energy content as the same as actual oil. Antonio Turiel, staff researcher at the Institute for Marine Sciences of Barcelona, in research reported in the January 3, 2013, Reliance website, recalculates the IEA's own figures for 2035, correcting for the fact that liquefied natural gas, bitumen (Canada's oil sands) and ethanol "have a gross energy content per unit volume that is approximately 70% of conventional crude oil, and, for this reason must be counted in terms of 'equivalent barrels.'" Turiel presents two graphs, the first, the IEA's own projection for 2035, the second, the same data adjusted for actual comparable energy content:

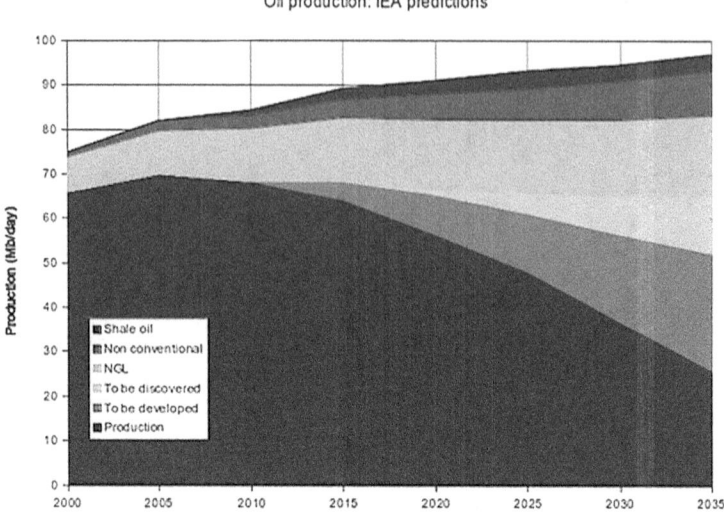

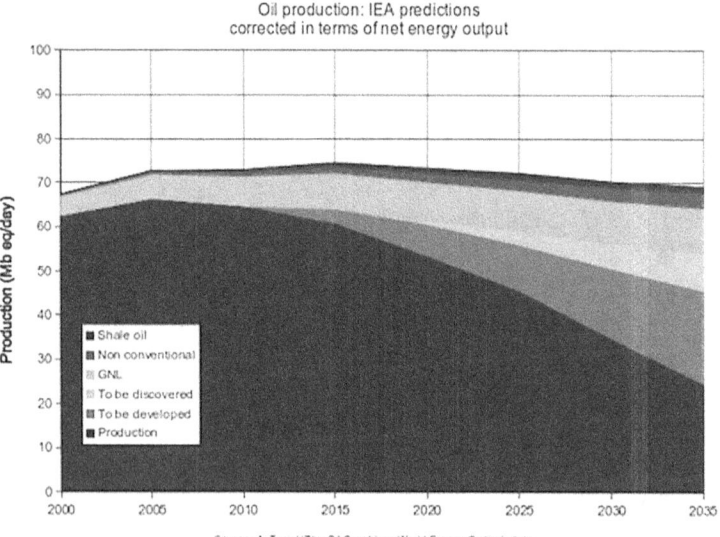

To have effective energy of only just under 70 mbd when you had counted on 97 is a shortfall of almost 28 percent.

Prospects for Shale Gas

The issues around shale gas are different from those for oil. This material is not a substitute for crude oil, and cannot be made into gasoline to run cars. It is a principal energy source for generating electricity and for heating. But supply is currently outpacing demand, due to what is called "dry gas" fracking, which has created a glut that has tumbled prices. Unlike oil, which is easily transportable and therefore priced at the world level, natural gas is localized. It can only be exported by pipeline or by the expensive process of liquefaction at ultralow temperature. U.S. (natural) gas prices started to inflate around 2000 from under $3 a thousand cubic feet (tcf) and reaching $7-10 in 2008. Then, as fracking expanded, in 2012 prices fell to under $3 for most of the year. Today shale gas provides 25 percent of U.S. natural gas consumption and is being promoted as a reliably available and cheap energy resource for utilities and manufacturing.

Expecting, mistakenly, that they can count on these low rates indefinitely, utility companies and factories are in process of massively converting from coal, and some from oil, for generating electricity and for heating. The press frequently opines that there is a century of plentiful and low-cost natural gas, and it is even being considered as an alternative to gasoline to fuel automobiles, which would require a massive retrofit of the country's gas stations and automobile design. (In fact, only liquefied natural gas, with its requirement of constant refrigeration, can match ordinary gasoline for driving range. Simple compressed natural gas has very limited range, more like that of electric vehicles.)

The *New York Times* in mid-2011 began to raise red flags about the economics of shale gas production, saying they had uncovered "hundreds of industry e-mails and internal documents and an analysis of data from thousands of wells" that cast serious doubts on the industry's viability:

> In the e-mails, energy executives, industry lawyers, state geologists and market analysts voice skepticism about lofty forecasts and question whether companies are intentionally, and even illegally, overstating the productivity of their wells and the size of their reserves. Many of these e-mails also suggest a view that is in stark contrast to more bullish public comments made by the industry, in much the same way that insiders have raised doubts about previous financial bubbles.
>
> "Money is pouring in" from investors even though shale gas is "inherently unprofitable," an analyst from PNC Wealth Management, an investment company, wrote to a contractor in a February e-mail. "Reminds you of dot-coms."

"The word in the world of independents is that the shale plays are just giant Ponzi schemes and the economics just do not work," an analyst from IHS Drilling Data, an energy research company, wrote in an e-mail on Aug. 28, 2009. (June 25, 2011, NYT)

The *Times* cites data for more than 10,000 wells that reveal a pattern of a few high-producing wells

often surrounded by vast zones of less-productive wells that in some cases cost more to drill and operate than the gas they produce is worth. Also, the amount of gas produced by many of the successful wells is falling much faster than initially predicted by energy companies, making it more difficult for them to turn a profit over the long run.

Rolling Stone ran a major exposé of the shale gas industry in its March 1, 2012, issue, titled "The Big Fracking Bubble." It profiles Aubrey McClendon's Chesapeake Energy Corp., which right-wing owner McClendon boasts is "the biggest frackers in the world." McClendon funded the Swift Boat attacks on John Kerry, was a big donor to Rick Perry's presidential campaign, and pumped $500,000 into efforts to make gay marriage illegal. Inconsistently, he voted for Barack Obama in 2008, but not in 2012.

A clue about the real value of fracked gas, as *Rolling Stone* puts it, is that for Chesapeake Energy,

the primary profit in fracking comes not from selling the gas itself, but from buying and flipping the land that contains the gas. The company is now the largest leaseholder in the United States, owning the drilling rights to some 15 million acres — an area more than twice the size of Maryland. McClendon has financed this land grab with junk bonds and complex partnerships and future production deals, creating a highly leveraged, deeply indebted company that has more in common with Enron than ExxonMobil.

As an example, in 2010 Chesapeake made $2.2 billion selling land it bought in Texas for $2,000 an acre to a Chinese company for $11,000 an acre. They also made $1 billion selling the future production rights for the next fifteen years to 4,000 wells to Deutsche Bank and a Swiss investment firm. Of course, at 38 or more percent annual depletion, the wells should all be worthless long before the leases expire. Caveat emptor.

And there is a caveat for Chesapeake as well. Government leases require that drilling be undertaken within three to five years or the lease is forfeit. Fracking wells cost $10 million each, and the more of the early output there is, the worse the current gas glut and the lower the prices, which, at less than $3 a thousand cubic feet, are already far below costs, so that no one is making money just now on all the fracked gas being produced. Chesapeake was $3.5 billion in the red at the beginning of 2012. *Rolling Stone* concludes:

> If the bubble bursts, Chesapeake's stockholders won't be the only ones who pay the price — the shock waves will be felt throughout the economy, from homeowners who rely on natural gas for heat to manufacturers who were betting on it to power their new factories.

This is apart from the millions of gallons of water diverted to fracked mines, then becoming a huge disposal problem when mixed with methane and toxic chemicals.

Wolf Richter, in the June 5, 2012, *Business Insider*, writes:

> The economics of fracking are horrid. All wells have decline rates where production drops over time. But instead of decades for traditional wells, decline rates in horizontal fracking are measured in weeks and months: production falls off a cliff from day one and continues for a year or so until it levels out at about 10% of initial production. To be in the black over its life under these circumstances, a well in the Barnett Shale would have to sell its production for about $8 per million Btu, pricing models have shown.
>
> At today's price of $2.43 per million Btu at the Henry Hub—though up 28% from the April low — drilling is destroying capital at an astonishing rate, and drillers are left with a mountain of debt just when decline rates are starting to wreak their havoc. To keep the decline rates from mucking up income statements, companies had to drill more and more, with new wells making up for the declining production of old wells. Alas, the scheme hit a wall, namely reality.

Of course, $8 per million btu is not an economically impossible figure, but it would leave scores of utilities and hundreds of factories with energy costs a magnitude greater than they expected when they did their conversions to natural gas. Meanwhile, drillers have been fleeing the supposedly cutting edge industry, pulling out their rigs by the hundreds and relocating them where fracked wells have some chance of hitting oil or at least natural gas liquids.

In an interview on oilprice.com published November 12, 2012, oil geologist Art Berman adds:

> Shale gas has lost hundreds of billions of dollars and investors will not keep on pumping money into something that doesn't generate a return.

The second thing that nobody thinks very much about is the decline rates shale reservoirs experience. Well, I've looked at this. The decline rates are incredibly high. In the Eagleford shale, which is supposed to be the mother of all shale oil plays, the annual decline rate is higher than 42%.

They're going to have to drill hundreds, almost 1000 wells in the Eagleford shale, every year, to keep production flat. Just for one play, we're talking about $10 or $12 billion a year just to replace supply. I add all these things up and it starts to approach the amount of money needed to bail out the banking industry. Where is that money going to come from?"

A commonly quoted claim, based on reports by the authoritative Potential Gas Committee, is that the United States has natural gas resources from all sources, including shale gas, that will last 100 years. Even President Obama has repeated this figure. The November-December 2012 issue of *Public Power* reports Art Berman's deconstruction of that number:

> "A resource is everything that is in the ground without consideration of economic value," he said. "People look at shale gas resources and say they are immense. However, the next question is, of that total volume of resource, how much can you make money on? And the answer is a much smaller percentage."

Public Power summarizes:

> Berman's math: If you divide the "technically recoverable resource" of about 1,900 Tcf (trillion cubic feet) of gas, as identified by the Potential Gas Committee's (PGC's) report by annual U.S. consumption, you come up with 90 years. However, the PGC's report also says the "probable recoverable resource" is only about 550 Tcf — approximately one fourth of the "technically recoverable resource."
>
> Furthermore, if you divide the 550 Tcf "probable recoverable resource" by three, which represents the component of the resource that is actually provided by shale gas, you get about 180 Tcf. (The remaining 370 Tcf includes conventional reservoirs plus non-shale/non-coalbed-methane unconventional reservoirs.)
>
> The result: There is about eight years' worth of shale gas supply available in the United States, he said.

Conservation and Renewables

This section and the next, on climate change, are the subjects of other articles. All I am doing here is making a few basic points. The problem, as all but the most pessimistic peak oil theorists agree, is not that we will run out of oil soon, but that conventional crude oil is declining steadily while the replacements all require a much greater investment of money and energy to extract and the volumes that appear likely don't match rising world demand. This is most pressing on liquid fuels for transportation, somewhat less so for electricity generation. What, then, would be a prudent course? We can reasonably expect that oil for transportation will become gradually more and more expensive, placing a growing burden on expenditures for other essential needs, such as maintaining infrastructure, health care, and Social Security.

Frankly, world population growth, coupled with rapidly rising standards of living in the developing world, pose an essentially insurmountable problem on a planet on which a wide panoply of resources from oil to potable water to arable land and fish in the sea are all in sharp decline. Human societies, especially the most advanced, which make the most profligate use of our depleting resources, will have to sharply reduce a variety of resource demands, most especially oil and using living animals for meat. That reduction would be less wrenching if it were begun early and managed sensibly at the government level. Given the gridlock in American politics, the institutionalized denial promoted by the Republican Party and the fossil fuel companies, and disbelief by the majority of the citizenry, it is pretty certain that these issues will be faced only when they irrupt at crisis proportions, in runaway prices or massive shortages. There are things that can mitigate the downward slide, and while it will be hard to implement them when the need is already on us, here are some.

First, there should be greatly increased investment in electric transport; in light rail, and electric trolleys and buses, for urban and interurban transport, and development of long-distance electric freight rail. Republican politicians adamantly oppose this fairly obvious step, which requires only existing technology already in wide use.

More than 80% of transportation depends on oil in the form of gasoline and diesel. But according to the EIA, non-fossil-fuel sources produced 31.4 percent of U.S. electricity during the twelve months ending in October 2012. This is good news, but doesn't solve all our problems. The lion's share of that was from nuclear, at 19.2%. There are 104 nuclear power plants in the United States, construction on all of which began in 1974 or earlier. No new plant has been built in thirty-nine years. For opponents of nuclear power that is a good thing, but as other sources of electricity become scarce, people may well reconsider their nuclear options. Still, it takes a very long time to get approvals and then to complete construction of a nuclear plant..

And for those who blithely toss off the idea that we don't have to worry about declining oil because there is always solar and wind power, they should consider that these sources provide only 5.3% of U.S. electricity. As for personal transport, through December 2012 a total of 75,000 highway capable plug-in electric vehicles had been sold in the United States. Things look only slightly better when we include hybrids: 2.4 million hybrids were sold in the U.S. between 1999 and the end of 2012. Of course, not all of those are still on the road, and there are 254 million registered passenger cars in the United States, making hybrids something less than 1%.

This brings us back to the IEA's forecast, which now doesn't look so optimistic: that in 2030 the U.S. would be importing only 30% of its oil, provided Americans reduced their per capita consumption by 40%. The Obama administration in August 2012 ordered auto manufacturers to reach average fleet fuel efficiency standards of 54.5 mpg by 2025.

Environmentalist Chris Martenson in a December 19, 2012, interview with oilprice.com stressed the need to radically improve electric battery storage. Buildings need to be constructed or retrofitted to require less heating and cooling. Martenson is convinced that existing technologies can be used to greatly reduce both oil and electric usage, but that this is unlikely in an economy that requires constant growth to maintain its equilibrium. Further, that private enterprise is simply not equipped to fund or carry through a major reorientation of the country's energy usage. Only a major government effort of the kind that carried us through World War II can successfully confront such a grandiose undertaking.

Climate Change

Lastly, there was the worst bad news contained in the International Energy Agency's *World Energy Outlook 2012*, which the press largely passed over in silence. Kurt Cobb commented:

> Of all the findings in the 2012 edition of the World Energy Outlook, the one that merits the greatest international attention is the one that received the least. Even if governments take vigorous steps to curb greenhouse gas emissions, the report concluded, the continuing increase in fossil fuel consumption will result in "a long-term average global temperature increase of 3.6 degrees C." [6.8 degrees Fahrenheit. Total warming to date since 1880 is .8 degree Celsius or 1.4 degrees Fahrenheit.]

This should stop everyone in their tracks. Most scientists believe that an increase of 2 degrees Celsius is about all the planet can accommodate without unimaginably catastrophic consequences: sea-level increases that will wipe out many coastal cities, persistent droughts that will destroy farmland on which hundreds of millions of people depend for their survival, the collapse of vital ecosystems, and far more. An increase of 3.6 degrees C essentially suggests the end of human civilization as we know it. (November 27, 2012 TomDispatch.com)

Taken together, America's energy future is more threatening than rosy. The comparatively small increments from tight oil do not promise a new era of prosperity.

February 1, 2013

Animals and the English Language

Our language is filled with metaphors and similes comparing people to animals, and the very names of many animals are often used as epithets to characterize people. Most of the metaphors and similes (someone is LIKE or AS something) are so long in use that they have become cliches. The terms mostly date from the days when most people lived on farms and many in wooded areas where most of the animals enlisted were actually familiar to the speakers. Today American city dwellers on a daily basis see mainly dogs, cats, pigeons, crows, and squirrels. Less often, rats, mice, and hawks. Still less often, live horses, goats, pigs, and sheep. Except on television and trips to the zoo, many of the others are known only by reputation.

Our predilection is for anthropocentric feelings of superiority to other animals. It allows us, as our numbers swell into the many billions, to construct an ever larger and more horrific and cruel industry that raises animals and birds for food. Pigs whose lives are spent in pens so small they cannot turn around, chickens with their beaks amputated and without room to take a step, slaughterhouses where the cows whose life's goal is to become part of McDonald's billions and billions of burgers end in terror and pain.

All animals feel hunger, fear, and pain. The higher animals, particularly elephants, primates, wolves, dogs, pigs (the most mistreated), the great cats, and, perhaps surprisingly, birds such as parrots and crows, share all the emotions that humans have: love, anger, affection, shame, depression. Gorillas if trained in sign language can carry on a limited conversation. Koko reads children's picture books and has favorite videos. Chimpanzees, our closest relative, share 98 percent of human DNA. The relationship is so close that the two species can accept blood transfusions from each other. Chimps, like humans, have blood types A, B, and O. Their DNA is closer to human than the DNA of horses to donkeys, which can interbreed and produce infertile mules. DNA evidence shows that humans and chimps did interbreed for the first 1.2 million years after the human bloodline diverged from chimpanzees, and a number of scientists today think that a human-chimp hybrid is possible, although a number of experiments by Russian scientists in the 1920s were unsuccessful. Chimps use sticks as tools and hunt in organized groups. They perform better than humans on matching tests on a computer touch screen.

Dolphins hold a sponge in their mouths when foraging on the sea floor to protect their noses.

An NBC online article on the "The 10 Smartest Animals" said of pigs that in experiments in the 1990s, "Pigs were trained to move a cursor on a video screen with their snouts and used the cursor to distinguish between scribbles they knew and those they were seeing for the first time. They learned the task as quickly as chimpanzees." (retrieved June 30, 2013). The article added that if allowed to follow their own inclinations that pigs are the cleanest of domestic animals. At worst, they roll in mud because they have no sweat glands and are trying to keep cool. The Humane Society of the United States website writes: "They easily learn to operate levers and switches to obtain food and water, and to adjust ambient temperature to their liking. Pigs have also been observed to work in collaboration to free themselves from their pens. According to Donald Broom, Professor of Animal Welfare at University of Cambridge Veterinary School, who has been conducting mirror reflection tests with pigs: 'Pigs have the cognitive ability to be quite sophisticated. Even more so than dogs and certainly [more so than] three-year-olds.'" The article concludes: "Pigs share many similarities with humans with regard to emotions and cognitive states, and increasing scientific inquiry into the true nature of these animals continues to recognize their substantial mental abilities and so-ciable nature, as well as their capacity to experience pain, pleasure, fear and joy."

Dogs who live with humans learn to understand a surprising amount of human speech. The extreme example is a border collie tested at recognizing 1,100 English words.

Alex, an African Grey Parrot trained by Prof. Irene Pepperberg at the University of Arizona for thirty years, 1977 to 2007, had a vocabulary of more than 100 words that he could use intelligently to communicate. He could iden-tify fifty different objects, could distinguish seven colors and five shapes, and understand the concepts of "bigger", "smaller," "same," and "different." When he was told to fetch a specific hidden object that he discovered wasn't there and he had been tricked, he became angry.

Elephants have been known to recognize other elephants from whom they had been separated for thirty years, and to hold a grudge against humans who had abused them for just as long, They, like the higher primates, have close knit families that persist for a lifetime. They are able to recognize an image of themselves in a mirror, an attribute shared only by humans, great apes, and dolphins.

Surprisingly in the list of the most intelligent animals there is also the octopus. An article in the December 2011 issue of *Orion* magazine reports that octopuses can open a child-proof Tylenol bottle, and like to play with little plastic bottles like balls by blowing water at them to bounce them off aquarium walls, a behavior limited to only the most intelligent animals. At the New England Aquarium an octopus was shown a clear plastic cube with a crab inside that it would want to eat. The cube had a latch to secure the lid. The octopus soon learned to open the latch. In the end the crab was in one box enclosed in a second, which in turn was enclosed in a third, each with a different kind of latch. In a few days the octopus could quickly open all three of the boxes to get its crab.

Yet our language is filled with demeaning, and hostile views of animals. I have collected some of the more common phrases comparing humans to animals and birds, and as you can see, the negative heavily outweighs the positive. I'm sure I have missed some but these are the most common. I collected them without considering their attitude and sorted them only after I had found them all.

Animal Metaphors (Zoosemy)

Positive

cash cow
coltish
doe-eyed
eagle-eyed
foxy
horse sense
lion-hearted
memory like an elephant
out-fox
straight from the horses mouth
the lion's share
top dog

Negative

alley cat
badgering
barked
barking up the wrong tree
beating a dead horse
bird brain
black sheep
bovine
bull in a china shop
bull-headed
catting around
catty
chicken out
chicken-hearted
chicken livered
clammed up
cold fish
cowed
crocodile tears

dead duck
dog tired
dogged
eating crow
fat cats
ferreted it out
fish eye
fish out of water
funny duck
get on (off) a high horse
get someone's goat
go hog wild
gull
harebrained
have a tiger by the tail
have bats in one's belfry
hen-pecked
his goose is cooked
his tail between his legs
hog
hold your horses
horse face
hounded
in the dog house
it sounds fishy
kangaroo court
monkey around
monkey business
mousy
mulish
old crow
old goat
pack rat
parroted
pawed
pigging out
piggy
play cat and mouse with someone
play possum
pussy foot

ratted
sheepish
silly goose
sitting duck
sloth
smell a rat
snake in the grass
ugly duckling
weasel out of it
wolf down
wolf in sheep's clothing
wolfish

Neutral

800 pound gorilla
deficit hawk
doggedly
elephant in the room
hoof it
horsing around
lone wolf
night owl
separating the sheep from the
goats
squirreling something away
the straw that broke the camel's
back
walrus moustache

Similes

Positive

brave as a lion
busy as a beaver
crazy like a fox
eager as a beaver
fought like a tiger
free as a bird
gentle as a lamb
graceful as a gazelle

happy as a clam
happy as a lark
hungry as a horse
strong as a bull
strong as an ox
swims like a fish
wise as an owl

Negative

blind as a bat
breed like a rabbits
crazy as a loon
dead as a dodo
drunk as a skunk
like a bat out of hell
like herding cats
naked as a jaybird
packed like sardines
poor as a church mouse
prickly as a porcupine
sick as a dog
slippery as an eel
sly as a fox
spineless as a jellyfish
stubborn as a mule

Neutral

eats like a bird
quiet as a mouse
silent as a clam
weak as a kitten

Animal Names Used to Characterize Humans

Positive

bear
eagle
fox
lion
mouse (can be affectionate toward a woman but can also be a negative)
stallion
tiger

Negative

albatross
ape
ass
baboon
bird
chicken
cobra
coyote
dinosaur
dog
donkey
frog
goat
goose
gopher
gorilla
guinea pig
hippopotamus
hyena
jackal
lemmings
lizard
magpie
monkey

octopus
ostrich
pig
pigeon
rat
shark
shrew
shrimp
snake

swine
toad
turkey
viper
vulture
whale

Neutral

June 1, 2013

The Hip Dictator and His Opponents

The Dictator's Learning Curve: Inside the Global Battle for Democracy.
William J. Dobson. New York: Doubleday, 2012. 341 pp.

Former *Foreign Affairs* editor William J. Dobson has been making the rounds
of dictatorial states for the last half decade, interviewing the autocrats' top
functionaries as well as leaders of their democratic opposition. From Putin's
Russia to Mubarak's Egypt, Mahathir Mohamad's Malaysia, Chávez's Venezuela, and, of course, the very model of the modern authoritarian state, China.
He concludes that dictators have smartened up since the heavy handed days of
yore, when they had to give themselves 99 percent in every election and
sealed their borders, preventing people from leaving and trying to prevent
information about the outside world from getting in.

    The totalitarian regimes of the far right — National Socialism and fas-
cism — were destroyed in World War II. Those of the left — the Soviet
Union and its East European client states, Maoist China — collapsed at the
beginning of the 1990s, or in the case of China, underwent major reforms.
This has left North Korea as the sole indisputable exemplar of the totalitarian
model. Cuba stands somewhere between there and the states labeled
authoritarian.

    During Ronald Reagan's presidency the United States was excoriated by
progressives for adopting UN ambassador Jeanne Kirkpatrick's Cold War
doctrine of supporting authoritarian dictatorships against totalitarian ones, on
the claim that they were more likely to be reformable. In those days right-
wing military juntas were plentiful, from Greece to Argentina. Today the shoe
is on the other foot, as a list of today's ten worst dictators would most likely
comprise Kim Jong-un (North Korea), Bashar al-Assad (Syria), Omar al-
Bashir (Sudan), Robert Mugabe (Zimbabwe), Islam Karimov (Uzbekistan),
Gurbanguly Berdimuhamedow (Turkmenistan), Seyed Ali Khamanei (Iran),
Aleksandr Lukashenko (Belarus), Isaias Afwerki (Eritrea), and King Abdullah
(Saudi Arabia). Of these, nine have a generally leftist or anti-imperialist ori-

gin, only King Abdullah being unequivocally of the political right. Dobson's subjects are drawn from the runners up, a lighter shade of pale due to the smarter tactics that are the subject of his book.

The murderous scale of the old tyrants seems to be a thing of the (recent) past. A hundred million murdered by the Communist states, 35 million of them deliberately starved to death during China's Great Leap Forward when Mao refused to call off grain seizures to meet impossible quotas, because doing so would lose him his post as head of the regime. Two million executed by Pol Pot in Cambodia. And among the noncommunist despots, 500,000 killed by Idi Amin in Uganda, 250,000 by Saddam Hussein in Iraq, 25,000 in a single month in the Syrian city of Hama by Hafez Assad, Bashir's father. Bashir, over a somewhat longer time spread, is now around the 60,000 corpse mark in his determination to remain in power. The newer, gentler despots try to avoid this kind of Grand Guignol. In part this is because it is no longer possible to keep such carnage secret. It was decades before the true toll of the Great Leap Forward was established with any certainty.

After the fall of the Soviet Union in 1990 there was a sharp upturn in the number of liberal democracies, a trend that briefly seemed unstoppable. Then, in 2005, the reverse set in. Movements for democracy have become more widespread, but, as Dobson writes, today's dictators "are far more sophisticated, savvy, and nimble than they once were." Instead of arresting or shooting members of a human rights group, they send out health and building inspectors to shut down their offices. "Today's dictators pepper their speeches with references to liberty, justice, and the rule of law. . . . Today, the Kremlin's operatives typically stop stuffing the ballot boxes when they reach 70 percent."

In the old USSR a black van would drive up to a dissident's street in the night. They would be taken away and never seen again. Nowadays they have an accident or are the victim of a random mugging.

Back in the 1960s in its fight against Soviet and Chinese Communist influence, the United States backed whatever government or movement was fighting on the other side, commonly, but not always, something right-wing or dictatorial. Today most of the battles for democracy are internal to the country involved, while the U.S. is committed to strong economic or political ties to many of the more regressive leftist governments. As Dobson writes:

"The United States is one of China's largest trading partners, is the biggest buyer of Venezuelan oil, sends billions in aid to the Egyptian military, and courts Russian diplomatic support on a range of crucial strategic issues."

The pseudo democratic autocracy is becoming more the rule than the exception. Dobson writes:

Forty years ago, before the beginning of the democratic wave that began in 1972, the line that separated democracies and dictatorships was clearer. At that time, only a handful of authoritarian states masked themselves behind a democratic façade. Today, several dozen states — many that were once thought to be on the road to democracy — have become only a few shades less dark than their authoritarian past. Asia, Africa, and central Asia are littered with governments that are more democratic in form than function.

Putin's Russia

Vladimir Putin began to housebreak other centers of power in Russia in 2003 with the arrest of oil billionaire Mikhail Khodorkovsky on trumped up charges. Khodorkovsky remains in prison. When Putin took office there were three major television networks, of which the government controlled only one. The two independent networks were forced to sell to the state under threat of imprisonment and their owners fled abroad. Dobson reports that the Russian government now controls 93 percent of all media outlets. Media editors are instructed on a daily basis on what to present and what to say about it. When Medvedev, due to term limits, succeeded Putin as president in 2008, the media were instructed to open each broadcast with a story about Medvedev, followed immediately by a story of equal length about Putin, whether or not Putin had done anything that day.

To sustain the illusion of a multiparty state, Putin's United Russia party itself invented loyal opposition parties to represent nationalists, the poor, and old people, with the Kremlin writing the scripts for them. The only actual opposition party of any size is the Communist Party of the Russian Federation, a neo-Stalinist, ultranationalist and antisemitic body thoroughly hostile to liberal democracy.

Dobson interviews Boris Nemtsov, a former provincial governor and Minister of Fuel and Energy in the national government, now a critic. Asked what is the difference between Communism and Putinism, Nemtsov puts his finger on the dividing line between the old totalitarians and the new dictators:

> Putinism looks smarter, because Putinism comes just for your political rights but does not touch your personal freedom. You can travel, you can emigrate if you want, you can read the Internet. What is strictly forbidden is to use TV. Television is under control because TV is the most powerful resource for ideology and the propaganda machine.

The Russian state has instituted punitive regulations for nonprofit organizations, which can be shut down at will for building code violations, use of pirated software, or even typos in documents, essentially at the government's discretion. Fire inspections are a favorite.

As they have done with political parties, the Putin government has created dummy nonprofits, officially independent of the government but actually controlled by the Kremlin. Notable here is the Moscow Bureau for Human Rights. When, in 2008, the New York-based Human Rights Watch issued a report on kidnappings, executions, and torture in the Russian republic of Ingushetia, Alexander Brod, the head of the Moscow Bureau for Human Rights, held a press conference to give the government a clean bill of health.

Between 2000 and early 2012 nineteen Russian journalists were murdered, the most famous, Anna Politkovskaya, in 2006. Scores more are beaten with impunity.

Russian functionaries defend the system by pointing to the economic success of authoritarian China and Singapore. This is a tricky case, that I will come back to. Dobson concedes that over the last forty years, planetwide, autocracies have matched the democracies in economic growth. But this parity disappears if East Asia is excepted. Outside of that region the autocracies displayed a median per capita growth rate 50 percent lower than poor states that were democratic. In the Russian case, Dobson notes, while the Asian authoritarians built their economies on manufactures, especially automobiles and high tech electronics, 70 percent of Russian exports in 2008 were gas and oil and only 1.7 percent were goods and services.

Moreover, while China nominally remains a Communist country, total state employment there in 2009 was only 10.2% of the working population, while in Russia it is almost 40 %. The World Bank estimates that close to half of the Russian economy consists of bribes and other forms of corruption.

The Russian government at all levels rigs elections. One official told Dobson that Putin is popular enough that he doesn't need to do this, but that mayors and regional officials do it routinely to head off any sign that their power is weakening. In 2009, for example, in elections for the Moscow city Duma, Sergei Mitrokhin, the head of the liberal Yabloko party, was not credited with a single vote in his home district despite the fact that at minimum he, his family, and friends all voted there.

In 2009 Putin succeeded in abolishing elections for provincial governors, replacing popular votes with appointments from the Kremlin.

Dobson tells the story of Yevgenia Chirikova, who became an ecological activist in defense of Khimki Forest. The forest is part of the green belt surrounding Moscow, and abuts the suburb of Khimki on the city's northwest border. Comprising twenty-five hundred acres, the forest is supposed to be inviolate under Russian law. In 2008 the government, without public notice, began constructing a highway to go from Moscow to St. Petersburg that would run through the middle of Khimki Forest. Developers were also lined up to build housing along the roadway. Chirikova called meetings of her neighbors, set up a website, and began organizing demonstrations to save the forest. Mikhail Beketov, publisher of a small local paper, supported the protest. He was beaten with baseball bats almost to death, losing a leg and four fingers and suffering brain damage. He never regained the power of speech and died on April 8, 2013, at the age of fifty-five.

In July 2010 an environmentalist tent camp, set up in the forest to give advance warning if construction went forward, was attacked by almost a hundred masked men. When police finally came it was the environmentalists they arrested.

Construction was halted briefly while President Medvedev called for further study but was finally approved in December 2010. In March 2011 government agents raided Yevgenia Chirikova's husband's electrical engineering firm. Authorities threatened to take her children, on anonymous and false accusations of child abuse. Construction is still underway but the environmentalists won a case in a Moscow court in December 2012 that the construction company was cutting a swath more than three times wider than allowed under their permits.

Mubarak's Egypt

Dobson next turns to Mubarak's Egypt. He talks to Omar Afifi, now an attorney, but back in 1995 he was a cop. The night before parliamentary elections the Cairo police chief called a meeting of seven or eight hundred of his men. They were ordered to go to the polling places in plain clothes and hand out pre-marked ballots choosing the government party. They were instructed to start fights, and during the disturbances to go into the polling stations and stuff the ballot boxes. In later years as a lawyer he conducted classes in Egyptian law to help people defend themselves in court. When he published a book on this subject state security agents seized all the copies.

Ayman Nour, an attorney, founded El Ghad, a liberal secular party, in 2004. The following year he was arrested on spurious charges of improprieties in El Ghad's founding documents. He was released from prison and ran for president against Mubarak in the 2005 elections, getting 600,000 votes, or 7 percent. This was the second-highest total in the rigged elections. Nour was returned to prison in December 2005, where his case became an international issue. In November 2008 his party headquarters were burned to the ground.

He was released from prison in February 2009, but the government ordered him dropped from the bar association. His contract to teach at a university was canceled. He was unable to sell a house he inherited from his father when the government ordered all of the country's notaries to refuse to notarize the sale documents.

El Ghad split going into the post-Mubarak parliamentary elections, held from November 2011 to January 2012. The official El Ghad Party ran as independents, while Nour formed the Ghad El-Thawra Party, which took part in the Muslim Brotherhood's slate.

Back in the United States, Dobson in March 2010, while Mubarak was still in power, talked to long-time Egyptian human rights activist Saad Eddin Ibrahim. The regime, Ibrahim said, uses intimidation, prison, and character assassination against its critics. And if those fail it tries to destroy its victim's livelihood. "They are draining my resources filing cases against me," he told Dobson.

> At one time, there were twenty-eight cases filed against me by different people from different places around the country. . . . They filed a suit [against me] for inciting El Baradei to run and therefore destabilizing Egypt. I don't know the guy [who filed it] but for the next year or two it will be like a sword hanging over me.

Mahathir Mohamad's Malaysia

Dobson spends a day in February 2011 with Anwar Ibrahim, leader of the People's Justice Party, the principal opposition group to the authoritarian regime of Mahathir Mohamad in Malaysia. Anwar had been Mahathir Mohamad's deputy prime minister, 1993-1999, when he fell afoul of the dictator and spent six years in solitary confinement on almost certainly fabricated charges of corruption. He received an additional nine-year sentence in 2000 on the charge of sodomy, but he was eventually acquitted on that count. His party won more than a third of the seats in parliament and five of the thirteen state governorships in elections of April 2008.

Mahathir ruled Malaysia from 1981 until 2003, and has been replaced by his hand-picked successors. When in power he made wide use of the Internal Security Act that allowed him to arrest critics without filing charges and to hold them indefinitely. His arrests included ten members of parliament. He also closed down three opposition newspapers. He promoted an act of parliament that stripped the High Courts of the power of judicial review of laws. When the judges tried to appeal this, Mahathir fired five of them, effectively eliminating an independent judiciary. Mahathir is best known in the West for his antisemitic rants.

The regime remains relatively stable because the economy has been far more successful than in Egypt.

Chávez's Venezuela

Dobson visited two of Venezuela's most famous political prisoners: former Defense Minister Raúl Baduel and Judge Maria Lourdes Afiuni. Baduel had joined with Chávez in founding the Chavista movement in 1982, used his units in the military to restore Chávez to power after the 2002 coup against him, and was commander-in-chief of the Venezuelan army from 2004 to July 2007, when he resigned in protest against the extensive constitutional amendments that would have made Chávez president for life. Chávez had him arrested at gun point, charging Baduel with responsibility for missing military funds. Baduel is treated as a political prisoner by both Human Rights Watch and Amnesty International.

Dobson visited him in the Ramo Verde military prison in July 2010. He writes:

"Baduel told me he was bothered by what he saw: his longtime friend ruled like an autocrat and was surrounded by people who told him he could do no wrong." He quotes Baduel directly:

"They say I know him well, but now I think I met an impostor. He wanted power. He was able to hide that well through the years. He takes actions to sustain his only political project, which is to be president for life."

Judge Afiuni's case is even clearer. Under Venezuelan law people cannot be held without trial for more than two years. In December 2009, the case of businessman Eligio Cedeño came before her. He was accused of evading currency regulations. He had been illegally held for three years at that time. The government's tactic was to have the prosecutors repeatedly fail to show up for scheduled hearings. In their absence, Judge Afiuni granted Cedeño bail. This was the required action under the constitution. She was immediately arrested. Chávez went on national television to order that she be given a thirty-year sentence. The government accused Afiuni of taking a bribe to release Cedeño, but never produced any evidence.

William Dobson interviewed Judge Afiuni in her cell in the country's only women's prison, on the outskirts of Caracas, in July 2010. She told him about her arrest. She had just been placed in a jail cell when,

A senior intelligence official came in and said, "We have good news, and we have bad news. The good news is that we have found nothing against you. The bad news is that Chávez just condemned you to prison for thirty years on national television."

While in prison she contracted cancer, and was raped. She became pregnant from the rape and underwent an abortion that became a hysterectomy. After undergoing cancer surgery she was transferred to house arrest in February 2011. At the end of 2012 a trial began, which she refused to attend, as she said it was a political frame-up. It appears to have been suspended, as she remains under house arrest today, in April 2013, after Chávez's death.

Numerous human rights organizations, including Amnesty International, have demanded Maria Afiuni's release. Unusually, the United Nations has taken up the case. In February 2013, Margaret Sekaggya, the U.N.'s special rapporteur on the situation of human rights defenders, issued a statement declaring, "Judge Afiuni's situation represents an emblematic case of reprisal." The U.N.'s special rapporteur on torture, Juan E. Mendez, also challenged the Venezuelan government's refusal to investigate Afiuni's affirmation that she was raped in the infirmary of the women's prison in 2010, saying, "Rape and other grave acts of sexual violence by state authorities" amount to torture.

Chávez came to power in popular reaction against the corruption of the traditional party governments, which catered to the rich and ignored the plight of the poor. Using the country's considerable oil wealth, he subsidized major improvements in the living standards of the bottom thirty percent of the population, and provided generous foreign oil aid to leftist governments in the hemisphere, most importantly, Cuba, whose economy had been in the doldrums after the fall of the Soviet Union at the beginning of the 1990s.

But along with the tilt toward the poor, Chávez increasingly tilted the system toward disfranchising voters of all classes and concentrating power in his own hands. In the process the economy, despite it oil wealth, descended into chaos, inflation mounted to the thirty percent annual rate, threatening the survival of both the poor, and the elderly who live on fixed incomes. In response, he rigged elections to less and less reflect the real wishes of the Venezuelan masses.

Dobson interviewed Teodoro Petkoff in November 2009. Petkoff, today the editor of *Tal Cual,* was, at different stages of his life, a leftist guerilla fighter under Douglas Bravo, a professor, a member of the Venezuelan Communist Party, and a government minister. He calls Chávez a fascist. He concedes that Chávez, at least early in his presidency, was wildly popular, but says that his support steadily eroded and by 2009 was below 50 percent. Chávez compensated by closing off avenues through which he could be challenged:

Is this an authoritarian government? Of course. Is this an undemocratic government? Of course. There is not an inch of separation of pow-

ers. There are no checks and balances. Chávez has encroached on all political powers, all of them — parliament, justice, attorney general, comp-
troller, ombudsman, and the National Electoral Council.

So just how does this system work? Chávez established a new national assembly with rewritten rules, which, Dobson says, give him 93 percent of the
seats with only 53 percent of the votes. The Senate was abolished, leaving a
unicameral legislature. Public funding for political candidates was outlawed,
but Chavista candidates, especially incumbents, have virtually unlimited access to the public trough. Exclusion of opposition candidates from television
coverage, prohibition of some of the more popular ones from running for office, and free use of television by regime supporters, along with Chávez's
initial popularity, left the government free to hold frequent elections and ref-
erendums with no need to stuff ballot boxes as other authoritarian regimes
commonly do. One former member of the National Electoral Council told
Dobson:

"Election Day is not a problem. All the damage — the use of money,
goods, excess power, communications — happens beforehand." Dobson
comments:

> While the new constitution had banned public financing for the po-
> litical parties, the prohibition was only applied against the opposition.
> Government ministries openly flouted the ban, pouring millions of dol-
> lars into pro-Chávez banners, leaflets, and billboards, as well as sending
> state employees to convass for the president.

Other tools have been gerrymandering, and massive distribution of voter IDs.
This last doesn't work the way American Republicans do it, to fight nonexistent in-person voter fraud in order to suppress minority voters. In the Venezuelan case all voters already had IDs. Between 2003 and 2009, the number of
voter IDs issued jumped from eleven million to eighteen million, and 40 percent of the total in 2009 did not list an address. The fraud risk here is people
who collect multiple, unverifiable IDs, to allow them to vote many times.

The gerrymandering strongly favored rural areas over the cities. There is
no lack of poor people in Venezuelan cities, but there they tend to support the
opposition while the rural poor are more likely to go with Chávez. Dobson
gives as an example of the new districts, Amazonia, a rural state strongly pro-
Chávez, where it takes 42,000 votes to get a member of parliament, compared
to Zulia, where the opposition is popular, where it takes 708,000. In the September 2010 legislative elections, the Chavista candidates won 48.3 percent
compared to the opposition's 47.2 percent. But the Chavistas got 96 seats

while the opposition got only 64. In Carabobo and Caracas Capital District the Chavistas lost the popular vote but took seven of the ten seats in each district.

Chávez also used intimidation. In 2004, nationwide petitions qualified for a referendum calling for Chávez's recall. Before the vote Chávez had the names of all three million signers of the petitions posted to a public website. The health minister announced that any doctors or nurses who had signed the petition would be fired. Workers for the state oil company were also fired, as well as state bank workers. The next year the government distributed CDs with the names, addresses, and voting history of twelve million citizens, a list known as the Maisanta. One ninety-eight-year-old woman was denied her medical prescriptions because the Maisanta showed she had voted for the referendum. Others were turned away from hospital emergency rooms when admitting nurses checked their voting records.

The claim that the Chávez government has championed the poor, which has won it the admiration of leftists around the world, is a mixed bag. It is true that large numbers have been lifted out of poverty, mainly by subsidies from Venezuela's oil wealth. At the same time, Transparency International, an NGO that monitors political corruption, ranks Venezuela at number 164 out of 178 countries, on a level with Angola. There are more murders in Venezuela than in Mexico, and 91 percent are unsolved. Inflation is running at 30 percent. Government price controls require food stores to sell staples at fixed prices, but with the rampant inflation this is often below the price the merchants have to pay, leading to bankruptcies and empty shelves.

In North Korea loudspeakers blast continual propaganda that can't be shut off. In Venezuela while Chávez lived, all radio and television channels, including such apolitical venues as Animal Planet and National Geographic, were required to interrupt their programming to carry any presidential address, called a *cadena*, in full. In his first eleven years in office Chávez delivered almost two thousand of these addresses, some lasting for many hours. Dobson says the total of these speeches came to almost 1,300 hours. Apart from the *cadenas* Chávez had a weekly Sunday television show, *Aló Presidente* (Hello President), in which he monologued, on average, for just under five hours.

The law prohibits "defaming the president," which is punishable by thirty months in prison. People also face stiff fines for "offending" public authorities. When Chávez was first elected the government owned one television channel and two radio stations. When Dobson made his survey the government had six TV channels, two national radio stations, and three thousand community radio stations, as well as three print media companies. In December 2010 a law was passed making it a crime for any Internet provider to permit content that causes "anxiety or unrest among the public order."

Chávez's justification for his many antidemocratic measures was that he was defending the interests of the poor against the rich. But by 2008 large sections of the urban poor were starting to vote for the opposition, one reason why the electoral system was reconfigured to give greater weight to rural areas over the cities.

People who live in areas that vote for the opposition are severely punished. When in 2008 Henrique Capriles won the race for governor of the state of Miranda, with a population above three million, the central government retaliated by closing nineteen hospitals and 250 emergency and primary care centers. The state budget was cut by $200 million.

The Chavistas were shocked that same year when opposition leader Carlos Ocariz was elected mayor of Sucre Municipality, one of the poorest sectors of greater Caracas, home to two million people, 80 percent of whom are below the poverty line. Ocariz won 55.6 percent to 43.8 for the Chavista. He told Dobson, "The day after the election, the government took away sixteen garbage trucks, which was 60 percent of garbage collection." Water pressure for the hillside town suddenly dropped, leaving many residents without water. Ocariz said, "It's a mixture of negligence and political revenge."

Ocariz responded by getting water trucks to deliver to the poorest sections and installing stronger pumps.

Chávez, following an example set by the Iranian theocracy, on his personal authority alone ordered the government to ban candidates he disapproved of from running for public office. In February 2008, 400 political figures, 80 percent of them from the opposition, were declared ineligible to stand for election. A particular target was Leopoldo López, mayor of Chacao, who was the favorite to become the next mayor of Caracas. By the time Dobson finished his book the number of the banned had reached more than 800.

After López was forced out of the race, the Chavista candidate was defeated by another opposition figure, Antonio Ledezma. Chávez retaliated by effectively overturning the election, stripping the city of 80 percent of its budget and replacing the power of the mayor with a new, unelected, "head of government" for the Caracas Capital District. Dobson recounts how armed Chávez supporters "seized city hall and other municipal office buildings and refused to relinquish them. Offices were ransacked, equipment and city vehicles destroyed or stolen." In a meeting with Ledezma a year after his election the powerless mayor told Dobson, "Chávez wins when he wins, and he wins when he loses. If he doesn't win, he just takes it."

The death of Chávez, paired with the downward spiral of the Venezuelan economy, puts the future of the Bolivarian Revolution in doubt. The April 13, 2013, election was devastating for Chávez's successor, Nicolás Maduro, despite his eking out a paper-thin victory, 50.78% against 48.95% for opposition candidate Henrique Capriles Radonski. This was despite the fact that the ruling party totally controlled the airwaves, granting the opposition candidate four minutes a day. At the least the election dispelled the claim that the population, including the poor, are solidly with the Chavistas, as approximately half went for the opposition. Also notable was the fact that while Capriles carried only 8 of the country's 24 states, he won 6 of the 9 largest, Zulia, Miranda, Lara, Bolívar, Anzoátegui, and Táchira.

The Rebels' New Style

From Serbia to Egypt to Venezuela, as dictators have learned to cloak their rule in trappings of populist pseudo democracy, their opponents have evolved as well. The old Marxism has largely gone by the board and with it notions such as the Leninist combat party and of revolution aiming at a proletarian abolition of private property. The goals are political rights, civil liberties, and democratic institutions, not overturn of property relations, much less a one-party dictatorship.

In Venezuela when students mobilized to oppose Chávez's May 2007 closure of the country's most popular television station, RCTV, followed later that year by his proposed constitutional referendum that would make him president for life, their demonstrations were attacked by the police and the national guard. In response, instead of large gatherings the students dispersed in small groups to a hundred Caracas subway stations to distribute flyers. They set up roadblocks where they would let people pass only if they could name one article of the Constitution Chávez was trying to change.

The government accused the students of being CIA agents. They in turn staged a rally outside a bank, protesting that the government was delaying their checks from the CIA.

Soon young rebels were exchanging information and training on an international level. Prominent in this effort were veterans of the revolt in Serbia in October 2000 that brought down Slobodan Milošević. Central to that rebellion was the student group Otpor (Serbian for "resistance," formed in 1998). Otpor activists advised the leaders of the Rose Revolution in Georgia in 2003, and from there, the Orange Revolution in Ukraine at the end of 2004, which compelled a presidential revote, giving the presidency to an opposition candidate who had in the first count been declared defeated.

The Russian government immediately saw this as a threat, and preemptively founded their own progovernment youth movement, Nashi ("Ours"). William Dobson attended a Nashi rally in Moscow in April 2010 where Vasily Yakemenko, the group's founding leader, declared, "Our movement knows no authority except the authority of the policies of Medvedev and Putin." Nashi act as thugs to intimidate and often beat critics of the regime. In 2010 they held a summer retreat where photoshopped posters were displayed with the heads of leading human rights activists impaled on spikes. Nashi members are given paramilitary training including weapons training. One reporter who had been covering Nashi was attacked with steel rods, had one finger amputated, his skull fractured, his jaw broken in two places, and one leg crushed.

While Russia seems fairly impervious, the tactics pioneered in Serbia and perfected in the color revolutions of Eastern Europe have since made their way to Egypt and Latin America. Dobson had discussions of this with Ahmed Maher, a founder of the April 6 Movement that helped bring down Mubarak, and another young Egyptian activist, Ahmed Salah. Two elements are prominent in their strategy: widespread use of social media and the Internet to quickly disseminate information, and use of nonviolent tactics. The thinking is that the repressive regimes already have a near monopoly of armed force and would prefer to move the struggle to that plane. Nonviolent movements can succeed, but generally only if they can win over or neutralize large segments of the police and armed forces.

A popular handbook is Gene Sharp's *From Dictatorship to Democracy*. Sharp highlights little-used nonviolent methods to supplement demonstrations and strikes. These range from mock funerals to mass withdrawals of bank deposits. It always helps to recruit some children of high ranking government, military, and police officials, as it makes their parents a little less likely to shoot into crowds of demonstrators where their kids are in the front lines. Sharp, eighty-five in 2013 and three times nominated for the Nobel Peace Prize, runs his own organization, the Albert Einstein Institution, out of his home in East Boston. His books are banned in China and Russia, while the Iranian government has a special unit that studies Sharp's works in order to counter them. Hugo Chávez claimed Sharp is in league with the CIA.

Ahmed Salah in 2009 attended a five-day course in Boston by the International Center on Nonviolent Conflict. Another player is the Centre for Applied NonViolent Action and Strategies (CANVAS). Based in Belgrade, its staff includes veterans of democratic struggles from Serbia, Georgia, Lebanon, the Philippines, and South Africa. It operates clandestine training centers and has provided advice to movements in more than fifty countries. They will not work with any group with a history of violence, and do not offer tactical prescriptions. But they teach their trainees the necessity of planning for themselves. Srdja Popovic, one of the leaders of the Serbian Otpor and now of CANVAS, tells Dobson, "There is no such thing as a spontaneous revolution.

Spontaneity will only get you killed. The more you plan, the bigger your chance for success."

Asked how centralized the leadership of Otpor had been in the fight against Milošević, Popovic replied, "The top eleven activists never met in the same place." Didn't the government have informers and collect information on its opponents? Popovic said,

"When we saw our dossiers after the revolution, we had like two hundred pages each. They knew our movements. But there was no analysis. So, so what?"

How do you counter government shock troops? Popovic: "You need to create stronger bonds with the local police. We developed ties with the local police so they would warn us what streets to avoid. Every regime has a limited number of special units."

In Serbia Otpor had tried to win over every layer and group that it could, not automatically attacking them. Where it couldn't win them, it sought to neutralize them. In the case of a particularly brutal police chief, who personally beat and tortured prisoners, they got photos of him beating their members, then posted them where his wife shopped and where his children went to school.

Dobson cites a study by Erica Chenoweth that claims to show that between 1900 and 2006 something more than 50 percent of nonviolent insurgencies succeeded, compared to only 25 percent of violent ones.

While the mass tactics are nonviolent and seek to create a popular democracy, the thinking is that the movement during the struggle cannot be open and democratic, as an authoritarian regime will infiltrate and cripple it. Dobson says there are no hard and fast rules on which side will win. Victory goes to the most agile. Mubarak's government in its last days began to talk about reform and to admit the existence of police and military brutality. It made overtures to opposition movement leaders to work for the government to help reform it.

Economics, though, seem to be a strong predictor of outcomes. The huge spike in oil and food prices in 2008 led to food riots across North Africa and contributed heavily to the movement against Mubarak. This was despite the fact that the Egyptian economy grew at above 7 percent between 2005 and 2008. And even the fall of the old despot did not settle matters, as the military had been the backbone of the ancien regime and it remained intact, engaging in attacks on demonstrators in Tahrir Square long after Mubarak was gone. The election of Mohamad Morsi in June 2012 posed a new set of issues: was Egypt under the Muslim Brotherhood to become a theocratic state like Iran? The popular movement, through demonstrations of hundreds of thousands, was able to beat back Morsi's attempt to grant himself virtually limitless power, a project he had to publicly abandon in December 2012.

One positive sign Dobson sees, writing before Morsi's election and its aftermath, was the formation of Officers for the Revolution, a prodemocracy group within the Egyptian army. This was started by First Lieutenant Sherif Osman with a Facebook page.

Egyptian scholar Maha Abdelrahman in an April 22, 2013, post on opendemocracy.net, critiqued the limits of the new loose style of rebellion, at least for Egypt. While rejecting resurrecting the elitist Leninist vanguard party, she points out that the Egyptian opposition movements were focused on specific reforms, such as limiting presidential terms, ending the emergency law, calling free elections, and ending the Mubarak dynasty. They did not aim at taking over the government themselves. After their success in ousting Mubarak they confronted the two remaining entrenched powers in the country: the army and the Muslim Brotherhood.

The Brotherhood, while nominally illegal from the days of Nasser, was tolerated under Mubarak and had built a large infrastructure of social service and charity organizations. When elections followed the Mubarak era, the Islamic parties, through the Brotherhood's connections, had massive advantage over the many new and still unknown parties hastily created by the opposition groups. Abdelrahman also points out that the many opposition groups fall into three broad types that have little coordination between them: the mainly student and youth based movement that was most prominent in the Tahrir Square demonstrations; unofficial trade union organizations operating on the fringes of the state-controlled Egyptian Trade Union Federation; and the many small local protest demonstrations over the high cost of food and fuel and inadequate water and sanitation.

What to Make of China

A few days after Mubarak fell an anonymous post on social media called for a Chinese Jasmine Revolution, the name of the movement that had just toppled Tunisia's President Zine El Abidine Ben Ali. China's top leadership quickly banned any use of the word jasmine on websites and discussion boards. Soon calls for a Jasmine Revolution spread anyway. Their demands were limited to reforms: that the ruling Communist Party fight corruption and that it accept "supervision" by the people. Messages called for protestors to come out for strolls on specific streets in a dozen cities. One designated location was in front of a Beijing McDonald's. William Dobson went to see what would happen. Hundreds of police, reinforced by security volunteers wearing armbands, lined the street while plainclothes cops with walkie-talkie ear buds circulated through the crowd of pedestrians. A street sweeper rolled up and down spraying water to keep people moving along, while police with dogs kept pedestrians on the sidewalk. A popular folksong about the jasmine flower was pulled from websites, while flower stores were prohibited from selling jasmines.

Dozens of dissidents and human rights lawyers were rounded up and detained before stroll day, some held for weeks afterward. Critics of the government routinely have their phones tapped and are followed around by the secret police. If they are too outspoken they end up in prison.

China's constitution requires that the country be governed by the Communist Party. The press and online media are heavily censored. Freedom House in its 2011 world survey ranked China's press as "not free." International mail is monitored. Fifty-five distinct crimes are subject to the death penalty, including embezzlement and tax fraud, with executions running at around 5,000 per year, though accurate statistics are hard come by.

By most standards, China is a police state. Yet it bears little resemblance to the totalitarian cult of Mao's Cultural Revolution. What has changed is a massive retreat of party control over people's personal lives, private beliefs, living standards, occupations, and places of residence. Political freedom does not exist, or is highly restricted, but the state, in contrast to the regime's first thirty years in power, largely leaves people's private lives alone. The main exception is the one-child policy, which, given China's extremely limited arable land and potable water, has been a desperately needed necessity, no matter how much it outrages Western sensibilities.

Unlike the Mao era, or the Soviet Union in its heyday, China has a genuinely flourishing literary life and world-class film industry. But certainly it is its economic successes that have made the restrictive regime palatable and even popular. Unlike Chávez's Venezuela, which sought to sharply polarize its population, relying on unsustainable top-down subsidies to win the loyalty of the poor, China's leaders have promoted national unity and strongly encouraged their people's historic, but long-suppressed, bottom-up entrepreneurship. It is true that the children of high party functionaries got more than their share of privatized state assets and opportunities for insider trading that offered a short road to wealth. But by the UN standards of poverty, China has gone from 85% of its people in poverty in 1981 to 13.1% in 2008. Real average income for a Chinese household has grown from an annual $280 in 1980 to $3,000 in 2010. Ideology, once omnipresent, has been toned down, with national development given priority, and not in the ham-fisted manner of the old USSR.

William Dobson, for all of his championing of resistance movements to the new authoritarians, plainly admires the Chinese. He writes:

> The fact is that most Chinese have a far freer life today than ever before. Chinese citizens increasingly live where they want and with whom they want. Limits on one's personal lifestyle have all but disappeared. In the past two decades, more than 200 million people have opted to move from the countryside to one of China's new metropolises. They can own property, maybe even a car, and choose their own career or line of work. . . . The commercialization of Chinese media has led to a lively news and entertainment environment, with newspapers, magazines, and television stations pushing the boundaries to compete for audiences. As long as journalists tread carefully, government censors remain silent. . . . The party, unlike a couple of decades ago, no longer hounds citizens about their "socialist purity."

The Chinese authoritarian state is certainly smarter than most of the others, as well as more successful. Unlike Russia or Venezuela, it is not built around the rule of particular individuals. They have instituted term limits and local elections. In the 2002 and 2007 party congresses more than half of the Central Committee and Politburo members were dropped and replaced by others. In contrast to the closed off Mao years, some 20 percent of the party leadership have spent at least one year at a foreign university.

Dobson interviews Yu Keping, deputy director of the Central Compilation and Translation Bureau, who is reputedly close to then-party general secretary Hu Jintao. Yu told him,

"The lesson we can learn from the chaos in the Middle Eastern countries is the need for better public service and people's participation — transparency, accountability, and social justice."

Dobson tries to understand how people committed to the Chinese system conceptualize their work. Professor Pan Wei at Beijing University argues that China's system is more effective than the American one, pointing to the paralysis in Washington by the Tea Party movement. He proposes that the American system is based on accountability while the Chinese is based on responsibility. For Pan this means a centralized balancing of three groups of competing interests:

> Number one is partial interest versus the interest of the whole. Number two is to balance the interest of the present versus the interest of the future, for example, the environment versus people's demand for wealth today. And thirdly, it is to balance the interest for change and the interest for order. . . . I think the politics of responsibility is much more sophisticated than the politics of accountability.

But what keeps the government honest when there is little accountability? Dobson notes that in 2005 there were 87,000 strikes, demonstrations, and marches in China. This may be surprising in an authoritarian state. Most of these were protests against corruption or abuses by local leaders, pollution by local companies, police brutality, bad working conditions, or disputed land ownership. The government has responded by larger investment in its security forces and stepping up arrests of dissidents.

Authoritarian regimes everywhere look to China as their justification. But few of them other than Singapore have China's cultural tradition of subordination of the individual to the group, its people's entrepreneurial and craft skills, and, even in a Communist state, its largely meritocratic rather than personal system of rulership. What works in China, and even there with considerable unease, doesn't work where these essential elements are missing.

Looking back on the triumphalism that swept the Western capitalist states after the collapse of Communism at the beginning of the 1990s, it seems that they were only half right. Totalitarian state socialism, the Marxist alternative to decentralized ownership of productive property, has remained dead. But within the broad parameters in which decentralized property forms operate, the idea that liberal democracy was also the inevitable future has faded. If the United States is the extreme variant of rampant individualism and the north European social democratic welfare states are the most democratic and humane, there is also clearly a third pole, the more or less stable undemocratic and authoritarian capitalist states. Some of these rest on religious theocracies of the far right, such as Iran and Saudi Arabia, others on varieties of leftism. In most cases people of humane and progressive sensibilities should find themselves on the side of the rebels trying to reform or bring them down. In the case of China, we should support democratic activists, but recognize that in this case, at least, the system functions far better and with greater fairness if not greater freedom, than a great many of the world's governments.

May 1, 2013

Thinking about Oz

Oz Reimagined: New Tales from the Emerald City and Beyond. Edited by John Joseph Adams & Douglas Cohen. Las Vegas, NV: 47North, 2013. 365 pp.

The Living House of Oz. Edward Einhorn. Illustrated by Eric Shanower. San Diego: Hungry Tiger Press, 2005. 238 pp.

The land of Oz is a beloved American legend. It is known to most people from the 1939 musical film starring Judy Garland, Ray Bolger, Bert Lahr, and Jack Haley, still revived regularly on television and available on DVD. The film captured the look of the place much as it had been envisaged by its creator, L. Frank Baum, back in 1899: a vividly colored fairyland filled with odd but simple people and many magical creatures, from witches to live trees, winged monkeys, and Oz's famous automatons, the Scarecrow and the Tin Woodman. These images are engrained on the American psyche.

Still, the film misrepresented Oz as its history unfolded in Baum's thirteen later Oz books. One oddity was the decision to cast the Munchkins as dwarfs (today: little people). It works well in the film, but as the tales go on into many volumes there is no way to have the people of one of Oz's composite four countries — Munchkins in the east, Winkies in the west, Gillikins in the north, and Quadlings in the south — be far smaller than the others. Actually in *The Wizard of Oz* Baum describes them:

"They were not as big as the grown folk she had always been used to, but neither were they very small. In fact, they seemed about as tall as Dorothy, who was a well-grown child for her age." In the later books Munchkins are no smaller than anyone else, and the American habit of referring to cute little children as "Munchkins" would make no sense in Oz.

The greatest false note was the decision by MGM executives, fearful that such a flamboyant fantasy would corrupt the minds of American children, to make the whole thing a dream. That, and its concomitant and ever repeated message, There's no place like home. Kansas couldn't possibly compete with

Oz and anyone who knows what happened to Dorothy afterward knows that she soon left Kansas far behind and Oz has been her home ever since.

Baum styled himself the Royal Historian of Oz. His records show that the Scarecrow and the Tin Woodman, left to rule Oz after Dorothy and the Wizard departed for America, were overthrown by an army of women led by General Jinjur. She in turn was permanently replaced by Ozma, a descendant of Lurline, the fairy queen from the Forest of Burzee, who had first enchanted Oz so that its people never grew old and imbued it with its magic.

Important Oz personages (from left): Captain Bill, Scraps the Patchwork Girl, Jack Pumpkinhead, Ojo the Lucky, the Tin Woodman, the Wizard, Princess Ozma, the Scarecrow, Dorothy Gale, Glinda.

The Wizard, in one of his less savory deeds before the days of Dorothy, had kidnapped the baby Ozma. To prevent her ascending the throne he gave her to the Gillikin witch Mombi. Mombi transformed Ozma into a boy named Tip. Tip's adventures are recorded in the second Oz book, *The Marvelous Land of Oz*, which ended with the, for that time, daring transgender transformation in which Glinda turns Tip into Ozma, a young girl. Ozma has ruled Oz ever since, and appears in all of the succeeding books.

Dorothy returned to Oz four times. She is blown off a ship in a storm, falls into an underground kingdom during an earthquake in California, walks there on a magic road, and finally, is brought there by Ozma to live permanently, along with her Uncle Henry and Aunt Em. Dorothy is made a princess of Oz and never returns to Kansas.

The great attraction of Oz is that it is an American fairy tale. It's a you-can-get-there-from-here place. Its heroes and heroines are mostly American children, not the princes, princesses, or wood cutters of traditional European fairy stories. There is not only Dorothy Gale but Betsy Bobbin, Trot Griffiths,

Button Bright, Peter Brown from Philadelphia, and William "Speedy" Harm-stead from Long Island, New York. A few adults make it as well: Dorothy's Uncle Henry and Aunt Em, the Shaggy Man, Captain Bill Wheedles, and of course, the great original, Oscar Diggs, better known as the Wizard.

Dorothy and Ozma

The other unavoidable conflict between the film and the histories was the necessity to make Dorothy's film companions men in costumes. They did it marvelously well. Ray Bolger's Scarecrow was inimitable, and Bert Lahr's Cowardly Lion was a classic act. But in Oz the lion was a real lion, the Tin Man, depicted thousands of times over forty years in John R. Neil's illustrations, was really made of tin, with arms and legs that were thin jointed rods with no place in them to conceal a meat arm or leg. And the Scarecrow was filled with nothing but straw, his mouth only painted on. I suppose his voice materializes like the sound from a television speaker which only gives the illusion it is coming from the person pictured on the screen.

Oz is now more than a hundred years old. L. Frank Baum had written fourteen volumes before his death in 1918. After that his publisher, Reilly and Lee (they were Reilly and Britton during Baum's lifetime but changed their name in 1918), engaged Philadelphia children's author Ruth Plumly Thompson, who penned nineteen more, taking the series up to 1939. Then, like Sherlock Holmes, any number of authors have tried their hand at adding to the oeuvre, from artist John R. Neil, who had illustrated all but *The Wizard of Oz*, who added three undistinguished titles, to Jack Snow, who wrote two more in the late forties, all under the Reilly and Lee imprimatur, to many others in later years from other publishers.

I remember my father reading *The Wizard of Oz, Ozma of Oz*, and *The Road to Oz* to me and my sister when I was eight or nine. I looked over his shoulder and absorbed images that have remained with me for a lifetime: The mechanical giant with a hammer who guards the mountain cave in Ev that leads to the vast underground kingdom of the Nomes. The silhouette of the Shaggy Man after the king of Dunkiton had given him a donkey's head, brooding in a wilderness by moonlight. The lost boy Button Bright in his sailor's suit sitting idly and unconcerned by the side of the road, digging in the dirt with a stick. Johnny Dooit's sand boat that will take Dorothy and the Shaggy Man across the Deadly Desert to Oz.

I started collecting Oz books when I was about twelve and by my mid-teens had the whole thirty-three. I gave the set to my first wife's younger sister when I moved from San Francisco to New York in 1967. After I returned to Los Angeles in 1982 I collected them all again.

So today we have *Oz Reimagined*. Editors John Joseph Adams and Douglas Cohen have collected fifteen stories by sixteen widely published authors of fantasy, science fiction, and in some cases, other children's books. The mission seems to have been to offer an adult and mostly dystopian take on the fairyland.

Gregory Maguire, author of *Wicked*, provides a Foreword. And though his own Oz books emphasized the negative, he seems, of all the contributors, to best understand what Oz is about. He describes himself "as a man nearing sixty who recognized in Oz, more than half a century ago, a picture of home." I have thought of it that way for even longer. Every Oz story contains an adventure. They are filled with bizarre and often hostile creatures. Eight of the thirty-three Baum and Thompson books involve attempts to conquer Oz. But at the core there is Ozma's court. We know that in the end Ozma, with aid from Glinda, the good witch of the South, and the Wizard, who now knows a good bit of magic, will prevail. The stories epitomize what Jan Struther in her poem *Sleeveless Errand* called "The savour of the strange, The solace of the known."

Maquire puts his finger on how this juxtaposition is achieved, by a radical disconnect between a large part of the population and even their nearest neighbors. The peaceful portions and the malevolent little enclaves are mostly separated by a remarkable lack of interest in exploration:

"I found the insularity and even parochialism of Oz's separate populations puzzling and, maybe, worrying. Racist even, though I hadn't a word for it yet. Troublingly myopic, exceptionalist. Certainly lacking in intellectual curiosity. When Dorothy first arrived in the land of Munchkins, the kindly Munchkin farmers told her what they'd been told about the Emerald City and about the Wizard. But none of them had had the gumption of Dorothy to pick themselves up and go see for themselves. No firsthand experience. Few of them could predict what kind of population lived over the horizon. None of them cared."

This is true not only of the large subdivisions with their predominant color schemes — blue for Munchkinland, yellow for the Winkies, purple for the Gillikins, and red for the Quadlings — but for the endless subcountries with their own kings and courts, and downward from there to city-states, towns, and finally communities of just a few individuals living in clearings in the forest. The larger subdivisions are populated by humans: Oogaboo in the far northwest, whose queen, Ann Soforth once raised an army to try to conquer Oz, Mudge at the diagonally opposite corner; "kingdoms" named Pokes, Patch, Corabia. Then there are the endless magical enclaves: China Country where all the inhabitants are made of porcelain; elsewhere we encounter communities of living books, living torpedoes, mist maidens, people whose feet are fastened to the ground while their furniture runs around as needed.

There are little towns and kingdoms under the ground, on high mountains, and even invisible in the air overhead. Most seem oblivious to the larger Oz, and either hostile to people who wander into their territory or intent on converting them to their own peculiar way of life by transforming them in some usually unpleasant way.

In *The Lost Princess of Oz* (1917) Dorothy, the Wizard, and several others find their way to the city-state of Thi, a small town surrounded by a thicket of thistles, inhabited by Alice-in-Wonderland type creatures with heart-shaped bodies and triangular heads. On telling their leader, the High Coco-Lorum, that Thi is part of Oz, this person replies:

"It may be, for we do not study geography and have never inquired whether we live in the Land of Oz or not. And any Ruler who rules us from a distance, and unknown to us, is welcome to the job."

These small kingdoms and enclaves usually appear in only a single book and are never heard of again. In some cases, such as Oogaboo or Rash, they are central to the plot of a particular book. Most of the others are just impediments along the way, such as Chimneyville in *Jack Pumpkinhead of Oz* or the Hoppers and Horners in *The Patchwork Girl of Oz*. I have come to think of most of these ephemeral places that don't figure in the central story as filler.

In *Oz Reimagined* only a few of the authors show any awareness of the Oz of the written canon. Nine of the fifteen stories get no further than having a Dorothy, a Wizard, a Scarecrow, a Tin Man, and a Lion. They could have been written after watching the movie. There is some justification for this because of the far wider distribution of the film than the books, but it is also like commissioning a book of new tales about King Arthur in which most only take us as far as the youth removing the sword from the stone and leave out Camelot, Lancelot, Guinevere, and Sir Galahad. And far too many stories have winged monkeys, characters that after the first book are extremely rare in an Oz story.

First, the retellings of the original story:

Rae Carson and C.C. Finlay in "The Great Zeppelin Heist" offer a pre-Dorothy tale in which the newly arrived Wizard proposes marriage to the Wicked Witch of the West, but is tricked out of his engagement gift.

In "Dead Blue" David Farland imagines Dorothy as a technomage, the Tin Man as a cyborg, his flesh parts replaced with microcomputer-controlled bionics, the Wizard a harmless conman who ended in Oz when his star ship slipped through an unexpected wormhole. Dorothy and her companions are on the way back from killing the Wicked Witch of the West and intend to depose the imposter Wizard.

The darkest story in the set is Robin Wasserman's "One Flew Over the Rainbow," where Dorothy, "Crow," "Tin-Girl," and "Roar" are all patients in a mental institution.. Crow got her name because of a massive tattoo of a flock of crows running up her back to her neck. The narrator, Tin-Girl, so named because she cuts herself and is covered with hard scars, tells us that Crow's brains don't work right while she, Tin-Girl, has no heart. Get it? Roar is a big thuggish fellow. Tin-Girl trades painful sex to "the Wizard" in exchange for drugs, and a chance to escape. The man who prescribes their daily tranquilizers is Doctor Glind. Dorothy has hair dyed electric blue and paints her nails black. There is nothing Ozish about this one. It could be called Ozploitation.

Ken Liu appropriates the names of the first-book characters for "The Veiled Shanghai," a science fiction story set during the May Fourth Movement, the anti-imperialist protests in 1919 over the ceding of Chinese territory to Japan in the Treaty of Versailles. This also has nothing to do with Oz. It is given a fantasy gloss by adding an other-dimensional second Shanghai. There is an Uncle Heng and Aunt En and a Dorothy Gee who uses her English name because it is more chic. She lives on Kansu Road, which gives her the opportunity to intone "I'm certainly not on Kansu Road anymore" when she shifts to the other dimensional Shanghai. In the second Shanghai she follows a trail of yellow bricks mixed into the cobblestone streets to find the Emerald House of the Great Oz. She picks up the obligatory companions, a scrawny English boy nicknamed Scarecrow, a robot lumberjack called Tin Man, and a big opium addict called Lion. The Great Oz turns out to be Sun Yat-sen and the Wicked Warlord who Dorothy vanquishes is the real warlord Yuan Shih-kai.

Kat Howard's "A Tornado of Dorothies" runs the film back to the beginning again, with the events of *The Wizard of Oz* as an endless *Groundhog's Day* loop in which new Dorothies enter by falling on the Wicked Witch of the East, progress through the story, then become ghosts to be succeeded by the next "Dorothy." The most successful Dorothies move on to become other characters, a Glinda, for instance.

Jane Yolen in "Blown Away" has Dorothy carried off in her house by the tornado, but returning years later, grown up and having been a high wire walker in a circus and never gone to Oz at all.

Orson Scott Card sets his "Off to See the Emperor" in Aberdeen, North Dakota, while Baum and his family lived there before he wrote *The Wizard of Oz*. He has Baum's son Frank Joslyn Baum go on an other-dimensional adventure where he seeks the Emperor of the Air, making Baum's later wizard story a much altered version of his son's wanderings.

Even the stories that get past 1899 and the first encounter with the Wizard are often dispiriting. Dan Baily in "City So Bright" follows a Munchkin building polisher whose dangerous work high on scaffolding far above the ground is made still worse as his workmates are murdered by the government for even mildly criticizing the Wizard. In Jeffrey Ford's "A Meeting in Oz"

Dorothy has grown up back in Kansas and become a murderer. Returning to Oz she tries to assassinate the Wizard but he has her killed instead.

These tales are well written by respected authors, but they have little to do with Oz, even an adult Oz where the perils of sex, old age, death, and betrayal would reasonably find their place. The best of the lot are "Emeralds to Emeralds, Dust to Dust" by Seanan McGuire, "Lost Girls of Oz" by Theodora Goss, "The Boy Detective of Oz: An Otherland Story" by Tad Williams, and, the most authentically Ozish in the collection, Jonathan Maberry's "The Cobbler of Oz."

Seanan McGuire imagines that the steady stream of outsiders who have found their way to the fairy country has expanded into a flood. The natives become bitterly resentful of the "crossovers," who end in massive slums, wracked by crime and drug addiction. Even Dorothy has to be expelled from the palace, as popular resentment is too great for Ozma to retain a foreigner in her inner circle. In this fraught situation Ozma asks Dorothy to solve the murder of a Munchkin in the center of the crossover slum. As tantalizing asides, Dorothy's roommate is Jack Pumpkinhead, who has had a falling out with Ozma, and she herself is gay and having an affair with Polychrome, the Rainbow's daughter.

Theodora Goss takes an opposite tack on crossovers. Rather than trying to keep them out and stigmatizing the ones who arrive, Ozma is deliberately transporting sexually abused girls to Oz. Outraged at their treatment in America, she is building a massive army of rescued girls to conquer the United States and place it under a more civilized ruler. The girls are supplemented by Wogglebug hatcheries producing thousands more of the country's leading intellectual, the giant insect H. M. (Highly Magnified) Wogglebug, T. E. There are Tik-Tok factories turning out legions of the wind-up mechanical men, and Jack Pumpkinheads are being made by the thousands, their wooden bodies being vivified by Dr. Pipt's Powder of Life, now being produced in huge vats in the Gillikin country. Lots of Oz characters make cameos in this story, from Jellia Jamb to Ojo. And the Shaggy Man proves to be no mean fighter with an assault rifle in an encounter with a detachment of hostile nomes.

Tad Williams' story, as promised, is an Otherland tale. Otherland, which I highly recommend, is a four-volume science fiction saga published between 1996 and 2001. The premise is that a group of fabulously wealthy billionaires undertake a secret project to build a series of persistent-world virtual reality simulations with the aim of uploading their consciousness into them to achieve a form of immortality. In his Boy Detective ramble the action takes place within the Kansas portion of a once bilateral Oz simulation. Code corruption has shut down the Oz part, but in this Kansas the Tin Woodman runs a factory while the Cowardly Lion is the leader in the nearby forest. Omby Amby, the Soldier with the Green Whiskers, who here instead of comprising the entirety of the Royal Army of Oz is known as the Policeman with the Green Whiskers, is found dead, beheaded. The Wizard appears as Senator Wizard of Kansas. The Glass Cat is up to her usual mischief, while the eponymous Boy Detective is a system troubleshooter named Orlando Gardiner. In the real world he is a dead teenager. Here in the Otherland simulations he lives on as an immortal technician, the only character aware that the simulation is not real. This all works rather nicely even if it isn't Oz and isn't "real."

And finally we come to Jonathan Maberry's "The Cobbler of Oz." This is the closest to a traditional Oz episode. A young winged monkey whose wings are deformed and too tiny to fly visits the cobbler's shop seeking a pair of walking shoes. He tells her about an ancient pair of magical walking shoes with which a long-gone princess was able to cross the whole country in a few steps. In fact, he produces from a cupboard the very shoes, now badly worn and missing many of the silver dragon scales that gave it its power. He offers to loan them to the little monkey if she will cross the Deadly Desert and try to get replacement scales from the original dragon. Only at the end do we come to understand that these are the silver slippers that will later play a part in Dorothy's first Oz adventure.

In summing up, I would think that the century that stands between L. Frank Baum's fairyland and the hopeless and oppressive Oz imagined by these authors must say something about what has happened to America. Oz had its share of witches - old Mombi long outlived her sisters in the Munchkin and Winkie lands. Ruggedo, the one-time king of the Nomes, was behind four of the eight attempts to conquer Oz. (Baum spelled it Nome, while Ruth Plumly Thompson reverted to the more standard Gnome.) There were the Kalidahs and the giant spider of the original book, and many more dangerous and evil-intentioned creatures who came later. Yet these people, entities, and beasts were all defeated, neutralized, or left alone in their own small corners. Oz is a sunny land with a contented people, happy with their fairy ruler and perfectly satisfied to live under an unelected monarchy.

Ruth Plumly Thompson published the last of her Reilly and Lee Oz books in 1939, the year that Hitler and Stalin invaded Poland, touching off World War II. After years of bloody fighting, the Nazi menace was defeated, followed by an unexpectedly short-lived period of American peace, prosperity, and international influence. With the civil rights movement, the Vietnam War, the Sixties radicalization, the rise of the Radical Right, and finally the onset of many measures of U.S. decline from the 1990s it has become more difficult to imagine that the future will be, as our Victorian ancestors believed, a steadily improving triumph of progress, improving standards of living, and a reign of reason and justice. It is easier to imagine Dorothy as a lunatic, a demented killer, a mere name to be pasted onto a long-ago struggle against warlordism in China — or a Wizard or an Ozma running an oppressive bureaucratic state complete with secret police and dehumanizing slums.

*　*　*

Edward Einhorn is a New York little theater director and novelist. This is his second Oz book. The first, *Paradox in Oz* (2000), was a time travel puzzle story that only partially captured the spirit of the place and got a bit too complex. In that book he introduced his parrot-ox (pun) Tempus, a creature with the body of an ox but the head and wings of a parrot who can fly backward and forward through time and materialize multiple versions of himself from different time streams. Tempus returns for a small fly-on in *The Living House of Oz*. This time around Einhorn shows a surer touch and can reasonably be added to the canon. At first I shied away from the live house concept. Center stage is one of those Oz houses originally drawn by John R. Neil: a dome with a wide row of windows on the ground floor that look like teeth, two large upstairs windows that look like eyes, and tall chimneys on each side pointed like arms at the sky.

What Neil added in his own *The Wonder City of Oz* (1940) was to bring his houses to life. They talked, and many of the household objects inside were alive as well, creating a cacophony that was unbearably frenetic. Einhorn has adopted this premise, but tamed it and given it a better grounding. There is only one living house, and yes, everything inside is alive and chatters away, from a mobile hat rack who styles himself the Earl of Haberdashery to every pot, chair, and doorknob. But there is a reason. The human inhabitants are thirteen-year-old Buddy and his mother Mordra. She, it seems, is a dead ringer for the long-deceased Wicked Witch of the West. And she is also a powerful sorceress. The pair are in flight from an other-dimensional Oz ruled by a Wizard every bit as dictatorial as the worst imaginings of *Oz Reimagined*. Happily this is an offstage land.

Mordra and Buddy are being sought by the Phanfasms. These were evil shape changers first encountered in L. Frank Baum's *The Emerald City of Oz*, one of the several peoples enlisted by Ruggedo the Nome King in one of his many attempts to become the ruler of Oz. The Living House has a pair of big wooden legs, so when Mordra fears she has drawn too much attention to herself she has the house stand up and walk away to a more secure location, usually setting down in some forest clearing. This is an engaging concept.

Eric Shanower's Living House

While the house is camped in the little kingdom of Tonsoria (naturally, a place absorbed with hair styling, wigs, and full of comb and scissors trees) Buddy is kidnapped. In trying to rescue him, Mordra's sorcery is discovered by Glinda and she is arrested for illegally practicing magic. There are various adventures that get Buddy to the Emerald City to rescue his mother from Ozma and Glinda, Tempus the parrot-ox gives a helping hand, there is a really unexpected surprise, then the Phanfasms appear and, as an old fellow I used to know would say, it's Katy bar the door.

There is at least to some degree a welcome adult sensibility about the *Living House*. Mordra suffers from her ugliness and is not made pretty at the end. She is unwilling to give up her magic, which protects her child, no matter what the law says. Ozma and Glinda try to resolve the problem and do not become monsters in doing so.

Oz books have always been visual as well as textual. Baum, happily for us, got rid of W. W. Denslow, who illustrated *The Wizard of Oz*. Denslow limned the first patterns for the Tin Woodman and the Scarecrow, but his Dorothy was chubby and far too young, while his other characters were overly rotund and a bit goofy. John R. Neil took over with *The Marvelous Land of Oz* (1904). Neil's first Oz book owed much to Denslow but by his second entry, *Ozma of Oz*, in 1907, his own style had solidified. Dorothy became a slim, blond, stylishly dressed young girl. The Tin Woodman and the Scarecrow became slimmer and more sober. When Ozma joined the cast at the end of *The Marvelous Land of Oz* she had red hair and looked like a ten-year-old. By *Ozma of Oz* she has black hair, looks to be in her late teens, and wears a more form fitting dress. She is always seen thereafter with one large red flower covering each of her ears.

Under Reilly and Britton and Reilly and Lee the Oz books contained full color paintings, usually twelve, by Neil. These were canceled to save on printing costs after Thompson's 1935 *The Wishing Horse of Oz*. Thompson's last four books had only black and white drawings. Except for some facsimile editions by the International Wizard of Oz Club and Books of Wonder, all the editions after 1935 omitted the color plates.

Neil did his most elaborate paintings for the sixth book, *The Emerald City of Oz* (1910), in the belief that this was to be the very last of the series. But when Baum found that his other books didn't sell as well and that thousands of children were writing to him demanding new stories about Oz he resumed the series with *The Patchwork Girl of Oz* in 1913.

Neil slacked off a bit a few years into Ruth Plumly Thompson's reign as Royal Historian. At an Oz conference this year one speaker claimed that Neil would dash off all the illustrations for the annual Oz book in a single day.

W. W. Denslow's concept of Dorothy,
the Tin Woodman, and the Scarecrow

No matter, his work became so identified with the look of Oz and its in-habitants that post-Thompson writers have often failed to find traction in large part because their illustrators were too inauthentic. On this score Einhorn has been fortunate in teaming with Eric Shanower. A talented artist, Shanower is the author as well as illustrator of his own series of Oz graphic novels such as *The Salt Sorcerer of Oz* and *The Forgotten Forest of Oz*. For *The Living House,* apart from the full color dust jacket, he offers a generous number of fine pen and ink drawings.

His work is more meticulous and detailed than Neil's. His frontispiece for *The Living House* shows it at rest in a leafy glen, adding greatly to the story's credibility. And in his several crowd scenes, all of the traditional Oz characters, both by Baum and Thompson, are readily recognizable, from the Woozy to Tik-Tok, Kabumpo the Elegant Elephant, and Sir Hokus of Pokes.

Shanower is not slavishly copying Neil, but stays close to Neil's patterns as the canonical originals.

The character of Oz shifted somewhat when Ruth Plumly Thompson replaced its creator, with *The Royal Book of Oz*. Baum's folksy dialog disappeared, and Dorothy no longer said "I s'pose" and "it's terr'ble." Gone also were the quaint philosophical discussions and debates between the magical creatures over the relative advantages of their particular construction and the limitations of "meat people." Thompson wrote more traditional fairy tales, used even more puns than Baum, and favored her own characters, such as Peter from Philadelphia and Jinnicky, the Red Jinn, whose body was a large jar in which he lived like a turtle in its shell. Though her tales were smooth and had a good bit of Oz feeling, some of the mystery had departed with Baum's old fashioned prose and odd discussions, usually carried on during the night, when the magic creatures sat up talking, as they had no need for sleep. For those of us who wanted to see Oz continue we accepted Thompson, with just a few silent reservations. Some people speak of a canon of forty books, including John R. Neil, Jack Snow, and the now mostly forgotten Rachel R. Cosgrove and the Eloise Jarvis McGraw and Lauren Lynn McGraw writing duo. Beyond a certain point the image of Oz shimmers and becomes opaque, no longer authentic.

The more recent efforts often go still further afield, as in Philip José Farmer's *A Barnstormer in Oz* (1982) and *Oz Reimagined*. In the end, Oz can take only so much adultifying. Whatever evils or dangers are found or added, it must still be home and a refuge for those of us who must live our regular lives in one or another version of Kansas.

August 1, 2013

Index